Data Governance Handbook

A practical approach to building trust in data

Wendy S. Batchelder

‹packt›

Data Governance Handbook

Group Product Manager: Apeksha Shetty

Publishing Product Manager: Apeksha Shetty

Book Project Manager: Aparna Nair

Senior Editor: Sushma Reddy

Technical Editor: Seemanjay Ameriya

Copy Editor: Safis Editing

Proofreader: Sushma Reddy

Indexer: Rekha Nair

Production Designer: Prashant Ghare

DevRel Marketing Coordinator: Nivedita Singh

First published: May 2024

Production reference: 1210524

Published by Packt Publishing Ltd.
Grosvenor House
11 St Paul's Square
Birmingham
B3 1RB, UK

ISBN: 978-1-80324-072-5

www.packtpub.com

To my husband, for supporting my weekly writing sessions, encouraging me to keep going and pour my heart and experience into this book, being my life partner, and sharing this beautiful, messy, and incredible life with me.

To my children, who inspire me to stay curious, ask questions, and help others see the beauty in simplicity, love, and inclusion, every day.

To my father, who told me I belonged in tech, even when I was asked if I was in the wrong room on the first day of my first IT class, and who encouraged me to keep showing up and taking up space, no matter what others thought. Your encouragement inspires me every day, which in turn, impacts others, long after your passing.

To my teammates, mentors, mentees, and sponsors – thank you. You have taught me more than I can ever put into words. Thank you for inspiring me.

– Wendy S. Batchelder

Editorial Reviews

Much more than an innovative reference work for data governance professionals alone, this text is a beacon for anyone leading data-driven initiatives. Wendy is an exceptional guide through the complexities of data governance while maintaining a rigorous perspective on the business impact of data. A must-read for those aspiring to transform an enterprise through the power of information.

Dave Mayer, Vice President | Program Director, Gartner Data and Analytics Research Board

As a sales leader, there is nothing more critical than understanding and interpreting data. One of the biggest challenges is assessing integrity, and data governance has a direct impact on integrity. What I love about Wendy's work is it's not about data in a vacuum; she provides a level of business acumen and outcome orientation that far exceeds many practitioners in this field.

Melissa Steffen, General Manager Sales and Customer Success, Thomson Reuters

Wendy's most recent Data Governance Handbook, "A practical guide to building Trust in Data", for me, proves to be an industry-agnostic roadmap for success; with two of its primary on-ramps being 1) Trust and 2) Data! Wendy offers a pragmatic and reusable framework that can be adapted and adopted by all enterprises and organizations, unlocking meaning for every reader and organizational role from the "Boardroom to the Back Office". Wendy's transparent approach in unveiling the journey to building Trust in Data is refreshing, and her methodical principle-based approach, using practical industry-proven techniques, hints, and use cases, undoubtedly equips and empowers data and non-data practitioners, business leaders, and executive sponsors with a roadmap to success!

Stephen Harris, Former Corporate Vice President, Cloud + AI, Microsoft

Wendy Batchelder's guide to data governance is an essential resource for anyone looking to harness the vast potential of data in a structured and effective manner. With her extensive experience as a Chief Data Officer and her clear, insightful approach, Wendy not only demystifies complex data governance concepts but also connects them directly to tangible business outcomes. This book is a must-have for leaders who are serious about making informed decisions that drive company success. Her practical frameworks and real-world examples equip professionals to launch and sustain impactful data governance initiatives with confidence. A compelling read, highly recommended for those committed to transforming their organizations through data.

Sadie St. Lawrence, Founder and CEO, Women in Data

The relevance of this book expands well beyond just data governance professionals and applies to GTM operations professionals as well, especially as many look to leverage AI capabilities to make every customer engagement more intentional. Wendy simplifies the complexity of data governance, making it easy for multiple functions within a global organization to apply her best practices accordingly. I recommend this book to any GTM or revenue operations leaders.

Ryan Mac Ban, President of Americas, UiPath

Contributors

About the author

Wendy S. Batchelder is a three-time chief data officer with a wide understanding of how to take highly technical aspects of data and analytics and translate them into simple, concise business-valued solutions that are practical and easy to understand. Her background has led her to lead global data and analytics organizations at four Fortune 500 companies, including Wells Fargo, VMware, Salesforce, and now, Centene. She approaches situations with curiosity and humility, which has led to applying innovative data solutions to challenges with increased complexity to deliver value that companies can measure.

A lifelong learner, Wendy graduated from Miami University with a BS in accounting with a minor in information systems, from Drake University with a master's in accountancy, and from the University of Iowa with an executive MBA, and she has completed ongoing professional education at Harvard Business School.

Wendy resides in West Des Moines, Iowa, with her husband and six children.

About the reviewer

Ankur Roy is a solutions architect at Online Partner AB in Stockholm, Sweden. Prior to this, he worked as a software engineer at Genese Solution in Kathmandu, Nepal. His areas of expertise include cloud-based solutions and workloads in a diverse range of fields such as development, DevOps, and security. Ankur is an avid blogger, podcaster, content creator, and contributing member of the Python, DevOps, and cloud computing community. He has completed all the available certifications in Google Cloud and several others in AWS and Azure as well. Moreover, he is an AWS Community Builder.

Table of Contents

Part 1: Designing the Path to Trusted Data

1

2

How to Build a Coalition of Advocates   35

3

Building a High-Performing Team   61

4

Baseline Your Organization   89

5

Defining Success and Aligning on Outcomes   113

Part 2: Data Governance Capabilities Deep Dive

6

7

8

Data Quality   171

9

Data Architecture   197

Part 3: Building Trust through Value-Based Delivery

12

13

14

Data Automation for Impact and More Powerful Results   289

15

Adoption That Drives Business Success   309

16

Delivering Trusted Results with Outcomes That Matter   325

Part 4: Case Study

17

Case Study – Financial Institution   341

Index   353

Other Books You May Enjoy   366

Preface

The world generates ~2.5 quintillion bytes of data every single day (and growing!). As a result, understanding and managing the data created becomes more complex every single day. It's our job to drive simplicity, understanding, and ease of use to make accessing and using data as easy and understandable as possible.

As a data professional, our role is to ensure we can govern data and empower our businesses with the right data, at the right time, with the right controls. This book is a comprehensive guide on how to better understand what data governance is, its key components, and how to successfully position solutions in a way that translates into real, understandable business results. After reading this book, you will be able to successfully pitch and gain support for a data governance program, with measured outcomes in terms the business will understand and deeply value.

We will move from establishing a Chief Data and Analytics Office and building a business case to successfully implementing the more technical capabilities that any CDAO will need to deliver to drive successful data management. You will notice in this book that I emphasize the "why" behind these capabilities. In my experience, simply explaining what the capabilities are without being able to see how they can impact a business is a recipe for failure.

There are many more technical books available on each of these topics, and where I hope this book will provide a variance from what is already available is that: business value. I will spend time explaining the technical capabilities in terms your business stakeholders can understand, with the aim of creating a business-led program.

Ultimately, if you want to get into details about a specific tool or technical implementation, there are loads of other great resources (including books) you can head to drive your implementation, including a wonderful inventory from the publisher of this book, Packt.

Who this book is for

This book is for chief data officers, data governance leaders, data stewards, engineers who want to understand the business value of their work. It is also for IT professionals seeking further understanding of data management. Any business leader who wants to better understand data governance would also benefit from learning the basics, as well as any executive finding themselves managing a chief data and analytics officer who wants to better understand the discipline at a higher level. You should have a basic understanding of working with data and understand the basic needs of a business and how to meet those needs with data solutions. You do not need to have the knowledge or skills needed to sell solutions to executives, nor coding experience.

What you will learn:

- Exactly how to position data governance to obtain executive buy-in

- How to launch a governance program at scale with measured impact

- Real-world use cases that enable you to take action quickly

- How to obtain support for data governance-led digital transformations

- How to launch strong, with confidence

- A detailed step-by-step guide from ideation to delivery and beyond

What this book covers

Chapter 1, What Is Data Governance?, introduces you to data governance. At face value, data governance may seem like a cost center, if not approached with value generation in mind. Many companies start a data governance program without the right support, structure, or funding model. First, you will learn the basics of what data governance is and how it relates to adjacent capabilities. Then, you will learn the components of data governance programs, why each component matters, and finally, why to treat data governance as an enabler for business value.

Chapter 2, How to Build a Coalition of Advocates, explores gaining support for your program, which is arguably the most important part of launching a data governance program that drives impact. First, you will learn why and how to identify and secure the right executive sponsor for the data program, and then how to bring in additional leadership support. Lastly, you will learn how to engage and energize the entire company to collaborate toward value-based outcomes that matter to them.

Chapter 3, Building a High-Performing Team, focuses on establishing a high-performing data governance team, which is a critical and long-term investment in the success of a company's use of data. First, you will be introduced to the key roles in a successful data governance function, how they should optimally structure for results, and finally, how to establish routines and rhythms to support the operations of the team.

Chapter 4, Baseline Your Organization, teaches you the importance of defining a baseline, not only for the organization as a whole but also for individual projects. A key component of measuring success is measuring where you start. You will learn how to capture a baseline and who to communicate it to. Finally, we will discuss how to ensure agreement on the baseline before beginning work.

Chapter 5, Define Success and Align on Outcomes, focuses on the area where many data transformations fall flat – aligning on outcomes that matter to a business. Most data transformations stop with data outcomes and fail to reach the final mile – where the business uses the delivered data capabilities to drive operational efficiency, increased revenues, and better insights. In this chapter, you will learn why defining success beyond data and with the business matters, how to successfully map all relevant stakeholders (including secondary and tertiary stakeholders), and how to translate results into business terms.

Chapter 6, Metadata Management, delves into establishing a high-value, high-return metadata management capability, which is required for any data governance program. The success or failure of a chief data and analytics officer hinges on being able to answer a few fundamental, core questions. Where is my data? Who owns it? How is it classified? Is it safe and secure? Can I leverage it for value? Do I know how to reduce risk? You will learn the answers to these questions and be guided through how to tactically set up a metadata management capability for success.

Chapter 7, Technical Metadata and Data Lineage, explores establishing a high-value, high-return data lineage capability, which is a core capability for any data governance program. Following on from *Chapter 6*, this chapter focuses on the data supply chain. You will learn the answers to the questions in *Chapter 6*, with a focus on data lineage, and will be guided through how to set up data lineage for success.

Chapter 8, Data Quality, examines understanding the quality of data and being able to have a defendable stance when it comes to "Can I trust it?", which is key for any user of data or information that is used to make decisions. Establishing a data quality capability enables the CDO/CDAO and their teams to stand behind their data, being able to defend the quality of the information. This solution can also, when coupled with metadata management and data lineage, lead to a data certification process. You will learn the answers to the questions and be guided through how to tactically set up a data quality capability.

Chapter 9, Data Architecture, delves into data architecture. Designing the patterns and optimal flow of information throughout an organization is sometimes more art than science. With data architecture, you will learn just that. First, you will be grounded in what good data architecture is, when and how it should be applied to an organization, why perfection is not the goal, and when *not* to involve data architects in a program.

Chapter 10, Primary Data Management, focuses on primary data. One of the core capabilities of any organization is the ability to standardize and conform its most critical information – customer, product, and reference data. By nature, rationalized data provides a solution, whereas data used by multiple divisions for many uses is standardized and cleansed for the benefit of the organization as a whole. First, you will understand what primary data is and is not, clarifying misconceptions. Then, you will be guided through the various types of primary data, how to prioritize, and how to implement a strong and centralized primary data solution that will impact and elevate the power of data into a strategic asset. All the capabilities introduced so far will be woven into this powerful capability to tie them together.

Chapter 11, Data Operations, explores how to run the operations of a data organization, including support for the running of primary data management, data warehouses, data lakes, and other authorized provisioning points managed by the data organization. First, you will learn what data operations are, how to scale effectively, and when to pull in engineering. Lastly, you will learn how to optimize DataOps as a core capability and what opportunities there are to automate.

Chapter 12, Launch Powerfully, examines how to launch a good data governance program, which can quickly lose impact if not launched properly. The importance of the launch cannot be underscored enough. You will learn how to create simple and strong core messaging to engage and clearly articulate to the stakeholder community what and how delivery will be accomplished. Then, you will be led through the creation of a launch plan, a design of feedback loops to ensure continuous improvement, and finally, how to report on an ongoing basis for impact.

Chapter 13, Delivering Quick Wins with Impact, delves into the post-launch period, when the data governance team must quickly begin to deliver results. The time to first value metric should be as short as possible while producing impacts that matter to the business. You will learn how to create momentum through the delivery of quick wins, how to communicate the wins to the business, and how to ensure that the business not only understands the results but also becomes an advocate for the future success of the data governance program.

Chapter 14, Data Automation for Impact and More Powerful Results, focuses on automation, which is a lever that can be pulled to expedite data product deliveries. First, you will be introduced to what automation techniques can be applied to data governance. Second, you will learn how to select the right automation solutions for their transformation. Finally, you will learn how to power their transformation with automation across all solutions.

Chapter 15, Adoption That Drives Business Results, explores business adoption. Now that you have learned what data governance is, how to gather support, design a program, baseline the organization, launch, and deliver against the plan, you need to be able to ensure that your solutions are used by the business. Building an adoption roadmap, you will be able to articulate to your stakeholders how to use the solutions, ensuring a lasting impact of the solutions provided to the organization. Lastly, you will double the impact by ensuring ongoing supports are in place.

Chapter 16, Delivering Trusted Results with Outcomes That Matter, teaches you how to ensure consistency in what was promised to stakeholders versus what was actually delivered. As the implementation of data governance occurs, the chief data/analytics officer and their leadership team must keep all messaging focused on results. You will be guided through how to explain variances in expected delivery versus real results, and how that builds trust. Finally, you will learn how to message back to stakeholders powerfully, during delivery for impact.

Chapter 17, Case Study – Financial Institution, walks you through how to apply the topics covered in this book to an organization with a high degree of regulation (i.e., a financial institution). First, you will find use cases that are unique to this type of entity. Second, you will learn how to pull out the unique requirements and how to adjust messaging, sequencing, and results to accommodate the special needs of a highly regulated organization.

To get the most out of this book

You will learn how to design trust in data governance, starting with a fundamental understanding of what data governance is and the path to align an organization around the need for data governance. You will learn about the subcomponents of data governance, how to implement them, and how to drive adoption within the organization that creates value and ease of use for the business. To get the most out of this book, you should embrace a beginner's mind, allowing you to relearn your approach to data concepts with fresh perspectives.

Get in touch

Feedback from our readers is always welcome.

General feedback: If you have questions about any aspect of this book, email us at customercare@packtpub.com and mention the book title in the subject of your message.

Errata: Although we have taken every care to ensure the accuracy of our content, mistakes do happen. If you have found a mistake in this book, we would be grateful if you would report this to us. Please visit www.packtpub.com/support/errata and fill in the form.

Piracy: If you come across any illegal copies of our works in any form on the internet, we would be grateful if you would provide us with the location address or website name. Please contact us at copyright@packtpub.com with a link to the material.

If you are interested in becoming an author: If there is a topic that you have expertise in and you are interested in either writing or contributing to a book, please visit authors.packtpub.com.

Share Your Thoughts

Once you've read *Data Governance Handbook*, we'd love to hear your thoughts! Scan the QR code below to go straight to the Amazon review page for this book and share your feedback.

https://packt.link/r/1-803-24072-5

Your review is important to us and the tech community and will help us make sure we're delivering excellent quality content.

Download a free PDF copy of this book

Thanks for purchasing this book!

Do you like to read on the go but are unable to carry your print books everywhere?

Is your eBook purchase not compatible with the device of your choice?

Don't worry, now with every Packt book you get a DRM-free PDF version of that book at no cost.

Read anywhere, any place, on any device. Search, copy, and paste code from your favorite technical books directly into your application.

The perks don't stop there, you can get exclusive access to discounts, newsletters, and great free content in your inbox daily.

Follow these simple steps to get the benefits:

1. Scan the QR code or visit the link below

https://packt.link/free-ebook/978-1-80324-072-5

2. Submit your proof of purchase

3. That's it! We'll send your free PDF and other benefits to your email directly

Part 1:
Designing the Path
to Trusted Data

In this part, you will get an overview of how to design a data governance program, starting with the basic definitions, how to design a successful and scalable team, how to gain support, and how to define what success for your team and your company will be when it comes to data governance.

This part contains the following chapters:

- *Chapter 1, What Is Data Governance?*
- *Chapter 2, How to Build a Coalition of Advocates*
- *Chapter 3, Building a High-Performing Team*
- *Chapter 4, Baseline Your Organization*
- *Chapter 5, Define Success and Align on Outcomes*

What Is Data Governance?

As a data professional, some of the most frustrating conversations you will have about data governance will be about data programs feeling like a series of constraints versus a strategic enabler and that you are slowing business down vs. enabling excellence. Having led data transformations in three Fortune 500 companies, I have heard my fair share of these same messages. In my humble opinion, this is feedback; feedback that we are speaking in "data speak" and have not created a business case that is centered on value generation from the lens of our stakeholders. Rather, we have delivered a business case that is focused on data needs vs. business needs.

From a stakeholder's perspective, there are a plethora of forces at stake in driving business: generating revenue through the sales teams, marketing to existing and potential customers, economic factors, and supply chain challenges. Data is a part of all of these critical business components, but it is not the first thing that comes to mind for our stakeholders. It is embedded in how business runs. It is a part of the day-to-day. It does not and should not feel like a standalone function.

Therefore, it's our job to serve the business and to make it feel seamless to the business stakeholders we enable. When things feel like friction, it's not necessarily because we're not supported; it's because we are one of many problems leaders are facing. Often, this comes in the form of a lack of buy-in or pushback, a seemingly endless number of questions, or simply a lack of engagement. For data professionals, conversations like this often end in frustration and the underfunding of the data governance program. I have seen this scenario over and over again in organizations firsthand and have heard it from data executives in every single industry. Far too often, it ultimately ends in the failure of a chief data & analytics officer to survive in the organization.

The question is, why?

Over the course of the next 17 chapters, I will explain why Chief Data and Analytics Officers fail to establish themselves as strategic business partners in their organizations and how you can overcome these common pitfalls and succeed. I will cover everything you need to know to build a case for data governance, rally your organization to support you, deploy a strong data governance program, leverage core data governance solutions, and apply all of this in a case study for a fictitious financial institution. Let's dive in.

What you can expect to learn

Throughout this book, I promise to be transparent and direct about my experiences, and we're going to start strong: governance programs fail because we have failed. We have failed to explain data governance in a way that makes sense to our business stakeholders. We have failed to deeply and intimately understand how our solutions will drive business success. In short, we have failed to explain in terms of business value. Conversely, the most successful data executives I have had the opportunity to work with have been successful because they deeply understand their company. They have spent the time to intimately understand the business, have crafted data solutions that enable business success and have successfully explained the benefits in terms of business results vs. data results.

As we go deep into these topics, I will not make assumptions about your experience implementing a successful data governance program. I will start with the basics by grounding you in definitions and the foundational capabilities and will build on how to launch a successful and impactful program, complete with the measures for success that will resonate with executive management and, ultimately, the board of directors for your organization. In the end, we will complete a case study to bring it all together. By the end of this book, you will have all you need to launch a program and deliver with excellence in your own organization. No longer will your organization be overwhelmed by data and underwhelmed by insight. We will change the narrative together.

In this chapter, we will ground ourselves in the basics of data governance and how it relates to adjacent capabilities. Then, we will define the components of a data governance program, why each component matters, and why we treat data governance as an enabler for business value. Subsequent chapters will dive deeper into the fundamental capabilities of a data governance program and how to implement them.

We will cover the following main topics:

- What is data governance?
- What's driving the increasing need for data governance?
- A brief overview of the data governance components
- Data governance as a strategic enabler
- Building a business case for your company
- When and why to launch a data governance program

What's driving the increasing need for data governance?

As I meet with data professionals across industries, it is abundantly clear that data governance is more important than ever. Executives are expecting more from data, but without the proper investment, it is harder than ever to respond at the speed of business.

So why is it increasingly difficult to respond to our executives at the pace of the business? There are a number of key factors, including the continuous rise in the following:

- **Data volume**: We have more data today than yesterday (everyday!). In fact, the amount of data doubles every two years. Yet, we cannot expect to double our efforts or double our staffing or technology spend.

- **Regulation**: The regulatory landscape is evolving, increasing expectations for how data is handled. In the United States, at the time of this writing, six states had signed privacy and data protection legislation into law. This increases the complexity of compliance for data handling.

- **Expectations**: Executives' expectations are rising, but our use of data is not. In a recent Tableau survey, >80% of CEOs wanted their organizations to be data driven, but less than 35% percent of employees felt their data was used in decision making.

- **User base**: More individuals than ever are engaging in data, wanting it for their own use but needing to trust it. It puts our governance professionals in a position to add tremendous value by providing trusted, well-governed data to our organizations.

We have to become more innovative and more embedded, leveraging more technologies (e.g., automation and AI) than ever before. We talk about what that means for our customers. But what does it mean for us? If it's difficult to answer key, basic business questions today, how do we expect to do it in two–three years with more data than ever? We must take this sense of urgency and build capabilities that will scale and last as our volume, complexity, expectations, and user base continue to grow at an unprecedented rate.

What is data governance?

Before we dive in, it's important that we ground ourselves in basic definitions. During my first role in data management, we made the mistake of assuming that our stakeholders around the organization were aligned on what data we were referring to when we were discussing a particular domain of data. After several months of having difficult conversations on scope (if a particular data element, report, or system were in scope), we realized that we needed to go back and ground all stakeholders in a few very simple questions.

Data governance is the formal orchestration of people, processes, and technology by which an organization brings together the right data at the right time with the right controls to enable the company to drive efficient and effective business results. This formal orchestration should control, protect, deliver, and further enhance the value of data and create equity for an organization. Data governance is active and is delivered through capabilities, including the following:

- Metadata management
- Data lineage
- Data quality

- Data architecture
- Mastering data
- Data operations

We will explore these core capabilities, among other methods, in detail in subsequent chapters. The capabilities that make up a successful data governance program are defined slightly differently in just about every organization. Therefore, it is important that we define them here for the purposes of this book. Feel free to use the vocabulary in this text within your organization or the common language of your business.

> **Important note**
> Take the time to build a quick reference guide that defines the most basic terms used around your data governance program (e.g., data, governance, metadata, and so on). Make it accessible to the whole organization as a quick reference guide. Add to it as needed.

Data versus information

I want to point out that there is a passion for the use of data versus information terminology among industry veterans. Some practitioners are firm in their beliefs that these terms are not the same and should not be used interchangeably. Others use them synonymously without much thought. In my humble opinion, either can be appropriate for your organization. The important point is to distinguish between the two so that your organization understands the definitions and how to use them appropriately in your organization. Personally, I do not believe either position is correct or incorrect. It is far more important that you meet your stakeholders where they are and that your organization agrees on the alignment you choose to use. For the purpose of this book, I will use the term "data" primarily, and I will be sure to be specific about what that means.

Use case – financial services company

In my very first data governance position, we launched a robust and multi-million dollar transformation to comply with a regulatory requirement around data management and regulatory reporting. About six months into the effort, we found we were really struggling to define what was "in" vs. "out" of the scope of the program. After several curricular and passionate conversations, we learned that we were not able to scope well because, ultimately, our stakeholders had differing views about what constituted "data" vs. "metrics." We ended up building a full-blown methodology to ground the company and our regulators on how we thought about the reports so as to be in scope, built a full list of all reports, and documented whether each one either met the criteria or did not meet the criteria, and this was to be available for a credible challenge to anyone or any group interested. Instead of debating it theoretically, we documented the criteria with specificity and then clearly articulated the justification.

What I learned in this experience was two-fold: you cannot make assumptions regarding what people know or don't know when scoping a data program, and that you must have grounding definitions that can be socialized, agreed to, and documented so that all involved could remain grounded.

I'll ask us to do the same throughout this book. Please come back to these definitions as needed so we can be aligned.

What data governance is not

Too often, companies have a tendency to blame problems on the data and/or the data team. Data governance (team or program) is not the solution to every problem. Data, like air, is everywhere in an organization, and it truly takes the entire organization to manage it well. Similar to the quality of air when a fire breaks out, poor data moves through an organization like smoke moves from a fire. The strong management of data requires prevention, detection, and correction, and to manage data well requires the entire company to be on board. A single data team cannot unilaterally solve every data problem. It will take the involvement and action of the organization at large to drive change and manage data effectively.

Secondly, data will never be perfect. If you or your executive team is expecting perfection from data governance, I would urge you to adjust your expectations. To ensure we align on what the appropriate expectations and objectives of a successful data governance program are, we must define success. To do that, we must start with the objective of data governance.

The objective of data governance – create business value

To put it simply, companies exist to increase value for stakeholders. When it comes to data, there is one very important objective of data to increase equity for stakeholders. Managing data effectively is one of the ways companies can increase value for their organization.

Figure 1.1 – A simple value equation

An asset is something of economic value that is owned by an organization. A liability is an obligation (either current or future) that decreases the overall value of the organization. Thus, when assets minus liabilities result in a positive value, the organization has an increase in value (i.e., has created equity), whereas when assets minus liabilities results in a negative value, the organization has a decrease in value (i.e., has reduced equity).

The same mindset can be applied to data. Data can impact equity in a number of ways. Equity can be created through addressing and minimizing operational risks by sustaining regulatory compliance, avoiding fines and penalties, and increasing or creating revenue. I break this concept down into two key subcomponents to manage data governance more specifically. These two subcomponents (assets and liabilities) are directly influenced by my formal training as an accountant and IT auditor, and this tends to resonate well with management when they translate data solutions into measurable value (ideally, monetary value, but may also consider the time value of employees).

> **Important note**
> Data is an asset when it creates value for the organization.

A few examples include:

- Curated datasets that are used for multiple purposes
- Customer health scoring
- An authorized provisioning point
- A data model used for predictive modeling

> **Important note**
> Data is a liability when it creates risk for the organization. Data can be both of these things but cannot be either (for example, a data solution may create value and reduce risk).

A few examples include:

- Non-cataloged data
- Data that has not been classified and, therefore, not appropriately secured
- Data leaks/breached data

Ideally, organizations should manage the liability of data while maximizing data as a strategic asset, such that data equity is created. Depending on your business and the maturity of your data governance practices, either asset management or liability management may be a bigger priority.

Data governance should create data equity by increasing the value of data as an asset and minimizing data liabilities. I encourage you to come back to this framing as you apply the principles in this book to your own organization. As you pitch data solutions, consider this:

How is this solution increasing the value of my data (increasing the asset) and/or decreasing the liability?

Both are of value. The momentum created by delivery should translate directly to an increase in data equity over time.

An example of a data asset might be a curated dataset that is reliable because it has clear ownership, is of high quality, and can be leveraged for multiple business purposes organization-wide. An example of a data liability might be as simple as an organization not knowing what data it has, where it lives, or what to do with it. This carries a risk to the company from a security perspective, but also, the lack of accountability means that individuals may be using the data inappropriately for decisions that it is not fit for, increasing the company's risk of making a decision that it shouldn't be based on data that were never intended to be used for that particular purpose.

The measurement of the value of an asset is unique to each organization, but in short, being able to tie back the impact to the organization is a good guiding principle. The following are a few example questions to consider as you attempt to value the data asset:

- Does this asset enable additional revenue? How much?

- Does this asset save time? Can you calculate the hours saved by an hourly rate for an individual to calculate the person-hours saved?

- Does this asset improve customer satisfaction? Can this satisfaction be translated or calculated into value for the organization in terms of additional spending or increased customer retention?

Figure 1.2 – Data assets, liabilities, and equity formula

Data assets may provide value across these components, and value should be calculated accordingly. The most important part of this valuation exercise is not the calculation itself; rather, it is the alignment and agreement with the business. Once you have calculated the value, it is important to go to the business and ask for their feedback. Do they agree with your assessment? If yes, then you have a fully vetted value for your data asset. If not, work with the business to iterate on your data asset valuation until you reach an agreement. If you skip this important step (vetting the value), data teams often are seen to be overselling their value to the organization. This immediately undermines your credibility in the organization. Agreeing on the value of the business supports a strong business relationship and provides credibility of past success when seeking future investment into data solutions.

The measure of the liability portion of the equation is of equal importance. Like data assets, the measurement of the liability carried by an organization's data will vary based on your organization.

> **Important note**
>
> It is not as simple as more data equals more liability.
>
> Rather, the less the data is managed, the higher the liability. When data is unmanaged, the risk to the organization is higher.

A great example is security risk. When an organization does not understand where data is, it cannot effectively or adequately protect it. This comes at a high risk (liability) to the organization and could result in a data leak or, worse, a data breach. Here are a few questions to consider when calculating your organization's data liability:

- Do data liabilities increase the risk to the organization? How much? Are there fines or regulatory penalties we could be subjected to as a result of this liability?

- Does liability drive inefficiencies in our business? Can you calculate the hours incurred by an hourly rate for an individual to calculate the person-hours impacted due to the inefficiency (for example, a manual process vs. an automated one)?

- Does this liability impact customer satisfaction? Can this satisfaction be translated or calculated into a decrease in value for the organization in terms of additional spending or decreased customer attrition?

Once you have assessed your data asset value and data liability value, you can apply this to calculate data equity. The idea is to increase the equity over time. This initial calculation can serve as your baseline by which to calculate progress over time. Organizations also may like to leverage a data maturity model to measure progress; however, these models can be interpreted widely in an organization and do not take into account the business value associated with data solutions. Instead, they focus on the development of data capabilities, which do not always translate well for executive management. I prefer to focus on business value rather than an organization vs. a maturity model.

We will not dive into data monetization efforts in this book. The economics of the monetization of data is expertly described in Doug Laney's book, *Infonomics*, and I would highly recommend his book to anyone looking to dive into the monetization of data further.

A brief overview of the data governance components

Now that we have classified data solutions into assets and liabilities and defined how to calculate value, let's dive into the components in further detail. I prefer to group the components of data governance into building blocks. The reason I prefer this approach and have leveraged this framing in several companies is because it allows the organization to directly tie each building block to specific and straightforward outcomes. The first building block, **policy and standards**, is relatively basic and can be designed with a small team. This is a great place to get started in developing a data governance program.

Policy and standards

The purpose of this building block is to define data ownership and the structures needed to design accountability to manage your organization's data as an asset. This building block will ensure effective, sustainable, and standardized data governance on which the company can depend. This building block is a prerequisite for future building blocks because it defines **what** is required to drive effective data governance and **who** needs to be involved. Additionally, the components of this building block can be created in a simplified way and can be expanded as the company matures in its data journey.

An easy place to start is to draft a simple and straightforward data governance policy. The purpose of a data governance policy is to tell the company what they need to do, why, and who is accountable.

The objectives of a strong data policy include the following:

- Establishing a single policy and set of standards for data management
- Establish the capabilities and data assets that are in scope for the policy and, in turn, for the office of the Chief Data and Analytics Officer
- Define the accountability and responsibilities for the implementation of the policy and the operationalization of data management capabilities
- Set minimum standards for data management, specifically for governance, quality, and meta- and master data management
- Define the procedures and usage requirements for tools to drive the consistent and robust adoption of minimum standards in a consistent manner
- Enable flexibility where appropriate to allow for ease of implementation where possible
- Define what is out of the scope of the policy

As with any policy, it is important to identify the owner of the data governance policy, who will be accountable for managing the policy by refreshing it at least annually, updating the content, and evangelizing it to the company. It is also the owner's responsibility to ensure buy-in from key stakeholders across the company. Ideally, this owner would be a **chief data officer, head of data governance**, or similar role. If your company does not have a data leader in the role yet, another option would be a **chief information officer, chief information security officer, chief privacy officer,** or even a general council.

A policy does not need to be lengthy to be effective. Ideally, the policy would set forth the basics and would be supported by more specific and topically focused data standards. This approach often allows the policy to go through a more formalized corporate governance approval process while allowing for slightly easier updates to the data standards as your organization matures. I recommend implementing a data standard for each of the core capabilities addressed in *Part 2* of this book, plus any specific to your business requires additional guidance for data stakeholders. Remember, the policy sets forth the **minimum** expectations for the company.

To get started in developing your data governance policy, a suggested data governance policy outline may contain the following:

1. **Purpose and scope statement** (for example, to transform how the company utilizes data by creating additional revenue streams and simultaneously reducing data risk)

2. **The owner** (for example, a Chief Data Officer)

3. **Reviewers/contributors and titles** (for example, Head of IT, COO, and data stewards)

4. **Sign-off/approval** (For example, CEO, CFO, and so on)

5. **Data governance requirements**

6. **Roles and responsibilities for implementation**

7. **Feedback loops for improvements and/or additions**

8. **Measures of success**

9. **Compliance/audit expectations and frequency**

10. **Glossary of terms**

Data governance policy example

The following is an example of an enterprise data governance policy:

Owner: Chief Data & Analytics Officer

Last Approval: 12/31/2023

Policy Leader: Head of Data Governance

Contributors:

- Head of Information Technology/CIO
- Head of Human Resources/CHRO
- Head of Marketing/CMO
- Head of Sales/CRO
- Product/Business Unit Leaders
- Product/Business Unit Data Stewards

Purpose and scope

This data management policy applies to all data held or processed by the company, which may include customer data, transactional data, financial information, regulatory and risk reporting, and any other data related to the business of the company. This data may be first-party data, derived data, or data acquired from another company (third-party data). The outcomes of this policy are the following:

- Reduce risk
- Unlock revenue opportunities
- Drive operational efficiencies

Introduction

The company is responsible for ensuring all data is accurate, complete, secure, and accessible only to those who require access to fulfill their job responsibilities. This policy sets for the requirements for the enterprise to deliver on the outcomes established above.

Data governance

Data governance establishes the requirements and standards for all corporate data deemed "in scope" of this policy in the aforementioned policy and scoping section. The purpose of the data governance capabilities established within this policy are to drive enhanced transparency and accountability for our company's data and to drive improved consistency, control, and oversight for how data is managed, stored, and used going forward.

Roles and responsibilities

1. Enterprise Data Committee: An Enterprise Data Committee will be established, chaired by the Chief Data & Analytics Officer, to provide an oversight and prioritization body to manage data and analytics initiatives and issue remediation enterprise-wide. A Data Domain Executive will be required to sit on this committee to ensure appropriate prioritization across all data domains.

2. The Chief Information Officer will partner with the Chief Data & Analytics Officer to ensure technical requirements and systems are provided in support of the data and analytical needs of the organization, both for the Office of the Chief Data & Analytics Officer, but also for all functional data domains enterprise-wide.

3. A Data Domain Executive will be established for each functional area to ensure the appropriate focus, funding, and resourcing is established and maintained to manage data in accordance with both this policy and the needs of the business.

4. Data Stewards will be assigned by each Data Domain Executive to ensure the day-to-day execution of data requirements is completed in accordance with policy and the needs of the business. Data Stewards will also be required to work with the Office of the Chief Data & Analytics Officer to ensure that transparency of progress and ongoing operational effectiveness is maintained for leadership, regulators, and across domains.

Requirements

This section provides the minimum expectations for compliance.

Data Governance

Each data domain will develop a plan to drive compliance with this policy to operationalize the requirements within their data domain. The Data Domain Executive will ensure appropriate prioritization, whereas the Data Stewards will execute the plan on behalf of the Data Domain Executive. Additionally, Technical Data Stewards will support the delivery of all technical requirements to ensure compliance with this policy and the broader needs of the business. The minimum requirements are the following:

1. Identify all data assets and systems
2. Identify all data and technical data stewards for each asset and system
3. Assign each asset and system to the appropriate data domain
4. Develop a plan to meet the requirements for each asset and system and maintain compliance going forward

Data Cataloging

The purpose of data cataloging is to centrally manage and publish business and technical metadata across the organization to enable accelerated discovery of the data available across the organization in a clear, transparent manner. As data cataloging is implemented, the Chief Data & Analytics Office will evaluate metadata to determine the best source of truth for a given data asset and identify opportunities to reduce proliferation and redundancy across the company. This will further simplify our data ecosystem over time and reduce the costs of duplicate data handling/management and storage. The minimum requirements to be published in the Enterprise Data Catalog are the following:

1. Description of the data asset/system
2. Technical metadata
3. Description of schemas and tables
4. Identification of critical data elements (CDEs)
5. Business definitions for CDEs
6. Data classification for all data elements within the asset/system in accordance with the company data classification policy

Data Quality

The purpose of data quality is to ensure the data is fit for use. The following requirements have been set forth with the aim to centrally develop data quality rules, provide profiling resources and tooling, and monitor data hygiene to ensure the data can be trusted for analytical and business use and identify issues requiring disclosure and/or remediation. The minimum requirements are the following:

1. Define the data quality rules for each CDE and enter this into the enterprise data quality tool

2. Enable CDEs for data quality monitoring

3. Provide data quality dashboards to transparently report on current quality levels

4. Identify data quality issues and create plans to address material data quality issues

Policy Management

- **Feedback Loops**: Feedback about the policy and/or questions about policy implementation should be directed to the Policy Leader defined above.

- **Measures of Success**: A robust Enterprise data governance scorecard will be established for each data domain and at the corporate level. Periodic reporting of the progress of complying with this policy will be reported to the Office of the Chief Data & Analytics Officer and to the Enterprise Data Committee. Further measures of success may be required.

- **Compliance/Audit**: Internal audits, external audits, and regulatory bodies may audit this policy for compliance on a regular basis. All requests for audit should be disclosed to the Office of the Chief Data & Analytics Officer so that requests can be co-ordinated and driven through the Enterprise Data Committee.

- **Frequency**: This policy will be reviewed, updated, and re-approved at least annually.

Now that we've reviewed what makes up a great policy, let's pivot into the key roles and responsibilities for a data governance program.

Roles and responsibilities

Any data governance expert will tell you that people are the key to a successful data governance program. People are responsible for caring for the data and ensuring its accuracy, that it is fit for use, and how to improve it to make it better. This concept is called **data stewardship**. Data stewardship requires collaboration to drive success. The executive identified for each data domain appoints a data steward to drive day-to-day activities for the data domain.

The key responsibilities of data stewards include the following:

- Serve as the single point of leadership for their data domain

- Ensure the data domain executive is kept informed on key activities

- Ensure the funding necessary for adequate data management is secured and allocated properly to data management activities
- Collect data requirements for the data domain and execute the data management requirements across the data domain

The key responsibilities of the office of the Chief Data and Analytics Officer include the following:

- Define data policy, publish the policy, and review for updates at least annually
- Lead data domain executives and data stewards through requirements, ensuring a comprehensive understanding
- Provide data tooling to drive the enterprise-wide enablement of data management
- Streamline, to the extent possible, compliance with the policy
- Report regularly to the executive team and, when required, to regulators and the board of directors

> **Important note**
> One of the hardest parts of data governance is gaining the collaboration required to drive the outcomes the organization needs to leverage its data for results.

In every company I have worked in, the intention was almost always good: the people wanted to collaborate. Data governance experts wanted to collaborate to drive success; however, competing priorities, a lack of a clear vision, and difficulty measuring the impact of a data governance program often led to data stewardship being deprioritized. Ultimately, organizations that drive successful data governance initiatives recognize the importance of good data governance and that it is more than just understanding records, fields, and tables. They recognize that it is more than just building another data warehouse. They recognize that people are the center of success and that identifying the individuals responsible and accountable for strong data is the cornerstone of any data governance program.

For data to be good, stewards must be good. Good stewards take accountability for their data's quality, access, and overall management. The best data stewards I have worked with ensure the buy-in of the business users is achieved in every step of the governance process because the goal of data governance is not just clean data; it's enabling the users of the data to confidently and easily use data in pursuit of their business objectives.

Let's compare two examples to illustrate this:

- **Example 1**: A business user, person A, needs data X to report to a regulator. In a well-governed data environment, person A goes to the enterprise data catalog, where person A can search for data X. Person A finds the metric they need to report to the regulator, but they have a few questions. In the catalog, person B is identified as the data steward. Person A can reach out to person B to ask questions and learn more about data X to confirm it is the appropriate metric to share with the regulator.

- **Example 2**: Here is a company with little to no data governance. A business User, person A, needs to get data X for the regulator, but does not know where to start. There is no catalog for the data, so they ask the person they think might know about the data, person C. Person C suggests person A calls person D. Person A calls person D, and so on. Days or even months go by, and person A does not feel confident they have the right information for the regulator but provides the best information they know of. Ultimately, the regulator does not have confidence in the data because person A does not have confidence in the data.

Often, aligning data stewards in an organization is easier said than done. One of the easiest approaches to getting started is to begin at the executive level. I refer to these individuals as **data domain executives**. These are the individuals who are ultimately accountable for the data their division of the organization is accountable for. An example would be a **Chief People Officer (CPO)** being assigned the data domain executive for human resources data. This would make the CHRO ultimately accountable for human resources data. The CPO would delegate the day-to-day activities to their data steward, who would be responsible for ensuring human resources data is managed according to data governance policy and standards.

As a part of your data governance program, one of the first activities should be to identify the data domain executive for the organization. In my experience, defining the logical types of data into data domains and assigning a data domain executive is the best place to start. Upon defining the data domains and data domain executive, you will have the executives responsible for the data of the entire organization named. These individuals should make up your sponsors, and should you choose to start an enterprise data committee or council, they should become your voting members:

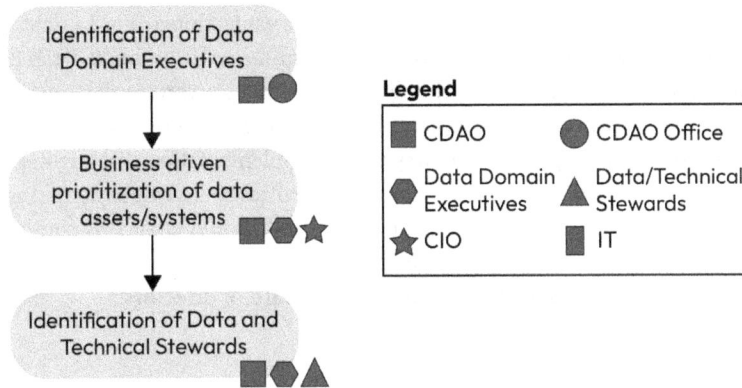

Figure 1.3 – Identification of data domain executives and data/technical data stewards

Depending on the size of your organization, you may have a third key role in the business side of data management. For larger organizations, you may consider establishing a more senior-level person to be a **data domain manager**. This person would have the role of the data steward, as described in the preceding section, and would likely have a 1:M relationship with data stewards who either report to them or have a dotted-line relationship with the business. In one organization I worked for, we had a data domain manager for the division of the organization, and for each sub-group, a data steward was defined. It looked like this:

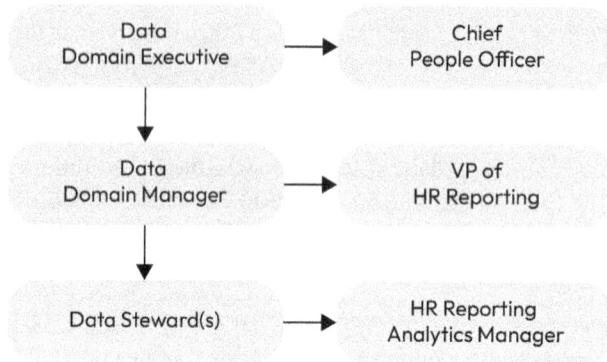

Figure 1.4 – Example of data domain appointments

Governance forums

An enterprise data committee is an effective way to align an organization around a data strategy and a data governance program, and it serves as a prioritization and escalation body. Each data domain executive who participates in the committee should assign a data steward to drive activities within their data domain. Often, organizations establish sub-groups (e.g., **human resources data councils** or **human resources data working groups**) to carry out the implementation and ongoing governance of the respective domain. This allows data governance activities to be implemented more deeply within the organization. The Chief Data Officer (or equivalent) should chair this committee and be responsible and accountable for managing the agenda, cadence, and facilitation, as well as reporting progress upward in the organization to the C-suite and the board of directors.

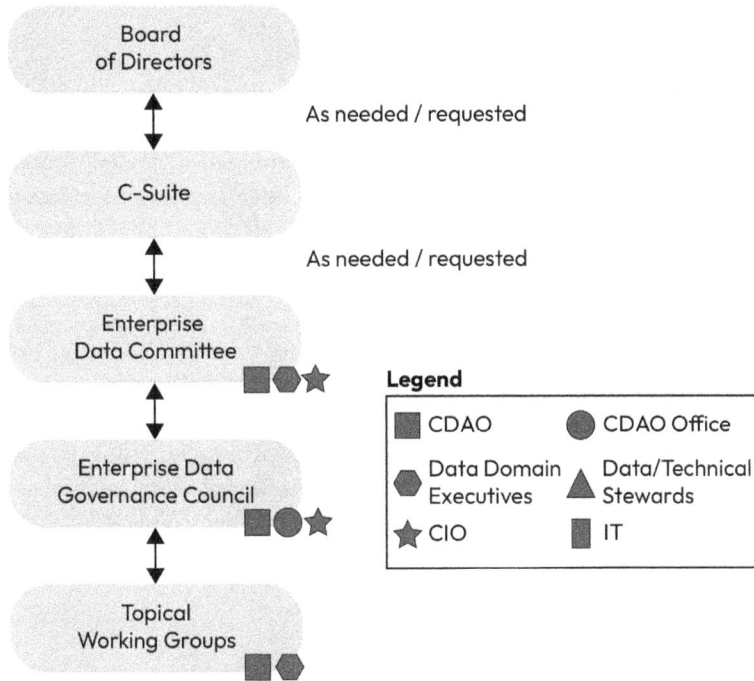

Figure 1.5 – Example of how various data governance forums work together

Important note

If you notice that the enterprise data committee is delegated below the data domain executive, you may have a problem. Having someone delegate once may not be of concern (e.g., for vacation); however, if you start to see a pattern, either by a particular domain or across the board, it is a signal that your committee is not providing value. Quickly reach out to the data domain executive and seek to understand what is driving the delegation. Simply ask, "I noticed that you have delegated the last few EDC meetings to someone on your team. Is there anything I can do to make the meeting more engaging for you? Your perspective is critical for the whole committee, and I want to make sure it's a valuable use of your time."

There are other key roles that may play a part in your data governance program, including BU stakeholders (often users of data) and the information technology team. We will dig deeper into the metadata chapter in *Part 2*, but for now, I also included the IT application owner in the preceding diagram (see IT). In any program, an IT application owner plays a key role in the success of a data governance program. The IT application owner is the individual responsible for the technical implementation of any data governance requirements set forth by the enterprise data governance policy and by the data domain executive or their delegate. We will get deeper into operating models in *Chapter 3*.

Reporting on governance progress

Ideally, as implementation progresses, the enterprise data committee should receive ongoing reporting to demonstrate improvements in data governance. One way to report this information is through the use of an **enterprise data governance scorecard (EDG Scorecard)**. The EDG Scorecard should provide a transparent status of how well the company is doing in implementing data governance capabilities and how well this remains implemented post-implementation. Ultimately, the EDG Scorecard should communicate to its users how the company is doing in terms of making data easier to find, understand, and, ultimately, trust.

Before trying to design and implement the EDG Scorecard for the entire company, I recommend selecting one data domain to pilot this process. I prefer to start with a data domain that has at least slightly more mature data governance practices than other domains. One data domain that tends to be a bit more mature in most organizations is finance and/or regulatory reporting. By piloting a data domain, the other data domain executives, who make up the enterprise data committee, get a sense of what an EDG Scorecard looks like and how they should be implementing it for their respective data domain.

Sample implementation metrics

Metrics should be defined to measure the implementation of the data management policy as well as the operational effectiveness of capabilities on an ongoing basis. To measure the implementation of the policy across domains, each domain should measure progress and report that progress to the office of the chief data & analytics officer on a regular basis (bi-weekly, monthly, or quarterly, based on your organizational expectations).

Examples for the office of the Chief Data and Analytics Officer include the following:

- The total number of data domains (this becomes the denominator for the following metrics)
- The number of domains with an identified/confirmed data domain executive
- The number of domains with identified/confirmed data stewards(s)
- The number of domains with systems of record identified
- The number of domains with systems of record assigned to system owners
- The number of domains with critical data elements identified for each system of record
- The number of domains with data quality rules written and executed for each system of record
- The number of domains with business glossaries established for each system of record
- The number of domains with data dictionaries established for each system of record
- The number of domains with reference data adopted for each system of record

Use case

A large multinational company has seven business units and four corporate functions. A chief data & analytics office was established to advance the use of data, analytics, and AI. As a part of the office's first-year strategy, the CDAO organized a team focused on data management maturity. With this focus, the head of enterprise data governance was tasked with the formal development of a data policy and a scorecard to track the implementation thereof.

The head of enterprise data governance developed an enterprise data policy to establish expectations for the organization and defined the key roles and responsibilities to drive compliance with the policy. The team identified 12 data domains: one for each of the seven business units, one for financial data, one for risk data, one for marketing data, one for employee/HR data, and one for master and reference data, which is owned by the CDAO.

To track the implementation progress across the 12 domains identified, the following scorecard was developed for the office of the chief data & analytics officer. This report is updated bi-weekly and reported to the executive team, the data domain executives, and the data stewards, and it is reviewed in the enterprise data committee meetings on a monthly basis.

Implementation Scorecard for the Office of Chief Data and Analytics Officer								
Owner: Chief Data & Analytics Officer								
Primary Contact: Head of Enterprise Data Governance								
Purpose: The following scorecard is designed to report on the progress in implementing the core requirements of the Enterprise Data Policy. Twelve Data Domains have been identified and established to manage the data for the company. The following scorecard is for monitoring the adoption by domain.								
Data Domain Executives Identified	**Data Stewards Identified and Appointed**	**Systems of Record (SOR) Identified**	**SOR System Owners Identified**	**Critical Data Elements Identified for each SOR**	**Data Quality Rules Written and Executed for each SOR**	**Business Glossary Established for each SOR**	**Data Dictionary Established for each SOR**	**Reference Data Adopted for each SOR**
9 of 12 domains	9 of 12 domains	6 of 12 domains	5 of 12 domains	5 of 12 domains	3 of 12 domains	5 of 12 domains	4 of 12 domains	0 of 12 domains
75%	75%	50%	42%	42%	25%	42%	33%	0%

Key Updates:

- Data Domain Executives: Since our last update, two additional data domain executives (HR and Marketing) have been confirmed. Both HR and Marketing have appointed Data Stewards for their domains. Community Banking, Wholesale Banking, and Wealth Management are pending appointment. ETA: 2 weeks.
- Data Stewards: HR and Marketing both submitted their Data Steward appointments shortly following their Domain Executive appointments. Further, the three domains with outstanding Domain Executive appointments have yet to identify Data Stewards. ETA: 1 month.
- Systems of Record (SOR) Identification: No update since the last report.
- SOR Owner Identification: No update since the last report.
- SOR Critical Data Element Identification: No update since the last report.
- SOR Data Quality Rules Written and Executed: No update since the last report.
- SOR Business Glossary Established: No update since the last report.
- SOR Data Dictionary Established: No update since the last report.
- SOR Reference Data Adoption: This track is not due for 12 months. As SORs are identified and reference data needs are identified, formal plans will be created.

Status: Green—On Track | Yellow—At Risk | Red—Past Due

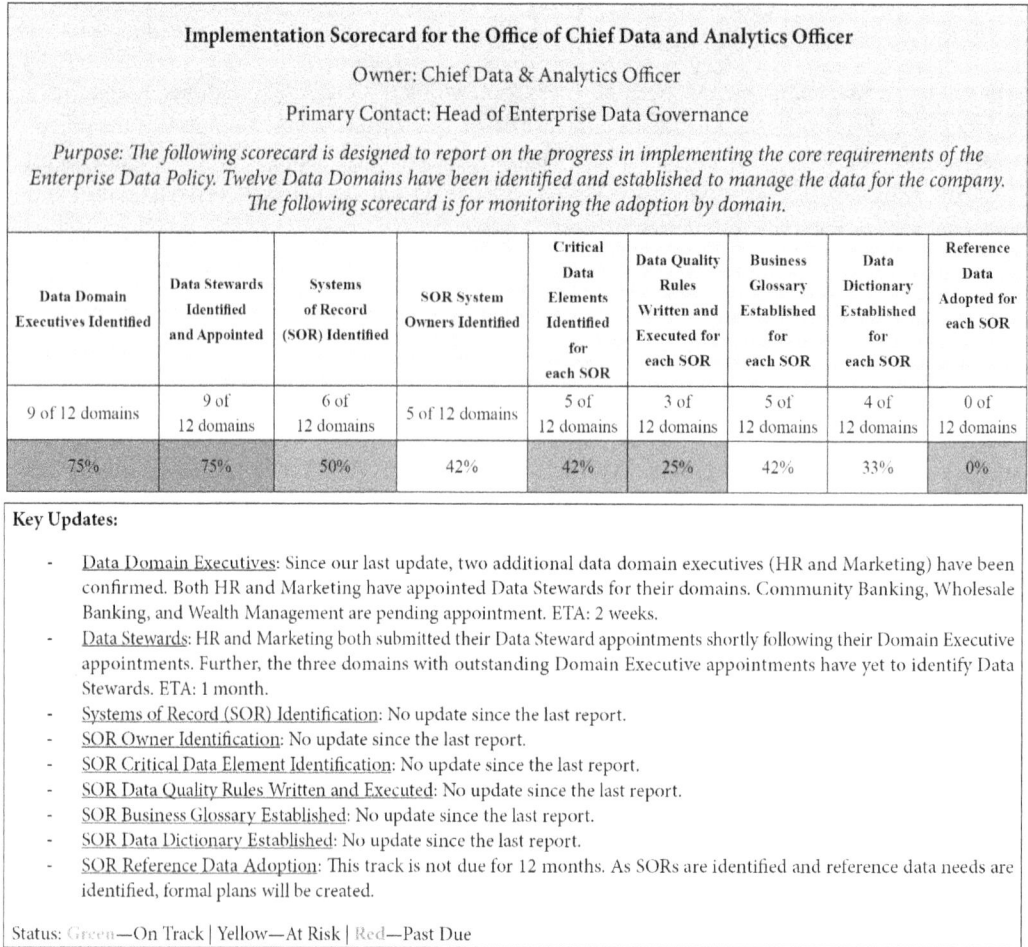

Figure 1.6 – Example of a data governance scorecard for the chief data and analytics office

Examples of the data domains/data stewards include the following:

- The total number of system of records assigned to the data domain (this becomes the denominator for the following metrics)
- The number of system of records with critical data elements identified
- The number of system of records with data quality rules written and executed
- The number of system of records with business glossaries established
- The number of system of records with data dictionaries established
- The number of system of records with reference data adopted

Each data domain should track its own respective metrics and submit the report to the office of the Chief Data and Analytics Officer on a bi-weekly basis.

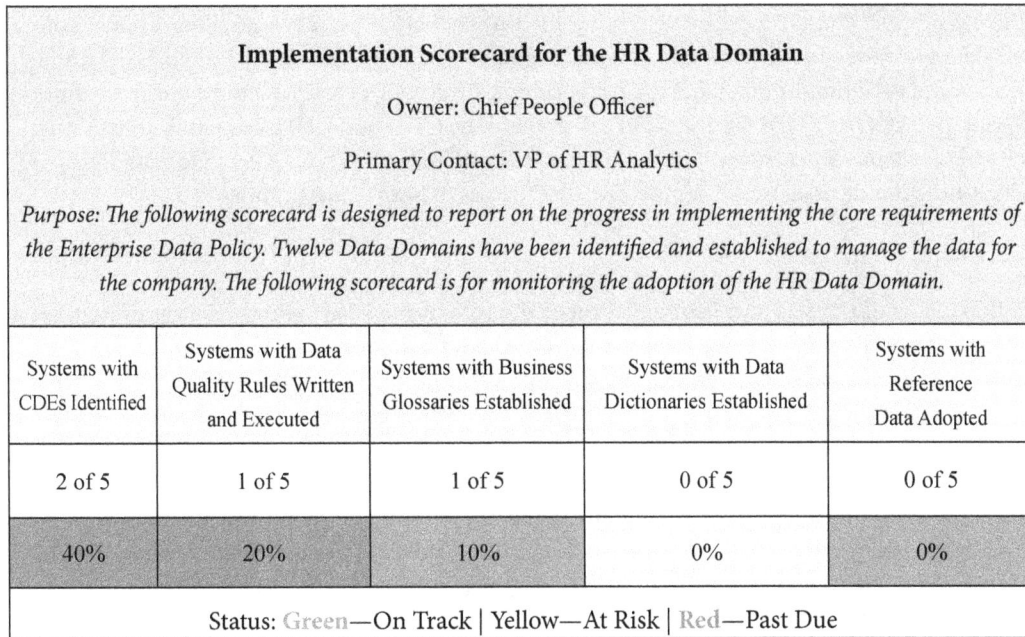

Implementation Scorecard for the HR Data Domain				
Owner: Chief People Officer				
Primary Contact: VP of HR Analytics				
Purpose: The following scorecard is designed to report on the progress in implementing the core requirements of the Enterprise Data Policy. Twelve Data Domains have been identified and established to manage the data for the company. The following scorecard is for monitoring the adoption of the HR Data Domain.				
Systems with CDEs Identified	Systems with Data Quality Rules Written and Executed	Systems with Business Glossaries Established	Systems with Data Dictionaries Established	Systems with Reference Data Adopted
2 of 5	1 of 5	1 of 5	0 of 5	0 of 5
40%	20%	10%	0%	0%
Status: Green—On Track | Yellow—At Risk | Red—Past Due				

Figure 1.7 – Example of a data governance scorecard for a data domain

Related teams and capabilities needed for success

No data team will function alone. To be successful in implementation, partnership is the most valuable skill at your disposal. There are a series of key functions that you will need to build strong and sustainable relationships with. First, the business functions. You must build trust with each business function you support. This begins and ends with deep listening. Deep listening requires you to listen with the sole purpose of learning. **You are listening to learn not to respond**. Your business function leaders will provide you with their needs. It is your job to listen and be able to take their needs back to your data team to inform and build out the data strategy. Trust will be earned as you deliver against their needs. Initially, hearing them out, regardless of their past experiences with data, is the most important place to start.

Information technology

Your company's **information technology team (IT team)**, led by a chief information officer (CIO), will likely support your success by delivering the infrastructure (at minimum) to support your team's data solutions. The relationship you build with your CIO and their key leaders is critical to your success. I've found the quality of the relationship between CDO and CIO to be one of the most powerful indicators of a CDO's success. In cases where the CDO and CIO have a high-functioning and trusting relationship, I have witnessed success for both leaders. In cases where the relationship is not high-functioning or, at worst, competitive, the success of **both** leaders is hindered.

Information security

Additionally, with the rise and formalization of the role of the CISO and the increasing threat landscape across all industries, the importance of the CISO has never been higher. One of the core tenants of the liability side of the data equity equation is the protection of your company's data. This shows up in data security, of course, but also spans and tightly connects with technical metadata management. In short, you cannot protect data if you don't know where it is. Technical metadata is a critical enabler that supports an understanding of what data you have, where it is stored, where it moves, how to classify it, and then what controls are needed to properly protect and secure it. We will cover more about this topic in *Chapters 6 and 7*. As a data leader, this capability will enable the success of your CISO, and therefore, I suggest you engage early and often with them throughout your data governance implementation.

Chief financial officer

As you work through building relationships and, ultimately, building out a stakeholder list, I encourage you to think of both business functions and corporate functions. Your stakeholders should include the CIO and CISO, as mentioned in the preceding section, as well as the CFO, head of privacy, general council, human resources, and operations, in addition to business functions. If you work in the technology field, product and engineering leaders are critical, whereas in financial services, groups such as risk management and regulators may be relevant. The point is to look at the company at large, including all the stewards and users of data, and identify the key leaders you need to work with to partner effectively. Most data leaders who do not succeed in their role fail because they fail to build relationships and/or fail to build trust through value creation.

Human resources

Your human resources leader will be a key stakeholder and strategic partner in helping you design your organization and develop a hiring, training, and retention strategy for talent management.

Privacy and legal

Privacy and legal teams will be key drivers for many of the capabilities your team will enable. For example, while the legal team should define data retention standards and the privacy team should define the types of information classification (private or company confidential, for example), it is your team's responsibility to implement the capabilities to discover, inventory, and auto-classify the data in accordance with these policies. Regulations such as GDPR or CCPA drive much of this work across industries, but other industries have special considerations, such as BCBS 239 or HIPPA. Be sure to work with your legal and privacy teams to find the right relations to follow.

Additionally, be mindful that emerging state regulations are coming quickly. At the time of this writing, the State of Iowa was the most recent state in the US to release a privacy law. It will go into effect January 2025.

Defining value

As you are starting to formulate your vision for the future, it is important you take into account all the input you receive from the stakeholders you interact with. As we work toward building your business case, building a coalition of support, and building a team throughout the next few chapters, it is important to note that no two companies will have a consistent message or vision for success. You will need to address each opportunity with fresh eyes. Despite having led data transformations in three Fortune 500 companies, each data strategy I have had the opportunity to lead has required a unique perspective. Companies are on their own journey to excellence, and even the most established firms have work to do to improve their data governance capabilities. You must assess each situation from this perspective, or you will risk applying the wrong strategy to the situation before you start.

Who to meet with

As you prepare to customize your vision for the company, build your list of stakeholders thoughtfully, as introduced in the preceding section:

1. What are the business divisions?

2. Who leads each division? Do they have a chief of staff or chief operating officer you should meet with also?

3. What corporate functions do the stakeholders have? Who leads each one?

4. How does funding get disbursed in an organization? Seek to understand the process and who influences the release of funds.

All of the individuals you list out in response to the preceding questions become key individuals to meet as you prepare your vision, your business case, and begin to socialize your vision. Many of these individuals may become data domain executives in the future.

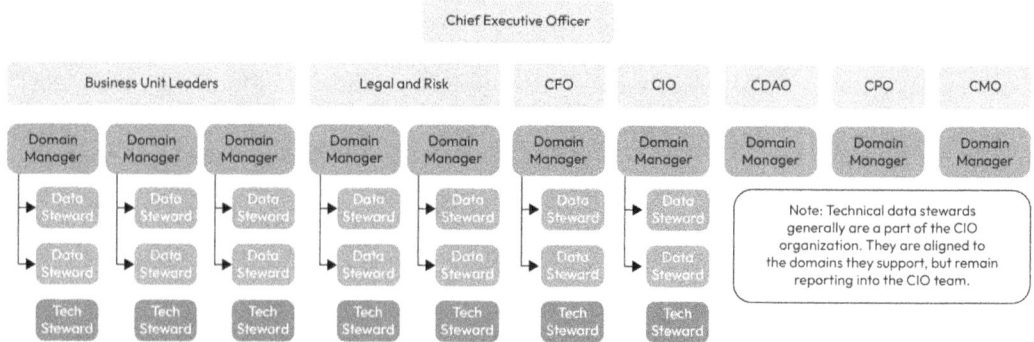

Figure 1.8 – Example alignment of domain model with corporate organizational chart

> **Important note**
>
> CDAO, CPO, CMO, and so on will also have domain managers, data stewards, and technical stewards aligned with them.

During your first interaction, simply listen to what their business priorities are. This is not the time for a solution. You are gathering facts and opinions from them so that you can use that as input to your future vision. Take copious notes. Before ending the meeting, ask for a follow-up in 4–6 weeks, where you will bring forward the mission, vision, and objectives for your team from their input and feedback.

> **Important note**
>
> In your organization, your data domain executives should be no more than your CEO-1 or CEO-2. No matter how large your organization is (50 or 500,000), if your data domain executive is too far from the top of the organization, your program will dilute. You must create a value proposition that clearly defines why the senior leaders must drive this body of work together. If it is pushed too far down in your organization, you will risk losing the prioritization, funding, and focus of your C-suite. Ideally, the individuals reporting to the CEO would be your data domain executives. In larger organizations (i.e., 50,000 or more employees), a CEO minus two may be appropriate.

Crafting a powerful why statement

A powerful vision statement is not exclusively for the chief data & analytics office but for the data and analytics capabilities of the company as a whole. When drafting the vision statement, be clear and concise about your aspirations and goals for the future use of data and analytics for the company. Consider the following:

1.   What is it you aspire to do?

2.   Who will help you achieve it?

3.   How will you know when you've arrived?

A powerful vision statement should be clear, concise, and easy to understand and communicate. It should be to the point, and jargon should not be used (no "data speak"). The statement should be focused on the future, inspirational, and aspirational, bringing all stakeholders together to work towards this imagined future together. Make it easy, short, and memorable. It should be able to be committed to memory easily. While being future-focused, it should be achievable and in alignment with the company's values.

> **Important note**
>
> Let's consider an example. Perhaps you are the new Chief Data and Analytics Officer at a leading insurance company. You might craft a vision statement such as:
>
> Insights are embedded in the flow of business with highly trusted, relevant, and curated data at the speed of our need to proactively wow our customers with delightful and meaningful moments that matter. We trust our data, and our customers trust us.

Customizing the message

As you craft your vision statement, bring it with you to your one-on-one meetings with the leaders you identified and met with. Share it with them individually, and ask for their feedback:

- Does it make sense for the company's strategic direction?
- Is it visionary?
- Will it inspire your team members and drive meaningful focus to the future?
- Is it meaningful for your needs?
- What would you change?

Listen and incorporate feedback as you review with these individuals. The degree to which you remain open-minded and take into account their input will directly impact their buy-in. This does not mean you must incorporate each iota of input, but you should consider it thoughtfully and loop back with each individual, thanking them for their support and explaining what you changed, what you didn't, and why. It is critical to close the loop with any changes you did not make, carefully explaining why they didn't make the cut. This transparency will build trust with your stakeholders, which you can build upon over time.

After you have revised and have finalized your vision statement, it is time to bring it forward for final approval. I suggest you incorporate an approval in your enterprise data committee meeting to further establish that the vision is not just that of the chief data & analytics office, but of the entire company. By involving the company in this exercise, you are setting a precedent that data is part of everyone's responsibility, although the CD&AO is ultimately accountable.

Data governance as a strategic enabler

Before you can dive into building out the data governance business case, you must understand the business outcomes the company is driving. In order to draft data objectives, you need to first understand the entire company strategy. If you don't have it already, request a copy of the company strategy. Ask questions to understand it fully. Then, work with your data domain executives to understand both their priorities and how their business unit or corporate function is delivering upon the company strategy. What outcomes are they required to achieve to create the value the company requires? Ultimately, the definition of these outcomes will support the wider company strategy and lead to business outcomes that are highly relevant and critical to the success of your organization.

The point is that you must define a path that clearly demonstrates how data and analytics will power your company and not slow it down. Often, when individuals hear the word "governance," they equate it to bureaucracy, friction, and slowing down progress. You must show how what you and your team will do will add value and enable the business and to do so without a negative impact on progress. It's critical that you define a mission and clear objectives that demonstrate this point clearly.

The mission of the chief data and analytics office

The purpose of the chief data and analytics office is to drive the business outcomes needed with data and analytics solutions. It is not to sit on the side of business; rather, it is to achieve the organizational outcomes by serving this with the business. It is an accelerant to results. Success is determined by business outcomes, and thus, the chief data & analytics office must define its mission as such. Start by defining what your team is to do in business. It may contain guiding principles such as the following:

- Inspire enterprise thinking

- Deliver business outcomes powered by insights

- Define and implement the delivery model for common data and analytic solutions

- Curate solutions that embed insights when and where the business needs it

- Ensure business is executed with governance by design, which is embedded in the processes

- Drive operational efficiencies through automation

- Create revenue streams or speed revenue generation cycles

- Reduce risk and remediate compliance issues

Ultimately, you and your team should craft a powerful mission statement that encompasses the full suite of your service to and with the company. Think about the question, What is our intention?

> **Important note**
>
> Let's consider a couple of example mission statements:
>
> - Empower the company with timely, trustworthy, and relevant insights to drive revenue to USD 1B and beyond.
> - The chief data and analytics office will unlock revenue, drive efficiency, and reduce regulatory compliance risk for Bank XYZ.

The mission of the data governance program

Once you have defined the mission of the chief data & analytics office, you must next define the mission of your data governance program. Your data governance program will need to take into consideration what problems you need to solve for your company and how you intend to solve them. This program should be an enabler and collaborator in solving problems for the company in a way that serves their broad interests. It can be as simple as the following:

> **We do X for Y by doing A, B, and C.**
>
> *"We deliver enterprise-wide data governance capabilities for all corporate functions by enabling governance by design in our platforms, powering data management solutions, and delivering trusted, curated data solutions when it matters."*

Determine the projects, programs, and budgets needed to enable the enterprise activities required for delivery against the company data and analytics strategy. As we go through *Part 2* of this book and dive deeper into each data governance capability, think about where you are with your company. Do these capabilities exist? To what degree? What gaps are you seeing? These gaps become your programs, projects, and deliverables. I suggest you come back to this section as we baseline your organization in *Chapter 4*.

Building a business case for your company

As you are meeting with the stakeholders you identified in the preceding sections and iterating on feedback regarding your vision statement, it is a perfect time to ask your stakeholders about what is working well, what could be improved, their priorities for the coming year(s), and some of the burning challenges their team is facing. I've often found that asking key leaders across a company open-ended questions and deeply listening to their experiences is fruitful when it comes to identifying opportunities to help drive value for them from data governance.

For example, if a stakeholder tells you that they are having a difficult time in the board of directors meetings because the CEO is always questioning their data, you may have an opportunity to help them. Spending time unpacking the reporting process, the metrics on the reports, the definition of the metrics, how they are calculated, where they are sourced from, and the quality of the underlying data itself may expose that there are problems with the reporting going to the board. Conversely, this exercise may prove the data is accurate, and now the stakeholder is armed with strong backing from you, the leader of the data organization, to attest to the accuracy of the reporting. Often, the data is guilty until proven otherwise. It is your great privilege to support your stakeholder in providing reliable and highly trusted data to deliver their results to the board. Treat the experience accordingly.

No matter what your stakeholders tell you, the importance of these conversations is to listen. Very rarely are stakeholders going to tell you that they need better governance, or they need stronger technical metadata, or for a team to come in and profile their data more frequently. They are not going to speak to you in these data terms. What they will say is **no one trusts the reporting**, or **I can't get what I need when I need it**. They are giving you the symptoms. It's your job to identify the root cause to diagnose the problem and fix the underlying issue: data governance.

As you are executing these deep-listening sessions and learning about the challenges your colleagues are facing, start to identify common themes. It's helpful to keep detailed and organized notes that you can easily refer back to, but that also can begin to group like problems together. Pulling on the preceding example, perhaps you hear from a number of stakeholders that there is inconsistency in reporting where the results sound similar, but the numbers are actually different. The executive team is now calling the data and the leader into question. You now know one of the components of your data governance business case is going to be centered around key metric alignment for the executive team. You will need strong metadata capabilities (*Chapter 6*) and data quality (*Chapter 8*) to help you, along with strong reporting and/or data analysts to help drive this alignment. Most importantly, you need to bring people together and drive consistency.

As you are preparing to write your business case, your listening sessions will produce themes, and you will center your delivery around the strategic implementation of capabilities and iterative delivery (sometimes referred to as **quick wins**) to show progress throughout the delivery. As you build your business case, be sure to highlight what your building blocks will be (that is, the components in *Part 2* of this book) and the iterative delivery you will enact to drive impact along the strategic journey. As you iteratively deliver for your data domain executive in alignment with the themes you've identified, you will turn challenges into wins, naysayers into advocates, and you will become the trusted advisor the company needs to deliver excellent data governance for the company at large.

As you start to build out the business case, which you will do iteratively as we work through this book, there is some good news: you have already made progress. The preceding items are key components of your business case. You will need to include the following:

- Your company's strategic vision and objectives
- Your team's mission statement

- Your data governance program mission statement

- Your powerful objectives

From here, you can start to frame out the programs you'll need to launch for your business case. At this point, you won't know what most of them are; however, you may have already begun to identify thematic issues or problems through your stakeholder listening sessions. Perhaps you already know your company does not have a data catalog or a way to measure data quality with transparency. You can start to plot out the capabilities you will need to deliver as "Programs."

I prefer to use a memo format to define a business case. The six-page memo is a strong format for delivering depth of content without losing your audience. Some companies pitch by using slides. You will need to determine which format is best for your company's culture. No matter how you decide to pitch, writing a memo is a good exercise to ensure your thoughts are solid going into the business case process. Ultimately, how well you write your business case will determine your degree of buy-in from stakeholders and your degree of funding. An example template for a business case may look something like the following:

Business case template
Title:
Owner: Your CD&AO + title
Author(s): Your name + title, as well as anyone else who helped you draft it
Contributors: Individuals who offered input
Reviewers: Individuals who reviewed the document (ideally your supporters)
Purpose: What are you aiming to achieve with the document? Are you looking for support? Funding? Alignment on milestones? All of the above?
Executive summary and our ask of you: Start with the end in mind. What do you want a busy executive to know? Put that up front. The details go below.
Business case: Explain what you will deliver, why it matters, when you will deliver, and how you will measure success.
Financials: Define exactly what you need to deliver the program(s).
Measures of success: Define the return on investment. Are you driving new revenue? Will you create efficiencies? Will you reduce risk? Quantify them here.

Figure 1.9 – Business case template

I suggest you put together this framing now, and as we go through the remainder of the book, fill in the business case for what you need for your company. As you gather information from meetings with your stakeholders, make notes and start to build your business case over time.

The fact that you have picked up this book and are working through it is a huge step on your journey. Continue to read, chapter by chapter, and execute the steps as we go. You can move as quickly or slowly as you need to in order to go at the pace you need at your respective company. Use this as a reference, a guide, and most importantly, the framework for how to deliver strong data governance at scale. Before we move into the next phases, it's important to discuss a final constraint: when and when not to launch your program.

When and why to launch a data governance program

While a data governance program could be launched at any time, **successful** programs tend to precisely time their launch aligned with other adjacent business programs and ensure the impact is very clearly defined for the executive team, not just in the individual program, but as a suite of transformations. If management does not have a strong need, is not fully bought in, or is too distracted (for example, in the middle of a large merger or acquisition), you will not have a successful program launch. Said another way, timing matters.

Take the time you need to understand your business, the challenges, politics, and the other key strategic transformational programs in flight or about to launch. Align with your peers on any business functions and operations to ensure you have buy-in. Then, plan your launch. If you do not get this timing right, you will need to restart your program, and in my experience, that is a very difficult process, usually requiring a new leader.

Why you should launch now

There are a handful of reasons that lead to an organization's investment in data governance. There's no perfect time, but there are some common reasons:

- **Regulatory**: There are a number of regulatory reasons that may drive your company to implement a data governance program. In financial services, for example, large global systemically important banks (known as GSIBs) were required to comply with BCBS 239, which drove an earlier focus on data governance for risk reporting.

- **Crisis**: Data breaches are another common driver for data governance programs. This is especially true when companies do not have a good handle on where all their data is, how it's classified, and/or are not confident they have properly secured it (you can't secure what you don't know about).

- **Executive request**: The C-suite has come to understand that they need more from data, and they are willing to fund a transformation to enable you to deliver against their needs.

- **Business request**: There is a critical and visible business need that is well-defined and funded.

- **Experimental**: The company wants to explore data capabilities and has set aside a funding pool to support experimentation in this space. You have the remit to use this funding to demonstrate the power of the possible.

Why you might want to wait

Finally, the willingness of executive management to celebrate quick, iterative wins that align around a long-term roadmap with adequate funding is critical. The program is not going to be successful overnight, and you must align with the fact that a long-term, sustainable, and data-centric culture requires iterative and ongoing investment and support. Ultimately, if the company does not understand what it wants and/or is not prepared to fund appropriately, you should not proceed in launching a wide-scale transformation to establish strong data governance. Here are some warning signs to watch for:

- **Executive Request**: The C-suite has come to understand they need more from data, but they *do not* understand what it will take to transform and get what you need to be a success

- **Business Request**: The business has a critical need, but they do not have it well defined, and there is no funding set aside for delivery

- **Experimental**: The company wants to explore capabilities but is unaware of what it will take to drive results

- **Undefined**: The company wants to establish a data and analytics function but does not follow through with forming a complete function

The company cannot ever finish the job of data transformation. It is like exercise. Just like you can't get in shape for one race and then claim you have become in shape for life and go back to sitting on the couch and expect to maintain the results. Take the time to secure support and funding for the program upfront. Your success and the company's success depend on it.

How to build your delivery timeline

Once you have built the framing for your business case and you have decided what capabilities you need, you should come up with some options for a timeline and funding. I find it's best to put forward three options for management so you can have a healthy discussion about what to do, how fast to do it, and how much the company is willing to spend to deliver.

Option #1 – Your preferred timeline

Start to build your optimal timeline. If what you need to deliver is up to you, and you can obtain adequate funding to do the work at a pace you feel is appropriate, what is that timeline? When will you release new capabilities? What will the company be able to do at each release?

Option #2 – Fast and expensive

Build an option that delivers more rapidly but likely has an increase in resourcing (the funding, headcount, or consultants' involvement). This option gives a faster time to value but comes with the balance of an increase in costs.

Option #3 – Slow and cheaper

Finally, build an option that takes longer but will cost less. In my experience, this is often the option that is thrown out right away by executives. Once they decide to move forward with data, they want to see results. Having this option on the table demonstrates that you were thoughtful and considered all options, and although they are not your preference, you considered the expectations of others.

You may also find that a combination of the options is created out of these review discussions. Be open minded. If management is putting forth their time and energy to review these options with you, this is a good sign. Listen to their feedback and be willing to come back with alternatives. Ultimately, you are aiming to receive support and funding; the more flexible you can be, the more likely you are to gain support.

You now have all the framing and background you need to build your data governance program and start to put your business case together. As we explore the next several chapters, we will go deeper into each topical area, which will give you the detail needed to design a powerful data governance program that delivers excellent results for your organization.

Conclusion

Beginning a journey to establish data governance transformation in your organization doesn't have to be difficult. It can take time, and requires support, but you can establish a strong data governance function for your organization. There are a few key steps that you should focus on as you embark on this journey, starting with identifying a data governance leader to own and sponsor data governance for your company, which will establish authority over the data governance function. You will also need to define what data governance means in the context of your company, through publishing a data governance policy (and standards, if needed). By carrying forward that policy implementation through establishing clear owners (e.g., data domain executives), establishing appropriate councils and committees, and writing a strong business case.

As you proceed through the chapters of this book, I will walk you through how to drive data governance into the ethos of your company, first, by establishing a coalition of advocates. In Chapter 2, I will begin by explaining why a coalition matters, how to assess possible supporters, and how to gather broad support.

References

- https://www.forbes.com/sites/bernardmarr/2018/05/21/how-much-data-do-we-create-every-day-the-mind-blowing-stats-everyone-should-read/?sh=302772a160ba

- https://medium.com/callforcode/the-amount-of-data-in-the-world-doubles-every-two-years-3c0be9263eb1

2

How to Build a Coalition of Advocates

Arguably the most important part of launching a data governance program that drives impact is gaining support for your program. Given the velocity of data creation worldwide, the impact on company operations (positive when properly managed, not so positive when managed poorly), the degree of risk of data misuse and mismanagement carry, and the opportunity that comes with value creation, it is no surprise that data is a hot topic with staying power. In every company I have worked for, customers, employees, and peers across all industries are asking a very common and consistent question:

How can we build trust in our data?

The concept of trust is complex. You cannot buy it. You cannot snap your fingers and create it. It takes time to create and seconds to lose. What is interesting about applying the concept of trust to data is that users of data often presume the data is wrong and that they can't trust it, especially when the data is not what they expected it to be. I often joke that "data is guilty until proven innocent," and it is often the way data is treated in practice. As data practitioners, the burden falls on our shoulders to prove data is reliable and to drive trust. Our colleagues demand it. Our customers demand it. The burden is ours to bear.

But it goes much further than "Is the data correct and trustworthy?" as our job reaches far beyond simply reporting. **Chief Data and Analytics Officers (CDAOs)** are truth-tellers, architects, engineers, and monetization leaders. Without the broad focus across capabilities, the role of a CDAO dilutes to reporting only. You will not build trust by being a reporting shop. Our job is to build trust across the organization not just in reports but in data solutions that impact business outcomes directly.

In a recent study by *McKinsey* [1], it was determined that customers "*consider trustworthiness and data protection to be nearly as important as price and delivery time.*" It is no longer enough to be the most reasonably priced or have the highest quality delivery. Customers want to trust the company and believe their data will be protected appropriately while doing business, as well as after the transaction occurs. They want to trust *you* to care for their data well. The combination of the dramatic increase in the quantity of data and the customer expectation to care for their data well puts **Chief Data Officers** (**CDOs**)/CDAOs in the middle of the conversation about trust in a new and elevated way.

No pressure.

Historically, CDAOs have worked through the lens of risk reduction, operational efficiency, and/or increasing revenue. This focus and demand for a trust-first approach requires a new dimension of thinking and a new focus on expectations. How do we manage data well, at an ever-increasing scale, while meeting the expectations of customers, partners, and employees? How do you bring the company along on the journey to data governance excellence? How *exactly* do we build trust in data in this new world?

It starts with *you*. We have to build trust with the people we do business with.

In this chapter, we will cover the following main topics:

- Building relationships with impact
- Landing an executive sponsor
- Establishing feedback loops
- Key roles to support you
- How to gain the support of the masses

Knowing that relationships are a core component of building trusted relationships and excellent data solutions, let's dive into how to build relationships with impact.

Building relationships with impact

Because data and analytics are a core tenet of any digital business, CDAOs have to take accountability for measurable results tied to business outcomes. You serve the company end to end and top to bottom. You have to build support from this perspective. Without getting too deep into the foundations of neuropsychology, the coalition of advocates you need to build trust in data must start with building trust in you. Your colleagues and stakeholders must believe that *you* can bring order to chaos. They must believe that you can drive this change. Ultimately, the relationships you build early in your program can either make or break your success. According to *Gartner*, "*Culture and literacy are the top two roadblocks for data and analytics leaders.*" (*10 Ways CDOs Can Succeed in Forging a Data-Driven Organization*, published May 22, 2019, Gartner.) These two terms "*culture*" and "*literacy*" are thrown around in the data industry constantly.

Unpopular opinion: I don't like either of them. Let's explore this further:

- **Culture** is defined as *"the customary beliefs, social forms, and material traits of a racial, religious, or social group"* [2]. Thus, it's not about creating a data culture; it's about creating a culture where data is a foundational component of the culture of the company: a bias for data over opinion, and facts over feelings. It's about making data a part of the everyday workings of the company – not as a separate "data culture," but woven into the overall culture of the company.

> **Data culture failures**
>
> In my experience, when CDAOs push a "data culture," they send a message that data is more important than other components of culture, and I wholeheartedly disagree with this approach. I have seen CDAOs fail by pushing this agenda. Instead, it's far more effective to push the integration of data into the culture not as a separate initiative but as a part of the company's DNA.

- **Literacy** is defined as *"able to read and write; having knowledge or competence"* [4]. Thus, the purpose of data literacy programs is to empower the company as a whole to be able to read and use data and have competence in data use; however, launching a program for data literacy also tends to fall flat. Instead, I recommend incorporating data into all programs (that is, policy training, compliance, and alongside technical training as a technical competence). Treating the general knowledge around data like other general competencies will make the learning feel more organic to the average employee, and creating focused training for the technical creators (for example, data engineers), makes this focus more natural for the company to adopt. Forcing the executive team to sit through "data literacy" programs/trainings is often off-putting at best and insulting at worst. Find a way to make this learning natural, and you will find the program to be more successful and welcomed.

While some may suggest you need to create a data culture in your organization with force and formality, what I believe is more tangible, measurable, and appropriate: build trust. *Through* building trust, you will improve the overall data culture and increase data literacy. Don't make the mistake of launching a "literacy" campaign or a "culture" program. Build trust through *delivery*, and the culture will come; data-driven decision-making will improve (for example, literacy). You must establish yourself and your team(s) as business peers to core business leaders, not simply internal **service providers (SPs)**, driving tangible business impact.

- **Trust** is defined as "*assured reliance on the character, ability, strength, or trust in someone or something; one in which confidence is placed*" [3]. I would much rather focus on building confidence in data, in me, and in my teams' capabilities and deliveries than focusing on literacy or culture. In my experience, focusing on building trust in data is a far more elevated and mature level of data governance than launching a literacy campaign. Is literacy a part of the program? Yes, of course, but it is simply one part of the program. One must focus on building a trusted data governance program, and literacy will follow.

Therefore, for the purposes of this chapter and, furthermore, this book, I will focus on how to build trusted solutions that empower data-driven decision-making through the delivery of world-class data governance programs and solutions.

> **Building trust**
>
> As Anna Jankowska stated in *Forbes*:
>
> "*Until you know the other party and their needs well enough, you will not be able to provide value. Your judgment may be biased and grounded in previous business experiences. Instead, you have to provide a totally objective and emotionally uninvolved perspective. Only then are you qualified to discuss their business needs and pain points and show them how your solution can enhance their performance.*"

Building trust one relationship at a time

Building trust happens in each interaction you have with your stakeholders. They are not just looking for trust in the results – they are building trust in you to deliver those results. There are a few ways you can go about bringing the company on your journey to build trust in data. You could drive it as a compliance exercise (aka…the "stick" method), which is based on driving data governance activities because you "have to" do them. You could do it purely by incentive (aka…the "carrot" method), which is based on driving data governance activities through incentives. Or, you could build a coalition of advocates and drive data governance from all sides. The latter is by far the most effective and the method with the most staying power.

This approach also shifts the burden off of only your shoulders and creates an environment where the whole company plays a part in the success of the program. In other words, it makes data governance a team sport. In this team of advocates, you are the team captain and ultimately accountable for the success (or failure) of the program, but you are no longer alone.

A more traditional approach to onboarding into a new CDAO or CDO role would suggest you work with peers to gather information cross-functionally, across the organization. I have found this only gives you a filtered view of the workings of the company because you are working at a layer of management that receives a filtered view of the organization. A broader and more inclusive approach involves the following:

1. **Horizontal**: Speaking with peers across the organization (yes – the traditional approach).

2. **Up**: Speaking with your manager (maybe C-suite; maybe the CEO) and the Board of Directors.

3. **Down**: Listening to your team (direct and indirect reports) to hear what is happening in your org and where your opportunities are within.

4. **Across**: Talk to larger groups of individuals at all levels to get a well-rounded understanding. This may include groups of individuals working on a large cross-functional project or teams within another part of the organization. Be strategic about how you select these groups, but do sample across the organization widely to get a broad understanding.

5. **Out**: Connect with vendors, consultants, and individuals who have left the company (including your predecessor, if applicable). Outside-in perspectives can help you learn what people are unwilling or unable to tell you.

This well-rounded approach results in a broad group of people feeling engaged and willing to support you long-term. This group feels seen and heard and thus is more likely to support you and your team. Ask for recommendations and solutions. Stakeholders will feel like their input matters. Circle back to the broad group and share what you heard and what you did with their input. If you considered it and went a different way, that's OK! Share it anyway. If you included it, show them.

Additionally, I recommend you conduct 1:1 meetings, small groups, and larger group listening sessions to gather input. Some individuals are more comfortable 1:1, whereas others may prefer a larger group setting. No matter what models you use, establish trust and build rapport with the person or people you are meeting with. They need to feel seen and that you are truly listening to them.

Identifying stakeholders

While it's tempting to dive right in and try to speak to everyone, I recommend starting with building a stakeholder map. This exercise will be grounding for you when it comes to measuring impact and success on an ongoing basis. Remember – not all stakeholders will hold equal prioritization. It does not mean they are not all important; they are. You will need to evaluate each one and work together to prioritize the most meaningful and impactful outcomes as you build your business case and strategy. Planning these interactions has a direct correlation to your chances of success in this role.

Start by listing out your stakeholders into groups:

- **Internal**: Stakeholders who are employed by your company
- **External**: Stakeholders who are not employed by your company but have a relationship with the organization in some way

When identifying the types of stakeholders in each group, consider who will be impacted the most based on whether your team and work are successful or if you fail. Additionally, you will need to prioritize these stakeholders as you build out your business case and delivery plan, so it's important to get to a manageable level of granularity (too many, and it will be too much to track; too few, and you won't be specific enough to define what you will do for each business group).

In the next two tables, I will show an internal stakeholder and external stakeholder examples, to help contextualize the information above.

> **Internal stakeholder groups – a banking example**
> - Individual contributors – tellers or analysts
> - Managers – branch managers or credit managers
> - Divisional leaders – community banking district leaders or credit risk VP
> - Executive team – community banking executive VP or chief credit risk officer
> - Board of Directors

> **External stakeholder groups – a banking example**
> - Customers – checking account holders or loan applicant
> - Partners – loan origination third-party vendor
> - Vendors/suppliers – credit reporting agency (for example, Experian, TransUnion)
> - Investors – stockholders

As you consider your own organization, it can be helpful to model out the mapping by customer, partner, vendor/suppliers, and investors like the example above. However, the definition of external is broadening:

> **Hint for success**
>
> More recently, I have seen companies take a broader view with regard to external stakeholders. Some companies have started considering stakeholders such as the environment to define the duty they believe to have to support or protect the world. Depending on your company's business, you may have additional internal and/or external stakeholders that make sense.

For each group, identify what their most critical priorities are. Consider asking or researching the following:

1. What is their role within the organization?

2. Is their relationship generally positive or negative?

3. How do they contribute or benefit from the organization?

4. What does success mean to them?

Start by building out your stakeholder map with these answers into a table or template that you can refer to as you build out your business case and deliver against your program. There are a number of formats you can use, but a template such as this can get you started:

Internal stakeholder groups

Group	Role	Health Status	Contributions and Benefits	Measures of Success
Individual contributors	Deliver against company plan via individual performance plans	Positive	Compensated by hourly, salary, perhaps healthcare and financial benefits (401k, and so on)	Employee satisfaction survey Voluntary attrition/turnover rates
Managers	Manage individual contributors' delivery against company plan	Neutral	Compensated by salary, commissions healthcare, and financial benefits (401k, and so on)	Customer satisfaction score Sales target % attainment for the product under management
Divisional leaders	Manage division/area	Positive	Compensated by salary, performance bonus, healthcare, and financial benefits (401k, and so on)	Customer lifetime value (CLV) Aggregated sales target % attainment for product line

Group	Role	Health Status	Contributions and Benefits	Measures of Success
Executive team	Manage entire business units (BUs)	Negative	Compensated by salary, performance bonus, stock options/ grants, healthcare, and financial benefits (401k, and so on)	Sales attainment % for all products Customer Satisfaction Scores (CSATs) Sales funnel contributions by marketing
Board of Directors	Recruit, supervise, retain, evaluate, and compensate the CEO (including succession planning) Oversee the strategy of the organization Establish a governance system for the company	Neutral	Cash and stock; expense reimbursement	Stockholder elections for public companies; appointment by private companies (varies)

Table 2.1 – External Stakeholder Group Example

Internal stakeholder groups – a banking example

Group	Role	Health Status	Contributions and Benefits	Measures of Success
Individual contributors: tellers	Serve customers in bank branches; teller drive through line	Neutral	Hourly employees (tellers); salary employees (teller supervisors)	# of accounts opened / week >= 25 Time to serve <= 4.3 minutes/ customer

Group	Role	Health Status	Contributions and Benefits	Measures of Success
Managers: branch managers	Manage a single bank branch	Positive	Salary; performance bonuses, non-financial benefits (for example, health insurance)	# of accounts opened / week >= 250 Customer retention >= 90% Cost to serve reduction of 10% in 6 months
Divisional leaders: community banking district leader	Manage a district of bank branches (with many branches)	Neutral	Salary, performance bonus, healthcare, and financial benefits, stock grant (401k, and so on)	Improve cost to acquire customers by 10% YOY Improve average time to close complaints by 2 minutes/ complaint YOY # of accounts opened/week >= 2,500
Executive team: community banking executive VP	Sets strategic direction and delivers success of the community banking division of the company	Positive	Salary, performance bonus for meeting goals, stock options/ grants, healthcare, (401k, and so on)	Improve operating cash flow from the banking division by 10% YOY Improve revenue by 5% YOY Reduce customer complaints by 10% YOY Reduce expenses by 10% YOY

Group	Role	Health Status	Contributions and Benefits	Measures of Success
Board of Directors	Recruit, supervise, retain, evaluate, and compensate the CEO (including succession planning) Oversee the strategy of the organization Establish a governance system for the company (committees, approving policies, and so on)	Positive	Cash and stock	Retention of CEO Company strategic plan attainment Reelection of board members

Table 2.2 – Internal Stakeholder Group Example

As you work to identify and define your strategy, you need to answer the following question: How will you enable your stakeholders to achieve their goals through building trust in data?

Building a stakeholder map

To begin to identify and align outcomes for your program, start by building a stakeholder map. A stakeholder map is an evergreen document that you should build together with your team. The map identifies all stakeholder groups that you will be supporting and/or are already supporting. I recommend making this stakeholder map available for your team. You may also want to open it up to your stakeholders for transparency, alignment, and ongoing quarterly business reviews.

Getting started

To begin to make a stakeholder map, start by defining the purpose of the stakeholder map so that you and your team members are grounded on why the map is important and why it will matter in the future. One simple statement you can leverage is, *"The purpose of this stakeholder map is to identify who we are serving, what their objectives are, how we are enabling their success, and our measures of success in delivering for them."* To create the stakeholder map, gather the following inputs:

- Company strategy

- Company organizational chart

- Current portfolio of work

- Any existing measures of success, **key performance indicators (KPIs)**, or **objectives and key results (OKRs)** in support of key deliverables for each stakeholder

After you have these items gathered, you can start to build out the map with the details, starting first with a template.

Building the map

Next, build a template for this exercise. Any simple table can support this. I've seen great stakeholder maps built into a presentation, in a spreadsheet, or on virtual whiteboarding software. The format is less important than the content, so be flexible with the means and focus on the end result. If your team has a preference, lean in.

An example template could look like this:

Stakeholder Group	Stakeholder Objectives	Data Solutions	Target Business Results
Marketing			
Sales			
Technology, Product & Engineering			
Human Resources			
Legal & Privacy			
Security			
Business Divisions			

Figure 2.1 – Stakeholder map template

As you work with your team and your stakeholder groups, you will begin to understand the stakeholder's priorities in rank order of importance. You will then identify what you will do or what you have done to support that stakeholder and the target business results that your team has or will deliver.

An example for the sales division could look like this:

Stakeholder Group	Stakeholder Objectives	Data Solutions	Target Business Results
Sales	1. Increase Sales 12% YOY 2. Maintain customer attrition at or below 8.5%	1. Deliver propensity to buy models for top 5 products by end of Q2 2. Build Early Warning System to identify customers at risk of attrition to enable customer success to save the account from churning	1. Increase sales 3% from propensity modeling 2. Identify ˜200 accounts at risk of attrition and retain >= 50% of accounts (100+)

Figure 2.2 – Stakeholder map example: sales division

Once you have created the map, you will want to share and maintain the map with your stakeholder.

Maintaining the map

As you work with the **chief revenue officer** (**CRO**) or head of sales, use this format or one like it to anchor your ongoing one-on-one meetings. Ask the following questions:

1. Have your priorities changed? Have any new priorities emerged?

2. Are these priorities still aligned with what you need from my team? Is there anything missing?

3. Do these solutions still meet your needs? Are there any additional features or capabilities that you would like to see?

4. Do these target business results make sense? Are they what you expect from us? Are they ambitious enough? Not enough?

Finally, as you deliver against these solutions, you can add a fifth column, for actual results. Then, you can ask a very important follow-up question:

Are we aligned on the measured business results? Do you agree that my team provided this impact on your team's success?

If the answer is no, ask additional questions from a place of curiosity. A suggestion that has worked for me in the past: What isn't sitting well or doesn't make sense as written? Are you willing to dig into this with me? I'd really like to get this right for you. The reason this works well is it's not defensive; it's from a place of true partnership. You are showing your stakeholders that you are committed to getting this business result right, not just in the delivery but in the measured business result. Ideally, you want your stakeholders to tell others what you did to enable their team, and they need to believe it as much as you do.

The case for building trust in data

According to Gartner, "*only 23% of respondents to Gartner's Fifth Annual CDO Survey indicated that they defined and tracked metrics to measure the value delivered by data and analytics to stakeholder outcomes.*" (*Tie Your Data and Analytics Initiatives to Stakeholders and Their Business Goals*, published June 9, 2020, Gartner.) I see this day after day both inside the companies I have worked in and for peers. Most commonly, I see measurements that are about the immediate stakeholder:

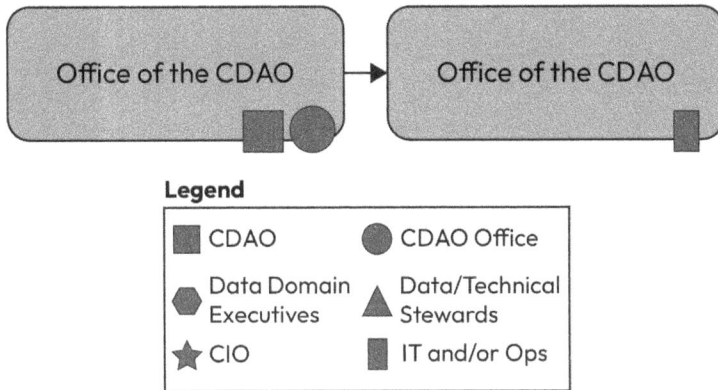

Figure 2.3 – Value chain to immediate stakeholder

For what it's worth, you're not alone. Data teams across industries and information technology teams both struggle with telling the ultimate value story. There are what I would call "traditional" data value metrics that matter for your data team. Data teams must go beyond basic metrics (that is, the percentage of improvement in data quality) and dive into stakeholder-impacting metrics.

For example, when delivering a propensity-to-buy model (that is, the likelihood of a customer buying a specific product), a data team often measures the time savings they created for the organization by implementing the model, meaning how much time was saved by the business from calculating the model manually, versus implementing an **artificial intelligence (AI)/machine learning (ML)**-driven model produced by the CDAO office's data science team. While this measure of success is a strong one (time savings of manual work versus model use almost always results in a positive investment story), it is not the ultimate measure of success. The account executive within the sales team is recommending more appropriate solutions based on the model created by the CDAO team. This real-life example provides the end customer with a felt impact.

Unfortunately, when data teams focus on their first-degree stakeholder (sales operations) we fail to see the ultimate impact of our work (sales teams and the customer), and lose out on the following:

1. Measurement of the value added to the enterprise

   - Increased revenue

   - Time savings

   - Increased customer value

2. Critical feedback loops from end users

   - Sales teams

   - Customers

3. Customer intimacy required to drive solutions that matter

   - Better measurement of buying behavior and ultimately increase sales

   - Better recommendations

   - More relevant sales

   - Increased customer satisfaction

   - Lower churn rate/customer attrition

To capture the full breadth of the impact, you must work more broadly, and work towards the ultimate stakeholder, as depicted below:

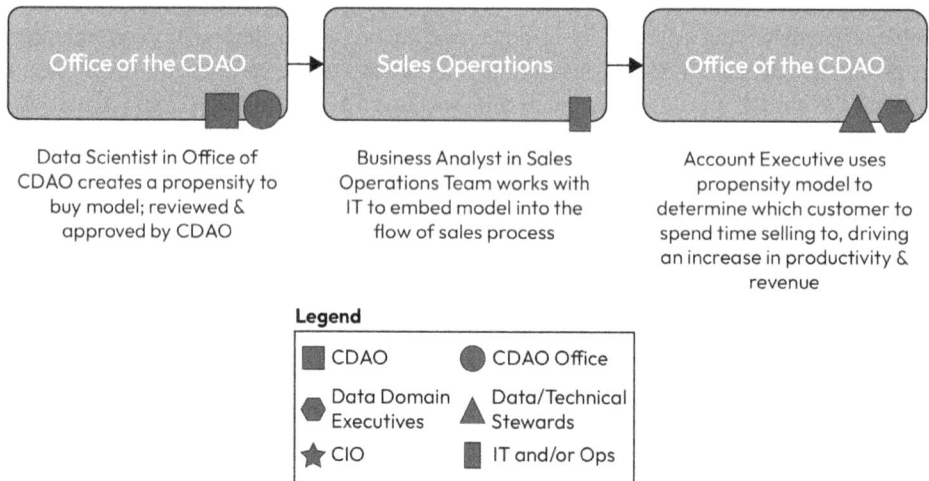

Figure 2.4 – Value chain from data office to business and to customer

In reality, the impact is much more significant. You should measure more specifically by determining the following:

1. How much did revenue increase?
2. How much productivity did the sales team save, by being able to rely on this model?
3. How much did customer satisfaction scores shift by being sold products that they actually want?
4. How much did customer trust increase?

Nearly every company fails to translate this into tangible, measurable, customer-impacting results. *What will the business gain? Why do it? Who benefits? By how much? Why? Who cares?* Success for CDAOs must be tied to stakeholders' strategic, critical priorities. This mindset will help you as you work towards securing an executive sponsor.

Landing an executive sponsor

Before you begin to deliver wide-scale initiatives, you must identify and secure an executive sponsor. An executive sponsor is a single individual who will be providing top-down support for your program. Over the next several pages, I will share how to identify an executive sponsor, what makes a great sponsor, who else needs to support you, and finally, how to bring the entire company along on the journey.

To gather support, the most effective place to start is from the top down in your organization. Ideally, you should seek to obtain full support from the entire C-suite. However, you do need at least one (ideally at least two) C-suite member(s) who will serve as your executive sponsor(s). Executive sponsors differ from other executives in that they will be more hands-on in your overall data governance work and should help you navigate gaining support across the organization, including obtaining funding. If you are new to your organization, executive sponsors may also help you understand how to navigate the organization, what underlying politics may exist, and identify who makes investment decisions, and ultimately, prioritization decisions.

Without an executive sponsor, gaining momentum and funding may be much harder. In my first few data transformations, I personally experienced much stronger headwinds when we did not obtain the support of the right executives at the right time. While we ultimately ended up with a program that achieved our goals, it took much longer to gain momentum and support. This ultimately had a cascading effect on our ability to make measurable progress quickly.

Identifying and assessing sponsors

One of the best ways to identify an executive sponsor is to find an executive who has data governance needs that are preventing their success from coming to fruition. In *Chapter 1*, we discussed conducting deep listening sessions to identify needs across the organization. Now that you have those needs identified, thoroughly review which executive leaders have the most significant and urgent needs that you can solve with data governance solutions. The result is your best possible executive sponsor.

Why business sponsors make the best sponsors

When it comes to finding a sponsor for data transformation, your best bet is to find a highly motivated business sponsor. Business sponsors are motivated because they have business needs. It sounds simple, but it is a simple driver that is often overlooked. The first thing to do is to evaluate their business strategy and identify opportunities for you to drive results for them within their business strategy through data solutions.

In the preceding section, I shared how to rethink how to identify the ultimate impact of your results. The ultimate internal stakeholder group (meaning the group you impact with your future delivery) makes the best candidates because they see, feel, and can measure the results of your data solutions. We will get into how to measure results more specifically in *Chapter 5*.

Use case – technology company

In one of my first roles in data, I had a big adjustment: learning to position a data solution without a regulatory driver. Although regulation can feel like a burden, it can also be helpful in driving change. During one of my earlier data transformations, I had to learn to position a data investment based on business needs exclusively.

Previously, I had been in the role of driving regulatory compliance, which required specific data solutions to be implemented. In this new role, I had to identify (clearly) what the business needed, why they needed it, and how I would measure success, and I had to do this all prior to securing funding.

While the solution was consistent (**Master Data Management** (**MDM**) platform), the positioning was completely different. In the technology company, I worked closely with the marketing division and **Chief Marketing Officer** (**CMO**) to define how we would master contact information for leads and what an improvement in master data contacts would mean for their business success. Therefore, the CMO became one of the business sponsors for the program. Additionally, we identified cost savings, and as a result, the **Chief Accounting Officer** (**CAO**) served as the other sponsor. Together, we proposed a solution, secured funding, and measured ongoing success throughout a 12-month delivery timeline.

Once you've identified opportunities to drive business results for your potential business sponsor, you should sit down with them and explain in business terms what data solutions you can deliver to help them achieve business success. You will need to articulate what you will do, how you will deliver it, what it will cost, how long it will take, how you will measure success, and the outcome that they will realize in business terms. We will spend more time in *Chapter 5* articulating how to craft these measurements.

Ultimately, **business sponsors** who believe you will drive business results for them will sponsor you. They have significant business needs, and when you help them win, you win. Additionally, when you drive success for them, they will tell your success story. The best success is one that your stakeholder tells on your behalf, so you should ensure they are fully bought into your delivery and that you empower them with outstanding results worth bragging about.

Hint for success
Make sure your measures of success go beyond "vanity metrics" of increased data quality and time or cost savings and truly measure business impact. While improving data quality, saving time, and lowering costs are all valuable, translating to business impact takes these results a step further. For example, if you improve the quality of your contact data, as in the preceding use case, it's far more valuable to articulate what the business was able to do because the quality of the contact data improved. In this example, we measured the improvement of the contact data (which was >40% higher quality) *and* what that meant to our marketing division. What it translated to was a higher-quality pipeline, which had a measurable impact on marketable contacts *and* a measurable increase in sales. We could specifically quantify how many dollars of additional revenue were created because of our implementation. Now, that was a data solution that got the entire C-suite talking.

Why your sponsor is not your CIO

A common mistake in alignment in many organizations (irrespective of industry) is for the **Chief Information Officer** (**CIO**) to become the de facto sponsor for the CDAO and data governance programs. There are four clear reasons why your CIO cannot be your primary sponsor:

- Your CIO is your partner.
- Your CIO is your enablement team.
- Your CIO may be working against you.
- Your CIO has their own challenges with the business.

The primary reason why your sponsor is not your CIO is simple: your CIO is your delivery partner. They are one of your most critical partnerships in the entire organization, but not as a sponsor. Both a CDAO and a CIO have a common sponsor: the business. The very best sponsors are the businesses that you serve, together. Your CIO is there to enable you. When it comes to implementing the technology behind your data solutions, your CIO is there to help you be successful. Additionally, the CIO is there to enable your businesses to be successful. This is why you may also run into challenges with your CIO. They may have an incentive to deliver directly for the business instead of for you.

Unfortunately, you may find that their CIO could be actually working against you, because of this dynamic. If it comes down to prioritization, your CIO may be biased to deliver directly to the business instead of for you in service of the business. This is why it's critical that the CIO works with you to prioritize appropriately with the business to ensure alignment enterprise-wide. Ideally, the CDAO, the CIO, and the business would sit down together to prioritize and align on priorities, measurable outcomes, and a plan for how to resolve issues when they arise.

Hint for success
While the CIO is *not* the most effective place for a CDO to report to, it is one of the more common structures. If you find the CDAO reporting to the CIO, it becomes even more critical to have strong business sponsorship in the event prioritization becomes a risk to the data governance program's success.

Characteristics of a great sponsor

If not the CIO, who should be your sponsor? The answer is the business leader who believes in you. So, how do you identify a great sponsor? It comes down to a few key factors:

- **They challenge you**: A great sponsor will challenge you in many ways, but primarily, they will challenge you to define success in business terms that matter to them. You will be required to define the problem you are solving, not only in data terms but in business results that impact the business as a whole.

- **They force you to dig deeper**: When you propose solutions, they will challenge you to make your business case stronger, more relevant, and aligned with corporate strategy in ways you wouldn't or couldn't see for yourself.

- **They define ultimate impact**: Your sponsor should have a well-established reputation for defining success in terms of the ultimate impact on the success of the company. They should help you to understand how to position the impact of your solutions in a manner that the company will understand so that you can communicate the ultimate impact of your solutions in a way that is culturally appropriate and will garner support.

- **They have CEO sponsorship**: The best sponsors are aligned with and supported by the CEO.

- **They are on the C-suite**: The sponsor you select needs to be a direct report to the CEO to ensure adequate sponsorship at the top of the organization and to ensure the CEO is involved in conversations about data governance.

Now that we've covered what makes a good sponsor, let's dig into how to build a great business case to help secure the sponsor you desire.

Building a business case to land a sponsor

As you deeply listen to your stakeholders, including your potential executive sponsor, this is the time to take all of those problems and needs that they share with you and craft them into a business case for your program. I would recommend you start with the executive sponsor's area of responsibility and define this as one of your key focus areas (that is, data domains). This data domain can become your pilot that will allow you to draft your enterprise data strategy and simultaneously deliver on a data domain's needs.

Key components

Key components of a strong business case include the following:

1. Value proposition/objective

2. Business outcomes that are specific and measurable

3. Value chain creation to demonstrate where and when you will deliver value

4. Timelines and key milestones

5. Key partners, roles, and structures required to support delivery

There are several pros to this approach, which include being able to demonstrate delivery of meaningful business-valued solutions, securing quick and meaningful wins, and being able to adjust your enterprise data strategy iteratively as you deliver for this data domain. By focusing on this domain, you are able to balance learning the ways the organization operates, developing meaningful feedback loops for your solutions to deliver iteratively better, and you can build trust with your presumed executive sponsor so that they feel confident standing behind you in delivering enterprise-wide data governance.

Depending on the size, scale, and quality of your team, you may be able to launch a second domain and deliver for your secondary executive sponsor (we will talk about the team in *Chapter 3*). However, it is far better to execute with quality in one area than in multiple areas with anything less than high-quality results. This is even more important when you are new to an organization and are working to establish your personal brand and credibility and working to align the company behind your strategy. Be cautious about overpromising and under-delivering. This is the fastest path to exit a company quickly.

CDOs have alarmingly short tenures. According to *Harvard Business Review*, the reason the CDO role churns so quickly is a combination of high expectations and low ability to deliver, given the complexity of the challenge ahead of them. Further, they are in high demand, making experienced CDOs a target for external recruiting. Having worked in three *Fortune 500* organizations, I can attest to having personally witnessed a high turnover rate for the CDOs I have worked with, and as a CDO myself.

> **Key learning**
>
> The objective here is to optimize for impact and timeline. High impact, delivered too slowly, and the CDO will run out of time to make a difference before the expectations of their performance fade. Low impact delivered quickly, and the credibility of the CDO is in question. The goal here is to find a high-impact area where you can make quick and visible progress. Choose wisely.

The business-case format matters far less than the content. I have seen great business cases exist in slide presentations, as documents or memos, and be recordings or videos. The most important part is the information contained within the business case. Working closely with your executive sponsor and their direct team members, you should craft a very powerful *why* statement. Why do you need to deliver the data capabilities included? What will you do? What will the results be? And, finally, what will be different in terms of the business once the capabilities are implemented? Your business results are not "implemented a data catalog;" they are very specific to what the business can do once the data catalog is implemented. It may be most important that the company standardizes on common business terms enterprise-wide. The outcome is aligned business terminology; the capability is the data catalog. This delineation is critical to your success.

Finally, I recommend your business case is kept evergreen. As you learn and deliver, do not be afraid to come back to your original business case and make edits based on what you learn throughout your journey. The executive sponsor should be willing and able to spend the time needed to ensure complete alignment of the business case content prior to any launch. I recommend you start by aligning the executive sponsor's direct reports first, and then when you go to the executive sponsor for final sign-off, you have already obtained the alignment of their team.

A very successful business case I wrote was structured as an approximately 10-page memo that was built by my enterprise data team, with inputs from sales operations, sales, marketing, operations, IT, and legal/compliance. The business case was built over approximately 10-12 weeks and ultimately presented to our transformation committee for funding and approval. The format is of lesser importance than the content, but what worked well in this example was the following:

Example business case for data program

The following outlines what a business case for a data program might include:

Title of program

Executive sponsor [C-suite member]

Business sponsor [CDAO; in this case, me]

1. Background and context

    A. Objective

    B. Key solutions

    C. Measurable outcomes from the program in the form of KPIs/OKRs

2. Organization of work into delivery tracks

    A. This named the tracks and provided the scope for each and what success would look like from a capability's perspective

    B. We delivered a simple summary visual that explained the drivers, the programs contained within the business case, and the outcomes

3. The near-term measurable outcomes that the business would benefit from in the next 6-9 months

4. Our needs from the committee

5. Breakout by track:

    A. What it was

    B. Clear capabilities delivered

    C. Why it matters

    D. Outcomes for the track

    E. What had been done to date, before formalizing it into a program

    F. Key near-term milestones

    G. What is needed for the track

    H. Measurable KPIs/OKRs we committed to delivering for the track

6. Link to further resources:

    A. Program landing page

    B. Detailed roadmap

    C. Training programs about data transformation

7. Program overview slide embedded in the document for easy reference

For each quarterly update to the committee, we returned to this format and simply updated it to reflect the progress and any wins beyond what we committed to, as well as any misses. We clearly articulated how far we were in delivering against our KPIs/OKRs and revised transparently and openly when we needed to adjust. In driving our program in this manner, we set a precedent not just for how data can be measured in terms of value but also in how seemingly "difficult to measure" programs can, in fact, measure results in terms the business can understand. It put credibility into the data team and was one of the biggest changes I made: that of trust in data.

Hint for success

Unpopular opinion: don't try to convert the "hostile" or openly dissenting stakeholder. In my experience, executives who are not supportive have their reasons. You could spend countless amounts of energy attempting to convert them to your "side." However, it is usually fruitless. My best advice is to show, not tell, them what good looks like. Deliver a capability that helps them, and they will come around in time.

A note on translating to business outcomes

To be successful, you must translate your work into business outcomes. Because of the importance of this component, and that in my experience, it is the reason a CDAO succeeds or fails, we will spend an entire chapter on this topic to ensure you are empowered with all the information you need to craft meaningful business outcomes for your success and that of your team. *Chapter 5* will focus on this topic exclusively.

Establishing feedback loops

As you deliver the right capabilities for your executive sponsor, it is critical that you continue to meet with them during your delivery. Since you should be creating the enterprise data strategy while you are delivering for your executive sponsor's domain, you should hold at least quarterly enterprise data committee meetings to share progress, prioritize additional needs of the company, and garner additional support from the rest of the domain leaders. One of the biggest mistakes you can make is meeting at the wrong frequency. There are two extremes to consider:

1. Meeting too often, without meaningful updates or progress to share

2. Meeting too infrequently, and the committee does not remember what you committed to deliver and loses interest

It is your job to find the right audience and the right frequency to match your enterprise needs. I recommend quarterly meetings at first unless there is a great deal of urgency (for example, regulatory commitment, sanction, or another crisis). You can adjust as the members of the committee desire. Ask for feedback and continue to adjust as needed.

There are a few signs to watch for which indicate you might be on the wrong pacing for meeting with your enterprise data committee and executive sponsors:

1. **Your membership shifts**: If you find that your meeting starts to get delegated to lower levels of the organization, this is a signal that your members are not finding your meetings meaningful and have pushed them to their team members.

2. **You get requests for off-cycle meetings**: If you find that your members are asking for information off-cycle or in between meetings, you may need to meet more frequently.

3. **There is silence**: If you find there is little to no participation or no questions off-cycle at all, you may not be providing relevant information, or your members may not understand what you are trying to communicate with them.

If any of these (or all) are true, I recommend you ask for feedback as soon as possible from your committee members. These are all signs you need to make changes regarding the frequency and/or content you are sharing with the group. If the membership has shifted, you may need to do a series of 1:1 meetings with your members to re-engage them and ask them to return to future cycles of the meeting. You likely have one additional chance to re-engage them before they stop coming for good.

Assuming all is going well with your pilot data domain and executive sponsor, you may be able to launch a second data domain on a slightly staggered start date. A word of caution: do not start a second data domain unless you are very confident you have strong support from the company *and* the delivery of the first data domain is going very well. Even then, it is critical that you maximize quality over quantity. It is far better to execute well with one domain than to deliver against two with mediocre results.

Key roles to support you

As a part of your delivery plan, for your first data domain, I recommend you spend the appropriate time aligning on roles and responsibilities between your team (the business of data), the technology team (the technology of data), and the business team (the data domain). This can be accomplished by working with the executive data domain leader's team, the CIO (or their delegate), and your team. Working together to define what you are responsible for versus what the data domain is responsible for versus what the IT function is responsible for upfront will enable better teamwork as you get into delivery together.

You will also need to establish a strong relationship with your finance business partner to assist you in managing the appropriate budget for your program, as well as the talent team (sometimes referred to as HR or recruitment) as you build out your team, which I will describe in *Chapter 3* in more detail. There are various other functions that you may need to engage with depending on the size and scale of your own organization. Regardless of size and complexity, I recommend identifying all the parties you need involved and what you need from them or what they may need from you throughout your program:

* **CIO**: While they are not your executive sponsor, they are a critical member of your support team. The CIO is critical to your success because their team will ensure you have appropriate systems and tools, as well as engineering staff, to drive the implementation of platforms and data management tooling and ensure your solutions have adequate infrastructure to successfully deliver on your commitments.

- **Chief financial officer (CFO):** The CFO makes an excellent supporting/secondary sponsor but is also the supporter you need to secure funding. It's paramount that you bring your CFO along on your journey, explaining what you are proposing, the value (in decreased costs, decreased/managed risks, increased revenue, time savings, and so on), and key timelines. They will be able to help you navigate how to secure funding, who needs to support you, and what their role will be in allocating funding.

- **General counsel/chief privacy officer (CPO)/chief information security officer (CISO):** These key roles will be outstanding partners for you in driving requirements (that is, must-do activities to maintain legal and security protections for the company). They serve as independent and excellent supporters because they need you. For example, these three leaders must know what data the company has, where it is located, and how it is classified so that they can adequately protect it. Between these three leaders, you will need to develop a comprehensive list of requirements to support the legal needs of the company and what is required to secure the company's data.

- **Chief people officer (CPO)/head of HR:** Your CPO or head of HR is another critical partner in your success. This leader will help you structure and hire your team, re-organize team members into your function from other parts of the business, and build ongoing talent management support. Often, they will assign an HR business partner to align with your organization. Work with this leader directly, but occasionally stay connected with the CPO to ensure they are fully aware of what is working well and how your team's priorities are progressing. They can help you identify key talent in the broader company looking for new challenges that may be a great fit for your team.

- **Business leaders:** Business leaders run divisions of the company and are your ultimate stakeholders. What you deliver for the company is to enable them to achieve results. You should build strong relationships with each business leader, as described previously. Further, ensure you are reporting progress back to them by showing them results your team drove for the entirety of the business. You need their vocal support for your program. In some companies, business leaders can also allocate a budget to support your efforts.

Your executive sponsor should sponsor you to present early and regularly at your company's most executive forum. Some companies refer to this group as the C-suite, the executive leadership team, or perhaps e-Staff (for executive staff). It may contain only the CEO's direct reports or it may include additional roles, depending on the CEO's preferences. I recommend having your executive sponsor set the stage for you, explaining why they have decided to play a role in your success and what value they believe you can bring, and endorse your program before they introduce you. This will grab the audience's attention so that they are focused on your presentation. Return to the forum regularly to share wins, adjustments, and impacts that you achieve.

The executive leadership team may also want you to present at the Board of Directors meetings, depending on the state of data at your organization and the importance of the issue. I highly recommend presenting to your board if the opportunity is presented. They can be incredible supporters and can ensure the CEO supports you. As a board member myself, I often ask questions about data presented in board packets and that management is using for decision-making.

How to gain the support of the masses

With the amount of data doubling by 2026 and the increased demand for a trust-based approach, it's critical we approach building our programs through that same lens: one where trust comes first. To build trust with the entirety of the organization, you need to show them they can trust you through your delivery. We previously discussed the importance of the enterprise data committee, which is critical for executive support. In addition, you should create forums and communication mechanisms to keep excitement and energy up about what you are doing to transform the company.

I recommend setting up a forum that does not have a restriction on the "who" or "how many" people attend. A broad and open forum is a great place to show what has been done versus telling what has been done. As you build capabilities, providing a demonstration as to what has been delivered and how the masses can start to take advantage and use the capabilities is how you will start to show your delivery and gain trust. Remember – you do not gain trust by talking about what you will do; you gain trust by showing what you did. Trust is built on actions, not talk.

Anchor your communications on a very basic model: What will the average employee be able to do upon delivery that they can't do today? Why does that matter? The answers to these two basic questions are your message. Be clear about this, specific, and with a strong bias for their lived experience in your company.

Make your progress transparent. Use internal wikis, electronic newsletters, and even short video clips to tell the masses what is happening and how delivery is progressing. Using a tool such as Confluence® to post key information about your transformation (such as your business case!), the roadmap, recent accomplishments, links to key artifacts (such as business requirements and technical requirements), as well as metrics will save you time in having to hold meetings every time someone has a question.

The preceding steps in which you bring together the power of a supportive executive sponsor, your enterprise data committee, and stakeholders enterprise-wide through forums and written communication is creating the energy that will carry you through the data governance transformation. It's your responsibility and honor to unite the masses in this way. Very few programs have the ability or the interest to unite this broad community in the way you can, by building trust in data. The cornerstone of the entire coalition is relationships. Invest early and often to drive the results you desire.

Conclusion

Building a strong relationship with stakeholders is a critical component of any data leader's success. As you think about building an entire network of supporters, be laser focused on which one or two would make the best sponsors. In this chapter I shared what makes a great sponsor, how to build a strong business case to secure a leader as your sponsor, and why a CIO is a great partner, but not your best selection for a sponsor. As a result of this chapter you should now be able to:

1. Build relationships with the executive team and key roles at all levels of the organization.
2. Identify at least one, ideally two, executive sponsor.
3. Write a compelling business case for your executive sponsor's data domain.
4. Establish feedback loops and communication mechanisms.
5. Communicate with the enterprise to gain the support of the masses.

As we pivot now into Chapter 3, where we walk through how to build a high performing team to drive success for your company, remember what your sponsor needs, and how you might build a great team to impact your sponsors desired outcomes. Chapters 2 and 3 can be executed concurrently, and both topics take time to complete. The best time to get started on both, is right now.

References

1. https://www.mckinsey.com/capabilities/quantumblack/our-insights/why-digital-trust-truly-matters
2. https://www.merriam-webster.com/dictionary/culture?utm_campaign=sd&utm_medium=serp&utm_source=jsonld
3. https://www.merriam-webster.com/dictionary/trust
4. https://www.merriam-webster.com/dictionary/literate#h1

3
Building a
High-Performing Team

Establishing a high-performing data governance team is a critical and long-term investment in the success of the company's use of data. By reading this chapter, I assume you are looking to build a high-performing data governance team and/or create an entire data and analytics function. Ultimately, your success will depend on the team you assemble to deliver excellent, high-quality impactful solutions for your organization. Given the scarcity of talented data professionals, this is the second most critical indicator of your success; that is, hiring the best possible talent you can afford for your company (the first being able to set and measure what success is, as I covered in *Chapter 2, How to Build a Coalition of Advocates* and *Chapter 5, Define Success & Align on Outcomes*).

Depending on your company's unique situation, you may encounter a few different scenarios that have led to your need to build a team. You might be the first hire for data and have to build an entire team from scratch. You could have been brought in to bring together disparate teams across your company to unify them under your leadership. Or, you could have inherited an entirely intact existing team in need of a transformation. No matter which situation you find yourself in, the performance of the team sits firmly on your shoulders from the moment you walk in the door.

In this chapter, we will discuss what roles matter and why, how to structure the team for success, how to implement the right routines and rhythms, and how to grow talent both within your team and across your company. As you might have assumed, establishing a high-performing data governance team is a critical and long-term investment in the success of the company's use of data. **Chief Data and Analytics Officers (CDAOs)** and offices of the CDAO only began to be established in 2002 (first, at *Capital One*), and as recently as 2012, only 100 CDAOs existed globally. However, in the last few years, the number of CDAOs has grown to over 152,000, according to *LinkedIn* data. The role of **Chief Data Officer (CDO)** is much more common, with 67.9% of major companies reported to have appointed a CDO, up from 12% in 2012. With demand for CDAO roles emerging at a rapid pace and the salary of these specialists rising to match demand, the **return on investment (ROI)** of these roles is under constant scrutiny. It is critical for the success of the office of the CDAO to build a high-performing team quickly, efficiently, and with effective measures of value.

We will cover the following main topics:

- Optimizing for outcomes

- Three common data organization models

- What roles are needed

- AI considerations

- How to structure the team for results (and why)

- Building the rhythm of the business of data

- Functional roles

- Talent development

Optimizing for outcomes

As you set out to design an organizational model and operational model for how your company will deliver data management and analytics outcomes that matter, you must begin with the end in mind. You are not building a single department; you are building a data-empowered enterprise. Long before you begin to design an organizational model, you must define what capabilities you need to deliver. The capabilities are a major outcome of the conversations you held when building your coalition of advocates out of the process outlined in *Chapter 2, How to Build a Coalition of Advocates*.

Use case

In one of my previous companies, there was a large and critical focus on the quality of data used in reporting. As a result, much of our data strategy was anchored on one major capability: rearchitecting the data infrastructure to drive a streamlined and curated data ecosystem that could produce high-quality reports with a high degree of reusability of common data elements that fed these reports. This ensured common data elements were reliable and of high quality. It was a clear and focused plan based on a specific outcome that the company organized and optimized around.

As a result, the largest portion of headcount was focused on creating authorized provisioning points, ensuring we had a comprehensive and reliable data lake and that we deployed strong data governance across all environments. Analytics and data science were combined into one leader, whereas the data management components were broken out and reported directly to the CDAO due to the importance of these capabilities and the low maturity level. This allowed for more direct oversight and focus of the CDAO over data management since that was our major investment and focus area.

Common outcomes

There are endless combinations of outcomes that a data and analytics team may be focused on at any given time, with new focuses emerging all the time. At the time of this writing, **generative artificial intelligence (GenAI)** has taken the forefront of much of the innovation space, and thus, the emergence of the importance of high-quality data is moving back to the top of the CDAO agenda. The important consideration is, as we discussed in *Chapter 2*, *How to Build a Coalition of Advocates* evaluating company strategy to ensure that what you are prioritizing is supporting the needs of the business. The following are 10 common outcomes expected from establishing a high-performing team that have held throughout my data governance experience:

- **Improved decision-making**: A high-performing data management team enables faster, more accurate decisions by ensuring the data that is relied upon is accurate, up-to-date, and easily accessible.

- **Increased efficiency**: By establishing clear protocols and processes for data entry, storage, and retrieval, a high-performing data management team minimizes time wasted on searching for data or correcting errors, thereby increasing organizational efficiency.

- **Data security**: They ensure that sensitive data is protected, compliant with relevant regulations (such as the **General Data Protection Regulation** (**GDPR**), the **California Consumer Privacy Act** (**CCPA**), and so on), and only accessible to authorized individuals.

- **Enhanced data quality**: They implement data validation and cleansing processes to maintain the high quality of data, reducing the risk of decisions made based on erroneous information.

- **Scalability**: A well-organized data management team prepares for the future growth of an organization, making sure data infrastructure is scalable and can handle an increased amount of data as the company expands.

- **Improved customer experience**: By managing customer data effectively, the team can help other departments in personalizing the customer experience, predicting customer needs, and promptly responding to inquiries or issues.

- **Innovation and insights**: High-performing data management teams can aid in identifying patterns and trends within data, leading to new insights that drive innovation and strategic planning.

- **Data literacy**: Such a team can also help improve data literacy within the organization, equipping employees with the understanding and skills needed to use data effectively in their roles.

- **Regulatory compliance**: Good data management ensures that the company is compliant with industry standards and regulations related to data privacy and management, preventing potential legal issues and penalties.

- **Cost savings**: Proper data management can lead to significant cost savings over time. These savings could come from improved efficiencies, reduction in errors, or preventing expensive data breaches and non-compliance penalties.

You can use this list of outcomes as a part of the justification for pulling a data team together. If you need a jumping-off point, select ones from this list that make sense for your business needs. You should customize areas of need, add new outcomes, and delete ones that do not apply.

Defining core functions

Up until this point, we have spent time defining data governance and exploring how to build outstanding partnerships, and now, the harder work begins. As the leader, your job is to take these inputs and start to shape your team. As there are an unlimited number of combinations of how to arrange data professionals into a team, I will walk you through some common patterns to get you started. Don't be afraid to deviate based on the needs of your company. Key questions to consider are the following:

- What are your core capabilities going to be?

- What will the team's priorities be?

- What is urgent and requires immediate attention versus what can wait?

- What do I, as the leader, need to be most engaged in? What do I need to stay closest to?

- What gaps in talent do I have within the team that may impact who needs my time and attention over others?

The answers to these questions will help determine which models make the most sense to drive the structure of your team. We will explore three foundational options for designing the data function and the pros and cons of each. As you continue to review these options, do not get hung up on which model is a perfect fit. A perfect fit does not exist. These organizational designs are templates to leverage for your team design.

Incorporating product management in organizational design

More recently, data governance teams and analytics teams have made an intentional shift to adopting core product management principles in data capability delivery. This shift has captivated companies both large and small due to the overwhelming benefits seen by focusing on doing fewer small, one-time deliveries, with a focus on long-term, sustained deliveries in lower quantity but higher quality.

Just as product management in the software development world focuses on creating and maintaining successful products, data product management involves treating data as a valuable asset and developing a strategic approach to its organization and utilization. Here's how you can incorporate product management in your organization design:

1. **Identifying stakeholders and their needs**. Just as in product management, understanding the needs of stakeholders is crucial in data organization design. Data organizations should identify the various teams, departments, and individuals that interact with data and gather their requirements. This helps in aligning data solutions with the specific needs of end users.

2. **Defining clear objectives and goals**. Data product management involves setting clear objectives and goals for data initiatives. This could include improving data accessibility and accuracy or enabling data-driven decision-making. By defining these objectives, data organizations can stay focused on what needs to be achieved and measure their success.

3. **Prioritizing data initiatives**. Similar to how product managers prioritize features and enhancements based on business value and user impact, data organizations should prioritize data initiatives based on their importance and potential impact on the organization's goals. This ensures that resources are allocated efficiently.

4. **Iterative development and agile practices**. Adopting iterative development methodologies and agile practices in data organization design enables continuous improvement. This approach allows data teams to iterate on their solutions based on user feedback, adapt to changing requirements, and respond to emerging business needs effectively.

5. **User-centric design**. Just as product managers focus on creating user-friendly products, data organizations should prioritize user-centric data design. This means providing data in a format that is easy to understand and use for end users and designing data solutions with the end-user experience in mind.

6. **Data documentation and communication**. Effective product management involves clear documentation and communication. Similarly, data organizations should document data definitions, data sources, and data lineage, making it easier for stakeholders to understand and use the data effectively.

7. **Performance measurement and metrics** (*yes, data about data!*). Data product management requires measuring the performance of data initiatives against set goals and KPIs. By tracking metrics related to data usage, data quality, and data accessibility, data organizations can continuously assess their performance and make data-driven improvements.

By adopting these product management principles, data organizations can ensure that their data infrastructure is aligned with business objectives, delivers value to stakeholders, and remains adaptable to evolving requirements in the dynamic world of data. As we explore common data organizational models in the rest of this chapter, I will pull through the concept of product management such that we incorporate these principles into our organizational design.

Three common data organization models

The roles you need should be determined by what you need to achieve. Truly, there are endless possibilities for how an organization could and should structure its team for success, and only you can design the right team for your unique situation. However, in the following pages, I will outline four types of data functions you may need to lead and suggest a few different organizational structures that will enable the four types to deliver successfully. It is your job, as the leader of the data function, to select which of the four types is appropriate for your organization's objectives.

Establishing the office of the CDO

Regardless of your company's data and analytic needs, organizations should have at least a small, central function. I will refer to this central function as the office of the CDO. Depending on your organizational structure selected, you may have a larger size and scoped office or a smaller size and scoped office. Ideally, this central office of the CDO will be responsible for setting the expectations, policies, and standards that the organization will adhere to. At a minimum, the central function will own the responsibility for setting these requirements and should also be responsible for implementation and ongoing monitoring of compliance.

Without establishing a central function that holds responsibility for requirements, implementation of the requirements, and ongoing monitoring of compliance, the various **business units (BUs)** will be left to their own requirements, implementation practices, and ongoing monitoring, which will result in inconsistencies in how data is managed as a company. If an organization wants to manage data well, it must establish this central group at a bare minimum. To maintain objectivity and remove bias in the policies and monitoring practices established by the office of the CDO, the leader of the Office of the CDO should report to as neutral of a location in the company as possible.

Federated data office model – office of the CDO

If a narrowly defined centralized office of the CDO is defined as outlined previously, the requirements set by this office will need to be implemented by the respective BUs. This model is "federated," whereas the office of the CDO does the bare minimum, and the BUs and respective corporate functions (for example, finance, sales, R&D) must do all the implementation work. In this model, divisions may or may not have divisional CDOs in place to drive the requirements within the respective divisions. They may also be empowered to design and implement their own capabilities to comply with the office of the CDO's enterprise policies:

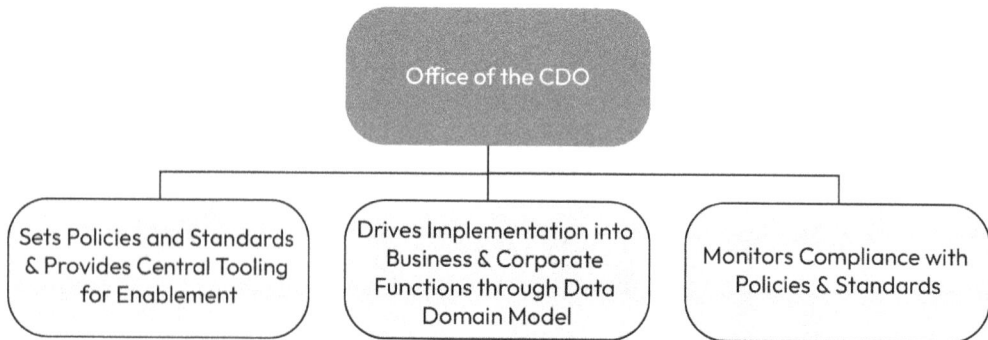

Figure 3.1 – Office of the CDO in the federated model

This model empowers the BUs and corporate functions to create capabilities that are needed for their own needs but makes it difficult to connect the capabilities together for an enterprise-wide view of data. Often, organizations begin with a model such as this, which favors the needs of each BU/corporate function without taking into account the enterprise and often necessitates a rationalization effort once data efforts become prioritized and more formalized.

To develop policies and standards, the office of the CDO should create an enterprise data council or enterprise data committee. This group should be chaired by the CDO and should comprise leaders from all major BUs and corporate functions. The requirements outlined in the policy should be approved by the enterprise data council/committee, published to the organization, and adopted by the BUs and corporate functions. Any tooling required to enable policy compliance should also be centrally maintained by the office of the CDO. Any policy exceptions or violations should be transparently monitored and reported to the respective BU or corporate function head, as well as to the CDO and the enterprise data council/committee.

Semi-Federated data office model – BUs and corporate functions

As BUs and corporate functions establish leaders to be accountable for policy and standard implementation within their divisions, each application, data asset, and service should be classified against the data domain model. The data domain model establishes a data steward for that asset, application, and/or service. The data steward is ultimately responsible for ensuring that asset, application, and/or service is managed in compliance with policies and standards set forth by the office of the CDO through the enterprise data council/committee and that the assets, applications, and/or services are used appropriately for their intended use:

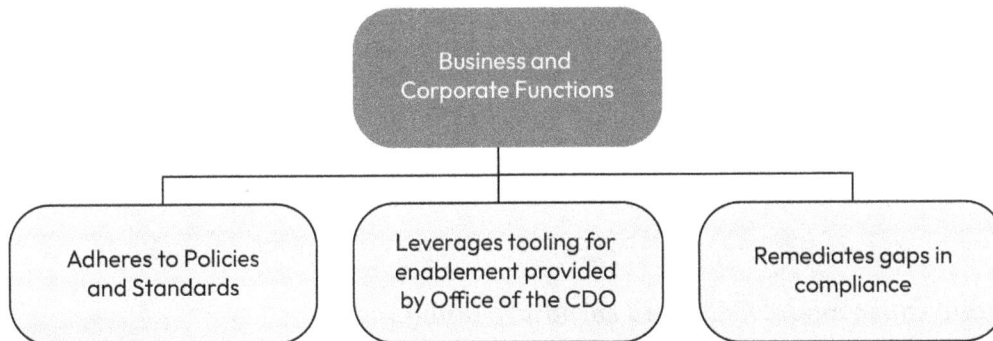

Figure 3.2 – BUs and corporate functions' responsibilities in the semi-federated model

Maturing and empowering through the hub and spoke model

A second model, the hub and spoke model, is designed such that the implementation of policies and standards may be through what is referred to as a hub and spoke model, whereas the central group provides the expectations, policies standards, *and capabilities*, and the spokes (the BUs and corporate functions) of the hub and spoke model drive the implementation down into the depths of the organization. Certainly, there are considerations for the type of business you're in, the regulations you may need to adhere to, as well as the size and complexity of your organization.

Hub and spoke model – Office of the CDO

The primary difference between the hub and spoke model and the federated model is that implementation activities fall firmly on the spokes or BUs and corporate functions in this model. In this model, each BU or corporate function may also have a divisional CDO, as with the federated model. While seemingly one significant difference exists in the federated model versus the hub and spoke model, this difference is *significant* because the heavy lifting of data governance is not in defining what needs to be done but actually in delivering capabilities to the business via the adoption of central capabilities by the business. The major benefit of the hub and spoke model is the standardization of capabilities across the organization, which enables consistency across the company:

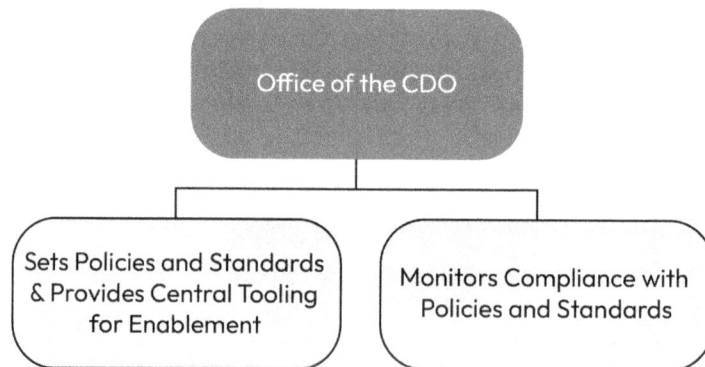

Figure 3.3 – Office of the CDO in the hub and spoke model

Hub and spoke model – BUs and corporate functions

This model shows how the BU or Corporate Functions should be designed:

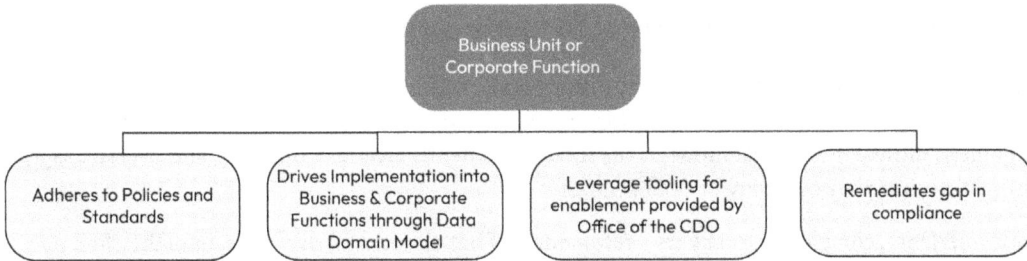

Figure 3.4 – BUs and corporate functions in the hub and spoke model

Driving consistency through the centralized model

In the centralized model, all responsibilities sit within the office of the CDO. This model is effective when there are large disparities between maturity across the organization, there are significant issues that require remediation, or the company is seeking to maximize consistency or cost savings in the short term. If your organization finds itself fully centralizing data and analytics, I urge you to advocate for this to be a short-term (12-24 months) solution, with the goal of moving to a hub and spoke model upon immediate remediation efforts being achieved. Long-term, the fully centralized model separates data stewards from their BUs and corporate functions, which erodes subject-matter expertise and decreases the effectiveness of the data steward over time.

Ideally, when centralizing, this allows all BUs and corporate functions to come together to take advantage of one another's expertise, rapidly adopt the capabilities enabled through the office of the CDO, and then push back out to the spokes of the hub and spoke model to manage data optimally across the organization long-term.

Centralized model – office of the CDO

The following diagram shows how the Office of the Chief Data Officer could be designed for a Centralized Model:

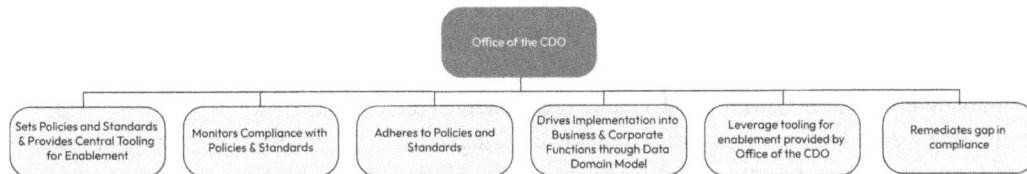

Figure 3.5 – Centralized model of the office of the CDO

How to select the right model for your organization

I have had the opportunity to drive data transformation within three *Fortune 500* organizations (to date), and I can confidently say this: no company manages data perfectly. While some do a better job than others, ultimately, the best model is the model that drives progress, maturity, and overall usage of insights to run your company or organization.

In my experience, companies usually try a few models (if not all of them) over time, until they find one that works well for their situation and/or corporate culture. If your company has yet to establish *any* data requirements or capabilities, I recommend starting with establishing an office of the CDO with a small starter team to first build the business case for data (see *Chapter 2, How to Build a Coalition of Advocates* for a deeper focus on building the case for data) and working toward the hub and spoke model over time, as functions buy into the outcomes for data maturity.

However, if your organization has some capabilities that are inconsistently implemented *and* you have major issues either with data quality, the appropriate use of data, or trust in your data insights, it may make sense to bring your data and analytics professionals together into a central team to drive consistency, rigor, and improve trust in your data function, capabilities, and output.

Lastly, if you have general support for your data initiative, strong leaders embedded in the BUs and corporate functions, and are looking to lift overall maturity, adoption of capabilities, or further strengthen the current state, the hub and spoke model is your best option. In my experience, the hub and spoke model is the strongest for lasting success *when, and only when* the central office of the CDO is also strong, well established, and appropriately funded (meaning staffing, tools, capabilities).

What roles are needed

The roles needed in an office of the CDO vary depending on the size and complexity of the organization. The CDO plays a critical role in helping organizations make better decisions by providing them with access to high-quality data. They also help organizations to comply with data privacy regulations. Therefore, the first role we will establish and define is that of CDO. The CDO is unlikely to be the first hire for data in an organization.

Most often, there are team members who exist and may even be excelling prior to the hiring or establishment of the CDO. Usually, some kind of organizational moment (a crisis, a need to make a shift toward using data, a realization that the company is failing to make timely decisions) has happened, which drives the hiring of a data executive. There are usually data professionals in a company ahead of this hire. They usually are not organized in a central function, or they are centralized but with lower-level professionals. As we structure the function, I am going to start top-down in defining the roles and structures of this function and begin with the CDO, but recognize they are often not the first role that exists.

CDO versus CDAO

The **CDO** is ultimately accountable for the success or failure of the company's use of data. The responsibility is distributed, but ultimately, the CDO is the individual who sets the vision, mission, and objectives for success in using and protecting data, as well as steering the company's data initiatives. Successful CDOs are true partners to the business, understand their needs and strategies, and enable their business partners with solutions that add measurable value to their success.

At the time of this writing, most industries now have an established CDO. What varies is the scope of this role. To help you get started in either agreeing to the scope of your role as the leader of a data function or to help you write a job description for your organization's CDO, I have shared a summary that you can start with and customize as you see fit.

The key is to ensure that the individual hired for this role can navigate the C-suite, create value from data exploitation, and enable business outcomes through data solutions. While some companies do not use the "chief" designation in the title of the role, I strongly believe it does matter, as it brings credibility to the rest of the C-level employees as a critical executive in the company.

Summary of CDO role

The CDO will oversee the management of their information assets, with a focus on establishing and ensuring adherence to a framework of data governance policies, standards, and practices, both at an enterprise and group level, with a goal of achieving a desired level of consistency and quality commensurate with business needs and outcomes. This individual should possess a balance of technical skills, business acumen, and people skills to navigate the technical and political hurdles of managing valuable corporate data assets.

Key responsibilities are the following:

- Defining a data strategy
- Sponsoring enterprise data councils, committees, and working groups
- Ownership of data policies
- Driving data integration for mergers and acquisitions (M&A) activities
- Oversight of data initiatives
- Data governance and quality
- Generating business value from data
- Ensuring data availability
- Master data management (MDM)
- Designing and implementing data architecture
- Managing data infrastructure and platforms

The following diagram depicts how the Chief Data Officer's team could be structured:

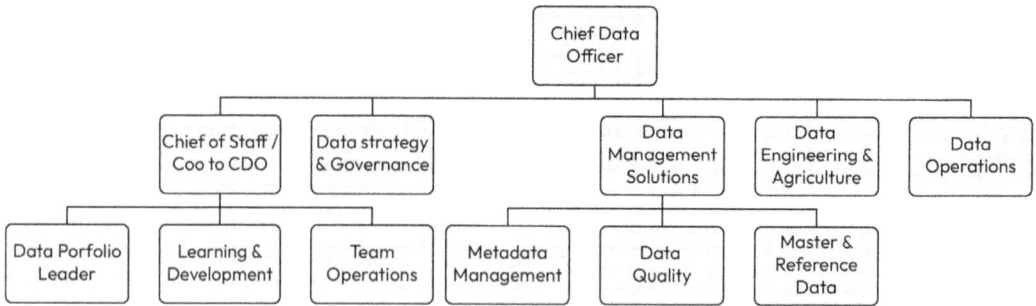

Figure 3.6 – Organizational model for CDO

Some organizations refer to their top data leader as a **CDAO**. Sometimes this is synonymous with CDO, and sometimes it is not. A CDO in one organization may be responsible for both data management and data analytics, whereas, in other organizations, a CDO may only have responsibilities for data management. I have been a CDO in both definitions. Less commonly, a **chief analytics officer (CAO)** may also be established. The title is less important between CDO or CDAO than a definition and clarity of the responsibilities of the role. What's important is to know in terms of what your organization refers to as the top data leader is what their scope of responsibility includes and that BUs and corporate functions are aligned. For the purposes of this book, I will use CDO to refer to an organization where analytics is *not* a part of the organization and CDAO to refer to an organization where analytics *is* included.

Summary of CDAO role

The company is seeking an experienced CDAO to lead the company's data and analytics vision and strategy. In this role, you will be responsible for assessing the current state of the company's data and analytics ecosystem, collaborating with both business and technical leaders to design and implement a truly best-in-class strategy that will support the company's near- and long-term vision.

You will build and lead a centralized data and analytics team focused on governance, data management, analytics, and data science.

Responsibilities include the following:

- Establishing data and analytics as a first-class, standalone function (for example, centralized)
- Defining the overall data and analytics vision and strategy for the company
- Together, with functional and business leaders, communicate the data strategy and North Star architecture, data infrastructure, and tooling for the organization at large
- Collaborating with security to define a data access strategy that protects and enables the democratization of data enterprise-wide
- Defining and driving critical data use cases to generate/unlock revenue opportunities, maximize operational efficiencies, and reduce risk
- Optimizing customer experiences and enabling higher-quality decision-making enterprise-wide
- Attracting, retaining, and upskilling/reskilling key expertise across data, analytics, and AI
- Providing subject-matter expertise on data, analytics, **artificial intelligence (AI)** partnerships, investments, and M&A activities

Data management roles

For the **data management** portion of the CDO/CDAO Office, there are four core sub-functions I recommend: data governance, data solutions, data engineering/architecture, and data operations. You may also want to supplement your leadership team with roles such as deputy CDO (exactly what it sounds like), chief of staff, and/or program manager. Depending on the size of your company and your team, you may have other roles you need to add as well. Let this be a suggested set of functions but not a comprehensive list. You may need specialized leaders based on your industry needs.

The most important hire when establishing a data function, and often underappreciated, is the **data governance and strategy leader**. This leader will be responsible for bringing together the critical mass of data professionals across your organization, defining the company strategy alongside the CDO, and be the individual principally responsible for rolling it out across the organization. This leader will also build out a team that will be responsible for managing the enterprise data council/committee and communities of practice, driving data literacy programs, and monitoring compliance with the policies and standards they will set for the company. Without this person in place, it will be extremely difficult to set expectations for the company to measure. In *Chapter 4, Baseline the Organisation* we will talk more about how to measure maturity, and ideally, the data governance and strategy leader will also measure the maturity of the organization, and you will need them in place to execute the content outlined in *Chapter 4, Baseline the Organisation*.

Summary of a data governance and strategy leader

The data governance and strategy leader is responsible for setting data strategy, in partnership with the CDO, and developing and implementing data governance policies and procedures across the organization.

This includes developing a data governance framework, identifying and classifying data assets, and establishing data quality standards. The data governance leader will also work with BUs to ensure compliance with data governance policies and procedures.

Responsibilities include the following:

- Developing and implementing data governance policies and procedures
- Identifying and classifying data assets
- Establishing data quality standards
- Working with BUs to ensure compliance with data governance policies and procedures
- Conducting data audits and assessments
- Developing and delivering data governance training
- Managing the data governance program

The following qualifications are required:

- 10+ years of experience in data governance
- Experience with data modeling, data warehousing, and data analytics
- Experience with data quality management
- Experience with data security and compliance
- Excellent communication and interpersonal skills
- Strong analytical and problem-solving skills
- Ability to work independently and as part of a team

Data solutions leader

The second hire I would recommend is the **data solutions leader**. This leader may also be called a data management solutions leader, data enablement leader, or something similar. The role may also be split across roles such as metadata leader, data quality leader, and master data leader. This leader and/or sub-function is responsible for enablement of data capabilities for the company. They should set the requirements for the capability, work with the IT department to select the proper tooling for your company's needs, and work with BUs and corporate functions to use the tooling in alignment with policy and standards set by the office of the CDO. The leader will also ensure that the office of the CDO uses these capabilities properly for any data that it is directly accountable for (that is, what's commonly known as master data; more on that in *Chapter 10, Master Data Management*).

Summary of a data solutions leader

The data solutions leader is responsible for delivering data management tooling for the company. This includes developing and implementing product management processes, as well as working with cross-functional teams to ensure the success of data management initiatives.

The ideal candidate will have a strong understanding of data management principles and technologies, as well as experience in product management. They will also be able to effectively communicate with and manage stakeholders across all levels of the organization.

Responsibilities include the following:

- Developing and implementing product management processes for data management tooling
- Working with cross-functional teams to ensure the success of data management initiatives
- Developing and maintaining relationships with key stakeholders
- Staying up to date on the latest data management technologies and trends
- Contributing to the development of the company's data management strategy

The following qualifications are required:

- 5+ years of experience in data management
- 3+ years of experience in product management
- Strong understanding of data management principles and technologies
- Excellent communication and interpersonal skills
- Ability to work independently and as part of a team
- Ability to manage multiple projects simultaneously
- Strong analytical and problem-solving skills
- Attention to detail

Information architect

The third hire I recommend is an **information architect**. The information architect is responsible for providing the company with accessible information. Ideally, this individual will design the way in which information is available for consumption through the architectural design of systems, solutions, and insights. This role is most effective when brought into the early stages of major programs, to ensure the company's data needs are designed as an equal capability to process, finance, and so on. Often, data isn't included until the later stages of major programs, which makes the opportunity to enable the company through transformation harder. Your broader **data architecture** team will also play a key role in designing data movement across the organization to ensure data flows are optimized and support the broad needs of the company.

Summary of an information architect

The information architect is responsible for the design and implementation of the company's data architecture. The ideal candidate will have a strong understanding of data modeling, data warehousing, and data governance. They will also have experience with product management and be able to work with cross-functional teams to design and deploy data-driven solutions.

Responsibilities include the following:

- Designing and implementing the company's data architecture
- Developing and maintaining data models
- Creating and managing data warehouses
- Implementing data governance policies
- Working with product managers to design and deploy data-driven solutions
- Analyzing data to identify trends and opportunities
- Staying up to date on the latest data technologies

The following qualifications are required:

- 5+ years of experience in data architecture
- Experience with data modeling, data warehousing, and data governance
- Experience with product management
- Strong analytical and problem-solving skills
- Excellent communication and interpersonal skills
- Ability to work independently and as part of a team

Data engineering leader

As you are hiring the roles outlined previously, as a priority, it would be useful to begin hiring or centralizing **data engineering** professionals. Data engineers are often a bit easier to hire compared to the aforementioned roles; however, there is still fierce competition for excellent data engineers, especially with specific skill sets in emerging technologies or niche areas such as master data, where there is a shortage of deeply experienced talent. Data engineers are responsible for engineering solutions within your data team and for use across the company. Your data engineering team may also create curated and trusted datasets or views that can be consumed across the company. Often, data engineers are responsible for building APIs, data exchanges, and broadly moving data across your organization.

Summary of a data engineering leader

The data engineering leader will deliver data engineering capabilities for the company. In this role, you will be responsible for leading a team of data engineers in developing and maintaining our data infrastructure. You will also be responsible for working with product managers to understand their needs and develop solutions that meet those needs.

Responsibilities include the following:

- Leading a team of data engineers in developing and maintaining our data infrastructure
- Working with product managers to understand their needs and develop solutions that meet those needs
- Designing and implementing data pipelines and data warehouses
- Developing and implementing data quality and governance policies
- Monitoring and optimizing data performance
- Staying up to date on the latest data engineering technologies

The following qualifications are required:

- 5+ years of experience in data engineering
- Experience with big data technologies such as **Hadoop**, **Spark**, and **Hive**
- Experience with data warehousing technologies such as **Redshift**, **Snowflake**, and **BigQuery**
- Experience with data visualization tools such as **Tableau**, **Power BI**, and **Looker**
- Experience with product management methodologies
- Excellent communication and teamwork skills
- Strong analytical and problem-solving skills
- Ability to work independently and as part of a team

Data operations leader

Finally, the **data operations** team is responsible for running day-to-day operations within the team and may be responsible for managing errors, manual movement, or matching of anomaly data or unmatched records in your master data platform. Ideally, the data operations team may also cover data remediation, which is the correcting of data issues. In many data transformations, there are times when data must be remediated in larger batches or groups to prepare for data migrations to new platforms. The data operations team can provide this service for the company.

Summary of a data operations leader

The data operations leader is responsible for developing and executing the company's data operations strategy. This includes designing and implementing data pipelines, managing data quality, and ensuring compliance with data governance policies. The data operations leader will also work with cross-functional teams to develop and implement data-driven solutions.

Responsibilities include the following:

- Developing and executing the company's data operations strategy
- Designing and implementing data pipelines
- Managing data quality
- Ensuring compliance with data governance policies
- Working with cross-functional teams to develop and implement data-driven solutions

The following qualifications are required:

- 5+ years of experience in data operations
- Experience with data warehousing and data lakes
- Experience with data quality and data governance
- Experience with big data technologies
- Experience with SQL and Python
- Excellent communication and interpersonal skills
- Strong analytical and problem-solving skills
- Ability to work independently and as part of a team

AI considerations

At the time of this writing, AI has become the topic of almost any conversation related to data. Most data practitioners, like myself, are excited about the potential that AI has to offer but also want to see governance applied to AI practices. Data professionals are in higher demand than ever due to the data governance needs to support AI. The top questions include the following:

- How do I ensure that the underlying data set used to train AI is appropriate?

- How are prompts protected? Are they retained?

- How do we protect **intellectual property** (**IP**; for example, source code) if entered into an open source AI solution?

- How is my data protected?

- How are GenAI products being trained? What happens to the data?

- How do we ensure that input and output are handled ethically and in accordance with our company values?

There is so much to be defined around AI, and the pace of change is only increasing. Many organizations are looking to their CDO to help define what they should do to establish appropriate practices around data use in AI and **machine learning** (**ML**). It is appropriate for you, as the data leader for your organization, to be responsible, and urgent for you to prioritize this area. With the expectation of oversight on the horizon by regulators across the globe, it's critical that data leaders are a part of ensuring the company defines governance and ethical use practices for how data is used for ML and, specifically, for **large language models** (**LLMs**) to be defined as a priority.

On the other hand, you may also consider how you might use AI to drive excellence in your data solutions. This topic is complex and emerging rapidly. I encourage you to look into these areas as new opportunities to leverage AI emerge. Key areas to consider are the following:

- **Data quality**: AI can be used to improve data quality by identifying and correcting errors, inconsistencies, and missing values. This can help to ensure that data is accurate and reliable for decision-making.

- **Data privacy**: AI can be used to protect data privacy by anonymizing or pseudonymizing data and by implementing access controls. This can help to ensure that data is not misused or disclosed to unauthorized individuals.

- **Data security**: AI can be used to protect data security by detecting and preventing cyberattacks and by implementing data encryption. This can help to ensure that data is not lost, stolen, or corrupted.

- **Data compliance**: AI can be used to ensure data compliance with regulations by identifying and remediating compliance risks. This can help to ensure that organizations comply with applicable laws and regulations.

It is important to note that AI is a rapidly evolving field, and the considerations for AI in a data governance team will continue to change as AI technologies develop.

How to structure the team for results (and why)

While we are focused on the data governance and data management portions of the team in this book, I do want to spend just a moment on the analytics side of the team structure. Candidly, I believe there are an infinite number of ways to structure the analytics side of the house, as you can read further in John K. Thompson's book, *Building Analytics Teams* (an excellent book for anyone looking to drive excellence in analytics). There are a few ways to optimize analytics that I have leveraged in my own teams. In all cases, it is based on the business outcome I have been aiming to optimize for.

First, if you are internally focused, aimed at driving operational excellence, aligning top-of-the-house metrics, or simply supporting internal operational functions, a simple single team may be your best bet. I have consolidated analytics teams under a single analytics leader in cases where we are optimizing for the company's internal needs. Second, if you are focused on improving products and engineering therein, I would recommend aligning the analytics teams by BU. For example, if you have a software and a hardware BU, divide your analytics team into a software analytics team and a hardware analytics team. The upside is your teams are now intensely focused and aligned with the business area they support, learn the drivers deeply, and can optimize for their stakeholders. The downside is you must personally be the connective tissue across these two teams and ensure alignment, as well as where the two teams need to come together for success.

Alternatively, depending on your business, you may also be intensely focused on the customer (and I hope that you are, regardless of business). This focus on external stakeholders (marketing, sales, customer success) may result in individual analytics teams for sales, marketing, and CXS, or a single team focused on customer analytics. In all cases, you should optimize for the outcomes you are aiming to solve and not be afraid to adjust as your priorities change. When you stand up your team, you may have burning needs that must be addressed urgently; optimize for those by structuring your team accordingly. However, as you mature your function, do not hesitate to adjust. The one constant, after all, is change.

Building the rhythm of the business of data

As you organize your team, another priority you must address early on is establishing the rhythm of the business of data. In all of the data programs I have led, I have underappreciated the importance of this early on and have had to learn from the consequences. While you are coming into your role and listening to the business, your team, and working on your strategy, your team is still working on… something. It is critical that you get your arms around what is happening within your team while you are working with your peers and senior executives to understand the priorities of the company and for the future of your team.

I recommend assigning someone on the team the task of building an inventory of the programs, projects, and **business-as-usual** (BAU) work that is occurring across your organization. A program leader or chief of staff is a great person to tap into to lead this effort. In my experience, program management is often not the priority of data leaders, and thus, I have yet to step into a data leadership role where this existed clearly and comprehensively. If you have this in your team, you are off to a great start. If you don't, get to work on identifying what the team is working on, and do it quickly. The sooner you can get your arms around the outcomes the team is already working on, the sooner you can identify quick wins and optimize the team for success.

As a part of this program management exercise, I recommend you set up a routine forum to review the business of data portfolio. You should ideally be getting regular updates on what the team is working on, progress made, stakeholder results (*note*: not data results, but what the stakeholders you serve are experiencing from the work of your team), issues and risks, and upcoming milestones. Does the team need your support to move forward? Are there barriers to success? This insight will also help arm you headed into executive stakeholder meetings so that you are not caught off guard as you are working to form relationships. You may want to establish a business of data program review for this purpose, on at least a bi-weekly basis. As you are getting up to speed in your role, you may ask each of your direct reports to set up a time to brief you more comprehensively on their portions of the program so that you can get a deeper dive before moving into the regular routine of review.

As you start to bring together key leaders across the organization, to manage data (as a team sport for the company), you should establish a few forums to continue to keep the key stakeholders actively engaged for the purposes of supporting data outcomes for the company. You will end up with a few different forums to do so, and I will provide a sample charter for each that you can leverage to get started.

Enterprise data committee

As you begin to engage with executive peers, invite them to join you in the **enterprise data council** or committee. As discussed in *Chapter 1, What is Data Governance?* and *Chapter 2, How to Build a Coalition of Advocates* this forum serves as the uniting function for your data domain executives. This forum also serves as a great place to prioritize initiatives, ensure the right funding is allocated to the right data programs, and ensure that issues that arise have the appropriate visibility and prioritization for remediation by your data operations team or data leaders across the company as appropriate. This group should influence and approve the company's data strategy and corresponding transformation. A curated summary of the business of data program may be a useful view to share with the council either as an appendix to materials or shared in offline updates.

Sample charter for enterprise data committee

Purpose

The data governance committee is responsible for developing and implementing a data governance framework for the organization. This framework will ensure that data is managed effectively and responsibly and that it is used to support the organization's strategic goals.

Importance

A data governance framework is important for several reasons. First, it helps to ensure that data is accurate, complete, and consistent. Second, it helps to protect data from unauthorized access, use, or disclosure. Third, it helps to ensure that data is used in a way that is compliant with laws and regulations. Fourth, it helps to improve the quality of decision-making by providing access to reliable and relevant data.

Key representatives

The data governance committee should include executives (C-suite leaders) from all areas of the organization that use data, including the following:

- Information technology
- BUs
- Legal
- Compliance
- Human resources
- Finance

Key roles and responsibilities

The data governance committee is responsible for the following:

- Developing and approving a data governance strategy
- Overseeing the implementation of the data governance strategy, policies, and frameworks
- Monitoring the effectiveness of the data governance framework, based on information reported by the CDO and enterprise data council
- Making recommendations for improvement to the data governance framework
- Sponsoring education and training employees on data governance
- Reporting on data governance activities to the CEO and Board of Directors
- **Meeting schedule**
- The data governance committee will meet quarterly.

Communication plan

The data governance committee will communicate with employees through a variety of channels, including the following:

- Email
- Intranet
- Town hall meetings
- One-on-one meetings

Evaluation plan

The data governance committee will evaluate the effectiveness of the data governance framework on an annual basis.

Enterprise data council

The council can be a forum ahead of vetting and reporting out to the C-suite in your organization. While some members of the C-suite may sit on your enterprise data council, others likely do not. Thus, ensuring that the right information is shared with the right individuals is a key component of your communication plan. Previewing information for the C-suite with the council is helpful in that: you can obtain feedback from the council ahead of presenting the C-suite, and, you can task council members with garnering support for your enterprise programs with their managers, often on the C-suite.

Sample charter for enterprise data council

Purpose

The data governance council is a cross-functional group of senior leaders responsible for setting the strategic direction and overseeing the implementation of data governance at *organization name*. The council will develop and implement policies and procedures to ensure the effective management of data across the organization.

Importance

Data is a critical asset for *organization name*. It is used to make decisions, develop products and services, and improve operations. Effective data governance is essential to ensure that data is used in a responsible and ethical manner and that it is protected from unauthorized access and disclosure.

Key representatives

The data governance council will include representatives from the following departments, typically 1-2 levels below the C-suite member they support on the data governance committee:

- Information Technology
- Legal
- Finance
- Human resources
- Marketing
- Sales
- Operations

Key roles and responsibilities

The data governance council will have the following key roles and responsibilities:

- Developing and implementing data governance policies and procedures
- Overseeing the implementation of data governance initiatives
- Monitoring data quality and compliance
- Resolving data governance issues
- Recommending prioritization across data domains
- Educating and training employees on data governance

Reporting structure

The data governance council will report to the data governance committee, which is the highest-level body responsible for data governance at *organization name*.

Functional roles

Functional data roles are the people within a BU or corporate function who are responsible for managing and using data. They include the typically thought-of roles of data analysts, data scientists, data engineers, and data architects. They also include governance roles that define data accountability, such as business data stewards, technical data stewards, and data operations leaders.

Functional data roles are essential for any organization that wants to make effective use of data. They help businesses to understand their data, identify trends, and make better decisions.

In a large organization, there may be multiple functional data roles within each BU or corporate function. The specific roles and responsibilities of functional data roles will vary depending on the organization and the industry. However, all functional data roles share a common goal of using data to help the organization achieve its goals. Functional data roles are a critical part of any organization that wants to be successful in the digital age. By using data effectively, organizations can improve their decision-making, increase their efficiency, and create a competitive advantage.

For every data domain (the logical grouping of like data; for example, sales, marketing, product, and human resources), accountability should be defined in three key ways:

1. Executive accountability through an *executive data domain leader*
2. Business of data accountability through a *business data steward*
3. Technical data accountability through a *technical data steward*

You may have noticed I did not say "owner" and instead used "accountability." Utilizing terms such as "data trustee" or "steward" drives behaviors that the individual named is simply accountable for ensuring the data is cared for appropriately for the use of others. This is a very different mindset than that of "ownership," which implies an environment where there is no sharing. The sole purpose of data management is to care for data and to use it for its intended value. Ownership creates barriers to achieving this purpose and thus is not recommended. Data is an enterprise asset and should be treated as such. The stewards are in place to ensure it can be used as just that—for the enterprise.

Executive data domain leader

An executive data domain leader is a senior executive, often a C-suite member for medium-sized organizations, or, in larger organizations, a -1 from the C-suite, who is ultimately accountable for ensuring that data within their data domain is managed appropriately, that the team complies with the expectations of the CDO, including the data strategy, data policies and procedures, and any supporting frameworks. They are also responsible for data sponsorship within their domain and ensuring funding is appropriately secured for domain-specific work.

The executive data domain leader is responsible for appointing business data stewards and technical data stewards to manage the day-to-day care of data assets in their domain.

Business data steward

A business data steward is responsible for ensuring the quality, accuracy, and consistency of data used by a business. They work with business users to understand their data needs and then develop and implement data governance policies and procedures. They also monitor data quality and identify and correct any issues.

These leaders are often in BUs and/or data domains and may be responsible for a large quantity of data assets or just a few. While a data domain must have at least one business data steward, they often have many.

Technical data steward

A technical data steward is responsible for the technical aspects of data management, such as data modeling, data warehousing, and data integration. They work with IT professionals to develop and implement data management solutions. They also monitor data quality and identify and correct any issues. These leaders are often in the technology department and/or within business IT functions and may be responsible for a large quantity of data domains or just one. While a data domain must have at least one technical data steward, they could have many. The variance comes down to the size and complexity of your respective company.

In short, a business data steward focuses on the business side of data management, while a technical data steward focuses on the technical side. However, they are close partners and should work as such to ensure data is managed well as an enterprise asset.

Talent development

Finally, the last, yet critical component of building a high-performing data practice at your company is managing talent. I would be remiss not to take a moment to discuss how to manage data talent effectively. In all of my various data roles, there has been some level of challenge in finding and recruiting the best possible talent. Nearly every company is hiring data talent, and thus, ensuring that you are both hiring for your near-term needs while also ensuring you are building a talent pipeline for the long term is equally as important.

Recruiting talent

As a leader, one of the best ways I've found to recruit talent is to be visible. By engaging in public speaking opportunities at local universities, mentoring high school students, and/or participating in local technology organizations, you can get to know the talent emerging in your market. You and your leadership team should be aware of high-quality emerging talent before you need them. Be mindful of the schools and organizations you work with so that you can ensure you are looking at talent from a broad and diverse perspective. Offering internships is a great way to work with emerging talent ahead of hiring the individual full-time.

Growing the pipeline of talent

There are non-traditional ways to grow your data talent pipeline that I have also had success with. First, consider rotations within your team across disciplines, but also with the business. Consider rotating your team members out into the businesses they support (along with someone from the business coming into your team) for a period of time agreed to with the business. Do you risk losing your team members permanently in the business? Yes – however, this may also place more data-literate individuals into the business who can become champions for your team and the work you do. This is still a good outcome if you allow it to be. Ideally, that individual comes back to your team with a renewed perspective of the business they support.

I also urge you to think about your hiring criteria. For all roles, do you *really* need a 4-year college degree to qualify? Or is 4 years of on-the-job training sufficient? What about a 2-year associate's degree? Do you accept certifications? What is it that you are attempting to obtain from a skills perspective from the requirements you outline? I am not discounting a college education; however, there may be roles where you can widen your aperture and tap into an entirely new population of candidates that you would not otherwise have considered.

Hiring related or adjacent roles is also a great way to widen your hiring options. For example, the business of data program leader defined previously could be hired and trained from your company's **project management office** (**PMO**). Perhaps they have been exposed to your team and could bring rigor from the PMO team to your organization. Overall, thinking beyond traditional hiring criteria may create a more diverse, innovative, and deeper talent pool than you may have originally considered.

Upskilling and reskilling

Lastly, as you consider implementing new technologies or designing new solutions, be thinking about how you might need to upskill or reskill your team. While supplementing your team members with experts in new technologies or solutions may be helpful, do not discount the desire of well-motivated team members to learn new things. I've seen data professionals replace entire teams of people upon migration to new technologies, which has led to enormous disruption of the business and a loss of institutional knowledge. Be open-minded and creative in how you solve your talent gaps.

This chapter contained plentiful considerations for how to structure the team, the key roles you might need, and how to manage talent acquisition/development. Arguably there are endless combinations and role combinations to consider. Ultimately, you can structure the team the way you prefer; however, if nothing else, consider the outcomes you are working toward. Ensure you have the closest distance between the hardest problems and yourself so that you can focus on the priorities of the company.

Conclusion

As you set out to establish the appropriate structure for your team, remember – perfection is not the goal. Get started. If you need to make changes over time, especially as your company's data management capabilities mature, you will need to adjust as you go. Don't be afraid to do that. I have found it is effective to set expectations with the team that you may need to evolve. The one constant is change, and with success will come the need to change, add team members, optimize, and restructure, and that's a good thing. It means that you are making an impact. Pick the right model for you, adjust it for your company's unique needs, and get going. The faster you make changes, based on the right information, the better off your team members will be, and the sooner they can focus on delivery.

References

- https://www.dbmaestro.com/blog/featured/the-evolution-of-the-chief-data-officer#:~:text=According%20to%20LinkedIn%20(Sep%20 2022,companies%20across%20all%20business%20segments

- https://www.forbes.com/sites/ciocentral/2019/06/24/chief-data-officers-struggle-to-make-a-business-impact/?sh=61092c90f1a4

4

Baseline Your Organization

A key component of measuring success is measuring your progress. To do that effectively, you need to know where you start from. In this chapter, you will learn the importance of defining a baseline, both for the organization at large and for individual projects. Next, you will learn how to capture a baseline and who to communicate it to. Finally, we will discuss how to ensure agreement on the baseline before beginning work.

There are many ways to baseline the organization to be able to measure your impact, but one of the most common is through the use of a data maturity model. Throughout the course of my last ten years in leading data transformations, one thing is for certain: having a strong baseline is beneficial not just for your stakeholders but also for you. It gives you an opportunity to demonstrate how much of an impact you've been able to drive through your tenure as the leader and the measurable progress of your team.

We will discuss the need to provide discrete value for a solution or a product-by-product basis. There is also a need to be able to demonstrate the systematic evolution of data management maturity at an enterprise level. We will discuss why it is important to measure maturity, the various ways to measure maturity, how to involve stakeholders, how to regularly reassess to demonstrate progress, and the importance of strong communication. Do not make the mistake of underappreciating the importance of measuring progress at this level. It is one of the best ways to show your value and to measure progress over time.

What is a data management maturity model?

A **data management maturity model** is a measurement framework used to assess the overall maturation of an organization's management of its data. Said another way, it measures how well the company is managing data. The assessment provides a score by category, provides the aggregate maturity level of the company, and identifies areas for improvement. The maturity assessment is subjective. There are a series of ways to minimize the degree of subjectivity, which I will outline over the next several pages. Data management maturity models are broken down into different categories, and further broken down into levels of maturity against each of the categories, which helps minimize, but does not eliminate, the subjectivity.

A very simple (non-data) example would be to measure how grey something is:

Figure 4.1 – Visual example of the degree of grey

In this example, none of these colors are wrong, they are simply progressively measuring the current state of the color from lightest grey to darkest grey. The current color simply tells us where we are. The delta, or variance, between the current color and the color we aim to be tells us how far apart we are, much like the data management maturity assessment measures the current state of data management. The level is not "wrong", but it can tell us how far away from our optimal state we are. It also tells us how far we've come since our last assessment.

If this is your first data management maturity assessment, you are embarking on establishing a baseline. This is simply a snapshot of where the company is today. It's important to frame this context for your stakeholders, who may need help to understand what a baseline means, not because they don't understand maturity models, but because some may struggle with having a low score representing a low state of maturity. You will need to ensure they understand it's simply a baseline and it will go up as you work together as partners.

This baseline will give the organization a sense of where it is today and can be used to compare against similar companies across the industry you operate in. For example, if you are a bank and your average data management maturity is 2.5, but the industry is averaging 3.5, you know you are behind your peer group.

Hint for success
Do not confuse a maturity model for a data strategy or a methodology. Methodologies are very useful (i.e., DAMA), but they define what a capability is, procedures to deploy it, and approaches to delivering data solutions. Maturity models aren't plans to implement. They assess where you are on your data journey.

Overview of process

Before we get into the details, let's start with a preview of the data management maturity process. The process can be broken into 10 simple steps:

1. **Define the scope of the assessment**: What data and processes will be included?

2. **Assemble a team of stakeholders**: This team should include representatives from all levels of the organization, as well as from different departments.

3. **Select a data management maturity model**: There are a number of different models available, so choose one that is appropriate for your organization's needs.

4. **Execute the assessment and collect data**: This data can be collected through surveys, interviews, and document reviews.

5. **Analyze the data**: Use the data to identify strengths and weaknesses in your organization's data management practices.

6. **Communicate results**: Inform all relevant parties of the results of the assessment.

7. **Develop a plan for improvement**: Based on your findings, develop a plan to improve your organization's data management practices.

8. **Implement the plan**: This may involve making changes to policies, procedures, or technology.

9. **Monitor progress**: Track your progress and make adjustments to your plan as needed.

10. **Reassess your maturity**: Periodically reassess your organization's data management maturity to ensure that you are making progress.

Phase 1 4 Weeks	Phase 2 12 Weeks	Phase 3 Ongoing
Define the Scope of the Assessment	Execute the Assessment & Collect Data	Develop a Plan for Improvement
Assemble the Stakeholders	Analyze the Data	Implement the Plan
Select a Data Management Maturity Model	Communicate Results	Monitor Progress Reassess

Figure 4.2 – Phases of a data management maturity assessment

Over the course of this chapter, I will walk through each of these ten steps and explain how to navigate challenging situations for each. I'll also share some of my lessons learned so you can avoid issues and have a great data management maturity assessment experience.

Why you should baseline data management maturity

While you are off *Chapter 2, Building a Coalition of Advocates*, and *Chapter 3, Building a High Performing Team*, you should also launch a data management maturity assessment (ideally, concurrently). This process will help you understand the company's data maturity horizontally across the organization leveraging a standardized approach, which will help highlight any blind spots you or your team did not uncover and help identify any biases (unconscious or not) you may have had in assessing the company's needs. Additionally, it will help identify areas where the stakeholders are aware of the maturity level for their areas or are unaware of the maturity level. This can help you build your relationship with your stakeholders by helping them understand the state of the union.

Foundational reasons to baseline

You will need to start by understanding and communicating the purpose of this assessment. Your communications will need to anchor on one basic question: Why are we doing it? There are five core reasons to execute a data maturity assessment to get you started:

- **To establish understanding**: As mentioned, the most well-understood reason to complete a maturity assessment is to measure the state of data practices at the company. The first assessment establishes the baseline you need to gain a comprehensive and fair understanding of the state of the company. Every subsequent time you execute the assessment will measure progress (more on that later).

- **To inform data strategy**: The outcome of the initial baseline will, in part, inform your data strategy. By taking inventory of where the company is with regard to data maturity, you will better understand what areas need improvement across the overall state of data governance. Note that just because an area is immature, does not mean you should put all your resources into improving it. See *#8 Implement the Plan* on how to consider these results.

- **To assess information risk**: One of the key outcomes of the assessment is to grasp how significant the risk of the current state of data management/governance poses to the organization. If limited controls are in place, it's worth investigating with the CISO to understand what protections exist for the data, if adequate data governance controls are not in place. You may have a serious problem on your hands if data governance is immature *and* information security is immature. The outcome of your assessment and the discussions with the CISO will be a key topic for your readout with senior management.

- **To prioritize your solutions**: As you gather an understanding of the state of data management at your organization, you will begin to see where opportunities to improve exist. In my experience, there are often outliers of opportunity, meaning areas of inherent weakness in the data management of the company. For example, if metadata management is low, it may be clear that you need to seek out prioritizing a metadata management improvement program.

- **To up-level the company's understanding of the value of data**: One of the best benefits of the assessment is not necessarily the assessment itself but the conversation about data that comes alongside the assessment. You will find questions emerge from individuals you may not have had an engagement with previously because of this work. Embrace it. Even an adversarial colleague, when met with an open mind and a curious disposition, can prove to be fruitful. Encourage their questions and welcome the opportunity to educate, even in micro-moments throughout the assessment. Additionally, individuals may not realize how much they are gaining from their existing work. The entire process will drive a better understanding of how data is or is not used today.

Be confident in why you are launching a baseline of your organization's data maturity. It may feel unnatural to you, and perhaps to some of your stakeholders, to go through this process. To some, it may feel like an audit or a compliance exercise. You will have the maximum support and success in your baseline if you are clear about the *why* upfront.

Communicate with your stakeholders that this effort may feel uncomfortable or even hard to discuss the reality of where the company is and/or its function. Be clear about the results and what they will do for the company. What do you intend to do with them? Share openly that the outcome may feel uncomfortable and encourage the collective stakeholder group to embrace it. This is a stepping stone to driving change.

Executing a data management maturity assessment

Executing the assessment can be a bit of a nerve-wracking process. You are likely to encounter some great supporters and some less supportive stakeholders. It's critical that you have a great value proposition and are able to explain why this benefits the stakeholder as an individual (what they will personally get out of the process), why it benefits their team, and why it benefits the company at large.

It may go without saying, but communication is the most important part of this process. Your primary responsibility is to remain unbiased, share information, translate to ensure understanding across the enterprise at the highest and lowest levels, and drive the assessment results to inform your strategy and ultimately the value of data at your organization.

[#1] Defining the scope

Before you prepare to launch your assessment, you will need to define the scope of the assessment. Often, it can be tempting to say "all" and move on. However, there are options when it comes to defining the scope of your data management maturity assessment. There are three primary options to choose from, and you should consider what the best option is for your organization. It is a time commitment to conduct, both for you and your team and for your stakeholders.

Enterprise-wide

Most companies choose to do an enterprise-wide assessment. This is my recommendation, with very few exceptions (that I will outline). If your objective is to assess the state of data management for the company, you need to assess the entirety of the company to achieve this objective. This is also the best way to determine if you have areas of strengths or weaknesses that you need to take into account as you set up your program, deliver on transformation, and/or build capabilities for the organization at large.

When following the enterprise-wide approach, you should leverage the data domains that you defined in *Chapter 2*. This will give you a better understanding of which groups are stronger or have matured beyond others. Whether you report on this domain model is a separate consideration (see *Section 6, Communicating Results*).

Hint for success

If you don't assess the enterprise as a whole, you should not claim the outcome to be an "enterprise assessment". I have seen this in a company; only about half of the company was included in the assessment, but the claim was made that it was an "enterprise" score. Unfortunately, once we baselined the entire company, the score was, in fact, much lower than previously reported. The groups who did not wish to participate previously had lower data maturity, thus, when they were baselined, the average score dropped.

Pilot and data office

If you are struggling to gain support for this effort, you could select a single data domain to pilot the process with. As you work with this data domain, you will be able to work individually with this pilot data domain and build a deeper relationship with them. However, it is easier to become biased when assessing a single group.

While you assess the pilot data domain, you should also assess your own data office. This can be a somewhat humbling experience, as you might find that the pilot data domain has a stronger maturity level than your own data office does (been there!). This should not be a concern or something to shy away from. Remember this is simply a baseline by which to justify future investment. Embrace the baseline and use it to your advantage. Do not be afraid of a low score for your team or the pilot data domain.

Oftentimes, these early assessments shine a light on the weaknesses of the company's data maturity and specifically highlight capabilities that need investment to drive adoption enterprise-wide (e.g., metadata management, reference data, lineage, etc.). The low score in the data office will highlight where the central data team needs to invest in the service of the data domains, such that consistent capabilities are built and then leveraged across the company. Embrace the opportunity to show how far you have to go.

Rolling assessment

A rolling assessment can be used if you are able to achieve buy-in for an enterprise-wide assessment but do not have the resourcing to drive an enterprise assessment concurrently. It's a great option for high interest in the process but low resourcing to conduct such an assessment. It becomes very important to maintain strong consistency as you roll the assessment across the company. You and your team will become more efficient, and perhaps effective, at executing the assessment as you progress through the data domains; however, you must take extra care to ensure that the first team assessed and the last team assessed are given an equal experience and an equivalent assessment.

The following chart can be leveraged to show the scope of your assessment. Enter the data domains on the left side, including one row for the central data office. In the second column, enter whether that data domain is in scope for the assessment or not (only use this column if not all groups are included). In the third column, enter the baseline score. In the last column, enter the current score. You should consider the full chart to be internal to the data office unless you intend to publish the disaggregated results (see Section 6 Communicating Results).

Data Domain	In Scope [yes/no]	Baseline Score [FY 1]	Current Score [FY 2]
Marketing			
Sales			
Technology, Product & Engineering			
Human Resources			
Legal & Privacy			
Security			
Business Divisions			
Data Office			

Figure 4.3 – Example scoping model

[#2] Identifying stakeholders

The next step in the data management maturity assessment is to identify who will be responsible, who will be accountable, who will be consulted, and who will be informed in the process. First, start by identifying the roles and groups before you assign names to the roles. This will help you create an evergreen approach you can maintain as people come and go from the company.

Here are some additional tips for identifying the roles needed to participate in a data management maturity assessment:

- Consider the different departments and functions within the organization that are involved in data management.

- Identify the people who have a vested interest in the success of the data management program.

- Look for people who have a deep understanding of the company's data assets and how they are used to support business decisions.

- Involve a mix of technical and non-technical people in the assessment. This will help to ensure that the assessment is comprehensive and that it gets the input of all the stakeholders.

Responsible

The role responsible for executing the data management maturity assessment, from defining the methodology, execution, and reporting, is your head of data governance. This individual usually reports to the chief data and analytics officer and has responsibility for the assessment.

Accountable

The **chief data and analytics officer** (**CDAO**) is ultimately accountable for the company's data management maturity assessment because they have the overall responsibility for data management within the organization. Since the CDAO is also responsible for driving data-driven decision-making throughout the organization, the data management maturity assessment is a critical tool for the CDAO to understand the current state of data management within the organization and identify areas for improvement.

The assessment will help the CDAO to do the following:

- Identify gaps in data management processes and procedures

- Assess the maturity of data governance policies and practices

- Evaluate the quality of data assets

- Identify opportunities to improve data-driven decision-making

The CDAO can then use the results of the assessment to develop a plan for improving data management within the organization. This plan should be aligned with the company's overall business strategy and should be communicated to all stakeholders.

By taking accountability for the company's data management maturity assessment, the CDAO can ensure that data is managed effectively and that the organization is able to derive maximum value from its data assets.

In addition to the reasons mentioned, the CDAO is also accountable for the company's data management maturity assessment because they have the authority to make changes to data management processes and procedures. This is important because the assessment may identify areas where data management needs to be improved. The CDAO can then use its authority to implement changes that will help the organization achieve a higher level of data maturity.

Finally, the CDAO is accountable for the company's data management maturity assessment because they are the public face of data management within the organization. They are responsible for communicating the importance of data management to the rest of the organization and for ensuring that data management is a priority. The data management maturity assessment is a valuable tool for the CDAO to use to communicate the importance of data management and to demonstrate the value that data can bring to the organization.

Consulted

The following groups of individuals should be consulted during the data management maturity assessment, both for broad context and for scoring purposes:

- **Data domain executives**: The data domain executives are responsible for data management within their data domains, so they should be consulted to get their perspective on the current state of data management and to identify areas for improvement.

- **Business data stewards**: Data stewards are responsible for ensuring the quality and accuracy of data, so they should be consulted to get their input on the data quality and governance processes.

    - **Data analysts**: Data analysts use data to make business decisions, so they should be consulted to get their perspective on the usability of data and the effectiveness of data-driven decision-making.

    - **Business users**: Business users are the ones who ultimately need to use data, so they should be consulted to get their input on the data that is available to them and the challenges they face in using data.

- **Technical data stewards**: IT staff are responsible for the infrastructure that supports data management, so they should be consulted to get their input on the data management systems and processes.

In addition to these key stakeholders, it is also important to consult with a variety of other people to gather context and examples of both successes and failures of data management, such as the following:

- Subject matter experts who have deep knowledge of the company's data assets

- People who have experience with data management best practices

- People who have been involved in previous data management initiatives

By consulting with a variety of people, you can get a comprehensive view of the company's data management maturity and identify areas for improvement.

Informed

As a part of the data management maturity assessment, you should inform several groups along the way. Ahead of the assessment, you should inform your data domain executives and the enterprise data committee. You need their support and buy-in for the assessment, so they can set the expectation with participants to prioritize the effort.

Upon completion of the assessment, you will want to go back to the data domain executives and enterprise data committee to inform them regarding the results and what will come next. Additionally, you should inform the C-Suite and the board of directors of the results so that they understand the needs of the company and can assist with funding and prioritizing any follow-up transformational work required in the data management space.

[#3] Selecting a data management maturity model

Before you get started, you will need to select the data management maturity model that is appropriate for your organization. There are several different models that exist with pros and cons that you can choose from, or you can choose to create your own. If your company has never done a data management maturity assessment before, I strongly recommend you select a widely used model, as it will help you to defend the criteria and the process overall. If your company is no stranger to data management maturity and has found that a more customized model may suit your needs better, then (and only then) you could create your maturity model.

Common industry models

Data management maturity models are frameworks that organizations can use to assess their current data management practices and identify areas for improvement. These models typically define a set of stages or levels of maturity, with each stage representing a successively higher level of sophistication in data management practices.

Some of the most common data management maturity models include the following:

- The **Data Management Maturity Model** (**DMMM**) by the **Data Management Association** (**DAMA**) (retired in 2021)

- The **Data Governance Maturity Model** (**DGMM**) by the IBM Data Governance Council

- The **Data Management Capability Model** (**DCAM**) by the EDM Council, is a non-profit organization that promotes the use of data management best practices

- The Gartner IT Score for Data and Analytics

- The Stanford Data Governance Maturity Model

- The TDWI Data Management Maturity Model and Assessment

Additionally, most consulting firms have their own proprietary models. The risk in using a consulting firm's proprietary model is that they are proprietary. Often, the company will require an engagement (i.e., funding) to continue to use the model over time. If you intend to execute your assessment over a series of years, this may not be the most cost-effective option for you and your company.

The model I've used the most is the DMMM model from DAMA, but it was retired in 2021. DMMM was replaced by DCAM. DCAM is more comprehensive than DMMM, and based on conversations I have had with other CDAOs, DCAM seems to be the choice of data maturity model for companies who had previously been using DMMM. My recommendation is to select a model that resonates closest with your company's needs and stick with it so that you can establish a consistent comparison of maturity over time.

Building your own model

Although less common, one approach could be to create your own model or blend models from various programs to fit your needs. It's critical to ensure you have a strong methodology heading into this approach, as you will need to be able to explain why your model is designed the way it is, especially in instances where someone or some team is scored low. I have seen situations where the team that scores low attacks the homegrown model versus looking at the results, and you need to be prepared for that.

Here's how to build your own model:

1. **Define the scope of your model**: Consider which aspects or areas of data management you will want to assess.

2. **Identify the thresholds for each level of maturity**: Consider what specific criteria are required for each level to be achieved. The stages in a data management maturity model may vary, but common stages include:

   A. **Ad hoc**: Data is managed in a reactive and ad hoc manner. There is no formal data management strategy or plan.

   B. **Basic**: Data is managed in a more structured manner, but there is still no formal data management strategy or plan.

   C. **Repeatable**: Data management processes are documented and repeatable. There is still no formal data management strategy or plan, but there is a commitment to improving data management capabilities.

   D. **Defined**: Data management processes are well-defined and documented. There is a formal data management strategy and plan in place.

   E. **Managed**: Data management processes are actively managed and monitored. There is a strong commitment to improving data management capabilities.

   F. **Optimized**: Data management processes are optimized for efficiency and effectiveness. There is a continuous improvement process in place for data management.

3. **Develop an assessment tool**: Consider how you might capture this information. The tool could be a checklist, an interview guide/questionnaire, or something more sophisticated. It should collect the data needed to produce the results of the assessment.

[#4] Execute the assessment and collect data

Now that we've gone through what a data management maturity model is, you've selected the participants, and you've selected (or designed) your data management maturity model, it's time to put the assessment to work. Let's execute the assessment!

Use case - gaming the system

Be mindful of *who* is executing the assessment.

At one of my previous companies, we executed an enterprise data management maturity assessment. At the time, the company had federated data offices established in each major division, plus a central data office. To conduct the assessment, each data officer (both federated and central) was given an assessment to score themselves. Seemingly efficient process, right?

Wrong.

Heading into the assessment, we knew which data offices had been established longer, had more resources and funding, and were more mature. But the results did not match the reality. Why?

Because funding was decentralized, some data officers used the assessment to game the results. This means they purposefully scored their maturity lower so they could use the results to advocate for additional funding for their data programs, despite being more mature than their peer data offices. What that looked like in aggregate was that the company overall was less mature than it really was, and the data offices with higher maturity scored lower than those with lower maturity. Further, some data officers over-scored their programs to demonstrate impact and progress. This is equally as bad, as it suggests the data office was more mature and had less work to do to build reliable, trustworthy data assets.

This invalidated the results, confused management, and ultimately undermined the credibility of the data management maturity assessment, along with the data officers individually.

Ultimately, we had to redo the assessment and hire a third party to conduct the assessment independently. This allowed the company to have an objective assessment, with results it could trust. Because of the way the first assessment played out, we had to conduct many interviews and collect evidence to support the assessment. We also added a layer of credible challenges by asking each data officer about what they knew from their peers to help validate the results and highlight any gaps in the interviews.

Preparing to launch

As you prepare to launch your assessment, I recommend you communicate a few different ways to ensure your stakeholders know what to expect. In your enterprise data committee and enterprise data council meetings, be sure to present on this topic well in advance of the annual exercise. In your enterprise data committee, I recommend a pitch deck that includes the following information:

- What is a data management maturity model?

- Why is it important to assess maturity? What are the benefits to the company, data office, and data domains?

- What will be done with the information?

- How will they be engaged?

- What do they need from the data team?

- What is the timeline of the assessment? How will we validate the results?

- When will we report the results? To whom?

- What is the time commitment you expect for each type of persona in the RACI?

Communicating expectations

Before you launch, you will need to set expectations about what this is, why you need to do the assessment, what you will do with the results, and why this process will benefit the stakeholders involved. You should also communicate the expectations to the individuals who are participating in the assessment. They need to understand what to expect during the assessment, what they should plan for from a time commitment perspective, what will be done with results, and why this process matters to them (as well as the company). Individuals involved will need to know what is coming and what will be required of them. Communication will become one of the most important parts of the assessment process.

Here's an example email you can send to your stakeholders kicking off the assessment:

> **Sample maturity assessment announcement email**
>
> To: All business data stewards; technical data stewards
>
> CC: Data domain executives, enterprise data committee members, chief data and analytics officer, and individuals conducting the assessment
>
> Subject: Announcing the enterprise data management maturity assessment
>
> Dear stakeholders,
>
> In the coming weeks, we will be launching an enterprise-wide data management maturity assessment. We have selected an assessment model to measure our company's progress against stated maturity levels across a series of data management dimensions. We have selected the industry-leading assessment model: DCAM. You can read more about the model here: `https://edmcouncil.org/frameworks/dcam/`.
>
> To support this effort, we are asking for two hours of your time over the next eight weeks. The first hour will be used to interview you and your teammates about the current state of data management in your area of the company. There are no wrong answers. We are simply taking a pulse of where we stand. There may be a request for supporting materials from that initial conversation, which we will send in writing following the first meeting.
>
> The second meeting will include a read-out of the results of your first meeting against our maturity model and will give you the opportunity to ask questions, challenge any of our assumptions, and edit to ensure we have the most appropriate score going into the aggregation process company-wide.
>
> Lastly, we will share the results with the enterprise data committee, the executive team, and, in aggregate, the board of directors. Your division's individual scores will not be shared—only at the company level. We will share the materials with you in advance, so you can see transparently what is being communicated. The results of the assessment will help with future funding, prioritization, and identifying where we can improve our data capabilities enterprise-wide in order to serve you better.
>
> Thank you in advance for your support of this important annual event. We are happy to answer any questions you might have. Meetings will be coming from our chief data and analytics officer's calendar in the coming days.
>
> Sincerely,
>
> Head of data governance
>
> CDAO Office

How to launch the data management maturity assessment

This is a great opportunity to both assess the current state and educate the stakeholders you engage with about the goals and objectives of a data management program. You can use this process to educate them on the core components while you also assess the state of maturity. Pay extra attention to the language you use. For example, not everyone will know what technical metadata is, but if you educate them on the term, they may understand it and be able to better share their understanding of the state of maturity for metadata management within their division.

By using these assessment sessions as dual purpose, you may be able to engage the stakeholders more fully in the conversation and use it to build your rapport with them. The more you can do in person, the better. You can use a workshop-style setting to bring common groups together. I have found this approach to be particularly helpful because it gives teams the opportunity to come together when they otherwise wouldn't.

Who you need to include

As mentioned, your assessment should target those closest to the data; business data stewards and technical data stewards. You may want to include a wide variety of individuals from across the organization, especially if the roles of business data stewards and technical data stewards are not yet formalized. At the very minimum, you should have a representative from every department with some additional focus from groups such as information technology and finance where there is heavier involvement in data.

Who you don't need to include

You may run into instances where you have individuals seemingly crawling out of the woodwork to join your workshops. It is OK to share and state clearly who was selected and why. You do not want to run into a situation where every data person in the company is included or you will struggle to complete your workshop in the time allocated. Stick to having a business data steward and a technical data steward from each data domain included in your assessment. If others want their voice heard, encourage them to speak to their data domain's representative ahead of the workshop.

Workshop versus one-on-one sessions

Depending on your stakeholders, you may want to consider whether it is best to schedule workshops or one-on-one sessions with them (or a combination). Ideally, you should conduct workshops as the default. They create the most inclusive environment and limit bias in the process. However, there are some specific instances where you may want to conduct a one-on-one session. See the following table for the rationale for both:

Workshop	One-on-one sessions
Should be the default	Best for adversarial individuals
Can help others hear ideas from each other	Can be used ahead of the workshop to help gain support of less supportive individuals
Helps remove bias	
Drives consistency	Can be used for extremely supportive individuals to help them understand the importance of their role in helping to guide a positive workshop

Execute one-on-ones

If you are conducting one-on-one workshops with those you need to bring on board with the process, you should do that ahead of the workshops. You may want to take time to explain the why and listen to what their concerns are. Common concerns include the following:

1. Wanting their individual results and not supporting aggregation
2. Fear of a low score
3. Fear of management's perception of their maturity
4. Not being included
5. Not being elevated to a data domain executive
6. Not being represented fairly

Be sure to hear them out and do your best to calm any nerves, explain why, and always use transparency. Facts matter in these situations.

Executing the workshop(s)

Your workshop needs to be executed very well. You should not cut corners in preparing the workshop and should facilitate your attendees. Remember to reiterate that a maturity model is simply a tool that you use to assess how well your company has done in using data to drive business outcomes. Most models break down into areas of focus or capabilities and provide a scoring approach to determine how mature the company or division is within that area of focus or capability.

Sample agenda

Welcome and introductions *[welcome the attendees and take time to do introductions for all participants]*

Aligning purpose: why are we here? *[Explain the purpose of the assessment and what the attendees can expect from the session]*

What the assessment is

Why we are conducting the assessment

Allow time for brief questions

Explain why this is beneficial for attendees

Explain why this is beneficial for the company

Goals and outcomes: what will we achieve together?

Topical discussion and assessment exercise

Scoring

Data office's next steps

Gathering example documents (avoid saying "evidence", as this can feel like an audit and may change the tone of the conversation)

Aggregating scores

Attendee next steps: explain what will come next, when, and how they will be engaged going forward

Thanks and adjourn

Bonus outcomes

As a result of conducting the maturity assessments in a workshop style, you will be able to gather additional outcomes that, while not the intention of the maturity assessment, will aid in your overall business case development and inform your strategy and initiatives going forward. Some bonus outcomes include the following:

1. Ideas for opportunity

2. Ideas for initiatives

3. Identifying common themes

4. Identifying troubled areas

5. Community building

[#5] Analyzing the data

Now that you've completed the workshop, the next step in the process is to analyze the data and prepare to communicate the results. As a part of this step, you have both quantitative and qualitative data to analyze. Both are valuable in this exercise.

The numbers – quantitative data

Arguably the easiest part of analyzing the data is looking at the scores themselves in isolation. Having collected the scores during the workshops, you need to add these scores into a common template and conduct a simple average to measure the company's aggregated data management maturity score. The average score is what you will use to report your results to the enterprise data committee, the executive team (C-suite), and the board of directors. The business data stewards and technical data stewards should also receive this information in advance of the executive communication plan.

The context – qualitative data

This analysis is more subjective and needs to be treated with care to ensure bias does not creep into the analysis. As you assess, please keep in mind the following:

- **Be objective**: Avoid making any assumptions or jumping to conclusions with your analysis. Imagine defending these results to stakeholders. Will your conclusions hold up? Use this thought process to help credibly challenge your assessment or that of your team.

- **Be realistic**: Don't expect to nail the assessment of the qualitative data overnight. This will be iterative and require back and forth with your participants to ensure you've captured their insights properly. Expect this in your timeline.

- **Be collaborative**: You will need to involve your stakeholders in this part of the analysis. You will ensure that your qualitative data is represented fairly and that no one is surprised when it comes time for the communication process. Try phrases such as "I think I heard you say ____, can you confirm that for me?" It will help build trust in the results.

- **Be iterative**: As you work on consolidating the findings and reporting on the results, you should expect to come back to the results again as you plan for improvement initiatives. Expect to iterate now and when you conduct next year's assessment. Keep the documents accessible for reference.

To analyze the data coming out of the assessment, take the following steps in sequence:

1. **Identify key findings**: Start by listing out all the key findings you heard during the assessment process.

2. **Group findings into themes**: Are you seeing a pattern of issues related to customer identifier data being low quality across groups? Lack of tooling? Group these types of findings into common buckets/themes to identify where you have consistency across data domains.

3. **Compare findings to the maturity model**: Look at these qualitative findings against the model. Align them into each topical area so you can see where you have specific areas that need improvement that may influence your scores.

4. **Compare findings across data domains**: Now assess these same themes across data domains. Are particular domains lower? These qualitative results are helpful during improvement conversations. It may be that a domain hasn't had any investment, or perhaps they were not aware of the central capabilities available to them. These qualitative data points are great for debriefing conversations and ongoing maturity planning.

5. **Look for root causes**: Is there a common reason why the qualitative results are what they are? Causation can be helpful when reporting results. Executives will likely want to know why the results are what they are. This is a good area to focus energy on, if possible.

6. **Prioritize findings**: Not every finding or comment is created equal. Focus on the findings that are the most impactful for your company's success in achieving its broader strategy to maximize impact and align on outcomes.

7. **Develop your plan for improvement**: You should gather at least a top-five list of what you believe the company needs to focus on going forward as a result of the assessment.

Alignment and agreement

The following steps speak to the alignment and agreement portion of the data management maturity assessment. The execution of the assessment itself is a challenge at times, but the hard work comes in alignment. It's critical that you gain the support of your stakeholders to ensure that they will buy into the results, support the implementation plan, and partner with you on your data strategy.

[#6] Communicate the results

Once you have the results of your data maturity assessment, you will need to decide how you want to communicate your results. You have options, and there are pros and cons to how you execute this step. You can make the decision on how to communicate these results yourself, as CDAO, or you could employ your enterprise data committee to make this decision collectively. Either can work in your favor equally (I have seen both work well in different companies/industries).

Communicating disaggregated results

Your first option is to communicate results by division. Communicating by division means giving the marketing division the marketing score, the sales division the sales score, engineering the engineering score, etc. Your stakeholders will most likely advocate for their own results because they feel more connected to their own scores versus their scores rolled up with the rest of the company. However, this is not my recommendation. In my experience across multiple companies, this disaggregation reporting approach generally leads to the separation of the data community, data funding, and capabilities. This leads to duplication of capabilities, disconnected results, and increased costs. There are only a couple of very limited reasons why I would recommend disaggregated results:

- **You have no central team**: This can be a good option when you do not have much of a team in place to help guide the company individually and you need to allow them to move the ball forward in the interim while you establish your team and hire leaders.

- **You have no data strategy**: When the company is in its infancy regarding developing a data strategy, reporting disaggregated results can show how disparate the results are across the organization. However, use caution. Sometimes this backfires and can result in individual groups (especially strong/mature ones) advocating for the company to work together on enterprise efforts.

Pros

The pros for disaggregated results are as follows:

- **Stakeholder preference**: Stakeholders most likely will want their own score so they can feel ownership of the result and action it independent of others

- **Accountability**: Stakeholders feel more accountable and thus may accept the results

- **Bias to action**: Teams may decide to take action right away, and they can because they know exactly what their teams' weaknesses are and what they can do to move it forward

Cons

The cons for disaggregated results are as follows:

- **Stakeholder disbelief**: The stakeholders may not believe the result without seeing the details, especially if it's a mismatch with their expectations.

- **Gaming the system**: When disaggregated results are shared, individual teams may be incentivized to overstate their maturity when they are looking to show off their maturity or understate their maturity if they are seeking funding.

- **Lack of collaboration**: Teams are not incentivized to work together to improve the scores when they have access to their own individual scores. They are now incentivized to improve their own area and not work together across the company. This can result in teams investing in their own capabilities instead of investing together toward company-wide capabilities, which are usually more cost-effective and efficient.

Communicating aggregated results

Your second option is to communicate a company aggregated score. Communicating at the company level only means that individual divisions will *not* receive individual scores and only the aggregated company score is disclosed. Be aware: some teams may agree to this and like the rationale only to attempt to disclose their score off the record after the fact. This approach only works if you maintain the aggregated score and do not disclose the individual team's scores. You can and should disclose what the individual teams need to work on where there are outliers (i.e., specific areas of weakness); however, the company score is just that. It's the score for the company as a whole.

Pros

- **Company view**: Providing exclusively aggregated results drives the organization to accept that this score is a reflection of how well the company is doing in managing data and thus can unify the company to take action collectively.

- **Partnership**: Aggregated results can drive divisions to work together to raise the bar vs. working in silos.

- **Learning**: Teams are motivated to share and learn from one another so that best practices can be driven across the company.

Cons

- **Individual team accountability**: Teams may not feel like they need to take action and they can rely on the greater organization to lift the scores.

- **Existing capabilities could atrophy**: By leaning more on the central team, if you do not carefully communicate the importance of existing capabilities, decentralized teams may not carry forward their existing capabilities, which can lead to a dip in short-term data management maturity.

Program baseline

Similar to the enterprise data management maturity assessment, you can perform an isolated maturity assessment for a specific program. This can be a great starting point for companies who are not ready to assess an overall company-wide assessment or in situations where they want to evaluate the lift provided by the data investment in a large transformational program.

You would execute the same steps, only against the program scope instead of across the entire data domain construct. You may desire to supplement this assessment by baselining data quality as well to measure the trustworthiness of the data ahead of program implementation and again at the end of the deployment to show the measured improvement for specific systems, data sets, or processes.

[#7] Develop a plan

As you finalize your communication plan, you should concurrently begin to work internally on your data office team, as well as with your stakeholders to develop a plan for improvement. This plan should focus on the high-priority findings you identified and come with assigned owners, timelines, and funding needs.

Bring your stakeholders along with you as you craft this plan. This is a super topic for a data community of practice or a data steward working group to develop together. I recommend prioritizing the common themes that came up during the assessment that benefit the whole of the data community, along with any glaring issues that impact customers, are a violation of law or contractual obligations, or have major ethical implications. Address any legal or contractual obligations in partnership with your in-house legal team and chief privacy officer.

Aside from major issues, focusing on building capabilities that will support the masses inside your organization is a great place to start. For example, if you have several concerns about low visibility into where data is coming from or going and the quality of the data, you may want to start with deploying a metadata management program alongside a data quality initiative. As you read *Part 2* of this book, we will dive into the specifics of these capabilities in detail.

While you are developing the plan, consider what capabilities will have the biggest impact and focus on why they will have the impact. For example, if your stakeholders mentioned concerns about low-quality and low-trust data, define what good-quality data would allow them to do. Why will high-quality, trustworthy data matter? This seems like a potentially obvious question, but try getting really specific. What will the stakeholders be able to do once they have this high-quality data that they can't today? Will it impact revenue? How? Can you measure it? How can you measure it? These answers will help you define exactly what you need to deliver and how to message it for buy-in at the top levels of the organization.

Once you have identified what you will do, who will drive it, when you will deliver it, and how you will measure success, build this into a program plan. This plan can be, and should be, part of your communication to your enterprise data committee, C-suite, and potentially board (depending on how much interest they have in your data program). You will use this for *steps 8, 9,* and *10.*

[#8] Implement the plan

Assuming you are successful in securing buy-in and funding for the plan you developed in *step 7,* you will execute the plan. Bring your stakeholders along on the journey by using your data steward working groups and enterprise data committee to report on iterative progress, results during delivery (i.e., quick wins), issues, risks, and how you are progressing against measured results.

As you deliver, do not be shy about claiming results. If you are seeing business impacts, don't just mark the milestone as complete and move on; ask the business user (not your data steward, the end user) to share a story about how they are experiencing the results of your deployment in their day-to-day business. Did they have lower customer attrition as a result of your data management deployment? Measure it and report it!

[#9] Monitor progress

As you implement the plan you developed in *step 8*, you should build in metrics to measure progress. For example, if one of the solutions you and your team are delivering is to catalog 500 data assets in your enterprise data catalog, you should create a scorecard to track that metric over the course of your program. As you deliver, the number of assets cataloged divided by 500 should give you a percentage of completion that you can then report to your stakeholders and executive team.

Reporting and monitoring progress is also a good way to keep everyone aligned on what you defined as success at the onset of the program. Scope creep is a very real risk to data programs because data is everywhere. There is also a risk of how data "feels" to stakeholders, and thus measuring and monitoring data initiatives is an important way to ground the improvement in facts vs. feelings.

The result of monitoring progress can also help build confidence in the team's delivery, which can be used for future funding, even ahead of final delivery. You can show that the investment to date is driving progress as agreed, and use that story to secure additional funding for the next initiative.

Report on a regular basis in a transparent fashion. You should bake measured results into all data-related projects and programs to show the impact of investing in data maturity for the company. As you reassess your maturity (see step #10), you can correlate the impact of these program investments to the uplift of your data management maturity scores over time. Win-win!

[#10] Reassess your maturity

Frequency of reassessment

You should develop a plan for reassessment. I find it most useful to decide on a pattern of reassessment and stick to it. It drives more credibility and consistency in the results, which translates into better buy-in enterprise-wide.

I'm a big fan of an annual assessment as the default timeline. There may be situations where you would vary from this frequency:

- **New acquisition**: If your company is acquiring new organizations, you may want to require a light version of the assessment within 90 days of the transaction being completed and then ramp the acquisition into the standard process from there. This will highlight areas of weakness that may need rapid focus as the acquisition adjusts to the organization.

- **Spin out**: If your company is going through a divestiture, you may need to execute a special purpose assessment as a part of due diligence.

- **Significant change**: If a division has made a significant investment in data, completed a major program, or has gone through a major restructuring, it may want a special purpose assessment to show the uplift as a measure of success.

Measuring success

As you reflect upon the data management maturity assessment, you should consider how you measure the success of your assessment. Some considerations include the following:

- Did all of your stakeholders participate?

- Did you achieve buy-in of the results?

- How many questions did you receive from the executive team?

- Was the board interested in your progress?

- Have scores improved over time? By how much?

You may also consider the amount of time it takes to conduct the assessment year over year to determine if your team is becoming more efficient at conducting the assessment and/or if the stakeholders are more engaged in the process (be careful in how you set up duration metrics to account for these two).

At the end of the assessment, what matters is how your company uses the information. If the assessment is conducted and then lands on the preverbal shelf until next time, it's likely a paper exercise and not one of value. Consider basing your value on how the assessment is used to feed additional investment, the dialog about data that ensues, and how your data community is engaging with one another. It's a great process to drive conversation, build community, and drive awareness of what trustworthy data can do to improve the value of your company.

Conclusion

It is important to ensure when you conduct this baseline, you do it well. Your credibility will be, in part, established by how transparent your baselining process is conducted. Ensuring that you communicate the methodology and the plans for sharing the results and to whom up front will help your stakeholders buy into the process. Be candid about the maturity of your team also. By being pragmatic about this process, you can gain credibility to help you design the program you need to lead for your company. Conducting this baseline of your organization is a great launching point by which to establish a credible and critical seat at the proverbial executive table. Take the time to do this well and thoroughly.

5

Defining Success and Aligning on Outcomes

Data management is bigger than managing a maturity framework. Managing a framework only focuses on the tactics to uplift a score. It may or may not drive the experience of using data, trusting data, and overall data management uplift. We need to approach data management with a renewed focus and a fresh set of eyes. We need to build foundational capabilities that scale without doubling the size of our teams as the amount of data doubles every few years. I challenge you to think beyond the maturity framework (although important), into the minds of your stakeholders.

Picture this: You've launched a Data & Analytics team. Your team is excited, they are focused, and you've even built out a great strategy, easy-to-understand policies, and specific milestones for delivering great results. You execute against that plan and are knocking the delivery out of the park.

There's just one problem.

No one believes that the team is adding value.

How can this be? You spent time listening to stakeholders' needs; you crafted a plan that is shaped around delivering against those needs. You've set up a strong program with great communication channels, yet the feedback from stakeholders is: this doesn't really help me.

What went wrong?

This oh-so-common problem happens frequently in data transformations and in the build of data capabilities when the crisp and clear alignment of expected business outcomes is not firmly aligned and signed off on by the business users before the work begins. Unfortunately, this type of scenario happens regularly, and the only remedy is defining success and aligning on outcomes during the planning phase.

This chapter will focus on the area where many data transformations fall flat: aligning on outcomes that matter to the business. Most data transformations stop with data outcomes and fail to translate to the final mile: where the business uses the delivered data capabilities to drive operational efficiency, increased revenues, and better insights. In this chapter, you will learn why defining success beyond data and with the business matters, how to successfully map all relevant stakeholders (including secondary and tertiary stakeholders), and how to translate results into business terms.

This chapter covers the following topics:

- Capabilities versus outcomes

- Business outcomes *AND* data capabilities

- What is success?

- Aligning on outcomes

- Barriers to achieving business value

- Building value measures into your stakeholder map

Capabilities versus outcomes

Before we can define success, we need to start by grounding ourselves on a few key definitions. First, we need to define what a capability and an outcome are, and then slice that between business and data flavors:

- **Capability**: The ability or capacity to do something and achieve a desired outcome.

- **Outcome**: The final result or consequence of an event or situation. This can be a positive or negative outcome.

Keep in mind that capabilities have outcomes. For each capability, a single or collection of outcomes should be prescribed. Before beginning to deliver the capability, you should take time to define the expected outcomes. But if you haven't, it's never too late to define the outcomes expected for each capability. You may also have expected outcomes and unexpected outcomes. For example, I exercised today, and I expect to experience muscle soreness tomorrow. I did not expect to be so sore it would hurt to walk.

Now, let's make this clearer to delineate between business capabilities and outcomes versus data capabilities and outcomes:

- **Business capability**: Defines "what" the business does at the core. This is separated from "how" things are done or "where" they are done. It contains a set of skills, resources, and processes that enable a company to meet an objective.

- **Business outcome**: Defines the result of the capability. This includes deeply understanding the result of delivering the capability.

- **Data capability**: Defines the combined skills, processes, technologies, and resources that an organization pulls together to utilize data to achieve a specific objective.

- **Data outcome**: Defines the result of the data capability. This refers to the result or consequence (positive or negative) that is achieved through the delivery of a data capability.

Because we are most concerned about data capabilities, let's dig into what the key components of data capabilities are before we move into data outcomes later in this chapter.

Capabilities

Specific data capabilities will be described in further detail in *Part 2* of this book, following this chapter; however, let's start by clarifying what makes up a strong capability:

1. **Skills and knowledge**: This includes the expertise of data professionals such as data analysts, data scientists, and data engineers. It also encompasses the data literacy of general users across the organization who need to understand and utilize data effectively.

2. **Processes and methodologies**: This involves established procedures for data governance, data quality management, data collection, data analysis, and data security. Standardized processes ensure consistency, efficiency, and reliability in handling data throughout its life cycle.

3. **Technologies and tools**: This encompasses the hardware, software, and infrastructure needed to manage and analyze data. This can include data warehouses, data lakes, data visualization tools, analytics platforms, and various software applications specific to data management and analysis.

4. **Resources**: This includes financial resources allocated for data initiatives, infrastructure maintenance, and personnel dedicated to data management and analysis. Effective data capability requires adequate resources to support the necessary processes, technologies, and personnel.

5. **Cultural aspects**: This refers to an organizational culture that values data, encourages data-driven decision-making, and fosters collaboration between different departments in utilizing data effectively. A data-driven culture is crucial for maximizing the adoption and utilization of data capabilities across the organization.

Together, these components make up a strong data capability. Each part is independently required and must be strong in aggregate to produce a high-quality, trustworthy data capability. Without all components, companies will struggle to have success *OR* align on outcomes. Overall, a well-developed data capability empowers organizations to do the following:

- **Gain deeper insights from their data**: By effectively analyzing and interpreting data, organizations can uncover hidden patterns, trends, and opportunities for improvement

- **Make data-driven decisions**: Utilizing reliable and insightful data allows organizations to make informed decisions based on evidence, leading to improved efficiency, effectiveness, and competitive advantage

- **Optimize operations and processes**: Data-driven insights can help identify areas for improvement, streamline processes, and optimize resource allocation for better performance

- **Enhance customer experience**: Analyzing customer data can help understand customer behavior, preferences, and needs, leading to improved product development, marketing strategies, and overall customer experience

Developing a strong data capability is no small feat, and it requires continuous improvement and adaptation as technologies and business needs evolve. However, by investing in the necessary skills, processes, technologies, and resources and fostering a data-driven culture, organizations can unlock the immense potential of their data and gain a competitive edge in today's data-driven world.

Outcomes

As we've clarified what it takes to build strong capabilities, what comes next is getting very clear on outcomes. As I articulated earlier, outcomes are what the business experiences as a result of the capability. It answers one of my favorite questions: *So what?*

My teams know this question well because it's one of my favorites to use, to help us get to the specific answer around what the outcome really is and what it means for the business. For example, imagine you are working on the following situation:

- **Goal**: Get in shape

- **Capability**: Running

- **Outcome**: Complete a 5k in under 30 minutes

Most goals fail when we do not get specific about the capability required and the outcome we are expecting. If we take this same framing and apply it to a data capability, it may look something like this:

- **Goal**: Ensure the company knows what data it has, where it is stored, how it is classified, and who is accountable for it

- **Capabilities**: Near-real-time metadata (business and technical), AI-powered classification, and data stewardship, as well as a data catalog

- **Outcome**: Searchable data environment to enable customer contract obligations and to identify their data in your ecosystem, with **points of contact** (**POCs**) within 24 hours

Note in both examples there is more than one capability that could support the goal, but when you take into consideration the outcome required, the capability has fewer options and you can be more focused on what you need to generate success. In the next section, I will build on how to marry business outcomes with data capabilities for more powerful alignment between your business stakeholders and your data team.

Business outcomes and data capabilities

Traditional data capabilities are managed from within IT departments, which is part of why they have historically not been as successful. IT measures of success are typically framed as project-based measures, such as meeting milestones, or in budget/time measures, dollars or hours saved. This early generation of data capability management inevitably led to difficult-to-measure-and-quantify outcomes, which is the basis of the evolution from IT outcomes toward business outcome-focused measurement of success.

Helpful Hint
If you continue to measure data capabilities in a traditional, legacy IT (project-based) way or exclusively budget/time, you may find that you create a conflict of interest between your business stakeholders and your incentives.
Often, your stakeholders need to have business outcomes that may not improve speed or budget but actually use an increase in budget to drive an increase in something else that is meaningful (for example, revenue, customer success scores, or lead identification).

You need both

You need to set up your outcome framework based on both business outcomes and data outcomes. First, you need to align with the business on what success looks like for them, in their terms, and then (and only then) you should align and map your data outcomes to their business outcomes to demonstrate how your deliveries match up with their outcome needs.

If we take the preceding example and structure it into a simple framework, it might look something like this:

First-Level Example	
Goal: Ensure the company knows what data it has, where it is stored, how it is classified, and who is accountable for it.	
Business Outcome	**Data Capability/Capabilities Needed**
Searchable data environment to enable customer contractual obligations to identify their data in your ecosystem within a 24-hour SLA	<ul><li>Near-real-time metadata (business and technical)</li><li>AI-powered data classification</li><li>Data stewardship</li><li>Data catalog</li></ul>

Table 5.1 – Example of first-level business outcome

You might notice that stacking the business outcome next to the data capability that will be delivered to support it allows the reader to understand what data capabilities are required for the business outcome.

Next, you should explain how these capabilities will support the business outcome:

Second-Level Example	
Goal: Ensure the company knows what data it has, where it is stored, how it is classified, and who is accountable for it.	
Business Outcome	**Data Capabilities Needed**
Searchable data environment to enable customer contractual obligations to identify their data in your ecosystem within a 24-hour SLA	• Near-real-time metadata (business and technical) for customer information systems (for example, that may mean 5-6 systems versus the entire company) • AI-powered data classification for customer information systems • Data stewardship – customer success data domain executive, business data stewards, and technical data stewards • Data catalog for in-scope systems

Table 5.2 – Example of second-level business outcome

If you pitched the first-level example to your company and asked for funding, it would be pretty difficult to align on success. Why? Because it reads like you won't be successful until you have metadata for the entire company, you classify all data in the company, you have all stewards identified, and you have a fully populated data catalog.

However, if you go back to the business outcome, which is more specific than the goal, you have a much more specific data capability to meet that outcome. This is far more ideal, focused, and has a far higher probability of **success**, which is the topic of our next section.

What is success?

Now that you've zeroed in on what success is (reminder: it's focused on the business outcome), you can work with your business stakeholders to define success. In our previous example, we aligned with our business stakeholders on a single outcome that was met by the implementation of four key data capabilities. In our example, these capabilities are focused on the customer data domain.

To be successful, you must ensure that you have a narrow enough focus so that you can define a simple and straightforward **definition of done**. A definition of done is best to describe success when it is specific and measurable (you may like to use the commonly known SMARTER framework to assist you with this). Ideally, you should take each of these data capabilities and define what it will take to deliver a capability of value.

What is the definition of value?

Value is defined by the shareholder; therefore, until you have their sign-off on the value provided to their business, what you believe is irrelevant. You can, and should, measure and produce the value measurement you believe you provided to your stakeholder; however, it should not be considered final until you both agree and will stand behind the results together. The worst-case scenario is when you have delivered a solution for the business and you believe it's added value and they do not. It will undermine your credibility instantly.

Let's keep pulling on the previous example. How do you define success, in light of value that the business will agree to?

Defining success

Starting with the business outcome, start by defining a set of core metrics that will measure value for the business, in terms they understand:

1. Align on the overall business outcome.
2. Define and map data capabilities needed to achieve the business outcome.
3. Define what will need to be done for each data capability to deliver value in part and in aggregate (for example, sub-milestones).
4. Align on how you will measure value.
5. Deliver capabilities.
6. Report progress iteratively.
7. Measure data capability success in data outcomes.
8. Measure data capability success in business outcome(s).

Together, these eight steps can be used to frame a strong delivery roadmap. Let's break these eight steps into an actionable plan, using the previous example.

Aligning on outcomes

Let's now break these eight steps into an actionable plan, using the previous example. These eight steps will explain how to, in specific detail, align with your business stakeholders. As you become more confident in this process, you will find it takes less time to complete this process. However, the first few times you go through it, you may find it takes a bit of time to map out. This would be a good process to work on with someone on your team or as a small team to ensure you capture all possible outcomes and work to refine them into a clear outcome prior to sharing them with your stakeholders for input and discussion. This is also a great process to work on with a stakeholder if they are open to collaborating more closely with you.

Step 1 – Aligning on the business outcome

Start by ensuring you and the business stakeholder (referred to as the business sponsor) are aligned on the business outcome they need, to support their business strategy. You may jointly write this outcome, or you might write it based on the listening sessions you conducted on your listening tour when you started out in the data role.

For the purposes of this section, I will present the components of this eight-step approach in a series of tables for easy reference. You can use this same format if it suits you for your own company.

Business Outcome
Searchable data environment to enable customer contractual obligations to identify their data in your ecosystem within a 24-hour SLA.

Table 5.3 – Example business outcome

Step 2 – Defining data capabilities

Next, you will define and recommend data capabilities you and/or your team will deliver to support the business outcome. This is a great opportunity for you to explain to your stakeholder what these capabilities are and why they are the right data capabilities to support their outcome. If you make the common mistake of simply providing a list of data capabilities to the stakeholder without explaining why they are the right capabilities, this is the first risk in your delivery. If the stakeholder does not fully understand and comprehend why these capabilities are the right ones to support their needs, this is where the first shred of doubt creeps in. The doubt may not manifest until later in the steps, but this is where you begin to lose them and your credibility. Do not skip this step. It's critical to your success and building trust with your business stakeholders.

Data Capabilities Needed
• Near-real-time metadata (business and technical) for customer information systems (for example, that may mean 5-6 systems versus the entire company)
• AI-powered data classification for customer information systems
• Data stewardship – customer success data domain executive, business data stewards, and technical data stewards
• Data catalog for in-scope systems

Table 5.4 - Example data capability requirements

Step 3 – Defining data capability deliverables

For each data capability defined, you will need to define what will need to be delivered for each. Typically, you will have 1:M (one-to-many) deliverables for each data capability. These can be delivered iteratively (as we'll see in *step 5*) and should be, wherever possible, so you can demonstrate progress. The following example is a view of how you might want to identify capability deliverables:

Data Capabilities Needed	Deliverables
Near-real-time metadata (business and technical) for customer information systems	• Identify and select metadata tooling vendors • Implement metadata tool • Identify each in-scope system that contains customer information • Build connectors for metadata tooling • Connect metadata tooling to each in-scope system identified • Validate completeness of metadata for in-scope systems • Build ongoing operations and observability for metadata tooling to ensure ongoing validity and trustworthiness of metadata
AI-powered data classification for customer information systems	• Enable data classification feature in metadata tool • Validate the appropriateness of the classification feature to ensure accuracy • Implement periodic recertification of data classification by data stewards

Data Capabilities Needed	Deliverables
Data stewardship – customer success data domain executive, business data stewards, and technical data stewards	• Identify customer success data domain executive and gain approval • Identify all in-scope business data stewards and gain approval • Identify all in-scope Technical Data Stewards and gain approval • Onboard and train data domain executive, business data stewards, and technical data stewards in their roles and responsibilities • Enable data domain executive and business/ technical data stewards
Data catalog for in-scope systems	• Train data stewards on data catalog requirements. • Enable data stewards with the required steps to implement data catalog requirements per data governance policy for in-scope systems

Table 5.5 – Example data capability for deliverable mapping

Step 4 – Aligning on value measurement

Once you have defined the steps in delivering each capability, based on specific deliverables, your next step is to align on the measurement of the value delivered. This is another step that requires a very tight partnership with your business stakeholders. Since you've defined the plan to get there (including what needs to be delivered, and for each capability), it's time to align that they agree with this approach, you answer any questions that they might have, and you affirm that once these capabilities are delivered, they will be able to meet the overall business objective.

In our previous example, the overall business objective was to meet customer contractual obligations, which was, essentially, to have their data well identified and governed.

Assume your company has 500 customers. Ensuring you are compliant with all 500 customer contractual obligations is critical to each of the customers' contracts, given the agreement language is consistent. You can use the 500 to calculate an impact based on SLA violation in the contract (for example, let's say the contract imposes a $10,000 fine for each violation). You can use the 500 customers * $10,000 per violation to determine the value of the impact to be $5,000,000. This is the value of the risk you are working to mitigate.

Data Capabilities Needed	Deliverables	Value
Near-real-time metadata (business and technical) for customer information systems	• Identify and select metadata tooling vendor • Implement metadata tool • Identify each in-scope system that contains customer information • Build connectors for metadata tooling • Connect metadata tooling to each in-scope system identified • Validate completeness of metadata for in-scope systems • Build ongoing operations and observability for metadata tooling to ensure ongoing validity and trustworthiness of metadata	Single location to view, understand, and report on customer data across the company's complex ecosystem Can easily extract a view of all customer data, by customer, to demonstrate control over their information in a succinct and easy-to-digest manner, saving ~3,000 hours of additional audit requirements per year *Note*: The value is not implementing the tool itself; it is what the tool enables the company to do.

Table 5.6 – Example data capability for deliverable-to-value mapping

Step 5 – Delivering iteratively

A rather simple step to describe; much less simple to do. This step involves delivering on the plan you defined in *step 3*:

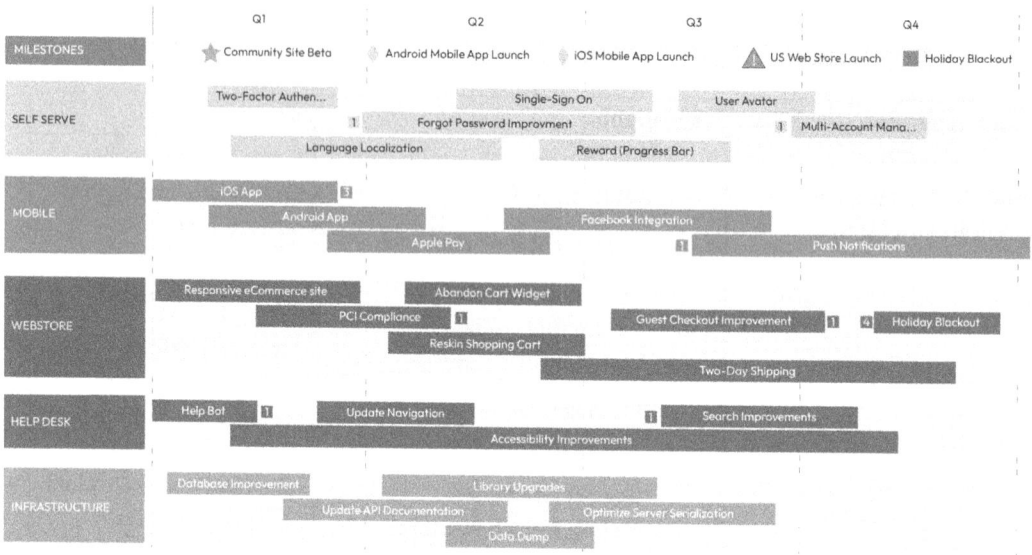

Figure 5.1 – Example roadmap slide

Step 6 – Reporting on progress iteratively

As you complete the delivery of the items in *step 5*, you should report progress to your stakeholders regularly. I suggest that you report at least monthly, if not bi-weekly. This ensures your team is motivated to make meaningful progress regularly, and that the stakeholders remain fully engaged in sponsoring the work you are delivering for them. Remember this isn't their only priority (most likely), and you will need to retain their focus and attention throughout delivery.

Because you've aligned on value measurement, you will be able to clearly articulate what they can do *AS* delivery occurs, and not just at the end of the delivery process. You could create a report to similar to the following:

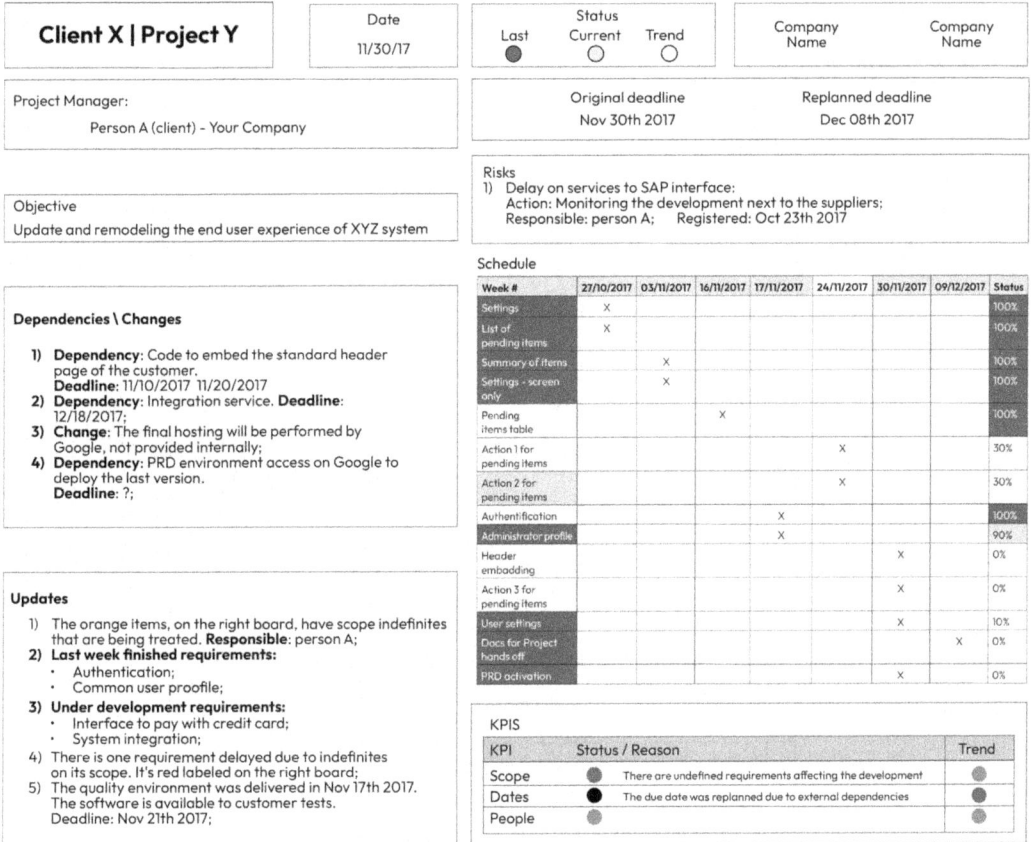

| Client X | Project Y | | Date 11/30/17 | | Status — Last (●) Current (○) Trend (○) | | Company Name | Company Name |

| Project Manager: Person A (client) - Your Company | Original deadline Nov 30th 2017 | Replanned deadline Dec 08th 2017 |

Risks
1) Delay on services to SAP interface:
Action: Monitoring the development next to the suppliers;
Responsible: person A;   Registered: Oct 23th 2017

Objective
Update and remodeling the end user experience of XYZ system

Schedule

Week #	27/10/2017	03/11/2017	16/11/2017	17/11/2017	24/11/2017	30/11/2017	09/12/2017	Status
Settings	X							100%
List of pending items	X							100%
Summary of items			X					100%
Settings - screen only			X					100%
Pending items table				X				100%
Action 1 for pending items						X		30%
Action 2 for pending items						X		30%
Authentification					X			100%
Administrator profile					X			90%
Header embadding						X		0%
Action 3 for pending items						X		0%
User settings						X		10%
Docs for Project hands off							X	0%
PRD activation						X		0%

Dependencies \ Changes

1) **Dependency**: Code to embed the standard header page of the customer.
Deadline: 11/10/2017 11/20/2017
2) **Dependency**: Integration service. **Deadline**: 12/18/2017;
3) **Change**: The final hosting will be performed by Google, not provided internally;
4) **Dependency**: PRD environment access on Google to deploy the last version.
Deadline: ?;

Updates

1) The orange items, on the right board, have scope indefinites that are being treated. **Responsible**: person A;
2) **Last week finished requirements:**
   · Authentication;
   · Common user proofile;
3) **Under development requirements:**
   · Interface to pay with credit card;
   · System integration;
4) There is one requirement delayed due to indefinites on its scope. It's red labeled on the right board;
5) The quality environment was delivered in Nov 17th 2017. The software is available to customer tests. Deadline: Nov 21th 2017;

KPIS

KPI	Status / Reason		Trend
Scope	●	There are undefined requirements affecting the development	●
Dates	●	The due date was replanned due to external dependencies	●
People	●		●

Figure 5.2 – Example status report

Step 7 – Measuring success in data outcomes

After your team completes the delivery of the implementation (and, ideally, concurrently as you deliver each capability), you should measure the success of the delivery in terms of the data outcomes first. This is helpful for your own team and to ensure that, first and foremost, you have met the expectations of basic data delivery. After you ground yourself and your team in the data outcomes, you should immediately move to measure success in business outcomes and report on these two measures jointly (*steps 7* and *8* together).

Finally, if you find that your data outcomes *OR* your business outcomes deviate from your expected results, be transparent about the variance, seek to drive to the root cause as to why it varied from your expected results, and work to determine the impact.

Data Capabilities Needed	Deliverables	Data Milestones	Data Outcomes
Near-real-time metadata (business and technical) for customer information systems	Identify and select metadata tooling vendors	Tooling vendor is selected [1 of 1]	Business and technical metadata capability is available for use
	Implement metadata tool	Tooling goes live (implemented) [1 of 1]	
	Identify each in-scope system that contains customer information	In-scope systems are identified [6 of 6]	System inventory for customer platforms is completed
	Build connectors for metadata tooling	Connections between in-scope systems and metadata tools are built [6 of 6]	Near-real-time business and technical metadata is enabled for systems for customer data platforms
	Connect metadata tooling to each in-scope system identified	Connections between in-scope systems and metadata tools are implemented [6 of 6]	
	Validate completeness of metadata for in-scope systems	Validation of metadata completeness is completed [1 of 1]	Customer metadata is validated
	Build ongoing operations and observability for metadata tooling to ensure ongoing validity and trustworthiness of metadata	Data observability deployed [1 of 1]	Data observability capability is enabled

Table 5.7 – Example data capability mapping to outcomes

Step 8 – Measuring success in business outcomes

As you close the loop to the final step, measuring success in terms of business outcomes, you will notice that these map to the original business outcome defined at the onset of this process. In the example, we tied out the data outcomes to the business outcomes. All paths start and end with the business. The middle of the process is where data capabilities are defined, delivered, and enabled to support the business. Depending on what capability you are focused on enabling, you will have different outcomes, but the same framework is useful.

Data Capabilities Needed	Data Outcomes	Business Outcome(s)
Near-real-time metadata (business and technical) for customer information systems	Business and technical metadata capability is available for use	Searchable data environment to enable customer contractual obligations to identify their data in your ecosystem within a 24-hour SLA
	System inventory for customer platforms is completed	
	Near-real-time business and technical metadata is enabled for systems for customer data platforms	
	Customer metadata is validated.	
	Data observability capability is enabled.	

Table 5.8 – Example data capability mapping to data and business outcomes

Summary

After completing all eight steps, it is helpful to put the entire story in order for your readout to the business. In all cases, I recommend doing a post-go live review not only on the outcome itself but also on the process. A feedback loop is a great optional ninth step to implement as a best practice:

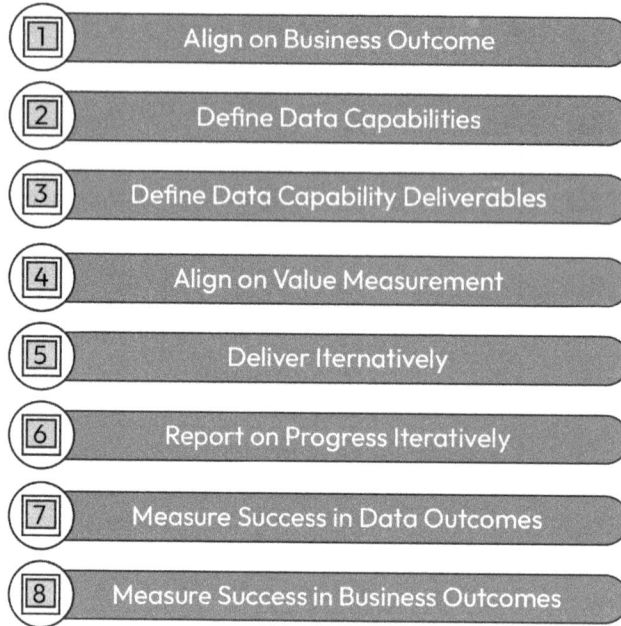

1. Align on Business Outcome
2. Define Data Capabilities
3. Define Data Capability Deliverables
4. Align on Value Measurement
5. Deliver Iternatively
6. Report on Progress Iteratively
7. Measure Success in Data Outcomes
8. Measure Success in Business Outcomes

Figure 5.3 – Summary of business success alignment process

From this point, you are ready to define success and align with your stakeholders – congratulations! Following this framework will enable you to successfully navigate specific and clear outcomes that matter to your stakeholders with ease. Remember to iterate through these steps so that you and your stakeholders are clear about expectations. Next, I will walk you through some barriers to success to be aware of as you operationalize these steps.

Barriers to achieving business value

After following the eight-step approach outlined previously, you have the strongest chances of success. However, there are always risks in delivering any program. I would be remiss not to point out the most common barriers to success:

- **Organizational culture and/or politics**: These are not always visible, and your chances of not fully understanding or seeing these risks are higher if you are new to the organization. It's harder to understand the invisible network of how the company gets to a win if you are new. If you are new to the organization, ask how success is achieved. Seek to understand unspoken cultural ways to get work done in your company.

- **Funding changes or challenges**: Securing and maintaining funding, especially in multi-year implementations, can be a challenge. If you are working on a multi-year delivery, ensure you have a commitment to the entire program, not just year 1.

- **Sponsorship turnover**: People make professional moves. You have to assume that your project sponsor might not be in the same role (or the same company) for the duration of your project. If you do not ensure that you have support, go a layer or two below the sponsor to ensure you have durable support.

- **Lack of support**: You did not get the full support of a sponsor, or you only received support at a junior (or simply too junior) level. The person you gained support from may not have the authority to provide the support you need to drive results to finality.

- **Lack of technical expertise**: Perhaps your team did not have the technical expertise required to complete the work. You attempted to let too technical work be done by not technical enough experts, and the result is a sub-par solution.

- **Regulatory or economic changes**: A material change occurs either economically or in the regulatory environment that impacts the prioritization of the project.

Drive unified data experiences internally and across our products to empower the organization and our customers with the right data at the right time with the right controls. Aim to achieve the following:

- Tech-enabled governance
- Transparent metadata
- Unified and trusted consent (for marketing)
- Trusted insights
- Results at scale and speed

Now that we've covered potential barriers to success, we can pivot into how to add value measures to your stakeholder map. This is a fantastic but often overlooked step: consolidate the outcomes by stakeholder so that you can have a comprehensive view of all the work you've done to drive measurable business outcomes for each stakeholder you serve. You can then use this information in periodic reviews with your stakeholders (annual, bi-annual, or quarterly business reviews, depending on your preferences).

Building value measures into your stakeholder map

As you work to build out your company's *value measurement methodology* (like we did previously), for each project, you can start to build out what this value measurement and value map look like for all of your stakeholders. This process is time-consuming but critical to demonstrate the value of your team's impact enterprise-wide.

Thinking back to *Chapter 2*, where we built out the stakeholder map, you can add in the value measurement methodology against each stakeholder group. A best practice is to sit with each stakeholder on a regular basis (I like to do this quarterly) to go through a *Quarterly Business Review* for the value your team has brought to bear for them. This idea of a Quarterly Business Review would walk them through the following:

- The scope of your engagement with the stakeholder

- A list of discrete projects you have completed for them in the quarter (or year)

- A list of enterprise services you provide to them (and everyone else)

- The value measurement for the quarter (or year)

- A look ahead to what is coming next quarter

Stakeholder Group	Stakeholder Objectives	Data Solutions	Target Business Results
Sales	1. Increase Sales 12% YOY 2. Maintain customer attrition at or below 8.5%	1. Deliver propensity to buy models for top 5 products by end of Q2 2. Build Early Warning System to identify customers at risk of attrition to enable customer success to save the account from churning	1. Increase sales 3% from propensity modeling 2. Identify ~200 accounts at risk of attrition and retain >= 50% of accounts (100+)

Figure 5.4 – Stakeholder map example: Sales division

Remember when we looked at how the office of the CDAO was supporting these objectives? We lined out the direct impact from CDAO to Sales Operations to Sales and clearly articulated how each role was involved in delivering that value. We also grounded ourselves in how the CDAO team was thinking about value.

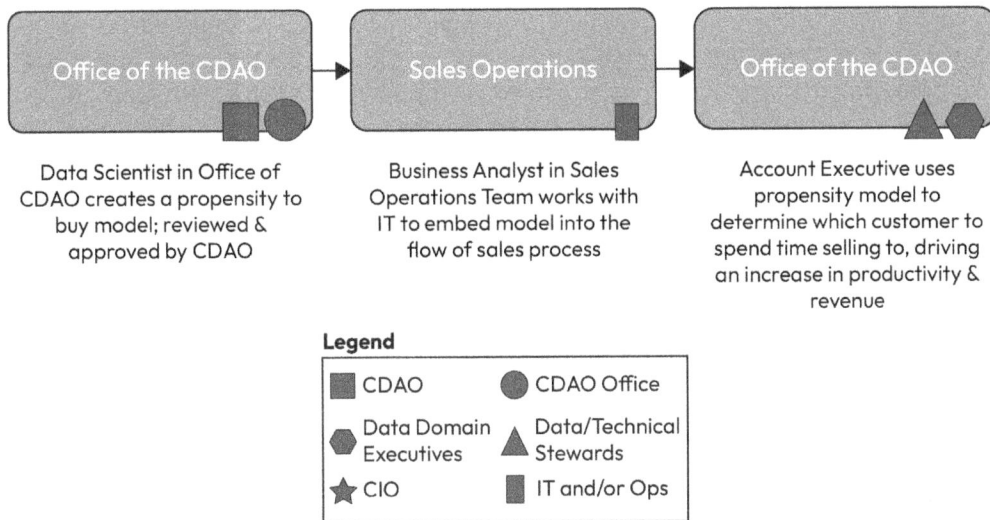

Office of the CDAO	Sales Operations	Office of the CDAO
Data Scientist in Office of CDAO creates a propensity to buy model; reviewed & approved by CDAO	Business Analyst in Sales Operations Team works with IT to embed model into the flow of sales process	Account Executive uses propensity model to determine which customer to spend time selling to, driving an increase in productivity & revenue

Legend

■	CDAO	●	CDAO Office
⬡	Data Domain Executives	▲	Data/Technical Stewards
★	CIO	■	IT and/or Ops

Figure 5.5 – Value chain from data office to business and to customer

Key measures include the following:

1. *How much* did revenue increase?

2. *How much* productivity did the Sales team save by being able to rely on this model?

3. *How much* did customer satisfaction scores shift by being sold products that they actually want?

4. *How much* did customer trust increase?

For this example, we would measure these specifically, as a part of our value measurement methodology, and present the results back to both Sales Operations and Sales executive leadership, to show them exactly how much we impacted their top and bottom lines, as well as customer satisfaction and overall customer health scores.

More advanced CDAO offices build their own value measurement dashboards to build out transparent and accessible reporting (ideally with the ability to drill into the details that support this aggregation, by stakeholder group) so that you can build trust with your stakeholders by showing (not just telling) them how you are bringing value to them every day. By reporting in this highly advanced way, you are reporting powerfully on the value you bring to the organization in a way that supports ongoing investment from the lasting impact of your team.

Conclusion

Measuring value for an organization is not easy. It takes thoughtful alignment with stakeholders about how to measure success, together. No one team can solve this independently; you must bring the discussion about value measurement into the early stages of the project, focus the stakeholders on the importance of alignment, and build a rigorous, transparent process into the normal flow of business. In my experience, many teams discuss having this capability, or may even claim to have something similar. In practice, very few teams do this consistently well across their entire company. Let's normalize this process so that as a practice, we can demonstrate that there is an incredible **return on investment (ROI)** in data. In this chapter, we walked through the eight-step alignment methodology to drive outcomes with your stakeholders, common alignment challenges, and how to carry forward the measured outcomes to your stakeholder map for aggregated value alignment.

This chapter concludes *Part 1* of this book. In *Part 1*, we outlined how to bring a data program together, how to baseline your company, how to build a great team, and how to align with your stakeholders for powerful results. In *Part 2*, we will dig into the major data governance capabilities in detail, covering what they are, how to deploy them effectively, and how to measure the success of each capability.

Part 2: Data Governance Capabilities Deep Dive

In this part, you will get an overview of each of the six key data governance capabilities, starting with key definitions, how to measure success, and examples of what works well and what doesn't. You will be guided through the implementation of foundational programs for each capability, and how to launch each capability in your organization.

This part contains the following chapters:

- *Chapter 6, Metadata Management*
- *Chapter 7, Technical Metadata and Data Lineage*
- *Chapter 8, Data Quality*
- *Chapter 9, Data Architecture*
- *Chapter 10, Primary Data Management*
- *Chapter 11, Data Operations*

6

Metadata Management

This chapter is intended for anyone interested in learning more about metadata management at a high level, understanding optimal implementation strategies, or anything in between. It is not necessary to have any prior experience with metadata management to understand the material in this chapter.

Establishing a high-value, high-return metadata management capability is absolutely required for any data governance program. The success or failure of a chief data & analytics officer hinges on being able to answer a few fundamental, core questions: Where is the company's data? Who owns it? How is it classified? Is it safe & secure? Can I leverage it for value? Do I know how to reduce data risk? You will learn the answers to these questions and be guided through how to tactically set up a metadata management capability for success as we dive into the critical capability of metadata.

Simply put, metadata is information about data. Metadata capabilities are used to make data more understandable, accessible, and reusable. Metadata management is the process of creating, storing, organizing, maintaining, and using metadata. In my experience, metadata is one of the most underappreciated data capabilities, but it is foundational to any data management program. Metadata is the root of success when deployed and managed well and the root of failure when underfunded and underutilized.

Metadata management is important for a number of reasons. First, it can help to improve the quality of data. By providing information about the data, metadata can help to ensure that it is accurate, complete, and consistent. Second, metadata can help to make data more accessible. By providing ways to search and filter metadata, users can more easily find the data they need. Third, metadata can help to make data more reusable.

By providing information about the data's context and usage, metadata can help users understand how the data can be used in different scenarios. In this chapter, we will cover the following:

- Metadata management defined
- The value of metadata management
- Core metadata capabilities

- Building optimal metadata capability

- Setting up metadata management for success

Metadata management defined

Before we get into the details, I find it important to align on basic definitions. In my experience, data professionals sometimes skip basic definitions in an attempt not to insult the audience when launching data capabilities. However, starting with grounding definitions can be done with grace in a way that does not insult the business leader and still grounds the audience on what we will accomplish.

I like to start with a simple slide with the title "Before we begin." This simple yet impactful grounding slide can be set up with a basic premise and with the following verbal statement: "Before we dig into the details, I want to spend just a moment ensuring we all have the same common understanding of what it is we are going to discuss today. I, for one, have not been a metadata expert all my life, and thus, let's take a moment to define what it is we mean when we talk about metadata today." This simple yet non-offensive grounding centers the team on the definition together without sounding like we are preaching to our stakeholders.

So, to that end, before we begin, let's ground on definitions. When we talk about **metadata**, it's important to state that all metadata is, is information about our data. You may hear it described as data about data. It's not enough to capture data about data, we must put it into action, and that requires **metadata management**.

What is metadata management?

Metadata management is a foundational capability that every company needs to understand and manage. Effective metadata management capabilities tell users basic information about the data, including the following:

- What data exists

- Who created the data

- When the data was created

- Where the data was created

- What the data means

- Where the data comes from

Metadata can be used to do many things, but at a minimum, it helps users to do the following:

- Discover data assets
- Understand data context
- Build trust in the information
- Consume data

There are three types of metadata that require active management: business metadata, technical metadata, and operational metadata. Together, these three types of metadata allow for data assets to be better understood and enable additional value to be unlocked from the data. Let's start with some basic definitions.

- **Business metadata**: This connects data domains to business data stewards, drives business data definitions, and is responsible for linking business metadata to the technical metadata across the enterprise.

- **Technical metadata**: This contains the physical data elements and attributes from physical data, enables data tracing, and drives an understanding of any data transformations. Technical metadata shows us where the data came from in terms of the physical databases, systems, and data flows across the enterprise. Technical metadata also describes the data structure, storage, format, and processing. This type of metadata usually includes data such as data types, column names, and table structures.

- **Operational metadata**: This contains information about how and when the data was created or transformed. It may include information such as time stamps, location, or job execution logs.

All three of these types of metadata are important for strong data management. They serve different purposes and are typically used by different users (e.g., business metadata is usually used in service of business data stewards, whereas technical metadata is more critical to the technical data steward persona).

Examples of metadata

Let's bring these definitions to life. Let's start with metadata about structured data, such as a customer data record, as shown in a database table for the Customer Data platform:

ID	First Name	Last Name	Street Address	City	State	Country	Zip Code	Phone Number
12345	Bob	Smith	123 Main Street	Anytown	IA	USA	11111	555-555-5555
67890	Nancy	Glad	456 Town Place	Anytown	IA	USA	11111	555-555-5556

Figure 6.1 – Example data records

Business metadata

The business metadata will include the following:

- The definitions of each of the fields (e.g., ID, first name, last name, street address, and so on).

- The business data steward

- The technical data steward

- The source of the customer data (i.e., the Customer Data Platform)

This business metadata may look like this in the data catalog system:

Business Term	Business Definition	Business Data Steward	Technical Data Steward	Authorized Source
Customer ID	The unique identifier assigned to an individual customer	Asha Sinha	Sally Smith	Customer Data Platform
Customer First Name	The legal first name of an individual customer	Bob Jones	Henrik Hans	Customer Data Platform
Customer Last Name	The legal last name of an individual customer	Bob Jones	Henrik Hans	Customer Data Platform

Figure 6.2 – Example of a data catalog record for customer data fields from the Customer Data Platform

Note that the Customer Data Platform may have table headings that are as simple as "ID", whereas, in the data catalog, the term is more specific (Customer ID). This is because the header "ID" may be used in various ways that are not unique to the customer. We must use unique terms and definitions in order to drive the appropriate understanding and specificity to enable a common language across the company.

Technical metadata

The technical metadata will include the following:

- The location of data stores

- Interface information

- Information about tables and field structure

- Data types

- Links to related fields

- Indexes

Metadata about unstructured data, such as a picture, may contain the following:

- An image title

- An image description

- An image date

- An image location

- The image copyright

The value of metadata management

When I think about the value of data management capabilities, I think about value in terms of what can I do after I deploy this capability that I am not able to do today. How do I measure this difference? It may be in dollars saved, fines avoided, hours of employee time that is saved, revenue that is generated, opportunity value unlocked, or some combination thereof. Any of these value vectors can make the capability worth deploying.

The difference with metadata is that subsequent data management capabilities (as we will explore in *Chapters 7–11*) will not reach their full potential without metadata capabilities in place. Thus, this capability is foundational, which also needs to be accounted for when measuring the value of metadata management. There are five core tenants to the value of metadata management capabilities:

- **Transparency**: Metadata management enables transparency about the data. Technical metadata tells us where the data came from, the systems the data was sourced from, if it was transposed or otherwise changed, and enables us to understand the data better. When we know more about the data's journey, we have increased transparency about the data, and therefore, higher trust in the data.

- **Stewardship**: Metadata management enables us to drive the accountability of the data. When we know what data we have, we can assign data stewards to the data, which enables accountability. When we know who is responsible for the data, we can create an environment where there is a point of contact to take care of the data for the company's use. This model of stewardship enables the company to be able to identify any responsible parties and drive further accountability for the management of the data. When stewards exist and have clear roles and responsibilities (as we outlined in the data governance policy), then the company gets to reap the rewards from the additional care over the data.

> **Important note**
> Remember, the key to high-quality stewardship is that of a service provider, not a data owner. The concept of ownership can lead to a "scarcity" mindset, which will prevent the stewards from sharing the data. Data represent an enterprise asset and should be available for shared use unless privacy, legal, or other regulations require confidentiality over the data assets.

- **Clarity**: Metadata management enables the company to gain clarity about terminology, sourcing, and ownership. By driving clarity, business units, analysts, engineers, and executives alike can align with ease.

- **Reusability**: Metadata management enables the company to locate, understand, and use (and reuse) enterprise data assets.

- **Foundational Capability**: Metadata management is a key foundational capability that is required for subsequent data management capabilities such as data quality, architecture optimization, and data operations. If we don't know what data we have, it's very hard to measure the quality of it, optimize sourcing, or manage it as a part of general data operations. We must have high-quality, reliable, and accessible metadata to drive these additional capabilities.

Why does metadata matter?

Metadata management provides the necessary capabilities to establish informational understanding and organization in a company. The active nature of metadata management allows a company to foster the use of data assets through sharing, enabling insights into data for change management, and allowing for the appropriate control and protection of regulation, policy adherence, and overall compliance.

The business outcomes that you can expect to drive through building out metadata management capabilities include the following:

- The ability to **search and locate** both business and technical data (saving the data user hours or potentially weeks of trying to find the data through their own internal social network, asking colleagues where the data and multiple iterations are when attempting to find the best source for that data)

- The ability to **rationalize common terms** enterprise-wide (aligning the business to a common taxonomy)

- The ability to **manage data well** and feed other key data management capabilities, such as governance, data quality, data architecture, and primary data management

Core metadata capabilities

Business metadata capabilities should be led by the data management solutions team under the office of the Chief Data & Analytics Officer. Business metadata must be driven centrally and should partner closely with business data stewards across the company to deliver end-to-end metadata process and technology solutions, including the tooling and processes required to enable business value from metadata management. In this section, we will cover the core capabilities that the data management solutions team is responsible for when deploying and managing enterprise-wide.

Metadata Framework		
Strategy: Approach, Standards, Connection to Enterprise Data Strategy and Enterprise Data Policy.		
Governance: Rolls and Responsibilities, Committee Structures, Reporting, Change Management, Traning, and Enablement.		
Define and Create: Organization of initial definitions, Stewards and collection of existing information for both business and technical Metadata	Integration and Tooling: Enablement via integration into tooling (e.g. collibra, Informatica, Alation	Analyze, Rationalize and Optimize: Processes to review, drive alignment, consistency, and adoption of common terms, sources and stewardship Retire legacy sources definitions and adopt enterprise sources
Measure, Use, and Continuous Improvement: Measure value, drive continuous adoption of enterprise terms and continue to optimize as new systems, sources, and reports all developed. Continuous improvement and adoption as new businesses, Products are integrated and/or developed.		

Figure 6.3 – Sample Metadata Framework

Metadata standards

Metadata standards are the guidelines or expectations for how the company should create, manage, and use metadata. These standards help companies define what must be done for data assets, systems, processes, and use such that there is consistency enterprise-wide and that the metadata can be relied upon.

Why do metadata standards matter?

Metadata standards are critical to the success of metadata management because the standards align expectations for how metadata management will be deployed, used, and leveraged across a company. There are four core tenants of a metadata management standard, and the following should be addressed in full in the standard:

- Metadata is an enterprise asset that has value and should be managed accordingly.

- Metadata management is an enterprise-wide capability and requires enterprise-wide leadership.

- Accountability is required; no one person or team can drive enterprise-wide metadata management alone or in isolation.

- Decisions around metadata management must be made through an enterprise lens and not in favor of one user or one group above the greater good of the enterprise

How to measure progress

A simple way to measure the progress of the deployment of metadata standards is two-fold: the publication of the standards and the adoption of the standards. For publication, you are seeking to publish one standard for the enterprise. There's no need to measure much beyond the publication date meeting the expected publication date and any regular revisions being on track.

The second measure of success is the adoption of the standard. You can set adoption metrics by division, data domain, system, or business data steward—whatever makes sense for your data management program. The important component is consistency across data management capabilities. If you are measuring by data domain, for example, measure all your data management capabilities by data domain to drive consistency in adoption.

Who manages metadata standards?

The office of the Chief Data & Analytics Officer is ultimately responsible for the business glossary for the company. Within the office of the CDAO, the data management solutions team, which manages all the metadata, data quality, and primary data, should drive the requirements that feed the metadata standards; however, generally, your data governance leader will be responsible for publishing all enterprise data standards through a consistent process and will ultimately be publishing the metadata standards.

The data governance Leader may also manage compliance against the company's data standards, with the metadata management leader being accountable for progress in deployment and adoption. Business and technical data stewards should be consulted in the development of the standards. Data domain executives should be informed about the standards.

How should you use it?

The metadata standards should be used to guide users on what is required for metadata management, defining the capabilities, what solutions are available to aid them in both complying with the standard, and also using metadata management. The standard should define the key terms, establish processes, inform users on what metadata tools should be used, and, overall, drive enablement to use this key data management capability.

In some organizations, the metadata standard may also inform the reader about the funding requirements, change management, and what is out of the scope of the standard.

Business glossary

Business glossaries and data catalogs both represent key metadata management capabilities, but they have different purposes and generally serve slightly different audiences. A **business glossary** is a lot like a common dictionary—it creates clarity. It contains the key business terms and their definitions for the data that matters to your company. The business glossary should provide search capabilities to enable users to search and find the data they are looking for, enable an understanding of the key characteristics of the data, and drive some level of workflow to suggest changes and approve the business metadata.

> **Important note**
>
> Sometimes a business glossary is referred to as a data dictionary.

Business glossaries are typically used by business users (but technical users may also benefit from their use) to help drive understanding and meaning about data, and they typically capture the following information:

- **Terms**: What we are defining
- **Definition**: A clear and concise description of the term
- **Synonyms**: Other terms that have the same meaning as the term
- **Antonyms**: Other terms that have the opposite meaning as the term
- **Examples**: Examples of how the term is used
- **Notes**: Any other relevant information (optional field)

Why does a business glossary matter?

A business glossary matters for any company because it serves as the common language the company uses to discuss key information. Aligning on business terms is helpful in everyday business, as it ensures everyone in the company, from the CEO down to the individual analyst, is speaking the same language.

> **Important note**
>
> At one company I worked at, we spent almost 18 months aligning on an enterprise definition for the term "customer." Because some of our business units were business-to-business and some were business-to-consumer, the definition needed to be broad enough to cover both business models but specific enough not to include prospects or leads. Aligning the entire business included a wide range of stakeholders, some of whom were very passionate about the term. However hard the alignment was, it was critical we defined it properly so that our enterprise reporting and decision-making were consistent. We could not report information to the C-suite or the board without this alignment.

How to measure progress

As you build out your business glossary capability, you will need to report on progress to your stakeholders, your manager, and perhaps the enterprise data committee. Several metrics can be used to measure and communicate the progress your team is making in terms of delivery. Here are some examples:

- The number of business glossaries completed by system/the number of systems
- The number of business terms uploaded to the business glossary/the number of terms defined
- The number of business terms approved/the number of business terms defined
- The number of applications without business glossaries/the number of applications
- The number of business terms without an assigned owner/the number of business terms
- The number of data domains with completed business glossaries/the number of data domains

How do you measure the value?

This is one of the harder components of a business glossary. Most of the value is qualitative. The lack of a business glossary is often felt enterprise-wide and all the way to the top of the organization. Let me share an example to explain.

Example

I once had a CEO ask me to drive alignment for the most important terms in our company. They said, "Don't take forever to do it through."

What was the problem? Why did the CEO need us to align our top terms?

We were in the midst of a business transformation and changing business models. He was running into issues when talking to various GMs across the business because the individual GM's revenue numbers were not aligning with the finance teams' numbers. When we dug in, we found that the definition of revenue used in the GMs varied widely between the GMs but also with regard to finance. The finance team had to make several adjustments to comply with GAAP, which created a notable delta between internal reporting and external reporting. This led to many cycles of discussion at very senior levels about data differences. Imagine the cost of these meetings.

When we aligned the business to the common terms and calculations, the teams had far more productive meetings rooted in data that everyone agreed to.

Here are a few ways you can measure the value:

- **Reduction of Errors**: A business glossary can be used to reduce errors in reporting by pulling the definition ahead of producing a report. By aligning on the definitions upfront, you can prevent cycles of the reproduction of reports when the business and the producer of the report align on what they really want ahead of report creation vs. after the report is finalized, where the numbers don't align with what they expected, leading to rewrites.

- **Increases in Efficiency**: Having a business glossary can improve efficiency by making it faster to find and use information. This can be exponentially impactful the larger the organization you are in.

As you might note, these are time savings. You could produce a model to measure these assumptions and validate the assumptions with the business users. For example, we believe that once we have a business glossary defined with adequate definitions and sourcing, we expect each report production time will be reduced by 20 hours due to upfront alignment vs. the back and forth experienced today. By using this assumption of 20 hours x 100 reports per year, we predict we will save 2,000 hours of labor per year (equivalent to one full-time employee). If your organization produces 1,000 reports per year (or 10,000), imagine the impact this simple solution can make.

Who manages the business glossary?

The office of the Chief Data & Analytics Officer is ultimately responsible for the business glossary of the company. Within the office of the CDAO, the data management solutions team, which manages all the metadata, data quality, and primary data, should drive the enterprise business glossary, as well as the tooling to support the enablement.

Most companies assign a leader who is focused on metadata management to drive the capabilities outlined in this chapter. In all of my previous data teams, I have had a team of anywhere from 3–15 people (sometimes more for larger companies) focused on this area. Why so big? If you are aligning on an enterprise glossary for a company with 6,000 applications, you're going to need robust processes, forums, and tools, as well as a roadmap to deliver. The work is never "done." As companies evolve and serve new markets, new customer bases develop and deploy new systems, all of which lead to more business glossary work for your team.

What does a mature business glossary capability look like?

As you work to mature a business glossary capability for your company, there are a series of actions you can take to drive more maturity and use of a business glossary. In maturing data governance programs, business glossaries are often created for a particular system or data domain, but in more mature companies, an enterprise glossary is created to standardize business definitions across the company. An enterprise business glossary usually enables the following capabilities:

- A synthesized and rationalized business glossary versus duplicates/divisional
- Drives the adoption of ontologies
- The rationalization of terminology and its association with data assets
- Enables the linkage of business terms across domains

Ultimately, the enterprise-wide alignment of the complete information associated with the business terms, including meaning, relationships, and lineage, helps drive a true enterprise business glossary. In the preceding example, in which I worked with the CEO to drive a common report of the top metrics across the company, we started the enterprise business glossary with the nine terms he was interested in standardizing. From there, the team built out a standard enterprise business glossary as we continued to add more standardized terms to our metrics as a service program.

However, it doesn't take a CEO request to begin this work; you should begin to synthesize and rationalize business glossaries across the company as a part of your standard program. The easiest place to start is identifying where you already have duplicates across data domains and/or systems, and you can easily determine the enterprise definition. These common definitions are your "enterprise" business terms.

You will find instances where an enterprise definition is agreed upon, but divisions have a definition that is a subcomponent that nests within the enterprise division uniquely for them. For example, you may have an enterprise term such as "revenue." For a division, you may capture revenue by product line. While the enterprise revenue term is inclusive of the common definition, when the division is specifying its product line, they may call it "product A revenue," which clarifies that it is revenue but for a specific product.

How should you implement a business glossary?

1. **Scope**: Define the scope of the business glossary. You could start with a system, a team, a data domain, a program, or the company at large. It's important to align on what you will be delivering against. Define success upfront to ensure alignment with your stakeholders.

2. **Onboard the stakeholders**: Define what the process will be and explain the expectations, timing needs, and what they can expect for outcomes.

3. **Gather any materials available**: You may be pleasantly surprised to find that pieces of a business glossary or definitions of terms may exist. Sometimes, teams capture this information in a spreadsheet or a presentation for shared use. Leverage what is on hand as a starting point.

4. **Define the terms**: Work with the business data stewards and users of the information to define the definitions, align on synonyms and antonyms, provide examples, and collect any relevant notes.

5. **Publish the glossary**: Put the collected information to work in your enterprise business glossary.

Data catalog

This stores information about the organization's data assets, such as data location, format, lineage, and quality. The **data catalog** is usually a key metadata capability for data engineers, data scientists, and other technical users. The data catalog may include other relevant information, such as links to source data, classification, or other pertinent information. The data catalog usually contains key information for each data asset, such as the following:

- **Name**: The name of the data asset

- **Description**: The description of the data asset

- **Location**: Where the data asset can be found

- **Format**: The Format of the data asset (curated data set, report, and so on)

- **Lineage**: The history of the data asset (see *Chapter 8* for more information about lineage)

- **Quality**: Information about the quality of the asset, such as accuracy, completeness, and so on (see *Chapter 9* for more information about data quality)

- **Tags**: These can be used to organize and search for data assets and may also use a format to be driven (e.g., report, customer, vendor, and so on)

I would expect a data catalog to provide business users with useful datasets that have already been created, which will speed discovery and time to insight for the company. Ideally, this capability should enable business users to augment the information in the data catalog with new information to continuously improve the data catalog.

Why does it matter? What matters?

As a company grows and data becomes more critical to the company's overall success, individuals and teams spend too much time searching for data they trust. In my experience, there is usually an inflection point: either something bad happens (a data breach, regulatory mandate, and so on), or it simply becomes too painful to continue to operate based on "historical knowledge" about the company, and scaling becomes a challenge. Data catalogs are the solution to help individuals and teams seek, find, and use data across the company by allowing individuals to reuse common data assets.

This problem is not new. According to an IDC white paper from 2001, "*A 1998 survey found that 76% of company executives considered information to be "mission critical" and their company's most important asset. Yet, 60% felt that time constraints and a lack of understanding of how to find information were preventing their employees from finding the information they needed.*" Furthermore, Forbes reported that in 2018, data professionals were still spending 50% of their time finding and governing data.

Here are some indicators that you may need a data catalog:

1. Your business analysts have a hard time finding the data they need to populate their reports and/or BI tools

2. Finding information in your data lake is difficult, if not impossible

3. When data can be found, understanding it is still a challenge

4. There is no ownership for data or data assets, so finding someone to answer basic questions is near impossible or very time consuming

5. Reusing data assets from other individuals requires you to know the data asset exists and who created it so you can use it, too

6. No process exists to verify the data is trustworthy

7. The source of the data is unknown, so blind reliance is required for use

How do you measure the value?

In my experience, most companies have not fully adopted data catalogs, which are the most simplistic way to address these very common problems. While there are many ways to calculate the value (i.e., cost of relying on incorrect data, fines for misreporting information, time, and so on), the easiest and least controversial way to calculate the value of your data catalog is an employee's time. Simply take the cost of a data analyst's salary, let's assume USD 100,000 for ease of calculation, and use the metric referenced in the preceding section of 50% of their time spent searching for information. That means 50% of their compensation annually is spent searching for and governing the data they manage:

$$\text{USD } 100,000 * 50\% = \text{USD } 50,000$$

How many data analysts does a company employ? 10? 100? Multiply your cost per analyst accordingly.

How much does a data catalog service cost? Usually, this is the total cost of ownership, which includes the licensing cost, the server costs, and the management of the tooling (metadata analysts).

What about the factor of time lost searching vs. more productive tasks?

All of these answers should factor into your company's decision to invest in an enterprise data catalog. Don't forget to consider the opportunities lost by not having this capability. What might you be able to do if you didn't have to deploy your analysts to search for data day after day? Could they be creating new revenue-generating ideas? The total picture of opportunity and cost is relevant to tell the real value that a data catalog can bring to your company.

What metrics should be used to measure maturity?

- The number of data assets checked into the data catalog

- The number of data assets with complete information

- The number of data assets certified by the data steward (meaning, validated source, data quality, and ownership identified)

- The number of data assets with data stewards

- The number of data assets being reused in total data assets

- The number of data assets with complete lineage

- The number of data assets from each data domain logged in the enterprise data catalog/the number of data assets

> **Example**
>
> In one of my previous roles, we had to rationalize data assets as a part of our customer data transformation. Originally, we had customer data spread across the entire company. As we deployed a unified customer data record system, we rationalized customer data assets in our enterprise data catalog. This provided the company with the approved or "authorized" definitions, assets, and location for the golden source data. Any other source of customer data was considered "non-certified," and the CDAO did not stand behind its reliability.

Who manages it?

Similar to the business glossary, you may have multiple levels of management for a data catalog. You may have divisional or data domain-driven data catalogs, which are managed by a business data steward or business data team.

These business data leaders will partner with your metadata leaders in the CDAO office to establish and effectively manage the enterprise data catalog. Optimally, an organization would have an enterprise data catalog exclusively, with ways to manage and tag information that is specific to a singular data domain. This transparency is ideal for data evolution, such as when a data asset previously used at a divisional level is discovered and adopted at an enterprise level. If the transparency into the divisional/data domain's data catalog is not visible to the enterprise, the data assets cannot be leveraged effectively.

However, having divisional or domain-based data catalogs are a great place to start if your organization does not have a data catalog capability. You don't need a tool to get started. You can use something as simple as a spreadsheet and mature into a tool when you are ready to invest.

What does maturity look like?

The enterprise-wide alignment of the complete information associated with the data assets includes the meaning, relationships, and lineage to drive a true enterprise data catalog. A mature data catalog capability should make it very easy for a business user to determine the following:

- What data you have

- Who is accountable for the data

- Where the data is sourced from

- Whether the data is trustworthy

- Where to find the data (ideally, there could be a link to it)

The seamless and secure access to data assets enterprise-wide, including integration with identity access management to ensure the right people have the right access to the right assets at the right time, is optimal. It can be quite frustrating when a data catalog makes the data easy to find, but then a user spends days, weeks, or months waiting for access approvals.

Easy discoverability/sophisticated search (e.g., powered by AI) makes this capability even more interesting. Some newer features will suggest additional assets given your search history. The recommendations embedded in data catalogs are making it even easier for users to find what they need and, sometimes, additional information they didn't know they wanted.

How should you use it?

- Business users should find the data they need by **searching** a data catalog
- Understand the data being used more easily and **consistently** with others (common language)
- Helps business users **better interpret technical information**
- Use the data to **create insights** needed to answer key business questions

Building optimal metadata management capability

In 2021, I participated in an interview where I boldly (at the time) stated that metadata was the most underappreciated data governance capability. Now, in late 2023, I stand beside that statement. It's my firm belief that metadata is the power behind all data governance. To this day, I am asked what companies should do to maximize their investment in data governance, and every time, I suggest a strong investment in metadata capabilities by creating and optimizing a data marketplace.

What is a data marketplace?

A data marketplace is what I would call a "business of data capability," meaning that it is driven by the data office. When powered and supported by technology, a **data marketplace** is a single location for a company to create a shopping-like experience for all data assets. The foundation of the data marketplace is powered by metadata and allows users to access data assets from a single platform with ease. Ease of search and discovery are critical features of a world-class data marketplace.

A data marketplace can solve a number of issues for a company, including, but not limited to, the following:

- Locating data from across the organization (1:M platforms/systems/sources)
- Identify duplicate data (proliferation of data assets) to drive simplification efforts
- Identify data quality issues to drive remediation efforts
- Drive the transparency of data definitions, calculations, sourcing, and the quality of data assets

What's in a data marketplace?

A data marketplace contains both metadata (business and technical) and data assets, providing workflow for stewardship activities, and it does all of this with unified transparency for the enterprise. You should include the following:

- Data governance policies (links to)
- Stewardship workflows to enable proposed definitions, approvals, and so on
- Business glossary
- Data dictionary
- Data lineage
- Data products (links, owners, and certification status)
- Certified data assets (reports and curated datasets)
- Standardized enterprise KPIs
- Data quality metrics for the above capabilities

Why does a data marketplace matter?

A data marketplace is a seamless, connected experience that provides the capabilities described in the preceding section to enable the company to find the data that it needs quickly, efficiently, and with trust and transparency by design. If time matters to your business, a data marketplace can accelerate the time to insight unlike any other capability. The best data marketplaces I have seen have focused ruthlessly on great user experiences by keeping the user interface simple, content-relevant, and focusing on quality content over quantity of content.

In the background, the CDAO office will likely spend time integrating a variety of features, systems, and processes to make the data marketplace a delightful experience for users. Do not hesitate to invest in this capability. The number one complaint from my stakeholders has always been around the challenge of finding trustworthy information, and a data marketplace solves this problem. If you can make it easy for your stakeholders at all levels of the organization to find the information they need to do their jobs well, you will be successful as a data leader.

Measuring outcomes and return on investment

- The number of unique users (you could track by business unit or region for more specific intelligence) per month (or any time horizon that's relevant to your business).
- The number of unique data products/assets onboarded to the marketplace.
- The number of unique certified data products/assets onboarded to the marketplace.

- The number of systems connected.

- Persona-based user counts. This tracks the number over a set duration (i.e., monthly or quarterly) and determines which personas are using more or less over time so you can explore why and drive additional use. Some examples include data engineers, data analysts, business analysts, and executive management.

Setting up metadata management for success

Ultimately, a great metadata program helps companies to answer fundamental data questions such as, What data do we have? How is it classified? Where is our data? Who is responsible for it? How can I find it? Can I use it? Being able to answer these fundamental questions is what makes a metadata management program successful. The CDAO and metadata management leaders, together, must share the value proposition of this capability. My advice is not to be afraid to share what can go wrong without strong metadata management but also what can go right when you have a strong metadata management program.

While at face value this capability may seem fairly straightforward, the implementation of a strong program across a large company takes time, focus, and clear communication about the value. I recommend starting with a data domain or a single system and working across your company to drive implementation. While you work to capture metadata, launching a data marketplace capability will enable the company to take advantage of all the hard work your team has put into building metadata management capabilities in an easy-to-digest format.

Conclusion

The remaining data governance capabilities in the subsequent chapters will build on this metadata capability. If you do not have a strong handle on your metadata, measuring data quality, building authorized provisioning points, optimizing architecture, and building authoritative sources for common datasets (i.e., customers or products) becomes a lot more difficult. Thus, it is critical to message the importance of this foundational capability early and often as you advance the maturity of data governance at your company.

As a result of this chapter, you should be able to adequately explain the importance of metadata management, including why it is required for all other capabilities to be successful, understand how to design a strong metadata management function, and how to define and implement the specific needs for your company's implementation. The next chapter will discuss the topic of metadata, but it will focus on the more technical aspects of metadata management.

References

- https://computhink.com/wp-content/uploads/2015/10/IDC20on20The20High20Cost20Of20Not20Finding20Information.pdf
- https://www.forbes.com/sites/forbestechcouncil/2019/12/17/reality-check-still-spending-more-time-gathering-instead-of-analyzing/?sh=4363228128ff

7
Technical Metadata and Data Lineage

Establishing a high-value, high-**return-on-investment** (**ROI**) data lineage capability is a fundamental capability for any data governance program. The success or failure of a Chief Data & Analytics Officer hinges on being able to answer a few key core questions:

- Where is my data?
- Who owns it?
- How is it classified?
- Is the data safe and secure?
- How does it change (or how was it changed) as it moves through the company?
- Can I trust the data? Is it of high quality?

Data lineage is the ability to see the journey the data has taken across your organization. Data lineage captures the source of any transposition changes and the overall journey of where that data has come and gone. It provides a line of sight into how the data has evolved across its source, journey, and evolution.

Building on the Metadata Management capabilities outlined in *Chapter 6, Metadata Management*, this chapter will focus on the more technical aspects of Metadata Management. We will focus on where the data is, how it's moved, and the technical requirements to better understand the data. While technical data stewards are most likely to be engaging with technical metadata, specifically with data lineage, business data stewards also benefit from this capability. Additionally, technical metadata will provide the foundation for the measurement of data quality, which we will cover in *Chapter 8, Data Quality*.

As of the time of this writing, full end-to-end data lineage is still a challenge for most companies. I will outline my experience in deploying data lineage, the challenges, and what we can do about it in lieu of perfection. We do not need to wait for the "magic bullet" tool or technology to lean into the development of data lineage capabilities for our companies. We can start right now with what we have and build as the capability matures. Let's start with some basic definitions to ground ourselves in a common language.

We will cover the following main topics:

- Technical metadata

- Data lineage

- Building an optimal data lineage capability

Technical Metadata

Technical Metadata is typically used by more technical data professionals such as engineers, data operations professionals, system engineers, and general information technology analysts. Technical Metadata is information that describes the more technical aspects of data and includes key information to manage and understand the physical aspects of data. Technical Metadata includes location and formatting information across the following areas:

- **Data schema**: The description of the structure of the database, including tables, rows/columns, and the relationship between them

- **Data dictionary**: Includes data definitions, data lineage, and data quality rules

- **Data lineage**: The history of how the data is created, processed, and used; it is used to enable data discovery, data integration, data governance, and data analysis

Why does it matter? What matters?

Documentation of physical data assets, movement, transformations, and relationships between physical data elements enables the users to better understand the data. Technical metadata capabilities are important for several reasons, including the following:

- Helping data analysts and engineers understand what data is available

- Helping to track the history of how the data was created and transformed, which can be useful for debugging and auditing purposes

- Can be used to assess the quality of the data to enable the users to identify and fix data quality issues, as well as identify where the data quality issue was introduced in the process (thereby enabling the business to fix the process issue that led to the data quality issue)

- Protecting data from authorized access and/or modification

Helpful hint

When you are getting started with technical metadata, you will likely need to pick one area to start with. You may want to start with a report that is important to your business so that you can provide assurance that the report is reliable. If this seems overwhelming, you might just start with a simple metric on that report.

For example, perhaps you are trying to understand if the customer count you are reporting to your stakeholders (and, perhaps, specifically stockholders) is accurate. Here are a few questions you might be asking about that metric:

- What is the definition of customer count?

- Where are we sourcing the customer count metric from?

- Is the source the right place to source the customer count metric from, based on our definition?

- What is the lineage of the customer count data? Who touches that data in transit?

- Are we confident the customer count data is of high quality? Can we trust it?

- Who is the owner of the customer count metric?

- Have we tested the lineage to ensure that the data is reliable? Have we tested the data quality for accuracy, completeness, and reliability?

By evaluating the answers to this question, we will be able to determine if A) there are issues with the customer count metric or B) we are confident relying on it. By exploring the metric in detail and documenting the results in a shared system of record for metadata, we can reduce our dependency on institutional knowledge and create transparency and visibility into this metric. Once it is evaluated, we can reuse it across the company with confidence.

How do you measure the value?

I often get asked how to measure the value of the more technical aspects of data governance (in addition to data governance in general). The root of this question is: how do you measure the value in terms that business users will understand *and agree to*? The important part of this answer is that the business user must agree that the value they received is as you described. Most CDAOs do not go the extra step to gather confirmation from the business that they did indeed receive the value the data office says that they did. In this case, CDAOs are found advocating that their team provided impact, and no one is agreeing, often causing the CDAO to lose credibility with the business and, ultimately, funding and support.

To avoid this issue, it's imperative that value is based on facts and that the business agrees with the facts upfront, before the deployment (often, this means aligning on the methodology by which value will be measured), aligning after the deployment of the capability that they did receive the value. There are several ways to measure the value of technical metadata.

The most straightforward way to measure the value is to start by measuring the benefits that technical metadata provides to the organization:

- The reduction in time spent to find and understand data [*# of hours saved x the number of people impacted * average cost per hour/per person = Reduction in cost saved by providing technical metadata*]

  - Assumptions to align with the business on:

    - # of hours saved

    - # of people impacted

    - Cost per hour/person

  - Note: Align the assumptions upfront so that when the results come in, there is less debate. Often, the number is higher than they expect, and it provides concerns about the methodology. This approach will reduce the friction in value alignment discussions.

  - *Additional note*: I have seen the "search and find" time for an analyst **reduce up to 80% by activating a metadata management capability in an organization**, so do not understate the importance and impact of this capability.

- Improved quality and accuracy of data analysis [*# of identified data issues * value of data issue remediation*]

  - Assumptions to align with the business on:

    - Value of data issue remediation [could be the actual dollar amount, could be materiality %, could be the value of the decision made from the number]

  - Note: You could simply track the number of data issues identified and remediated; however, that assumes all data issues are treated equally, which is not true.

An alternative or additive measurement of value is the measure of the cost avoidance that technical metadata provides to the organization. These tend to be a bit harder to define and align with the business but are equally as valuable. Here are some examples:

- Compliance violation avoidance (examples: GDPR fines, CCPA fines, external audit findings) [*# of violations avoided * average cost of violation*]

  - Assumptions to align with the business on:

    - Which violations were avoided (usually aligned with Chief Privacy, Chief Legal, or Chief Compliance Officer(s))

    - The average cost of violations

- Error avoidance [*# of errors avoided * Value of avoidance*]

  - Assumptions to align with the business on:

    - What is an avoided error?

    - What's the value of the avoided error?

Ideally, your technical metadata leader should track and report these metrics regularly. I recommend making the metrics stakeholder-facing, available for review at any time, and fully transparent. You can invite challenges from stakeholders regarding the assumptions to build trust in the metrics used to measure success, without being defensive. If the assumptions don't make sense to the business, change them. Ensure alignment on the assumptions, and let the value of the solution speak for itself from there.

Which metrics should be used to measure maturity?

When evaluating the maturity of the technical metadata management capabilities, the following metrics should be used internally to measure the implementation of the capability:

- Number of data sources with data schemas documented

- Number of data sources with complete information

- Number of data sources with technical data stewards identified

- Number of reports with technical metadata documented

- Number of metrics with technical metadata documented

- Number of data quality issues identified from technical metadata

---

Example

Where is our data?

A common, and somewhat terrifying question to be asked.

What's more terrifying is the common answer: *I don't know.*

This is the reality for most companies, unfortunately. Many have a "decent" idea of where the data is. They may know what system it's in…but what about the unknowns? Are you 100% sure that the data hasn't been copied? Replicated? Stored on a spreadsheet?

This is what makes technical metadata so important, to be able to answer the question, "*Where is my data?*" Many companies know where they expect data to be but struggle to have a complete picture of all of the locations of their data with certainty.

Who manages it?

Technical metadata should be managed by the **Technical Data Steward**. The Technical Data Steward is a technical resource within the organization, often within the Information Technology function, who is responsible for maintaining and caring for the physical data within your organization. While your **Business Data Steward** is responsible for policy compliance, business definitions, use, and business glossary accuracy, the Technical Data Steward is the technical counterpart to this Business Data Steward. Together, these two roles create trust in the data that is available to the company as a company asset.

What does maturity look like?

A mature, fully operationalized technical metadata solution will provide fully available, easily accessible, comprehensive technical information about the company's data, with clear stewardship (which answers the question: *Who is accountable for the data?*). The data will be transparent, clear, and easily understood by any user. Additionally, the solution will answer the following questions:

- What data do we have?

- Where is our data located?

- How is our data being used?

When we can consistently and systematically answer these questions of our data, then we have a mature technical metadata capability. If we have to go on a search and rescue mission each time a question (such as the preceding ones) is asked, we have more work to do. It usually takes one crisis, either customer-driven or regulatory-driven, where you can't easily answer the preceding questions to drive executive management to invest in this capability quickly and at scale.

How should you use it?

There are a number of ways a user (business or technical) can use technical metadata information to aid them in running their business and performing their respective job responsibilities. A few common examples include the following:

- **When you are looking for data**. *Example*: A user is trying to find the best source of revenue for a specific product.

- **When you find a problem and want to understand the source of the issue**. *Example*: The user identified there is an issue on a report. They look to the business and technical metadata to find where the data is coming from to discover the source of the error.

- **When you are trying to secure and protect data**. *Example*: You need to find **personally identifiable information (PII)** in the company and protect it from unauthorized access. First, you need to find where the PII is so that you can classify it as PII, and then work with your security team to protect it.

- **When you need to delete data**. *Example*: A new customer requirement to delete data within a specified time period is defined in their contract. They've asked the company to delete their data, and you need to find where all their data is in the organization.

- **When you are trying to understand a process end to end**. *Example*: You are a business analyst, and you are looking for ways to optimize the lead-to-cash process. You want to understand the path a quote takes through the company's systems to look for simplification opportunities.

- **When you are attempting to understand change management impacts**. *Example*: A new release of your HR system is going into production this weekend. You need to determine if any of the reports used for headcount management are impacted by the changes before they happen.

Data Lineage

Data Lineage is the capability that tracks and documents the journey data takes through an organization's systems. Data lineage shows how data flows through the systems, how it is changed or manipulated along the journey, and where it is stored and ultimately used. In short, data lineage provides transparency into the data. This is critical because transparency helps us drive trust in our data. When we know what the data is and where it comes from, we trust it more, and it is a key component in understanding the data and believing what it tells us.

The other key component of a data lineage capability is it tracks the flow of data over time. Unlike some of the other data capabilities in this book, data lineage provides information about the data life cycle. By providing a clearer understanding of where data originated, how it may have been changed, and where it ultimately resides, we are able to see all the transformations the data went through along its life cycle, what changed, and why.

Why does it matter? What matters?

Having trust in our data is paramount to ensuring a company is making data-driven decisions. At the last assessment, 83% of CEOs wanted their organizations to be data-driven, but only 30% of employees believed that they were (*Tableau*). Why the gap? Well, in part, because the data is not trusted, it's hard to get to, people do not understand it, and, therefore, it's considered in decisions but rarely used. Data lineage matters because it helps companies to see the data more clearly, understand where it came from, and, thus, trust it. This trust is foundational to data use. When we trust information, we can use it for decision-making, and, therefore, make better decisions. Ultimately, *data lineage brings integrity to data*.

Data lineage is the documentation of physical data assets, movement, transformations, and relationships between physical data elements. Data lineage tells us the following:

- Where the data is

- How it's stored (is it in a data warehouse, data lake, on-premises, or in the cloud (which cloud)?)

- How the data was created

- Where the data came from

- When it was last altered

- How it was updated (systematically, by a human, and determining which one by capturing the user ID)

Example

In one of my past experiences building out a Data Governance function, I had a consulting partner tell me that there was no need for end-to-end lineage so long as we could verify that the quality of the data at origination matched the quality of data at the output at the report. All that might be true for data quality purposes, but that doesn't tell us about any technical implications associated with change management for security purposes, and so on.

For example, if a change goes into production in System A, and the reports we are looking at come out of System D, we would not have visibility into the interim stops at System B or System C. Without data lineage, we would not be able to see that System B contains that data and is a potential impact from a change. This is simply one system that the data transfers through as a part of its journey. We would simply see that System A and D did not match, but not know that data from System B is extracted into a different report and is also impacted in the change process.

Data lineage also provides us insight into what kinds of changes might impact it. Imagine being able to query our data lineage repository. We can see where that data lives across its life cycle, not just at its beginning and respective end. It's important to consider all of the requirements for data lineage and all the use cases associated with it when making these types of decisions.

The benefits of data lineage are broad, as we will explore in the following sections. Please keep in mind that data lineage is the foundation for additional data governance capabilities, including data quality. We will cover data quality in great detail in *Chapter 8*, *Data Quality*.

How do you measure the value?

Consistent with the measures in the *Technical Metadata* section, the value of data lineage can be measured in terms of cost savings, time savings, risk avoidance, and value add. See the preceding section for specific examples and calculations you can use to measure the value of data lineage. More broadly, data lineage can be measured in a variety of ways, including the following:

- **Increased revenue/cost savings**: If you provide better information to the users, they are able to make better decisions about how to spend money, and thus generate revenue. This can also be leveraged to increase operating margin, by evaluating opportunities to reduce redundancies and cut costs. Costs can also be saved by identifying data errors early and preventing users from making decisions based on bad data.

- **Risk reduction**: You may be able to help save your company from the risk of a data breach by identifying data that carries risk and protecting it early.

- **Improved decision-making**: By using data lineage to provide a clear line of sight into the data, you can apply automation techniques to make reports quicker and higher value so that decisions can be made faster and with less human error risk.

- **Increased/improved innovation**: You can use data lineage to uncover new insights from existing data, which can be used to create new products and services.

Broadly speaking, data lineage is valuable for a number of key reasons, including the following:

- **Increased data quality**: Data lineage feeds data quality by providing insight into changes to the data to identify potential errors.

- **Increased compliance**: Data lineage helps companies meet compliance expectations that require an understanding of data sovereignty and support avoidance of fines or penalties for requirements such as GDPR or CCPA.

- **Enhanced auditing**: Data lineage enhances auditing capabilities due to the availability of data flows. By being able to see transparently where data has flowed, data lineage can help auditors understand a process before they have to meet with stakeholders.

- **Improved security**: Data lineage is a fundamental capability to drive precision in security practices. Instead of taking a blanket approach, a deep understanding of the data that needs to be protected allows security teams to act with precision, applying the appropriate level of control to the right data in the organization.

- **Faster troubleshooting**: Data lineage can be used to investigate data issues to be able to trace the data throughout the data supply chain. This traceability will help the user identify the source of the issue faster, saving (potentially significant) time.

- **Improved change management**: Data lineage drives improved change management by enabling teams to see what data will be impacted by a release or change ahead of time so that appropriate testing can be completed ahead of production releases and after to confirm changes are functioning as intended.

- **Stronger data governance**: Data lineage can be used to improve data governance and assist in the prioritization of efforts. By providing a systematic way to document data flow, the data governance team can leverage data lineage to prioritize focus areas and ensure data is used in a consistent and compliant manner aligned with data governance policy.

Leveraging the areas outlined here, you can use a basic calculation to measure the value of data lineage all in by calculating the aforementioned benefits, and then using a simple ROI calculation:

$$\textbf{ROI} = \textbf{(Benefits} - \textbf{Costs)/Costs}$$

You can calculate the ROI on your data lineage capability for the company. To calculate costs to serve this capability, you should include the following costs:

- **Cost of the software**: Cost of the contract to acquire the data lineage tool or tools used in your organization to provide the capability to users.

- **Costs of the implementation (over some period of time)**: The cost to implement the tool may include one-time costs such as an implementation consultant and increased headcount (such as contractors to stand up the platform or tooling needed to design processes or do initial data lineage collection).

- **Cost of the maintenance, including people, processes, and technology**: Cost for the people who will provide the capability on an ongoing basis, ongoing server space, and so on.

Together, this calculation can value the benefit in terms of cost and provide your company with confidence that the work to maintain data lineage is overshadowed by the significant benefits it provides.

What metrics should be used to measure maturity?

In addition to business value measurements outlined previously, the data governance team may track specific value measurements program-wide, such as the following:

- Number of data quality issues identified and resolved

- Number of compliance violations identified and prevented before impacting a customer

- Number of security incidents identified and prevented

- **Time to market** (**TTM**) for new products or services

- Increase in **time to value** (**TTV**) for data analytics

- Cost savings from data source retirement or simplification efforts

Who manages it?

As with other types of technical metadata (such as a data dictionary), the Technical Data Steward is often the responsible person (or people) who cares for data lineage and ensures the lineage accurately represents the physical data throughout the company. A business user may use the data lineage to evidence confidence in the data, given visibility into where the data has moved, the quality along the journey, and the overall reliability of the data; however, the care of data lineage is typically in the hands of the Technical Data Steward.

What does maturity look like?

There are a number of mature data lineage capabilities that are relevant, but simply, the breadth and depth of your data lineage capability is the primary indicator of success. As you start to roll out this capability, you may start with a single report or metric. Next, you may evolve to an entire data domain or suite of systems. Last, you may have all prioritized data assets across the company documented with sustainable data lineage. As you mature, you should be able to uncover problems and errors in your data lineage through validation. Validation is a best practice that should be implemented along your maturity journey. The validation should include connecting data supplies and data consumers to confirm the results are as expected. Let's explore validation deeper.

> **Best practice – validating lineage**
>
> By conducting end-to-end lineage, data analysts and business users can increase the trust of the data lineage capability. Validation provides confidence in the completeness and accuracy of the technical metadata capabilities.

To validate lineage, select a report that matters to your company; perhaps an executive-level dashboard with **key performance indicators (KPIs)** would be a good selection. Then, do the following:

1. Prioritize the relevant report and identify key business elements (data points) on the report.

2. Select a sample of line items to validate from the report.

3. Meet with the individual who either produces the report or is responsible for the automation to create the report (depending on how the report is created).

4. Document the end-to-end generation of the line items/key business elements identified in *steps 1* and *2* for each unique business element selected.

5. Identify any issues or concerns with the documentation provided.

6. Compare the narrative to the technical data lineage collected and assess any gaps.

7. Discuss with the report owner/producer any gaps identified, validate if the understanding or the technical lineage is inaccurate, reeducate for understanding gaps, and update technical lineage for any technical gaps.

Report

Revenue by Product

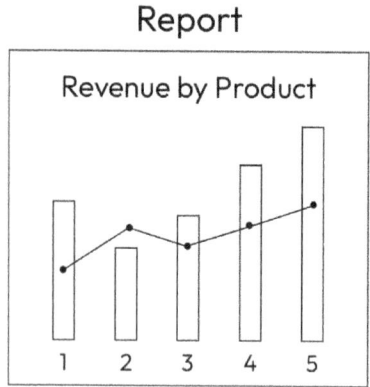

Figure 7.1 – Example report: Revenue by Product

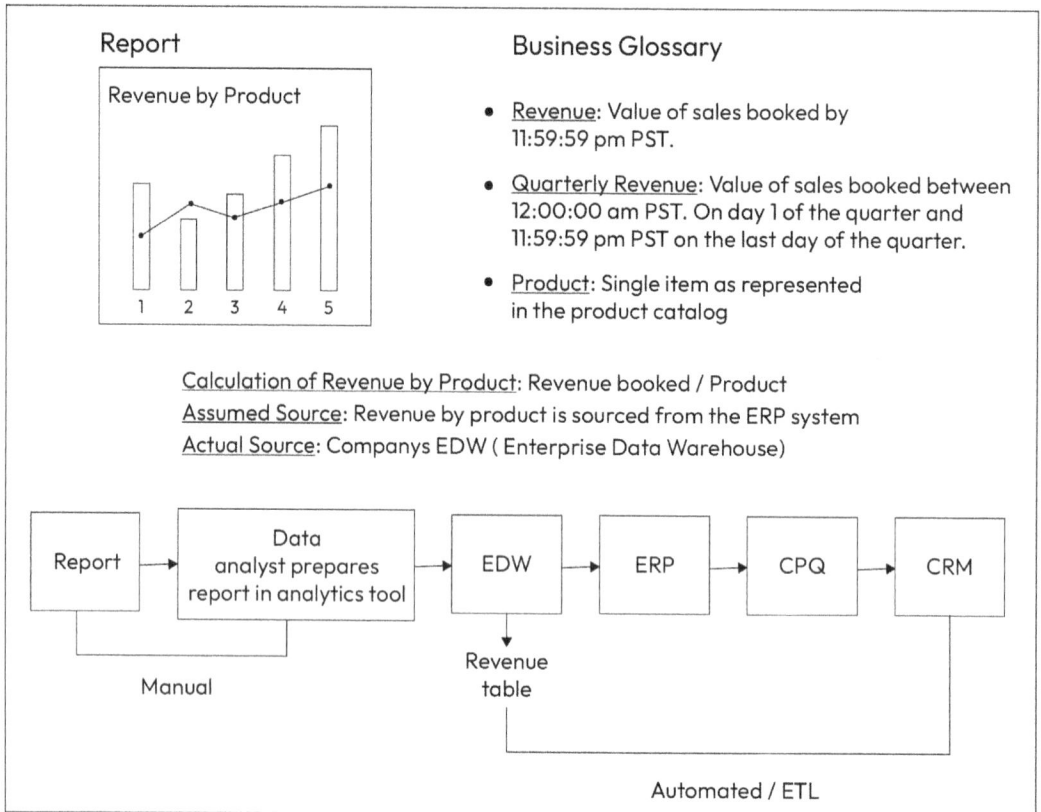

Report

Revenue by Product

Business Glossary

- Revenue: Value of sales booked by 11:59:59 pm PST.

- Quarterly Revenue: Value of sales booked between 12:00:00 am PST. On day 1 of the quarter and 11:59:59 pm PST on the last day of the quarter.

- Product: Single item as represented in the product catalog

Calculation of Revenue by Product: Revenue booked / Product
Assumed Source: Revenue by product is sourced from the ERP system
Actual Source: Companys EDW (Enterprise Data Warehouse)

| Report | Data analyst prepares report in analytics tool | EDW | ERP | CPQ | CRM |

Manual

Revenue table

Automated / ETL

Figure 7.2 – Example metadata process

> **Best practice – linking technical metadata to business metadata**
>
> To bring the power of business and technical metadata together, we must be able to link the two together. Ideally, your business and technical data stewards will work together to drive this capability so that the company can benefit from the work done.

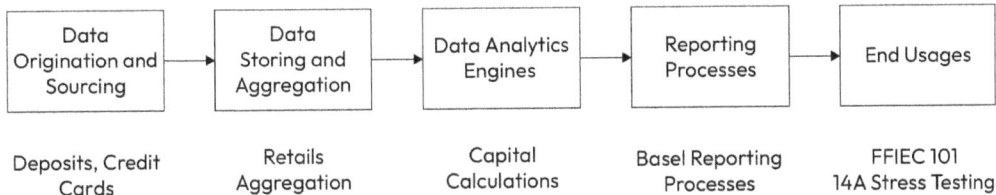

Figure 7.3 – Example data supply chain for retail bank division

Upon scoping a specific data asset into the metadata management capability, your business data steward will work to define business definitions and calculations and identify the appropriate, optimal source of the data. Then, the technical data steward will step in to identify physical data elements and extract the technical metadata (or read the technical metadata, depending on your tooling). The details about the physical data elements and the data supply chain should be reviewed and validated for quality, consistency, and accuracy.

> **Best practice – optimizing the data journey**
>
> By leveraging data lineage, the data team can identify data duplication enterprise-wide. When we have visibility into all the hops, skips, and jumps data takes across the data supply chain, we can identify inefficiencies across the supply chain. This allows us to identify places where the data can move more directly, reducing the risk of error and optimizing costs to maintain the same data in multiple locations.

How should you use Data Lineage?

Ideally, individuals should start with their question. What often happens is a data engineer or business analyst will start with something such as, "*I need access to database ABC.*" I always find this to be the wrong place to start, but it's *so common.*

My immediate response is "*Why?*" and is often met with a confused look.

It's not uncommon for the response to be something along the lines of "Because I need to do my job", "I need to produce a dashboard", or "My boss asked me to get some data to create an insight."

The problem with this line of thinking is that we are putting the data before the business understanding, and it's based on a series of assumptions about the data. In reality, what we should do is clarify the outcome we are searching for before we start asking for access to any data. Starting with "*Why?*" results in a much more specific and faster outcome. It allows the requester to think more deeply about why they are doing what they are doing and enables the data team to support them with a faster path to that answer because it is based on what they need versus where they want to start their search. This "give me access" approach is based on the assumption that the requester knows the location they are requesting access to is the best place to get the most trustworthy version of the data they need.

It's often wrong.

Pulling on the previous example, if access were to be granted to the database requested, without further dialog, the requestor would get access to the data and go about their merry way. However (and I can't stress this enough), it's likely that there is more to the request and more to the data than initially believed. There are a few things that could go wrong in this example:

- The database may not have the data in it that the requester believes it does

- The data might not be fit for use

- The data may have low quality

- The database might not be the best place to get the data as it may not be certified

- The analysis the requestor needs may already be readily available (the metric, the dataset, or perhaps a report)

Thus, the first step in any search for technical metadata should begin with the business metadata: specifically, the business glossary (see *Chapter 6, Metadata Management* for more information on business glossaries). I encourage you to go back to the requester and ask, "*What question are you trying to answer?*"

For example, the requester may have been asking for access to a finance database in order to gather information about revenue for a specific product. They wanted access to the database so that they could query the database for the data they needed. However, in this example, what they may not know is that your team already produces a certified dashboard with revenue by product that is available in the Data Marketplace (see *Chapter 6, Metadata Management* for more on Data Marketplaces). You can save the requester a lot of time and risk of producing inconsistent information by showing them the Data Marketplace and how they can more easily find what they need.

Because your Data Marketplace is full of certified, tested, and trusted data assets, the requestor can easily search for and find the data they need to answer their question. In this example, the requestor can locate the **Revenue by Product** dashboard and use the existing filters to sort by the time horizon they are interested in, with the additional comfort that the data is certified, validated, and trustworthy. Everyone wins.

Building an optimal Data Lineage capability

Now that we understand more about data lineage, what it looks like, who is involved, and the benefits, let's explore how to build an optimal data lineage capability for your organization. First, you need to assess the complexity of your organization. Are you a large, highly regulated industry or are you a small, single-product company? Not every organization will need a fully robust, state-of-the-art data lineage. You may also start by building data lineage manually to prove the capability before investing hundreds of thousands, if not more, into a more robust tool.

Prioritize the scope of your implementation. Begin with a single report or single metric as a pilot and prove the capability. Gather a small group of individuals who are a part of the production of this report and help them understand the value of understanding the journey of data across the organization to produce their report or metric. Trace the data's journey, identify opportunities for simplicity and remediation of issues, and measure the quality of the data.

Show the benefits of the pilot widely across the organization. Better yet, have the report or metric owner tell this story on your behalf. Have them share how their job has been simplified and/or improved because of this capability. Your next challenge will be to prioritize those who will step forward, wanting the same benefits seen in the pilot.

This is a great time to discuss and prioritize the following:

- Why you should have full end-to-end lineage (and for which use cases)
- Why you should *not* have full end-to-end lineage and alternatives

Not every data element enterprise-wide needs full lineage. You will need to prioritize the data assets that matter most. Remember the ROI calculation, and focus on the biggest ROI cases. The best approach for your organization will depend on the size and complexity of your data landscape and the resources available to make it a success. Start small and scale from there.

Conclusion

As you work to deploy a strong technical metadata capability within your organization, it helps to work in concert with your business metadata capability. As you are working to progress this capability across programs or data domains, having your data catalog updated as you go, defining key data elements, and aligning with technical metadata, including lineage, will help you build confidence in the quality of both business and technical metadata. Being able to show your users that you have both business and technical depth of understanding that is reliable will translate into strong reliance on your capabilities. Remember to start by defining the scope to help set expectations regarding what the business will get from this capability, and when. Ensure you have clear roles and responsibilities, along with clear, transparent, and published metrics to measure your success. Lastly, don't forget to tell stories of success as you go.

8
Data Quality

The quality of decisions is tightly linked to the quality of data that supports them. As a result, the quality of data impacts every facet of the organization. It's an (appropriately) bold statement that is often under-appreciated. From day-to-day operations to long-term strategic direction, having high-quality, reliable, and trustworthy information is not a "nice to have;" it's a must-have for any company. Having quality data is critical for the success of any company of any size. How you operationalize ensuring you have quality data in your organization should vary based on the size and complexity of your organization, but the need for data quality is static. It's at the very core of running any business.

In the ever-evolving landscape of data-driven decision-making, there exists a profound truth that we, as data custodians and stewards, must humbly acknowledge: the quality of our data is the cornerstone upon which all our analytical endeavors stand. In this chapter, I will delve deep into the vital realm of data quality, for it is here that we will confront the very essence of our responsibilities as guardians of the information our companies depend on. With a direct and unwavering focus, I aim to illuminate the significance of data quality in the context of data governance. In this chapter, I will uncover not only the intrinsic value of high-quality data but also the transformative potential it holds for organizations. I can't emphasize enough the undeniable importance of ensuring that our data is not just data, but reliable, insightful, and, above all, trustworthy.

It's quite easy to suggest that data quality is "everyone's job" (and it is); however, ultimately, it is up to you to define what is needed, define and provide the implementation of data quality capabilities, and drive the importance of data quality for the company you work for. You will be held accountable for the quality of data enterprise-wide, regardless of how much of it is under your direct control. This may feel unfair, but as the data leader, the duty is yours. When a major data error is uncovered, whether you are directly involved or not, you will be brought in to help solve it. The burden will rest on your shoulders. Therefore, this chapter and the guidance herein are critical for your success.

We will cover the following main topics:

- Data quality defined

- Core capabilities

- Building an optimal data quality capability

- Setting up data quality for success

One of the hallmarks of the success of a Chief Data & Analytics Officer is defining and implementing a trusted data capability. This will show the company not just that data is trustworthy, but provides transparency into *why* they can trust the data. When it comes to designing optimal capabilities for data quality, **Trusted Data** is one we will explore later in this chapter. First, let's start with some key definitions.

Data quality defined

Data Quality is the data governance capability that refers to the degree to which data is accurate, reliable, and fit for its intended purpose in a given context. There are several dimensions by which data quality is assessed; these include completeness, accuracy, timeliness, consistency, and relevance. As mentioned previously, data quality is an essential capability for all organizations. Overall data quality across the company is critical, as is data quality in individual data elements, on key reports, as a part of operations, and for the overall functioning of the business. Data quality is the core of building trust in our information. Next, each data quality dimension is defined, along with a few examples to help contextualize what data quality is and how it may show up in your company. We will move quickly into the core capabilities needed to apply these core dimensions after we ground ourselves on the basics:

Data Quality Dimension	Definition	Example(s)
Accuracy	Accuracy refers to the correctness of data. Accurate data is free from errors, and it reflects the real-world entities and events it is supposed to represent. Inaccurate data can lead to incorrect conclusions and decisions.	In a customer database, a person's birthdate is recorded as January 15, 1980, instead of January 25, 1980.
Completeness	Completeness refers to whether all the required data elements are present. Incomplete data can hinder analysis and lead to gaps in understanding.	An inventory database lacks records for certain products, leaving gaps in the list of available items.

Data Quality Dimension	Definition	Example(s)
Consistency	Consistency ensures that data is uniform and follows established standards. Inconsistent data can arise from variations in data entry, formatting, or terminology, leading to confusion and data integration challenges.	In a sales dataset, the currency is inconsistently recorded as "USD," "US Dollars," or "$," making it difficult to aggregate sales figures accurately.
Timeliness	Timeliness pertains to how up-to-date the data is. Timely data is relevant for decision-making and analysis, while outdated data can lead to missed opportunities or misinformed decisions.	A financial report for the first quarter of the year is not updated until several months into the second quarter, making it less relevant for decision-making.
Relevance	Relevance is about whether the data is suitable for the specific task or analysis at hand. Irrelevant data can clutter datasets and make it harder to extract meaningful insights.	In a marketing campaign analysis, data on customer shoe sizes is included, even though it has no bearing on the campaign's effectiveness.
Validity	Validity checks whether data conforms to predefined rules, constraints, or business logic. Valid data adheres to the defined criteria and ensures data integrity.	An email address field contains entries that do not follow a valid email format, such as `user(at)example(dot)com` instead of `user@example.com`.
Integrity	Data integrity ensures that data remains accurate and consistent throughout its life cycle, preventing unauthorized changes or corruption.	A database administrator accidentally deletes or modifies records without proper authorization, resulting in data integrity issues.
Trustworthiness	Trustworthiness reflects the reliability and credibility of the data source. Data from reputable sources is more likely to be of higher quality.	Data obtained from a well-established, government-regulated financial institution is considered more trustworthy compared to data from an anonymous online source.

Table 8.1 – Data quality dimensions

Data Quality Strategy

A Data Quality Strategy is a foundational capability of any data quality program. The data quality strategy defines the company's integrated, company-wide approach to achieve and maintain the quality level required to meet business goals. Set by the company's Chief Data & Analytics Office, the strategy should include the goals, key objectives, plans, and measures to improve and maintain data quality for the organization. While the strategy is set centrally, the strategy should clearly articulate the remit and responsibilities of the central team, as compared to business data stewards, technical data stewards, architects, data analysts, and so on.

The Data Quality Strategy should contain the following core components:

- **Data quality objectives**: Start by defining what the purpose of the data quality strategy is, what outcomes you will deliver through the strategy, and what success looks like, specifically for your company (for example, how data quality supports data strategy, including data governance outcomes).

- **Assessment of current state**: Tell the reader exactly how bad (or good) the company's data really is. Be as specific as possible, and provide powerful examples that explain what the business impact is of current data quality issues wherever possible.

- **Data quality standards**: Articulate the criteria for trustworthy data. Your standards may include minimum rules for data quality dimensions, as well as what is expected to be done for each critical data asset. The *Core capabilities* section is a great place to start if you aren't sure what to include.

- **Implementation plan for data quality enablement**: Define what processes and tooling are required to enable data quality for the company and how you and your team will implement the required enablement mechanisms.

- **Remediation and issue management approach**: Define how data quality will be measured, reported, and remediated.

- **Data quality ownership and accountability**: Clear articulation of which roles are necessary for effective data quality management and what is expected of each role.

For example, your objective might be "Establish an enterprise data quality framework that supports prioritization, governance, and oversight of data quality to improve transparency into critical data and improve trust in key reports," whereas an example assessment approach may be something like "You may benchmark a system, a report, or a process to show the current quality level for the data." The output of this strategy should be actionable and translated into a roadmap for implementation.

Purpose

The purpose of a **Data Quality Strategy** is to drive clarity and alignment across your company regarding what data quality is, why it matters, and how the company will know it has been successful in driving trust into its information. The strategy is a great forcing function to drive conversation about what the gaps are today and how you will be able to measure success in the future. Most executives struggle to understand the **return on investment** (**ROI**) of a strategy. I recommend focusing on the business outcomes that you will drive as a *result* of the strategy, not the strategy itself. The strategy sets the North Star for this work, but it will not deliver the results alone.

You may wish to implement a **Data Quality Standard** as a follow-on to your Enterprise Data Governance Policy. The Data Quality Standard should include specific information regarding the Data Quality Strategy, codifying the roles and responsibilities for managing data quality as outlined in this chapter (and curated for the needs of your specific business), and provide further detail about how to comply with policy, through adoption of the capabilities set forth in the *Data quality enablement* section.

Accountability

The Chief Data & Analytics Officer's organization owns the Data Quality Strategy for the company. Depending on your team's size and scale, you may have someone who is fully dedicated to running data quality for the company, or you may have someone who runs all Data Governance capabilities; either is a great candidate to own and drive this for the Chief Data & Analytics Office. If possible, establish a head of data quality who will be ultimately responsible for the delivery of the strategy and the implementation of the capabilities needed to drive the strategy for the company. Other interested parties should include the following:

- Business data stewards
- Technical data stewards
- Architects
- Data engineers
- Data analysts and business analysts
- Executives who use and rely on quality data for decision-making

> **"Are we there yet?"**
>
> Inevitably, when you are setting out to implement a data quality program at your company, you will run into a stakeholder who will ask something along the lines of "How long until we are done?"
>
> Data quality is like exercise. When you're out of shape, you need to pick a plan and do the work to get into shape, but then you also have to maintain it. Data quality is the exercise plan for your company. You will need to define a plan, create a get-well plan (implementation), and support data quality on an ongoing basis. The work is never "finished," and by failing to maintain it, your company will quickly regress backward.

Data quality enablement

Data quality enablement is the core of any data quality program. Data quality enablement provides the company with centralized and standardized capabilities that serve the company's data quality needs. Enablement usually includes people to support the enterprise needs, processes to power the data quality needs of the company, and technology, usually in the form of tooling, to support managing data quality effectively.

Purpose

By providing central capabilities for the company, you can ensure the company has consistent views into the quality of the data, a common process to remediate issues defined, a way to prioritize, and appropriate communication so that individuals who need to know about data quality issues know about them when they matter most.

It boils down to transparent information about the quality of data, common tooling, which focuses budget and costs on shared tooling (versus competing tooling), and standardized processes to enable people to maximize their time when it comes to data quality.

There's also the key vector of reusability. For example, data quality enablement can ensure we are measuring critical data assets once and using them over and over again versus measuring data quality every time a data asset is used. The enablement team or function can provide a certification process to critical data assets so that users can see which data assets have been evaluated for data quality, passed expectations, and are reliable for use. This builds trust and reduces time spent searching for and measuring the reliability of common-use data assets across an organization. The bigger the company is, the more likely we are to be using common data assets without realizing it, creating the risk of mass redundancy. Imagine the time that can be saved when we can transparently see what critical assets we have (see *data marketplace* in the chapters on metadata) and know that the data is reliable (that's data quality!).

Accountability

As with a Data Quality Strategy and data quality standards, data quality enablement should be a function driven by the Chief Data & Analytics Office. The central function is best positioned to create the capabilities necessary for the company's business and technical data stewards to drive data quality efforts for the data they are responsible for. Usually, this enablement team sits either within the data governance sub-team or with a tooling team. Given the close marriage of metadata management and data quality, it's often bucketed together.

I have seen very effective programs where the data governance team leads the data quality strategy, data quality standards, and the data quality program enterprise-wide, while the data solutions or data tooling team provides the technology solutions to enable these capabilities. This can work very well if you have a large company, as it aligns the business and technical skills with the solutions necessary to deliver excellence from your data organization.

Spreadsheets don't scale

When it comes to deploying great data quality solutions, perfect can't be the enemy of good. However, there is a balance of scalability that needs to be considered.

At one of my previous companies, we were enabling an end-to-end view of several key reports to manage the business at the executive level. Our objective was seemingly simple: Is this report trustworthy for our executives to make business decisions? Operationalizing this question, however, was much harder than we expected.

We had to deconstruct the key metrics being used. We did not have the technical solutions to make this efficient or repeatable, but we moved forward anyway. The problem? The content of the reports changed frequently. Instead of looking at the sources and measuring the totality of the source at a feed or system level, we measured the individual metrics. However, as the metrics evolved or new calculations were introduced, we had to go back to square one to validate the data. If we had taken a more holistic approach and used technology to enable this work, we wouldn't have been documenting data quality in spreadsheets (defining critical data elements, mapping to source systems, and manually measuring quality). Each change required a significant amount of manual work. We couldn't scale.

The value of measuring data quality

I have no doubt you've experienced this if you've been in a data role for more than a day: Someone reaches out to you, convinced that their data is "wrong." They want it fixed. Ultimately, what they are saying to you is: I don't trust this data.

When we think about measuring the value of data quality, we have to challenge ourselves to think more broadly than one might expect to. When we are thinking about how to measure the value of data quality, we are really asking: How do I measure the value of trust? What does it mean to my company to be able to trust the information we use for decision-making, every single day? What is it worth to us to know we can trust the information being used to run our business? To drive value for our customers? To operate effectively? If you could place a dollar value on that, what would it be?

The value of trust in our data is highly dependent on your business. Let's start with a real-life example.

Building trust in data quality

Marketing is a function in a company that many do not necessarily correlate with data, but in my experience, the best marketing functions are highly data-driven. I worked with a marketing department that was struggling to understand which individuals they could market to. They had a plethora of lead data, but they were having a hard time determining the following:

Which leads had accurate email addresses and quality data

If the leads had consented to marketing holistically or for only specific products (further complicated by M&A)

If the most recent consent was valid for their country's regulations (for example, how long is the consent valid for?)

Ultimately, the Chief Marketing Officer needed to measure how much the marketing team was contributing to sales, but without quality lead information that they could trust, measuring the impact of marketing on sales was very difficult. They believed their team was contributing more than they were able to measure, but they couldn't prove that with data.

At the beginning of the process to improve the trustworthiness of the marketing lead data, we baselined the quality of the data by completing basic data profiling based on what was determined to be "key fields." We defined key fields as the fields associated with a contact record that were required to be able to market to that contact, which included: first name, last name, email address, company, and valid consent. Our initial profiling put the quality of these key fields at about 43%, meaning only about 43% of the contacts had reliable data in these five fields.

We deployed an enrichment service to be able to improve the reliability of the contact data. It allowed us to overwrite low-quality data (such as initials in fields for first name and last name, and fill in blanks), and to validate email addresses with a third-party service. This improved leads where the address had been typed incorrectly. Therefore, we were able to take instances where we had consent but an invalid email address and use the email address. Overall, this effort increased our marketable contacts from 43% to over 85%. As a result, the CMO was able to demonstrate that their contact data was of higher value and was directly tracible to sales at a higher rate. It was also a measure of their success as a CMO, which led to their ultimate success as a leader. This individual became a champion of our data and analytics team and supported further transformation work we led.

Ultimately, the value of having trustworthy data wasn't just a simple calculation. But for the Marketing division, it was a combination of cost savings from being sure they could market to real leads, the confidence that they had consent to market to the quality leads they had, *AND* that they were compliant with laws. They also needed to measure the value of revenue contribution, generated from the quality leads. In short, it was a combination of cost savings + risk avoidance + fine and penalty avoidance + contribution to revenue. This calculation will vary based on the use case, based on division, and based on your company. The important takeaway here is that you measure the value in business terms.

Most data professionals measure the improvement in data quality based on the percentage of improvement or reduction in errors but don't take it back to the business context. That's where you, as a data leader, can demonstrate your value to your company, by showing them how data investments have a real business impact in dollars (increase in revenue and increase in savings), time, and risk avoidance. That's how you demonstrate trust in data and return on your data investments. If you take nothing else away from this book, it should be this.

Core capabilities

Implementing data quality capabilities can significantly enhance the integrity, accuracy, and reliability of data, making it a trustworthy asset for decision-making, analytics, and business operations. It's worth noting that roles can vary based on the size and structure of the organization. In smaller companies, a single individual might handle multiple responsibilities, while larger organizations might have entire teams dedicated to specific tasks. Collaboration and clear communication among these roles are crucial to ensure cohesive and effective data quality management.

Achieving maturity in data quality management indicates that an organization has not only implemented the core capabilities but also refined, optimized, and integrated them into daily operations.

Measuring the value of each data quality capability ensures that an organization can justify its investments in data quality management and recognize areas of improvement. For each capability, the value can further be translated into tangible benefits such as monetary savings and increased revenue or intangible benefits such as enhanced stakeholder trust, improved brand reputation, and organizational agility. Converting the value of data quality capabilities into dollars or time requires understanding the specific financial and operational context of an organization. To truly get an accurate dollar or time value for each capability, an organization would need to conduct detailed assessments, considering its operational costs, business context, and the consequences of data issues. The framework for calculating value should be defined by the data office; the inputs should be provided by the business. We won't go into specifics here, but use the framework defined previously in *The value of measuring data quality* section to apply it to your organization.

Data profiling

Building an understanding of the existing state of data, including inconsistencies, anomalies, and patterns is delivered through a foundational capability called **data profiling**. Data profiling is usually performed by business data stewards and technical data stewards together. The business data steward can provide expertise on the business meaning and usage of the data, while the technical data steward can provide expertise on technical aspects of the data:

- **Business Data Stewards** generally have a deep understanding of the business data they are stewarding/responsible for, which includes understanding (or defining) the meaning, how it should be used, and the quality requirements. They are best positioned to identify data quality issues and define the business impact of the issues identified. Business data stewards should do the following:

  - Identify business requirements for data quality for their data elements

  - Ensure data quality profiling is implemented for their data elements

  - Define business rules that govern the data

  - Determine the frequency of data profiling (consider how frequently the data is changing, the volume of data, and the volume of issues in the data elements they are stewarding)

  - Review and analyze data profiling reports to identify and understand data quality issues, and report relevant issues to users of the data

  - Work with data stewards (other business data stewards and technical data stewards) to resolve data quality issues

  - Ensure profiling is complete, measured appropriately, monitored, and published transparently for users

- **Technical Data Stewards** generally have a technical understanding of the data, such as structures, formats, and systems. Technical data stewards are responsible for assisting the business data steward in identifying the physical locations of physical data elements that must be measured in support of the business data stewards' needs. They use this technical understanding to identify and troubleshoot data issues at the technical level in support of business data stewards. Technical data stewards should do the following:

  - Design and implement data profiling jobs

  - Configure and use data profiling tools

  - Analyze data profiling reports to identify and troubleshoot data quality issues in partnership with business data stewards

  - Work with other technical data stewards to identify up and downstream impacts of data quality issues and remediation required

- **Data Engineers** are responsible for the technical implementation of profiling requirements within systems to provide business data stewards, technical data stewards, and ultimately, users of the data with transparent information regarding the state of the data.

- **Users** (data analysts, business analysts, executives) are responsible for understanding the results of the data profiling efforts and taking into consideration any issues identified through profiling when using the data for business needs.

The figure below illustrates the process flow of business data and technical data stewards' partnership:

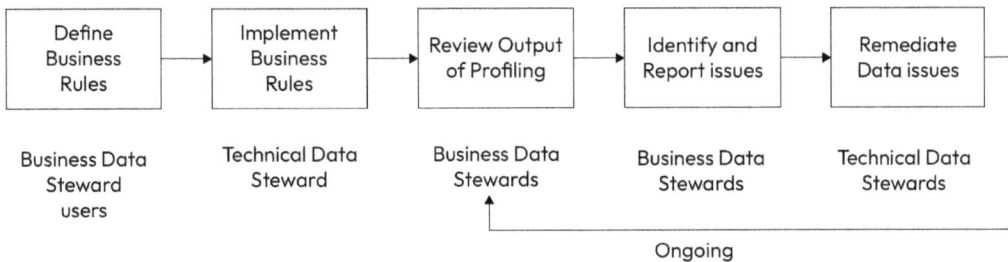

Figure 8.1 – Simple process flow of business data and technical data stewards' partnership

There are a few simple measures you can deploy within your team to show the progress your team is making in improving the quality of your company's data. Basic measures include the following:

- Percentage of datasets profiled per domain or system

- Reduction in surprises or issues when using data for analytics or operations (for example, how many issues you started with compared to how many you currently have)

- Cost savings from avoiding incorrect data-driven decisions or regulatory reporting errors (for example, did you catch a material error that would cause a financial misstatement?)

- Reduction in hours spent identifying and addressing data issues manually by adopting automated data profiling solutions

Data cleansing

The process of cleaning your data is referred to as **data cleansing**. Data cleansing identifies and rectifies errors, inconsistencies, and redundancies in datasets. In short, data cleansing corrects your data to meet the expectations of your users. Data cleansing should be conducted as close to the source as possible so that correct and trustworthy data flows through the organization already corrected. Wherever data is corrected, the business data steward and technical data steward have a shared responsibility to ensure users are aware of corrections (business data steward) and the corrected data is sent up and downstream (technical data steward).

When corrected data looks wrong

During a system implementation, my team improved the quality of the data for a specific dataset. The users of the data reported data quality issues. Why did this happen?

We hadn't appropriately notified the users of the data that they should expect changes and what the changes would look like. Thus, when the data changed, although improved, it appeared different from what was expected by the user, thus leading them to believe it was wrong.

Much like with data profiling, the partnership between the business data steward and technical data steward is critical to the success of this capability. The business data steward should identify which data elements should be cleansed (as every data element is not of equal importance, and there is a cost to cleansing) and work with the users of the data to determine the importance and priority of cleansing capabilities. The technical data steward is responsible for enabling cleansing activities in the system(s) and ensuring up- and downstream system(s) are aware of the cleansing being performed to preemptively alert consumers that the data is expected to change.

Because not every data element in a company can be cleansed, it is important to define what the strategy will be for data cleansing and which data elements are most critical for cleansing and to develop a prioritization mechanism to determine which data elements should be prioritized over others, and why. You may want to use your enterprise data committee or data governance council to support and approve your prioritization methodology.

Advanced data cleansing functions may offer a cleansing service centrally to support the company. One such example would be address standardization for contacts. Contact data often sits across an organization and may include marketing, sales, and customer service data. A central data cleansing service could be created to provide address standardization and enrichment for these divisions as a shared capability so that the company is paying for these services once and providing them out to multiple departments for value.

Much like data profiling, data cleansing value is measured in very similar ways: in terms of business value, dollars generated or saved, and time reduction. Some examples include the following:

- Percentage of reduction in data errors post-cleansing (or count versus percentage)
- Increased confidence in the analysis used in decision-making (*note*: it is important to align on how to measure confidence in terms of time or money)
- Money saved from preventing decisions based on erroneous data
- Reduction in hours spent manually correcting data
- Number of automated corrections made/number of errors identified
- Number of manual interventions required/number of errors identified

Over time, manual interventions should reduce, and the quality of data should uplift. You should be able to identify issues more easily as the overall quality of data improves. This should free up resources to dig into more critical issues and focus on business impact versus manually correcting data.

Data validation and standardization

The process to determine if the data is valid is called **data validation**. Data validation determines what values are appropriate for a given field. For example, it may be a range of values (0-99) or a specific list of values (for example, **North American Industry Classification System** (**NAICS**) codes) that the field is permitted to contain. Validation may also include whether a field can have characters or numerical values. Validation requires fields to conform to specific expected values.

Similarly, **Data Standardization** harmonizes data formats, units, and definitions so that there is consistency across the organization. Often defined alongside validation, these two capabilities ensure the data is formatted and consistent as expected. Standardization efforts ensure that the same data shows up consistently across systems and, at its most mature state, at the reporting level.

Much like data profiling and data cleansing, business data stewards and technical data stewards should work together to ensure these capabilities are adopted holistically:

- **Business Data Stewards** should define values that are appropriate for a field that meets the needs of the users of the data and are enabled across the company
- **Technical Data Stewards** should work with engineers to implement validation rules in the system(s) and ensure that the validation is consistent (standardized) enterprise-wide

Measuring the value of these two capabilities can be kept rather simple. A few easy metrics of success include the following:

- Rate of data entry errors (should be near zero over time)
- Number/rate of validation failures
- Reduction in operational disruptions and reduced data remediation/correction costs
- Savings from reduced data correction errors post integrations or ingestions
- Faster data processing speeds due to a reduction in validation failures
- Automated validation checks at all data ingestion points

Data enrichment

Data Enrichment is the process of adding new and supplemental information to existing datasets. This can be done by combining first-party data (your company's data) from internal sources with disparate data from other internal systems or third-party data (data from external sources). There are several ways to enrich data. Some common methods include adding the following:

- **Demographic data**: This could include information such as age, gender, income, location, and education.

- **Firmographic data**: This could include information such as company size, industry, and revenue.

- **Behavioral data**: This could include information such as website visits, product purchases, and social media engagement.

- **Contextual data**: This could include information such as time of day, location, and device type.

Data enrichment can be used to improve the accuracy, completeness, and relevance of data. This can be beneficial for a variety of purposes, such as the following:

- **Improving customer segmentation**: Enriched data can be used to create more accurate and detailed customer segments. This can help businesses to better understand their customers' needs and preferences and target them with more relevant marketing and sales messages.

- **Personalizing customer experiences**: Enriched data can be used to personalize the customer experience across all channels. For example, businesses can use enriched data to recommend relevant products or services to customers or to provide them with more personalized support.

- **Improving fraud detection**: Enriched data can be used to identify and prevent fraudulent activity. For example, businesses can use enriched data to verify the identities of new customers or to detect fraudulent transactions.

- **Making better business decisions**: Enriched data can be used to make better business decisions across all areas of the organization. For example, businesses can use enriched data to identify new market opportunities, optimize their pricing strategies, and improve their product development process.

Data enrichment can be a complex and time-consuming process, but it can be a valuable investment for businesses of all sizes. By enriching their data, businesses can gain a deeper understanding of their customers, improve their marketing and sales efforts, and make better business decisions. Simple value measures include the following:

- Increase in data attributes or features post-enrichment

- Enhanced insights and better predictive modeling capabilities

- Increased revenue from better-targeted marketing or analytics insights

- Reduction in manual data-gathering processes

More specifically, for the aforementioned examples, you can measure the value of these enrichment services with the following business metrics:

- **Improved customer segmentation**: You can track the accuracy of your customer segmentation by comparing the predicted segment membership to the actual segment membership. You can also track the performance of your marketing campaigns that are targeted to specific customer segments.

- **Personalized customer experiences**: You can track customer satisfaction and retention rates to measure the impact of personalized customer experiences. You can also track metrics such as **click-through rate** (**CTR**) and conversion rate to measure the effectiveness of your personalized marketing campaigns.

- **Improved fraud detection**: You can track the number of fraudulent transactions that are detected and prevented as a result of data enrichment. You can also track cost savings that are achieved by preventing fraudulent transactions.

- **Better business decisions**: You can track the number of business decisions that are made using enriched data. You can also track the financial impact of these decisions, such as increased revenue or reduced costs.

These can be difficult to measure concretely. Here's a specific example to show how you can break down the measure more specifically:

- **Business goal**: Improve the accuracy of customer segmentation.

- **Metric**: Percentage of customers that are correctly assigned to their customer segment.

- **Baseline**: 70% of customers are correctly assigned to their customer segment.

- **After data enrichment**: 85% of customers are correctly assigned to their customer segment.

- **Result**: Customer segmentation accuracy has improved by 15%.

Feedback loops, exception handling, and issue remediation

While users of data are engaged throughout the development of your data quality Program, the phase they are most engaged is once the program is up and running. As you operationalize business rules by configuring them into the systems through profiling, validation, enrichment, and so on, the results of the data quality program start to shine. The first set of results published is usually a bit jarring for business users to process. If data quality has never been an area of focus, the results are often alarming. As the data professional, your job is to help users understand that the first baseline of results is just that—a baseline. The initial results are used to show where we are today.

Feedback loops

As you start to work with users of the data and the various stewards, your role is to ensure the data quality program has appropriate **feedback loops** established for data stewards and your team so that you can improve the enablement of the data quality program and support the stewards as they work to improve the trust in their data. Feedback loops are required in a few different places in your program, but first, between the users and the business data stewards. You may want to help guide your business data stewards on how to set up appropriate forums for feedback about their data quality. They may find value in starting a **stewardship council** by data domain to help provide feedback and prioritization for where data quality remediation needs to be focused first.

You should also provide a forum for business data stewards and data domain executives to bring forward significant and cross-functional data quality issues for enterprise prioritization, where needed. The enterprise data committee and data governance council are great options for the escalation of these types of complex data issues that require enterprise funding, prioritization, or awareness. Let's start by exploring how a data issue would be escalated to such a forum.

Conversely, the business data steward may have identified a data quality issue that the user ultimately decides is not significant and isn't worthy of remediation efforts. It's important to document the process by which data quality issues are prioritized and dispositioned. You don't want to be in a situation where we're not sure if a data quality issue is a true issue or perhaps just a data defect that is not worth the time or energy to remediate. I recommend creating a disposition log so that you can track issues you identified and who signed off on the disposition to have a record to back your decision-making process.

Exception handing

There may be times in the data life cycle when exceptions are made regarding the data quality process. For example, a data lineage process may be defined for a specific data metric, and financial reporting purposes, the data must be at a specific quality level. However, for ad hoc analytical purposes, we may accept a lower level of quality to allow for speed to that insight. It's important to take the use of data into account when defining exceptions. In this example, the user may need a one-time pull of revenue data for a reasonableness check on progress to quarterly revenue targets. This extraction may not need to be perfect. The user should be informed that the data extract has not been through all the normal control processes, but if they understand this, an exception process may be very appropriate, especially if time-sensitive.

The importance of exception handling is to ensure that exceptions do not become the rule. You should define appropriate times when exceptions may be made. If you find that a specific request is being made somewhat regularly, consider whether that is truly an exception or is simply circumventing the expected flow of information.

> **Helpful Hint**
>
> Let's take a lesson from our IT counterparts and develop a severity methodology. In the IT world, IT issues are classified as *Sev1*, *Sev2*, and so on, based on a set of criteria. Based on that severity rating, a different process is followed to drive the sense of urgency.
>
> For data issues, we could follow the same methodology. If the issue is material or causes a system outage, perhaps that should be a *Sev1* and follow the highest level of escalation and remediation, versus a minor data issue, which can be remediated in weeks or months without much impact on the business and maybe a *Sev3*.

At a data element level, you might find that you have anomalies in the data, and that may also be considered an exception. You should work with the business data steward to determine if the exception is truly an exception, and why it is an exception. Did a control fail? Did the data get corrupted in transit? Did you receive a bad file from a third party? There are a number of reasons that data could come through with some kind of exception. The important thing is that you follow a standardized process to handle exceptions and follow them to closure. Here are some examples of how to manage specific types of data quality exceptions:

- **Missing data**: If you have a large number of missing values in a dataset, you may want to consider imputing the missing values. This can be done using a variety of methods, such as using the average or median value of the column or using a **machine learning** (**ML**) model to predict missing values.

- **Inconsistent data**: If you have inconsistent data, you may need to manually correct the data or update the data quality rules to allow for inconsistencies. For example, if you have a dataset with different formats for the date column, you may need to normalize the date format before using the data.

- **Duplicate data**: If you have duplicate data, you may need to remove duplicates or merge them into a single record. For example, if you have a dataset with two customer records with the same name and address, you may need to merge the two records into a single record.

Through this process, you might determine that the exception isn't an exception at all and that it is actually a data issue and needs to follow the issue remediation process.

Issue remediation

When a material data issue is identified, the business data steward should review and develop a comprehensive understanding of the issue and the source of the issue and identify options for remediating the issue. If the issue is significant, spans multiple data domains, or has a material impact on the company, it should get escalated to the appropriate forum. A simplified issue remediation process may look like the following:

Data Quality Issue Remediation

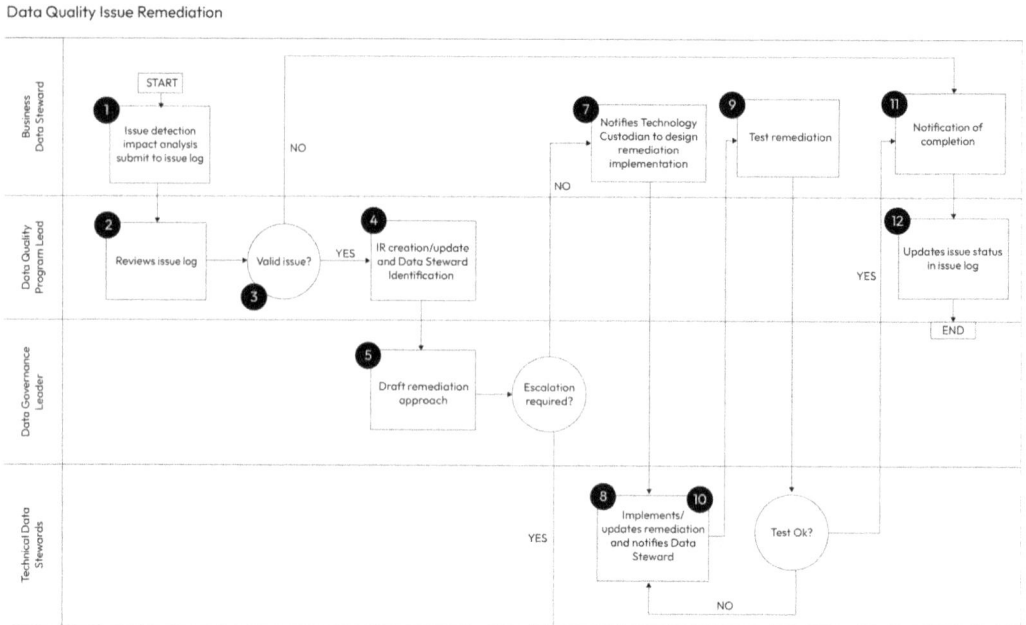

Figure 8.2 – Sample issue remediation process

What's most important is to define an issue remediation process. This will also enable you to define exceptions and feedback loops that make sense for your company.

In my opinion, the person closest to the data is the one most likely to understand the data the best and should be the one presenting the issue in these forums. That may mean that someone at an analyst level is presenting to senior executives. As the data leader, you should support the person with the most information and help them to shape the presentation for the right audience, which may result in a variance from the aforementioned standardized process.

There are a number of great ways to measure the value of feedback loops, exception handling, and issue remediation. One consideration: At the earliest stages of data quality management, you will have a surge in issues. I would expect that to normalize over 12-18 months, but it may be shorter or longer depending on the amount of time and resources applied to data quality measurement and remediation efforts. Either way, the following measures are a great way to show the value of your feedback loops, exception-handling processes, and issue remediation efforts:

- Number of feedback instances leading to improvements
- Increase in user satisfaction (similar to **net promoter score** (**NPS**))
- Efficiency gains from remediation efforts (time, money)
- Reduced iterative cycles in data processing

- Average time to resolve a data exception

- Average time to remediate an issue

- Number of open issues

Building an optimal data quality capability

A mature data-driven company not only implements the individual capabilities from the preceding section but also integrates them in a holistic manner, ensuring that data quality is embedded in the organization's operations and overall culture—a culture where trusted information is valued and expected. This state, where trusted information is the baseline and anything else is rejected, includes the expectation that the quality of the data used in reporting, operations, and analytics is measured, monitored, and reported for *all* in-scope data elements, assets, and integrations.

What does it mean to be in scope? It does not mean that every single data element, every single report or dashboard, or every single integration is measured, monitored, and reported. That would be just as irrational as measuring, monitoring, or reporting nothing at all (for the opposite reasons). Rather, optimal data quality requires thoughtful, intentional scoping of the right data elements, the right reports, and the right integrations to ensure that the company's assets (money, resources, time) are applied judiciously across the company's most important and relevant data.

Understanding the quality of data and being able to have a defendable stance when it comes to "Can I trust it?" is key for any user of the data, or information, that's leveraged for decision-making. Establishing a data quality capability enables the CDO, and their teams, to stand behind their data and be able to defend the quality of the information.

When we consider what an optimal data quality capability looks like, it comes down to a few key steps:

1. Identifying what data is critical, leveraging a prioritization framework

2. Profiling the data to deliver insights about the underlying data

3. Partnering with users to define appropriate business rules for the data

4. Writing and testing rules on data elements

5. Promoting rules to production to generate insights into the quality of the data

6. Monitoring and reporting on the quality of the data to business data stewards and users of the data

7. Remediating appropriate issues, leveraging feedback loops, exception management, and issue management processes, leveraging councils, stewardship groups, and data committees where appropriate

The flow of this process could look something like this:

Overview: DQ Monitoring Onboarding to Reporting

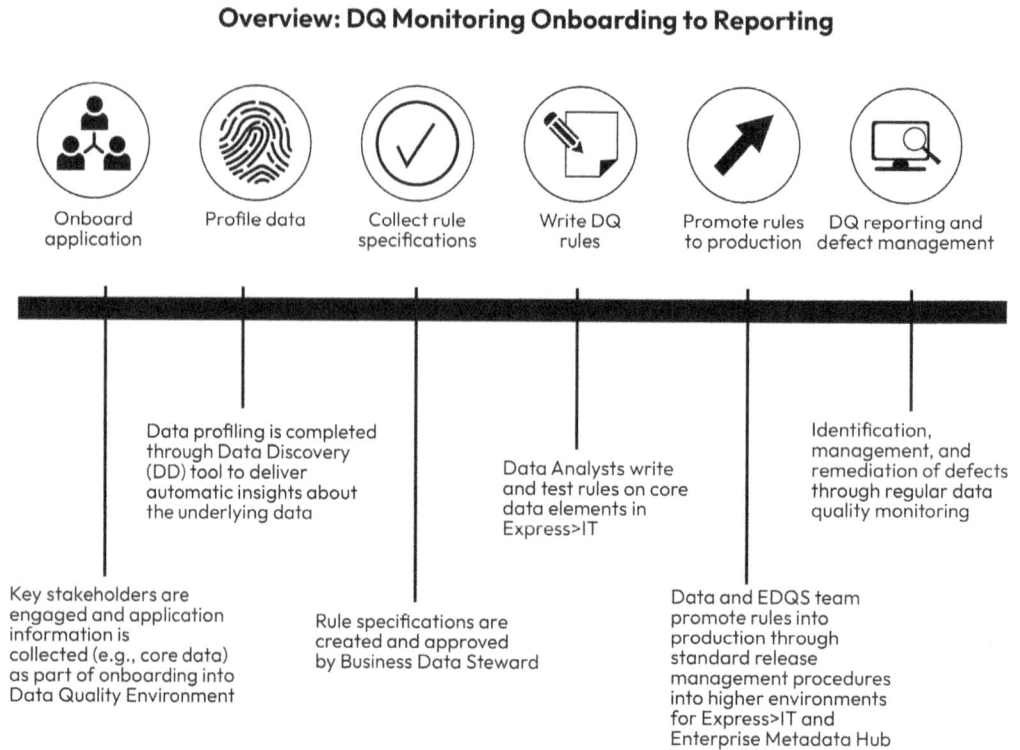

Figure 8.3 – Optimal DQ Monitoring from onboarding to reporting

The role of data stewards (both business and technical) cannot be overstated. They are the critical success factor in an optimal data quality capability. Without high-quality stewards who interact with users of information and have an intimate understanding of the data, its use, and the challenges, data quality will be a mere check-the-box activity. When stewardship is strong, the company's data will be highly trusted because it will be cared for exceptionally well. Therefore, ensuring your data stewards have accepted responsibility for data quality is of the utmost importance for the success of your data program.

Certified data

As you are standing up a strong data quality program, you may want to consider enabling a **certified data** process. When coupled with metadata and data lineage, data quality can lead you to deploy a data certification process that not only enables the reusability of common data elements or curated datasets but also increases the value of the data quality work.

To start, identify what data element or dataset is used often across the organization. You might want to start with a metric that is used for operational and reporting purposes (such as Customer Count). Average Customer Count is a good example because it is seemingly simple but often controversial. To certify Customer Count for the company, you first need to define who is the business data steward for Average Customer Count. This individual will work with relevant stakeholders to align on the definition of Customer Count. For the purposes of this example, let's assume the definition of a customer is: "An individual or company that has purchased one or more products in the last 12 months." To calculate the average, we will need to pull information from several systems.

The next step is to align on the calculation of the term "Average Customer Count" and the source(s) for the data. For this example, let's assume the calculation is as follows (as of 1/1/2023):

Number of customers = Total number of transactions in the last 12 months / Average number of transactions per customer

The average number of transactions per customer can be calculated by dividing the total number of transactions in a given period by the number of customers in that period. For example, if a company has 100,000 transactions in the last 12 months and an average of 2 transactions per customer, then the number of customers would be the following:

Number of customers = 100,000 transactions / 2 transactions per customer = 50,000 customers

This formula can be used for any company, regardless of industry or size. However, it is important to note that the accuracy of the calculation will depend on the quality of the data used. For example, if the company does not have a good system for tracking customer transactions, then the results may not be accurate.

Here is a step-by-step guide on how to calculate the number of customers that have transacted with a company in the last 12 months:

1. Gather data on the total number of transactions in the last 12 months. This data can be found in the company's sales records or **customer relationship management (CRM)** system.

2. Calculate the average number of transactions per customer. This can be done by dividing the total number of transactions in a given period by the number of customers in that period.

3. Divide the total number of transactions in the last 12 months by the average number of transactions per customer to get the number of customers.

Note: Once you have calculated the number of customers that have transacted with the company in the last 12 months, you can use this information to track customer churn, identify customer segments, and develop targeted marketing campaigns.

From here, you should identify the optimal sourcing for this data. For example, you may pull customer information from your **Customer Data Platform (CDP)**, and your sales information might come from your company's CRM platform. The business data steward would be responsible for determining the authorized source for this data.

Once a definition, calculation, and sourcing of the data are determined, the business data steward would then work with the data office to evaluate the lineage of the data, validate the lineage (see *Chapter 7* for details on lineage capabilities), and measure the quality of the data. Any issues with lineage and quality should be remediated (or disclosed to the users). You will need to use your data lineage capability to trace the data through the systems and identify where to measure data quality. Apply data profiling, enrichment, and de-duplication efforts where necessary to strengthen and improve your data quality. Once the metric is validated as trustworthy, the data office can mark the metric as certified.

If you've deployed a data marketplace, this should be the place where the metric is published for consumption and marked as certified. This will show any user of the data marketplace that the Average Customer Count metric is trustworthy and reliable for use. It also shows the user that any other metrics are *not* the authorized and certified metric and should not be as trusted as the certified metric. This process can be repeated for all key metrics in your organization and applied to common-use datasets, reports, and so on.

Transparency

The best way to build trust is through transparency. When the quality of data is low, the best way to lose trust is to not share the results openly. When the results of your data quality work show that data should not be relied upon, you should publish these results and leverage the response from users to drive remediation efforts. If important data is low quality, providing visibility into that deficiency will garner support for your remediation needs and, oftentimes, can lead to increases in funding and resourcing to help drive your data quality program. Don't be shy about reporting your deficiencies. It will help you.

Setting up data quality for success

My best advice for setting up your data quality program is to start small, be specific, be transparent, and scale rapidly. Pick a handful of metrics or a couple of key reports, and show the value of understanding the data, tracing the lineage, and measuring the quality of the data. Remediate issues quickly and visibly and show improvement in the data for these key metrics and/or reports.

Be very clear with your stakeholders, both users and executives alike: the goal is not to create perfect data for the enterprise. The goal is to deploy resources (time, money, people) for the most effective return on those resources. You could spend unlimited time and money remediating every data element, but it would be like trying to plug every hole in every boat in every ocean. Sometimes, you just need to build a better boat. You may run into instances where a report is incredibly low quality. It might be easier to completely recreate the report with different data sources or different metrics than trying to fix every single error. You'll have to use your professional judgment to determine the best course of action for your key metrics and reports. Choose wisely and deliver measurable improvements quickly.

The real-time request

You may run into instances when business users request "real-time" insight into the quality of their data. It's your job as a data professional to credibly challenge this request. From a position of curiosity, seek to understand the reasons why the business wants real-time measurement of the quality of their data. For starters, measuring real-time data quality requires you to test data in production, which can impact the performance of the production system. Oftentimes, data is profiled in a lower environment with a copy of production data, not to impact performance. Secondly, most "real-time" requests are satisfied with intra-day or hourly reporting instead of "real-time" reporting. Work to determine the business need driving the request, and then react accordingly. Sometimes, data professionals are eager to please and say yes without assessing the true business need against the cost to deliver. Real-time data often comes with a significant cost over even slight delays (a few hours) and requires different configurations of underlying system performance and integrations, often at a significant cost in infrastructure, processing, and people to monitor the delivery.

Real-time can backfire

Sometimes, real-time can backfire on you. When you have systems integrated in real time, in the spirit of ensuring high-quality data available for operations, that produces quick access to quality data. However, when things go wrong, you are propagating data problems in real time too.

It's not uncommon to design a CDP to push cleansed and enriched customer data into a CRM platform. Customer data is usually captured in the CRM, pushed to the CDP for enrichment, and then pushed back to the CRM. In one instance, a bug was introduced into the CDP, such that the hierarchy information (what connects individual companies to their parent company, which is used for transactions, sales territory mapping, and revenue reporting by geolocation, by account executive, and so on), was removed. When the hierarchy data was deleted in the CDP, it was replicated in the CRM. In the CRM, the now-orphaned customer records lost their parent company, which removed the territory assignment. The data was then sent back to the CDP without the territory assigned. This replicated blanks in the customer data records in both systems. We went from having a few orphaned accounts to thousands in a matter of minutes, to hundreds of thousands in a matter of hours, before we had to turn the synchronization process off. It took weeks to remediate and restore the full dataset in both systems to accuracy.

If the real-time requirement had been a few hours instead of real time, we would have been able to catch the replication issue without such a huge blast radius. Sometimes, intentional friction in the process can prevent these sorts of issues without such a big impact. A simple validation check for blank fields may have also stopped the replication job and alerted the team to the problem before causing such a widespread impact.

Integrations with other systems

Another facet of a strong data quality program is evaluating data pipelines. Often, data quality profiling and testing are performed at a system level or an integration level, versus an element level. There are reasons to do both, and the right application at the right time is the best way to allocate resources appropriately. Integration data quality can be measured in a few ways to determine the value of the integration measurement:

- Latency between the ingestion and its validation and subsequent correction
- **Time to decision** (TTD) from data ingestion from the source system to report
- Savings from immediate or real-time error detection and avoidance of downstream system implications
- Number of real-time corrections without manual intervention
- Number of successful integrations without data quality issues
- Speed of data flow between systems

Ultimate success with data quality comes down to understanding the business needs, what quality is required, and producing transparent results that business data stewards can take action to fix in a timeline that meets their needs. Start small, scale rapidly, and share results broadly. This is how you drive trust in your data.

Conclusion

In this chapter, we explored the fundamental concept of data quality and its critical role in driving informed decision-making. We established a framework for understanding the various dimensions of data quality, including accuracy, completeness, consistency, and timeliness. We further delved into different sources of data errors and imperfections, highlighting the importance of proactive data quality management practices. You should now have a firm understanding of the following areas:

- The importance of data quality, including why it is required for building trust in data.
- How to define a data quality strategy and framework
- Specific needs when it comes to implementation
- How to design a data quality solution with impact
- How to set data quality up for success in your company

By prioritizing data quality, organizations can unlock the true potential of their information assets. Clean, consistent, and reliable data empowers effective analytics, fosters trust in insights, and ultimately, fuels better business outcomes. Moving forward, the following chapters will delve deeper into specific data capabilities but keep data quality in mind. Data quality is key in the implementation of all data management capabilities and should be considered as you implement primary data and data operations, and will come to light in the use case in *Chapter 17*. You are now equipped with practical knowledge to assess, improve, and maintain the quality of your data for optimal results.

9

Data Architecture

Designing patterns and the optimal flow of information throughout an organization is sometimes more art than science. When it comes to optimizing for information accessibility, enabling governance, and powering the use of data in a company, the use of data architecture as a strategic driver is often considered once it becomes clear that the way information is flowing is causing problems. Unfortunately, this leads to a shift in paradigm regarding how traditional architecture falls short in leveraging the power of data for a company. Organizations then need to determine how to design architecture to support the evolving needs of a company with a new paradigm: optimizing for data.

Traditional IT architecture is concerned with the design and implementation of IT systems and infrastructure to support business operations. It encompasses a wide range of technologies and components, including servers, storage, networking, and applications. Data architecture, on the other hand, is focused on the design and management of data assets within an organization. It encompasses the definition of data models, data standards, and data governance processes. This is why traditional IT architecture does not usually meet the needs of data users: it's not designed with them in mind.

The key difference between traditional IT architecture and data architecture is that traditional IT architecture is focused on the systems and infrastructure that support business operations, while data architecture is focused on the data itself. In other words, traditional IT architecture is concerned with how data is collected, stored, and processed, while data architecture is concerned with how data is organized, defined, and used.

Characteristic	Traditional IT Architecture	Data Architecture
Focus	Systems and infrastructure	Data
Scope	Wide range of technologies and components	Data models, data standards, and data governance processes
Objective	Support business operations	Improve data quality, accessibility, security, and compliance

Table 9.1 - Key differences between traditional IT and data architectures

Data architecture is important because it helps organizations to get the most out of their data. A well-designed data architecture can help organizations to do the following:

- Improve data quality and consistency
- Increase data accessibility and usability
- Enhance data security and compliance
- Support data-driven decision-making

Data architecture is an essential component of any organization that wants to get the most out of its data. A well-designed data architecture can help organizations improve data quality, accessibility, security, and compliance. It can also support data-driven decision-making and lead to improved business performance. When designing a data architecture, it is important to keep the principle of simplicity in mind. A simple data architecture is easier to understand, use, and maintain. It can also help to improve the efficiency and effectiveness of data analytics.

We will cover the following main topics:

- Data architecture defined
- The value of data architecture
- Core capabilities
- Building an optimal data architecture capability
- Setting up data architecture for success

Data architecture defined

Data architecture refers to the design and structure of an organization's data systems, including databases, data storage, data integration, and data management processes. It is a critical component of an organization's overall IT infrastructure and plays a crucial role in how data is collected, stored, processed, and utilized within the organization. When building a home, blueprints serve as a plan for how the home is built. Similarly, in data governance, the data architecture serves as a blueprint for how data is built. Data architecture encompasses the design, development, and governance of data systems and processes.

Simple wins

When designing a data architecture, it is important to keep the guiding principle of *simplicity* in mind. A complex data architecture can be difficult to maintain and manage and can make it difficult to derive insights from data. A simple data architecture, on the other hand, is easier to understand and use and can help to improve the efficiency and effectiveness of data analytics. The scope of a strong data architecture includes the following aspects:

1. **Data sources**: Identifying where data is generated or collected, whether it's from internal systems, external sources, or user-generated content.

2. **Data storage**: Determining how and where data is stored, whether it's in traditional relational databases, NoSQL databases, data warehouses, or data lakes.

3. **Data integration**: Defining processes and mechanisms for combining and transforming data from different sources into a unified format for analysis and reporting.

4. **Data processing**: Deciding how data is processed, whether through batch processing, real-time streaming, or other methods.

5. **Data access**: Providing mechanisms for users and applications to access and retrieve data efficiently.

Data architecture is an essential component of any organization that wants to get the most out of its data. A well-designed data architecture can help to improve data quality, accessibility, security, and compliance. It can also support data-driven decision-making and lead to improved business performance.

The value of data architecture

Overall, a well-designed data architecture is essential for any organization that wants to get the most out of its data. By following the principles of simplicity and scalability, organizations can design a data architecture that meets their current and future needs. A well-designed data architecture can help organizations do the following:

- **Drive implementation of strong data governance**: By ensuring data is organized, stored, and processed efficiently, data architecture can reduce redundancies and inconsistencies.

- **Improve data quality and consistency**: By establishing standards and procedures for data collection, storage, and processing, data architecture can help to ensure that data is accurate, complete, and consistent across all systems.

- **Increase data accessibility and usability**: Data architecture can help to make data more accessible to users and easier to use for analysis. This can be done by developing data warehouses and data lakes, as well as by creating data models and dashboards.

- **Enhance data security and compliance**: Data architecture can help to protect data from unauthorized access and misuse. It can also help organizations to comply with data privacy and security regulations.

- **Support data-driven decision-making**: By making data more accessible and usable, data architecture can help organizations make better decisions based on data. This can lead to improved business performance and competitive advantage. A good data architecture facilitates data analytics, enabling businesses to derive valuable insights and make data-driven decisions.

- **Ensure scalability**: A well-designed data architecture should enable growth with the organization's data needs and business needs as the company grows and expands. A tight connection with corporate strategy and data strategy should enable scalability to be considered appropriately.

- **Enable security and compliance needs**: Effective data architecture helps in maintaining data security and adhering to regulatory requirements.

- **Drive cost efficiency**: By optimizing data storage and processing, data architecture can lead to cost savings by simplifying storage costs, reducing the quantity of processing, and removing redundancy.

Optimizing for aggregation

Consider a very large organization with decades of historical data. Data comes into the organization in hundreds of source systems, connecting and moving point to point, with no "target-state" or "North Star" architecture. You can imagine that this leads to redundancies, data quality issues, difficulty in extracting data needed, when needed, and a huge inconsistency in information enterprise-wide.

In this particular instance, the company built a plan to work strategically over time to better optimize the flow of information. This required a strategic approach to how particular datasets were managed, how they moved throughout the organization, what common data was needed (see *Chapter 10*, *Primary Data*), and where it should be conformed.

Some key decisions that worked well in this build-out were the following:

- What were we optimizing for? Cost? Simplicity? Aggregation?
- Who was responsible for making difficult decisions?
- How fast would we rearchitect the company?

These decisions were used to define the North Star by which the data architecture was designed. When you are considering a data architecture for your organization, these questions can help you define what the "target state" might look like and how you will chart the path to implementation.

Why data architecture is often overlooked

Data architecture is often overlooked in organizations for a number of reasons, including a lack of understanding of the benefits. Many organizations do not fully understand the benefits of data architecture, or they may not even be aware of it. Many organizations are focused on short-term gains, such as meeting quarterly revenue targets. Data architecture is often seen as a long-term investment, and it can be difficult to justify the cost and effort upfront. It's also an expensive endeavor to change, and thus, most companies lack the patience and focus to have the long-range plan realized. Furthermore, data architecture can be complex, and it can be difficult to know where to start. This can be especially challenging for smaller organizations with limited resources. There is also a shortage of skilled data architects, and it can be difficult to find and hire qualified candidates.

Together, these challenges often lead to data architecture being de-prioritized or simply a consideration but not a binding mechanism by which decisions are made. This often leads data and analytical professionals to additional hardship in serving their stakeholders due to underlying complexities within the company's technical landscape.

However, as a data professional, you must advocate for data architectural rigor, because data architecture is an essential component of any organization that wants to get the most out of its data. A well-designed data architecture can help organizations to improve data quality, accessibility, security, and compliance. It can also support data-driven decision-making and lead to improved business performance.

Here are some tips for overcoming the challenges of data architecture:

- **Start with a clear understanding of your business needs**: What are your business goals? What data do you need to achieve those goals? Once you have a clear understanding of your business needs, you can start to develop a data architecture that meets those needs.

- **Take a phased approach**: Data architecture is a complex undertaking, and it is important to take a phased approach. Start by developing a high-level overview of your data architecture. Then, you can start to implement the different components of your data architecture in phases.

- **Invest in training and development**: If you do not have the in-house skills to develop and implement a data architecture, you may want to invest in training and development for your staff. You may also want to consider hiring a consultant to help you get started.

Helpful Hint
Remember—implementing a target state data architecture is a multi-year, sometimes 5-7-year journey. Because companies are not likely to implement an entirely new parallel ecosystem, the strategic transition is typically executed in many phases. The most successful implementations I have been a part of had multiple phases: the first being what could be done quickly, and the second, where tools and platforms could be consolidated or retired. Subsequent phases are when more material changes must be made and require additional investment. It's critical to keep putting this in front of individuals making funding decisions so that they can be reminded where you are headed.

It can also be helpful to measure the success of data architecture as clearly as possible so that executive management can see the value in data architecture more clearly. In this next section, I will share some specific ways to measure data architecture value so that you can build your business case accordingly.

Measures of success

Measuring success in terms of business value and outcomes requires a combination of quantitative and qualitative metrics to ensure that the data architecture aligns with the organization's strategic goals and delivers tangible benefits. Regular monitoring and adjustments are essential to maintain the effectiveness of the data architecture as business needs evolve. Ideally, these measures will be defined by the head of data architecture, aligned with the chief architect, and supported by the users of data, business data stewards, and technical data stewards. The enterprise data committee should approve both the to-be architecture and these measures of success.

Example metrics could include the following:

- **Adoption**: The number of users who have adopted the new data services or components of the prescribed data architecture.

- **Data quality**: The number of data quality issues resolved due to the new design.

- **Requirements**: The number of data requirements met with the new design.

- **Costs**: Cost of replication saved due to new design. Measure cost savings achieved through optimized data storage and processing.

- **Accessibility**: How easily users and applications can access the data they need by measuring the time from request to closure of ticket.

- **Performance**: Speed of data processing and/or efficiency of data retrieval.

- **Security and compliance**: Track compliance with security and/or privacy regulations. Ensure that sensitive data is identified within the architecture and that the architecture enables compliance (for example, do not put sensitive data in multiple places; prioritize simplifying and reducing the number of locations with sensitive data as a best practice).

- **Scalability**: Number of programs that leverage the new data architecture without major modifications.

Additionally, be sure to design measures of success that quantify business impact. Assess how data architecture contributes to achieving business goals and objectives. This could include increased revenue, cost reductions, improved customer satisfaction, or other relevant business outcomes. These will vary greatly based on your business. Pulling users and business and technical data stewards in to help define business impact metrics is a best practice.

While not a specific measure, you should continuously gather feedback from users and stakeholders and use it to adapt and improve the data architecture over time. You may want to establish some "program" metrics to demonstrate early progress, such as the definition of guiding principles, first draft to-be state, and quantity of feedback provided. This will show engagement in the process and is a measure of success in the definition stage.

Core capabilities

Data architecture needs to be more flexible and dynamic than ever before. Companies are evolving quickly, and the speed at which **generative AI (GenAI)** has emerged is a perfect example of the ever-changing needs of corporations. You will note that the capabilities presented next are not specifying *which* technologies you need to deploy. That is up to you and your stakeholders to decide. The following capabilities tell *what* you need to define as a part of your data architecture program.

Establishing a data architecture program

Ideally, data architects should report to your chief data and analytics office. In some organizations, you will see the data architecture function report to the chief architect; however, in most cases, this results in data architects being less intimately familiar with the objectives of the company's data strategy and results in less data-friendly models. It can work well when your chief architect understands data complexities well and is supportive of enabling data to flow appropriately as a priority for the overall corporate architecture.

Regardless of reporting structure, your company should stand up a formal data architecture program. There should be at least two levels of data architecture defined: first, the overall top-down data architecture, which defines what the enterprise-wide data architecture is, the principles, the target architecture, and enablement across the company; secondly, from more of a bottom-up perspective, data architects should be embedded in individual solutions, to ensure that individual solutions are designed in accordance with the overarching company-wide data architecture program. Both are critically important. I have seen instances where the top-down component sits with the chief architect and the bottom-up component sits with the chief data and analytics office. This can work when there is strong alignment, but when alignment is absent, the separation will not be effective.

As a part of the data architecture program, the head of data architecture should establish a "North Star" for how data architecture will be defined, designed, and implemented. In all successful data programs I have seen, the North Star has had three common components: strong as-is and to-be models, clear roles and responsibilities, and strong executive support.

As-is and to-be modeling

As-is and to-be data architecture are two key concepts in data management. As-is data architecture is the current state of an organization's data landscape. It includes all of the data sources, systems, and processes that are used to manage and process data. As-is data architecture can be complex, especially in large organizations with many different departments and **business units (BUs)**. To-be data architecture is the desired future state of an organization's data landscape. It is a blueprint for how the organization wants its data to be managed and processed in the future. To-be data architecture is typically developed based on the organization's business goals and objectives.

Begin by documenting the current state. This as-is state will help the enterprise understand what the current landscape looks like. You can create this diagram in as much detail as you need to, but be prepared to define a high-level view that is consumable for executives and drill-down views that are more appropriate for architects and engineers. If your organization is like most, your as-is state may look like spaghetti. This is because data integrations are often added without data in mind, and over time become extremely complex:

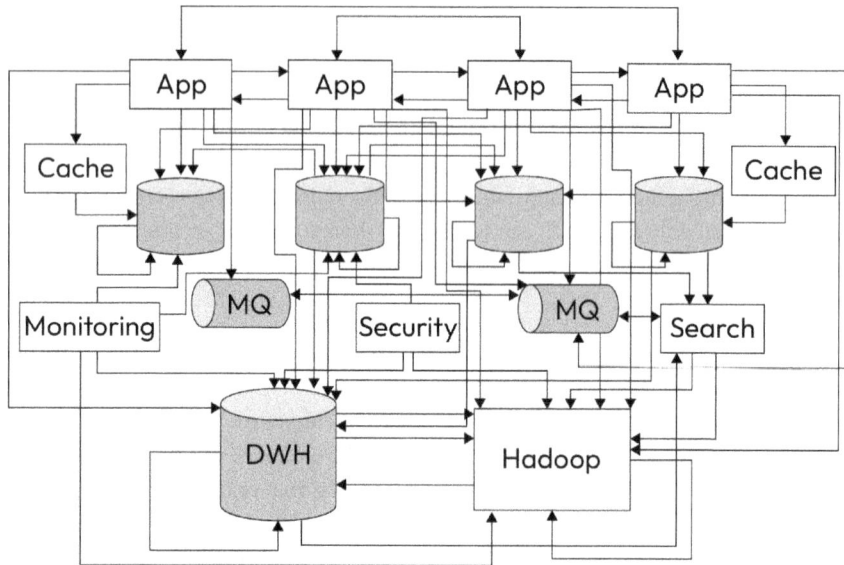

Figure 9.1 – Current state architecture example

Defining a to-be data architecture is no small undertaking, especially if the organization has not historically been intentional about how it designs systems, data, or business flows. It has the potential to be a huge lift, due to the significant amount of cross-functional alignment required to create a target state that serves everyone's needs. It will require compromise, thorough explanation, and time.

Once an organization has developed a to-be data architecture, it can begin to develop a plan to transition from its as-is state to its to-be state. This may involve making changes to existing systems and processes or implementing new systems and technologies. Here are some examples of the types of changes that may be involved in a data architecture transformation:

- **Consolidating data sources**: As-is data architecture may involve multiple disparate data sources, which can make it difficult to access and manage data effectively. To-be data architecture may involve consolidating these data sources into a single data warehouse or data lake.

- **Implementing new data processing technologies**: As-is data architecture may rely on outdated data processing technologies. To-be data architecture may involve implementing new technologies, such as big data processing platforms and **machine learning** (**ML**) algorithms, to improve the efficiency and effectiveness of data processing.

- **Improving data governance**: As-is data architecture may have poor data governance practices, which can lead to data quality issues and security risks. To-be data architecture may involve implementing new data governance policies and procedures to improve data quality and security.

A target or to-be architecture may look something like this:

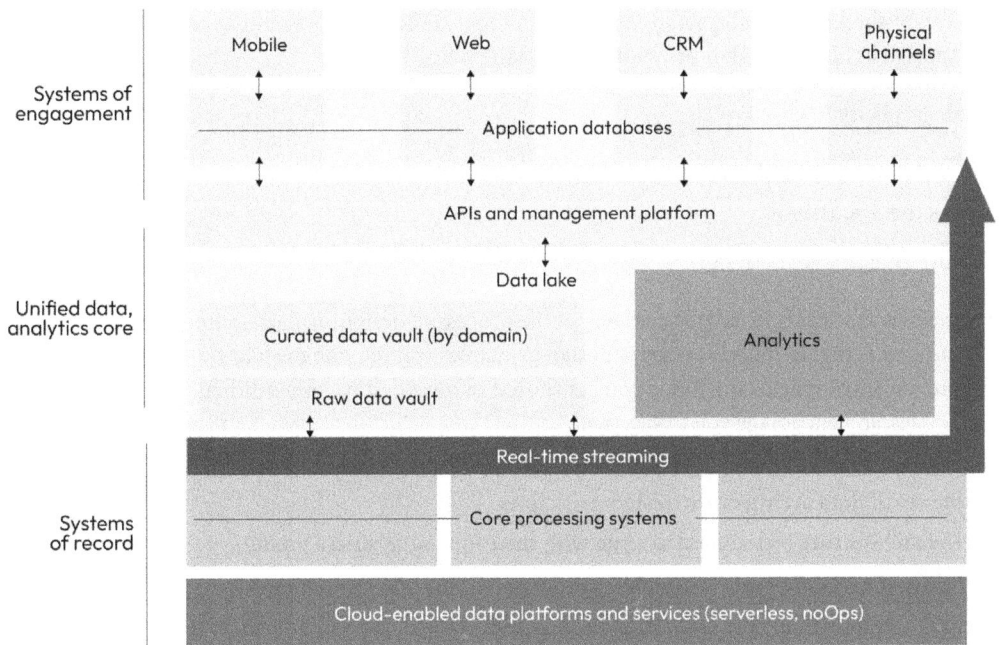

Figure 9.2 – Target state data architecture example

In this to-be data architecture, note data for analytics is separated from operations. This will allow your analytics teams to be nimble in response to business requests, without slowing down or impacting the operations of the company. This is an intentional use case that I encourage you to critically consider for your organization. However, do not let this be the first of many diversions from simplicity. My guess is your company would benefit from "only" having two stores for data versus multiple. Most organizations, when they are starting their journey, have dozens, if not more, of data stores (sometimes within each division). Be diligent in identifying sources and the purposes of what you have and what you need before you start making changes.

Building an optimal data architecture capability

In the previous sections of this chapter, we went through what data architecture is, the value of data architecture, and the two primary phases: as-is and to-be. In this section, I will step you through how to build out your optimal capability for success. The key to them: be purposeful and intentional in how you define your architecture.

Establishing design principles

First and foremost, you should define a set of **data architecture design principles**. Design principles should be established to align all participants in the process to focus efforts and align the design to a common approach. Ideally, design principles will do the following:

- Add simplicity to chaos

- Drive a simplified mindset

- Focus the discussion

- Ensure consistency in design

Design principles should serve as the backbone of the process of designing data architecture. Aligning all participants to a core, foundational set of design principles will provide the lens by which all design decisions are made going forward. Once you get started in design, it becomes difficult to revert to set design principles, so I encourage you to start with setting these principles upfront, to avoid rework later.

> Example set of data architecture design principles
> 1. The architecture is designed to scale with the evolving business model.
> 2. Business and data processes will be automated to the extent possible.
> 3. Data will be stored for central use and provisioned from the established authorized provisioning points.
> 4. Data will be reconciled or "mastered" according to documented business rules.
> 5. Users will have transparency into data quality and changes to the data model.

Developing architectural standards

A signal of a strong data architecture program is a defined set of data architectural standards. Data architectural standards set expectations for how architectural elements will be governed and what the approved models, access expectations, distribution models, and fundamental data assets control and set the use of information in a company. These standards should define what is expected for data for any solution.

Depending on the size and complexity of a solution, you may need to set expectations for involvement, approvals, and review processes. For example, if someone is making a small change (adding a column or adding a table to an existing solution), they may not need to go through a formal process, so long as they can attest that they are following data architectural standards. On the other hand, if a new ERP system is being deployed, the opposite should be true. An end-to-end design should be created documenting both current and future states, defining consumption patterns, establishing clear accountability and stewardship of newly defined or created datasets, and so on. You should ensure the standards include requirements, at a minimum, for the following:

- Metadata management
- Data quality
- Data access
- Data distribution and consumption

These standards should inform how the company makes platform choices and selects technology and tooling, and what integration patterns are used across the organization, in alignment with the design principles established previously. Business and technical data stewards should play an active role in designing data architectural standards so that their needs are met. Remember—these standards will set the evolution of data architecture and will not change everything overnight. They should serve as the North Star by which all future design choices are held.

Establishing a to-be state

I have seen two successful programs in my career (so far) that have leveraged the power of collective architecture across a company to enable the highest levels of optimization with technology and data investments. Both *could have* been more successful.

In both cases, the programs successfully and ruthlessly defined specific design principles by which the to-be architecture was defined; for example, tight expectations around the mandated use of reference data across the entire company, from a single source of truth. The result of this expectation would have led to a significant uplift in efficiency and ease in data aggregation enterprise-wide. However, in practice, the company was "softer" about the requirements of adoption. We entered the transformation with a firm expectation that we would require conformity and adoption of reference data within a 24-month period, but by the time we exited the program, we had relaxed this expectation to require the adoption of reference data only when "major" updates to the platforms occurred, which meant that the true benefit of reference data adoption would take years (5+). As with any long-term program, the momentum was lost, and the benefits were not realized early.

In the establishment of a to-be state, it's critical that momentum is leveraged to drive change. These changes are very expensive and require clear focus to achieve the **return on investment (ROI)** desired.

Tight integration with business architecture and IT architecture

One of the best ways to establish a strong architecture is to tightly integrate with business architecture, data architecture, and IT architecture. Most companies do not have a strong business architecture function. However, it can be the best way to evaluate the way in which the business operations should flow, the data that is required to support it, and the technology that will enable optimal operations.

The best practice would be to establish an **architectural council**. This should have representation from business, architecture, data, architecture, and IT architecture. Most companies do not focus on bringing these three types of architectural experts together, and therefore, when there are requirements for the business, data, or IT, they are often not considered holistically. By bringing these functions together, the company has an opportunity to streamline the design of simplistic and effective solutions.

Most companies do not focus on business architecture or assume it's happening as a part of basic operations. It's not. The architectural council can ensure that any architectural designs holistically account for all three vantage points. Selfishly, this ensures that data architecture is designed in a way that supports both optimal business processes and technology well. If either of these two other related architectural perspectives is not designed well, data architecture will not be effective. Thus, if your company does not have an architectural council, advocate for one. Ideally, this would be chaired by your chief architect and have representation across the business, inclusive of all three types of architecture.

Building data architecture into the systems development life-cycle process

Ideally, you will build a to-be state and transition plan with full funding and the support to transition in a few years. In reality, that is unlikely. Depending on the size, scale, and historical decisions of your company, the as-is state may be very difficult to unwind. You are going to be building the plane while it's flying, which makes these types of programs extremely complex. Because of this, it's much more common to see organizations build to-be design principles into the **systems development life cycle** (**SDLC**), for adoption over time.

The only way this will succeed, and that there will be a completion/end date to this program, is for a champion to continue to vocally drive the business value of the to-be state, have teeth in ensuring the to-be state is followed, and have the support of the executive team to make it happen. This can't be followed only when it's easy; it must also be followed when it is hard. The chief information officer can be a great advocate for you in this goal, as they typically hold the authority to approve or reject technical architecture in terms of programs. Ensure you have their full and unwavering support to bind the company to adopt the SDLC for optimal success.

Setting up data architecture for success

I'm confident you've noted that I have not defined *what* your data architecture should be in this chapter. I have given you the tools, the understanding, and the process by which to set up your data architecture program for success. Technologies change rapidly. The needs of companies vary widely. Only you can define what your company needs to use to build the optimal architecture for the data and analytical needs of your organization. I can't possibly tell you what architecture is right for your company; only you can do that.

However, there are key factors that will set you up for success. These *are* consistent across companies both large and small, and will ensure you have a successful program:

1. **Appoint a chief data architect**: Every company should have a person appointed to drive appropriate data architecture across the company. While you might not use this title per se, you should define the role and ensure they are empowered to make data architectural decisions for the enterprise as a whole.

2. **Define program routines and rhythms**: Set up key program forums, reporting, and value storytelling to ensure the data architecture program is treated as a formal program.

3. **Involve the right people**: Company historians who have a long-term history around why the company made the choices they did but who also have a futuristic view are excellent supporters of this work. They will understand why certain choices were made and what will break if changes are made. They can be the balance between urgency and thoughtful impact. Include your business architects, data architects, and IT architects from around the organization.

4. **Gain executive sponsorship**: Ensure you have the right sponsor. This is usually a chief information officer or chief technical officer. Ensure they are willing to advocate for you at the top of the organization and adequately fund the program long-term.

5. **Align with the chief architect and chief data analytics officer**: Ultimately, the chief architect must understand the importance of strong data architecture and why they need you to drive company-wide architectural success. Your chief data analytics officer also needs to sponsor this work. Ideally, the chief architect and chief data analytics officer co-chair this program, with the chief information officer or chief technical officer as the executive sponsor.

6. **Maintain a long-range mindset**: You must remember these programs take time; they are long-range, and they require significant investment. They will not happen overnight. You must have patience.

7. **Invest strategically**: Select a high-impact, shorter result window to show ROI. Invest in larger, more expensive components after you can show wins with impact. Do not wait to deliver the end result to show the value.

8. **Embed in the SDLC process**: Bind the program to the SDLC process to ensure you adopt a to-be state over time.

By appointing the right people, defining strong routines and rhythms, and following a ruthless prioritization process, data architecture can be a strategic driver for your data and analytics function over time. It is a long game. It requires long-term thinking and ongoing support from the top of the organization to be successful. Your role as a data professional will have significant influence over the data and IT architectures' ability to be successful and drive simple, elegant solutions that will drive optimized data for the company.

Conclusion

This chapter provided a comprehensive overview of data architecture within the context of data governance. We explored the critical role a well-defined data architecture plays in ensuring data consistency, accessibility, and reliability – all key pillars of effective data governance. We examined various architectural considerations, including data organization models, data storage solutions, and data integration strategies. You should now have a good understanding of the following areas:

1. The importance of data architecture, including why it is required for building successful data solutions

2. How to design a data architecture function

3. Specific needs when it comes to implementation

4. How to design a data architecture solution

Understanding these elements and their alignment with your organization's specific needs is crucial for establishing a robust data foundation. A well-designed data architecture fosters data quality, simplifies data management processes, and empowers data governance initiatives to thrive. As you move forward in your data governance journey, the following chapters will explore the practical application of these concepts. We will delve into data governance frameworks, policies, and implementation strategies to equip you with the tools and knowledge to effectively govern your organization's data.

10

Primary Data Management

One of the core capabilities of any organization is the ability to standardize its most core, most connected data: **master & reference data**. By nature, mastered data provides a solution whereas data used by multiple divisions for many uses are standardized and cleansed for the benefit of the organization at large. We will start with the basics: What is master data? Why is it critical? What makes it so complex and difficult to deploy and adopt? We will dive into what the different types of data are, and how it varies from customer data platforms.

I will explain how to prioritize this data governance capability and how to implement a strong and centralized master data solution that will impact and elevate the power of data for an enterprise into a strategic asset. All the capabilities introduced thus far will be woven into this powerful capability to tie them together.

Before we dive in; a note on the use of the term "Master Data Management"

At the time of this writing, the term and capability commonly referred to as "Master Data" is the prominent term in the industry. "Master" has inherent and historical racist roots in "ownership" of something from another source. In the data space, this is the act of identifying the single owner of an identifier. We have started to see a shift away from the term 'Master' in other industries (i.e. Master Bedroom in real estate listings, now commonly viewed as "Primary Bedroom" or "Grand Bedroom"). I have strong feelings about this term and urge the profession as a whole, to change this. My hearty recommendation is that we adopt "primary" data, to refer to this type of data.

If we are not changing it, we are choosing it. And I don't want us, as a profession, to continue to buy into this 'ownership' of types of data, with roots in racism. I'm choosing to refer to this type of data as "Primary Data" going forward, and I urge you to adopt this term in your companies, so that we can change the industry, together.

Defining Primary Data Management

Primary Data Management is a core data governance capability, which brings together a core set of processes and technologies that are used to create a single unified view of specific types of data. This capability helps ensure that these specific and critical types of data have, above all else, consistency, accuracy, and accessibility enterprise-wide. Examples of Primary Data include: customer, product, vendor, and contact data. Because these types of data (customer, product, etc.) are often created in various departments across the organization, they require a special handling to unify and provision, so that the entire organization can have the same view of the data. Without Primary Data Management, companies struggle with consistency, accuracy and quality overall, which leads to poor customer experiences.

Example – Customer Experience

Imagine you are a customer of a large financial institution, and you open up a checking account at a branch location. Months later, you call into a 1-800 number, to ask a question about your account. Since the time you opened your checking account, you also opened a mortgage account and moved into a new home. When you call customer service about your checking account, you are asked to verify your address for security purposes. Only there's one problem, your address on your checking account is your previous address.

Without customer primary data management, customer addresses are not updated across the enterprise when new products are sold to a customer. In this situation, you might be required to go into your local branch to formally update your address, instead of having it updated automatically, through the use of primary data management capabilities.

Primary Data Management is one of the more complex capabilities to establish in an enterprise, especially a large one. However, once fully adopted, this capability has the most significant impact on your organization's ability to deliver operational efficiency at scale. Establishing a **Primary Data Management (PDM)** capability enables your organization to:

- **Identify and Consolidate**. Establishing a PDM capability enables your company to identify the sources of the primary data, consolidate the data into a single process, and then replicate the databack to the original source better than when it came into the capability. This removes data silos and enables the entire company to work off of the same accurate data set.

- **Clean and Enrich**. By bringing the Primary Data into the central capability, the company is able to clean the data by evaluating the data quality, remediating issues with the data, and enriching the data with 3rd party data, thus elevating the quality and reliability of the data. This process removes inconsistencies, errors, and missing data. You can also add additional data to the records (e.g., demographic information, compliance flags).

- **Standardize and Govern**. Primary Data Management enables organizations to standardize and govern their primary data by creating and enforcing data quality rules to ensure data is consistent, accurate, and reliable. PDM drives trust in the company's most critical and core data.

- **Sharing**. Because Primary Data is centrally cared for and provisioned across the company, PDM processes make it easier for companies to share high-quality primary data enterprise-wide into other systems that require highly trusted data. This allows organizations to enable high-quality decision-making based on uniform data across the company.

In the section below on the Core Capabilities, we will explore how to enable these capabilities in your PDM deployment and garner the full value of the PDM investment.

Reference Data

Reference Data Management is a type of standardized data that drives uniformity across an organization. Examples of Reference Data are consistent across companies such as: zip codes, city names, industry codes (e.g., NAICS or SIC), or may be consistent for a particular company such as a chart of accounts. Regardless of what your reference data set is, these codes are considered a type of primary data because the company is following the same characteristics for primary data, including consolidation and standardization, central enrichment, deduplication, and simplification (meaning, the data is sourced and managed by a central team in service of the broader organization). Externally derived reference data can be sourced through government entities (e.g., Postal Codes) or through 3rd parties (e.g., Dun & Bradstreet). There are many providers of reference data.

A common business sponsor for Reference Data Management is your Finance Department. Generally, Finance is the central point of aggregation of information on various factors such as geography, industry, etc., all of which can be improved through conformity of reference data. Reference Data transformation typically comes up as a part of another major transformation, usually an Enterprise Resource Planning (ERP) transformation, where the company is forced to review all of its core data to run operations, report on financials, and provide regulatory reports.

In every company I have deployed Reference Data, the need for this generally comes up in release planning for ERP or Financial Statement design processes. The finance team realizes they have multiple conflicting versions of Reference Data, and need support to conform the data to a standard model. This is where the data team is usually brought in. Reference Data can typically be deployed rather quickly. Once you purchase software and can stand up the base capabilities, publishing the Reference Data isn't all that difficult. Because Reference Data is slow-moving data and does not change frequently, once you have the definitions defined, a steward identified, and have the capability to publish the data, actually putting the data into production is a relatively quick process (especially compared to other types of Primary Data).

Primary Data versus Reference Data

While reference data is a type of primary data, it is typically managed separately due to the slow-moving nature of reference data. Reference data is 'slow-moving' in that it does not change frequently. Consider industry codes such as NAICS codes. While there are new and emerging industries, these codes, commonly used for things like reporting or sales planning, do not evolve frequently. Thus, NAICS codes are updated every five years. Reference data also has a finite limit to the number of valid values. For example, there are only so many industry codes or area codes. An easy way to understand this is to think about reference data as being something you could select from a drop down menu. It could be a very long drop down, but a drop down nonetheless. Whereas, primary data (e.g., Customer Data) may have an infinite number of records or valid values that increases over time.

Types of Primary Data

In addition to Reference Data, there are other types of Primary Data. Primary Data is managed by type. Each type has a platform or system that is independent from the other types. However, each of these types may include some relevant reference data. For example, customer data may contain the customer's zip code, which may be selected from the valid values defined in the Reference Data system.

Customer

Customer Primary Data is all the buzz in customer-facing divisions (e.g., Sales, Marketing, Revenue). Companies who have not standardized their Customer Primary Data often struggle to see a full view of their customer. A tell-tale sign of a lack of a Customer Primary Data system is when each division has different information about a customer, and it's difficult to see the full customer journey across your company. Sales may have different information about a customer (like address) than revenue than operations than marketing. This is a great signal that your company would benefit from having Customer Primary Data implemented and deployed to unify the information about a customer for your organization.

Customer data can be sourced from a variety of sources including directly from the customer, from 3rd party enrichment services, from social media services like LinkedIn, and from marketing and events. Contact data (which we will discuss below) is also a great source for customer data. You may also source customer information from the sales process through order management.

Typical sponsors for customer data are usually Sales, Customer Success, or Sales Operations. Because this data is spread across these areas primarily, assigning an Executive Data Domain Leader for this capability is often the most difficult over other types of Primary Data. In my experience, it usually comes down to political power within the organization and funding. Whichever team has more power, authority, and budget often becomes the sponsor. A word of caution: It is relatively easy for that sponsor to then ensure the Customer Primary Data Management platform is in service of their needs over the needs of others. You are responsible for ensuring the data out of this platform serves the company, not just one division. A great way to combat this bias is to use existing governance routines and rhythms (like your Enterprise Data Committee) to codify the release schedule and the needs of the business in priority order.

Customer Primary Data Management usually becomes a priority when the sales and customer service teams begin to see lower quality scores from sales professionals, customer service representatives, and customers related to their experiences. Low quality and contradictory customer data makes it hard for sales professionals to process deals, to renew contracts, and to use the correct information to engage with a customer. Imagine being in the field, ready to call a customer, but having no phone number in the customer relationship management platform. Happens all the time.

As companies grow and their data is disbursed in more systems and platforms, keeping the data consistent becomes harder. Since customers are at the center of what companies do, having good quality, highly reliable customer information to run your business is more important.

Product

Like customer data, product data is centralized, unform data that is required to manage product information. Product primary data may include information such as product name, product description, product characteristics (e.g., color, weight, dimensions), manufacturer, model, price, and pictures. This information is used by a variety of departments such as sales, operations, supply chain management, and revenue operations teams.

Product primary data can be stored in a variety of places, including **enterprise resource planning (ERP)** systems, **product information systems (PIS)**, and **customer relationship management (CRM)** systems. However, it is important to have a single, central repository for a product's primary data to ensure that you have accuracy and consistency across all consuming systems.

Product data is often sourced from a variety of places as well, including supplier catalogs, websites, ERP systems, as well as internal production data. This is one of the reasons that primary data is so critical to managing well: the data is sourced from a variety of locations, is standardized and enriched in a single location (the primary data platform), and then pushed to the systems that need the data. If there was no primary data platform, then each individual system would need to do this work individually, leading to a huge increase in cost, complexity, and a high degree of inconsistency across systems, making aggregation and reporting extraordinary difficult.

Typical business sponsors for product data include engineering or product management, legal and compliance or revenue operations. Because it is highly universal across a company, and varies heavily based on industry, Product Primary Data, like Customer Primary Data, is a bit more difficult to identify the sponsor. Follow the same process outlined above for Customer Primary Data, and use your governance councils to aid you in nailing down a sponsor.

Vendor [or Supplier]

Vendor Primary Data Management (sometimes referred to as Supplier Primary Data] is a primary data platform that is specialized in goods and/or services providers that a company purchases from. It may include key information such as vendor name, address, company or industry code data, terms of payment, currency used, etc.

Vendor Primary Data is used for a variety of functions across an organization including procurement, accounts payable, supply chain management, and may also be used by HR for contractor information. The data from this platform may be consumed by ERP systems, procurement systems, and supplier relationship management systems. Like other primary data platforms, there are many potential sources for this data, and many potential consuming systems for this data. This drives the need to centrally manage the information well.

Contact

Contact Primary Data is a single, unified view of all of a company's contacts, which can include customers, prospects (i.e., leads), employees, vendors, and partners. The contact data includes information such as the name of the contact, address phone number, email address, and company affiliation. Contact primary data is often used by a wide range of departments in a company, such as sales, marketing, accounting, customer service, and human resources. Sponsorship for Contact Primary Data is typically in Marketing, given their role to acquire and create qualified leads for the company, through contact.

Contact Primary Data is used for a variety of business processes, including:

- **Lead Generation**. Contact Primary Data is used to identify and market to potential customers.

- **Sales and Marketing Campaigns**. Contact Primary Data is used to create and execute marketing campaigns that are targeted to potential customers.

- **Customer Service**. Contact Primary Data is used to provide customer support and resolve customer issues.

- **Human Resources**. Contact Primary Data is used to manage employee records and recruit new employees.

- **Accounting**. Contact Primary Data is used to pay expenses and suppliers.

Contact Primary Data is stored in a wide range of systems, including CRMs, ERPs, and HR systems. Data is sourced from a variety of sources such as business cards, email lists, social media, contacts themselves, event registrations, etc.

Building an Optimal Primary Data Management Capability: Core Capabilities for Success

One of the biggest misconceptions about Primary Data Management is surrounding what capabilities qualify a platform or system to be considered a Primary Data Management capability versus any other platform. There are a few core capabilities that are unique to a PDM system, and without these capabilities, you have not yet implemented a true PDM. It is common for non-experts to use the term "master" or "primary" to define a system of record, or simply a system that is the 'preferred' source for that particular type of data. That alone does not make a PDM. To be a PDM, a system must include the capabilities in this section, starting with deduplication.

De-duping or Deduplication

Also known as 'Match and Merge', **Deduplication** in Primary Data Management is the process of identifying and then merging duplicate data records. If your PDM Platform does not provide this capability, you do not have a PDM. This capability is a critical part of PDM because it ensures that the organization's data is accurate, consistent, and complete. Duplicate data can be created for a number of reasons, but often stems from similar data being entered into multiple systems, being entered in incorrectly, being updated differently in different systems or being sourced from different places (i.e., LinkedIn versus from an event attendance roster).

Approaches to Deduplication

There are few ways that a PDM system can approach deduplication to achieve the desired outcome of a single record for each customer, product, vendor, or contact.

1. **Fuzzy Logic**. Fuzzy logic is a type of artificial intelligence that is used to match data records that are not exact duplicates. The logic looks for errors such as typos, abbreviations and varying formats.

2. **Matching Algorithms**. Matching algorithms compare records to identify those that are likely to be duplicates using a variety of factors such as name, address, phone number, and email address.

3. **Human Review**. Human review is often necessary in PDM capabilities to confirm whether or not two records are duplicates. There is a degree of human review needed for unmatched records, and depending on the quality of your fuzzy logic or matching algorithms, you may need a high or low amount of human review. This is often the primary driver in the size of your PDM operations team, to review potential duplicate records that were not matched through the previous to deduplication methods.

You can see how well your deduplication process is working by measuring the number of 'unmatched' records, meaning, how many records you begin with before deduplication processes begin. This is the aggregate of the number of records are entering the PDM system from source systems. For a large enterprise, this may be 100-200 million records or more. Let's take a look at a simple example.

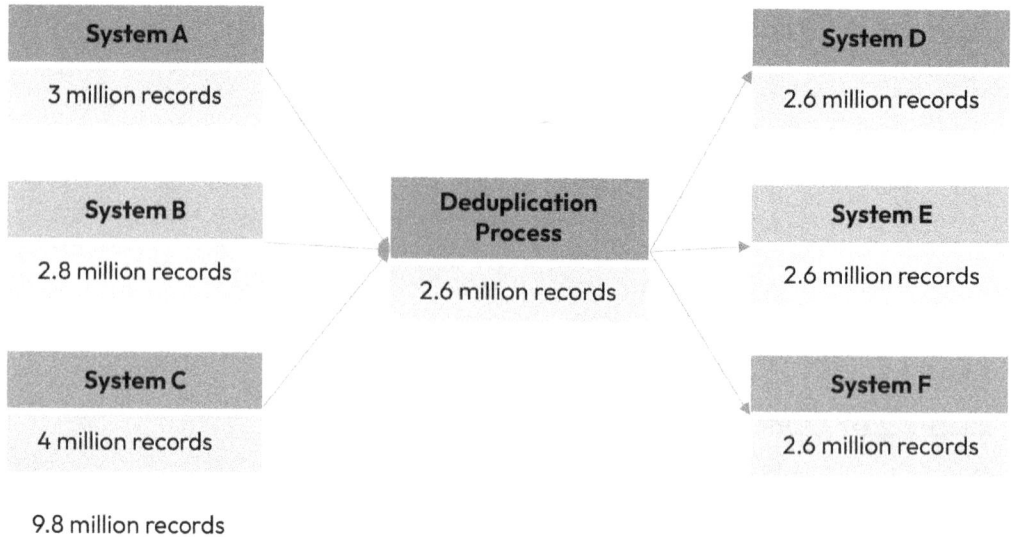

Figure 10.1 – Example Deduplication Process

In the example above, we are sourcing data from three different systems, each claiming to have customer data. As you can see, each system has a different record count for customers. In each system, there may be duplications within each platform as well as across platforms. When we send the data to the PDM platform in the middle, where the deduplication process is run (see "Deduplication Process" above, just one of many core capabilities in the PDM), that process standardizes and deduplicates common records across all records the PDM consumes.

When the data is pushed out to the consuming systems on the right, they all receive the updated customer records, deduplicated and ready for use. You can set up your data flows so that the sources on the left also receive the updated deduplicated data, but that is up to you and your business needs.

Metrics to Measure Success (Internal – Data Team)

1. Reduction in duplicate records (count)
2. Improved data storage efficiency
3. Cost savings in storage
4. Time saved managing duplicated or redundant data
5. Improved data quality
6. Accuracy of Customer Count (improvement score)

Metrics to Measure Success (External – Stakeholder)

1. Improved accuracy in analytics

2. Improved Customer Success Scores (from call center representatives being able to identify customers more easily and see a more unified, accurate view of the customer)

3. Reduced Costs (e.g., enrichment costs in a single location vs. many. Often companies buy the same enrichment service multiple times without realizing it.)

4. Reduction in marketing costs (from marketing to valid contacts a single time versus multiple times, or with bad contact information)

Common Definitions

One of the first steps in establishing a strong Primary Data system is to align the company on common definitions. First, you need to define what a customer is for your organization. Sounds simple, but is quite complicated.

Customer Data Definition Trouble

The first Customer Primary Data Management deployment I was a part of, we spent 18 months (not a joke!) working across the company to define what a customer was. We argued across definitions on elements such as whether the customer needed to be active, or if having a purchase within the last 12 months was sufficient. What did it mean to be "active"? What did they need to purchase? Was simply having an open account sufficient? What if there are no deposits in their account (for example)?

In my second Customer Primary Data Management deployment I worked on, I went straight to the Data Domain Executive for Customer Data, and proposed a definition to him. He made one minor tweak, we approved it together, and we announced the definition to the relevant stakeholders. It took less than 18 minutes. A stark contrast from my first experience.

What's the right approach? You need to make that decision for your company. But I would recommend you use your Data Governance routines and reporting processes to codify the definitions early before you get into the meta model design to limit rework later.

You will need to set a process to define what each data attribute for a Customer Record will be **rationalized** (others may call this process 'mastered' or 'mastering', but like the type of data, I am aiming to use a more inclusive term). For each attribute, you will need a definition to be aligned across the company so that when you refer to them in reports, in the system, and in your data catalog or dictionary, you have a common vocabulary and understanding.

Golden Source Attribution

Your Primary Data Management platform will have a finite set of attributes that you rationalize for each record. This is not the time to put 200 attributes into your primary data platform. Remember the purpose is to standardize the core attributes or common attributes that you intend to drive consistency with across your organization. It is not intended to be a customer data platform. We will walk through the differences in more detail later in this chapter, but for now, be mindful that this is simply the core data related to a customer, not all data related to a customer.

Based on my past experience, I would aim to rationalize no more than 50 core attributes about a Customer. That may seem like a lot or maybe not, depending on your company. The number can grow quickly, especially when you start to think of common attributes such as:

- Customer Unique ID Number
- First Name
- Last Name
- Shipping Street Address Line 1
- Shipping Street Address Line 2 (note: may include apartment numbers or building numbers)
- Shipping City
- Shipping State
- Shipping Zip Code
- Shipping Country
- Mailing Street Address Line 1
- Mailing Street Address Line 2
- Mailing City
- Mailing State
- Mailing Zip Code
- Mailing Country
- Country Code
- Area Code
- Phone Number

As you can see, this can grow quickly when you start to include variances like shipping vs. mailing address (+6 new attributes). Your business model will drive the types of attributes you need (B2B or B2C) as well as your industry (e.g., is gender and/or sex assigned at birth relevant for your product? It may be if you are in health care, but likely not if you are in technology sales).

For each of these attributes, you will need to define the meaning behind each attribute. I also recommend that you take this moment in your program to identify who the data steward is for each of these attributes. It may vary. For example, you may have a data steward for customer first name, customer last name, and mailing address attributes in sales, but your shipping attributes may come from fulfillment or your revenue operations teams. Each attribute should be assigned a data steward who will own and care for that data.

Hierarchies

Hierarchies are one of the foundational capabilities behind Primary Data. One of the unique features of Primary Data is the ability to provide **multiple hierarchy management** across a company. Multiple Hierarchy Management is the ability to apply multiple ways to roll up the same base data that has been standardized (or rationalized) to meet unique business needs. Common hierarchies for Customer Data include:

- Legal Entity Hierarchy
- Sales Hierarchy
- Account Hierarchies
- Location Hierarchies
- Organizational Hierarchies

Hierarchies also need business data stewards and technical data stewards. Business data stewards should define what the definition of the hierarchy is, and what the rules of the hierarchy are. Some could be defined by a 3rd party (e.g., legal entity) vs. others being defined by the business and unique to each company (e.g., Sales Hierarchy – which is how a company divides out which customers are in which sales territory).

Organizations could have an infinite number of hierarchies, but I recommend you deploy and manage a minimum number of hierarchies. They can be quite complex to manage given the speed of business and changes required. If your company is on a quarterly sales cycle, they may carve the sales territory quarterly, and thus, your Sales Hierarchy could change as often as quarterly.

> **Remember**
>
> The objective of PDM is to standardize commonly used data for your organization, so, if you deploy multiple versions of a single hierarchy type, you are violating the core tenant of primary data management: standardization.

Trust Logic

For each Primary Data Management platform you build, you will define **Trust Logic**. Trust Logic is the way in which rules and processes are used to determine the trustworthiness of your primary data. It is important to the success of your data model because it defines how your data will be brought together to drive accuracy, consistency, and reliability. Every company has a unique way of defining this trust logic, and the resulting model, and should be patented due to its proprietary nature. Especially if unique techniques are used, you should consider protecting this model.

As you are defining your Trust Logic, you will want to look at the raw data from the source systems you've identified. For example, let's assume you have identified just two desired sources within your company that will be providing data for your Customer Primary Data Management platform. You take a look at System 1 and you see the data looks something like this:

First Name	Last Name	Mailing Address Line 1	Mailing Address Line 2	Mailing City	Mailing State	Mailing Zip
Bob	Jones	123 Main Street	Apt 1	Chicago	IL	60606
Mary	Long	987 Lane Ave.		Middlebury	VT	

Table 10.1 – Source Data: System 1

That same data in System 2 may look something like this:

First Name	Last Name	Mailing Address Line 1	Mailing City	Mailing State	Mailing Zip
Bob	Jones	123 Main Street, Apt 1	Chicago	IL	60606
Mary	Long	987 Lane Ave.	Middlebury	Vermont	

Table 10.2 – Source Data: System 2

We also have standardization issues across these two systems:

1. Mary and Meredith are inconsistent for the customer's first name. How will we know which is the correct name? Are these the same person? Or are they two people at the same address?

2. There is no zip code for the second customer in either system. How will we find this information?

3. System 2 only has 1 address line, and thus, apartment number is appended to the mailing address field vs. being in a second field in system 1

Now, if these were the only two customers we had, we might be able to call each one and validate their accurate information and correct this data manually. What if you have a thousand customers? What if you have a million? 150 million? Manually correcting data is no longer scalable. That is why we need automated Primary Data Management capabilities to help us to improve the quality and reliability of this core data at speed and scale of our businesses.

Our first step to define the Trust Logic, is to define which system we will use as the source for each attribute. Each attribute can be defined independently of the others. To illustrate this example, I am going to use two shades of grey to depict the variance in the table below, showing how we have sourced the data in this example. Remember, you may have thousands or millions of rows vs. my example with just two records.

First Name	Last Name	Mailing Address Line 1	Mailing Address Line 2	Mailing City	Mailing State	Mailing Zip
Bob	Jones	123 Main Street	Apt 1	Chicago	IL	60606
Meredith	Long	987 Lane Ave.		Middlebury	VT	

Table 10.3 – Illustrative View of Where Each Attribute Was Sourced

In this example, the First Name attribute and Last Name attribute were sourced from System 2, whereas the remaining five fields were sourced from System 1. Why? In short—it's up to you. Usually there is a degree of data quality assessment for the various systems to determine which as the higher quality data.

Another factor in the Trust Logic is, you can also define that secondary systems are used when the first system selected provides a null or blank. For example, if the First Name for System 2 had a blank, you can configure your trust logic to pull System 2 data for First Name attribute first, and if null, pull in First Name data from System 1. You can define 1:M sources for each attribute and define which order you want the data to be pulled in from. This unique Trust Logic is specific to your organization.

Considerations

There are many factors to consider as you are building your trust logic. To determine which sources are being trusted first, second, third, and so on, should consider the following:

- The Source System. If the system that provides the data has higher integrity than another systems, you might consider consuming the data from the system with higher integrity over another.

- Age of Data. Older data tends to be less trustworthy than more recent data, as it's more likely to be out of date or inaccurate.

- Completeness. Incomplete data may be less trustworthy than complete data sets. You may want to consider if a source has more complete information.

- Consistency. Data that is more consistent with other data is more likely to be trustworthy.

- Changes. Data that is changed frequently is less likely to be trustworthy than data that is more stable.

- How the Data Was Collected. For example, if data was collected on a sign-up sheet manually, versus digitally acquired, the digital data is more likely to be accurate in most cases.

How does it work?

Trust logic can be used to assign a trust score to each data attribute by source system. The score can then be used to determine how the data should be used in its deduplication process, and how trustworthy the attribute is. Trust logic can also be used to automate data quality processes. The logic can be sued to automatically identify data that is inaccurate before it infiltrates the Primary Data Management deduplication process. This can help improve the overall quality of the Primary Data to make it more reliable.

Integration

When creating a Primary Data Management platform, one of the early steps in defining the target architecture (even conceptually) is identifying the integrations that are required. I often think about this in terms of left to right (left being the incoming integrations and the right side being the outgoing integrations). Integrations are no longer so simple. Many of the platforms that will be coming into your platform from the left side of the diagram, are also going to receive the output. This is called bi-directional integration. It is bi-directional because the data comes into the Primary Data Management platform is standardized, deduplicated, enriched and then pushed back to the source system.

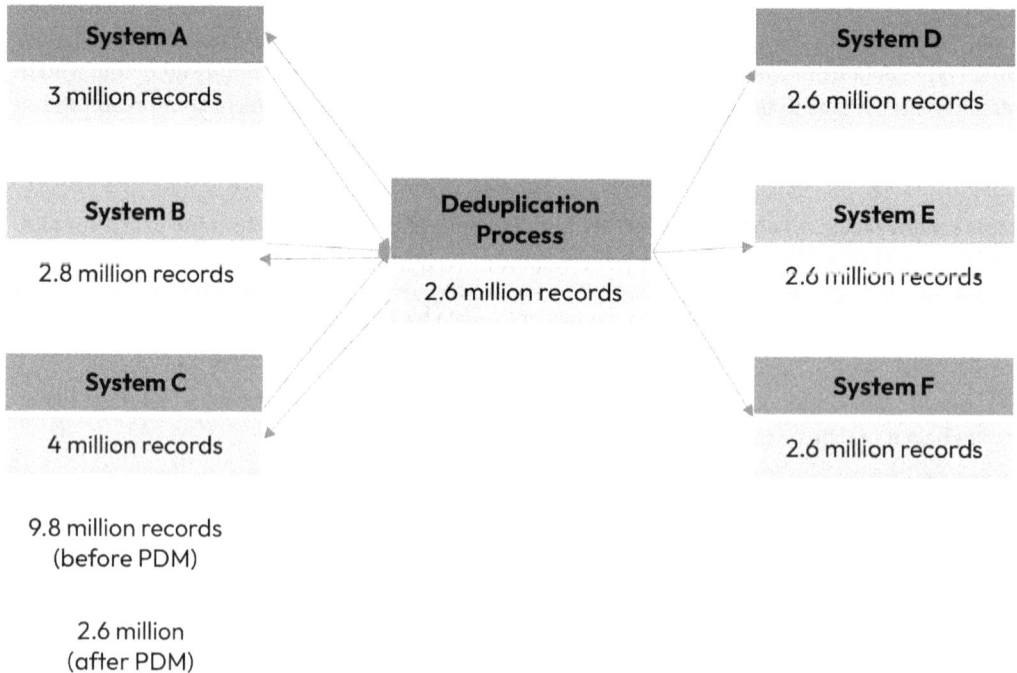

Figure 10.2 – Example of Integration Model

Quality Third-Party Enrichment

Third-party enrichment services are data files that are purchased from organizations outside of your own. The purpose of using a third-party enrichment service is to improve the quality of the data you have inside your company.

Back to our example, in the second record of our Customer Primary Data platform, we were missing a Zip Code for Meredith Long. A 3rd party address enrichment service could be used to enrich the quality of addresses in your Customer Primary Data Management Platform. The resulting output could look like this:

First Name	Last Name	Mailing Address Line 1	Mailing Address Line 2	Mailing City	Mailing State	Mailing Zip
Bob	Jones	123 Main Street	Apt 1	Chicago	IL	60606
Meredith	Long	987 Lane Ave.		Middlebury	VT	05753

Table 10.4 – Example of Enriched Addresses

In this example, the enrichment service was able to provide the correct zip code for the second record. Again, remember a simple search could be used to populate 1 missing field, but when you are operating at the scale of a large enterprise, these services replace thousands of hours of manual data quality clean up by using 3rd party enrichment to improve the quality of your data.

During the course of building out your customer and contact primary data, you may find you subscribe to dozens of 3rd party enrichment services, to ensure you have the highest quality data possible. Each service has its own pros and cons, so be clear up front in what you are trying to achieve with each enrichment. They can contradict each other. Make sure you have clear processes in place to assess the quality of the enrichment service, which ones you will trust over others, and how that fits into your match and merge processes.

Consumption Model

As a part of your Primary Data Management program, you will need to define how you will prescribe users to consume the data. Because of the nature of Primary Data, it is important that you take extra care in preventing poor quality data from entering into your PDM platforms. Thus, providing a standardized pattern for consumption will help your users receive what they need without compromising the platform.

Typically, you will be serving both operational and analytical user needs. This means that you will need to define the needs for these types of users and support consumption models for both. For example, for your operational use cases, you may need to consider regulatory reporting requirements like Sarbanes-Oxley but for analytical purposes, you may be able to support a less formalized and rigid control framework which enables you to move data faster and more seamlessly for analytical purposes.

It is likely you will push your Primary Data into a Data Lake and/or Data Warehouse to support analytics, while you push the data into your ERP and CRM for operational needs. You may also provide a pub/sub option for additional distribution of data across your ecosystem.

I recommend defining the consumption model for your company's needs, and enforcing a policy and technical process by which data cannot be further provisioned so that you maintain the data technical integrity of the data. If you do not enforce a strict consumption model, you risk re-creating the problem in which you set to solve: inconsistent primary data across the enterprise.

CRM vs. PDM

It is very common for technologists and business users alike to confuse these two types of platforms. To clear up a few misconceptions: these platforms do not compete with each other. Quite the contrary, they help support one another. Think about the CRM and PDM as being heart and lungs for a human. Both required, both need to work well for optimal health. The same is true for CRM and PDM. They are required to optimize each other.

What is CRM?

A Customer Relationship Management Platform or CRM Platform, is a system that enables sellers, customer service teams, and marketers to see a 360 degree view of a customer. CRMs help companies track their customer interactions, manage sales, provide customer support, and automate marketing campaigns. CRMs help businesses improve customer satisfaction, increase sales, reduce costs, improve operations, and make better business decisions.

While CRMs do tend to house much of the data attributes that are generally found in a Customer Primary Data Management platform, CRMs are not designed or generally governed in a way that fosters enrichment and reusability for the data for the entirety of use cases across a company. CRMs tend to be biased towards the sales cycle, versus regulatory or risk reporting purposes, analytics, or revenue operations.

According to Gartner, "CRM leaders who avoid MDM will derive erroneous results that annoy customers, resulting in a 25% reduction in potential revenue gains"[1].

Key Differences

There are some simple and profound differences between a CRM and a PDM platform. A CRM system can be used to identify and prioritize leads, while an PDM system will be used to ensure that the lead is accurate and complete. A CRM will be used to track customer interactions and purchases, while a PDM will be used to create the single view of the customer information. A PDM platform will be used to create and manage hierarchies, where the CRM system will consume the hierarchies and create more targeted marketing campaigns and product recommendations from the hierarchy information.

Feature	CRM	PDM
Primary Purpose	Manage customer interactions and relationships supporting sales, marketing and customer success/support.	Manage master data
Core Data	Customer contact information, sales leads, customer support tickets.	Customer data, product data, supplier data, employee data.
Key Features	Contact Management, Lead management, sales pipeline management, customer support, marketing automation	Data deduplication, data enrichment, data quality management, hierarchy management
Typical Users	Account Executives/Sales Leaders, Marketing Teams, Customer Service Representatives	IT Teams, Data Governance Team, Business Intelligence Teams.

Table 10.5 - Differences between a CRM and a PDM platform

Both platforms are of value to an organization, but they serve different users, with different capabilities. Both are better off when used together.

The Value of Primary Data Management

One of the most difficult challenges of Primary Data Management isn't the deployment of the platform or the complex integrations. It's actually the build out of the business case, which includes clearly articulating the value of a Primary Data Management investment. Because of the nature of the complexity of any Primary Data Management platform (regardless of customer, contact, vendor, etc.), the number of sources, and the number of adoptions, it can be difficult for business stakeholders to understand how such a large financial investment will result in business outcomes.

Most PDM investments fail when the business value is not clearly documented early in the program. In more challenging implementations, the reason the company struggled to understand the value of the investment, was when the business case we largely driven from a technology lens versus a business lens. While there is good reason to invest in PDM from a purely IT perspective (efficiency alone is a strong factor), because the cost tends to be quite high relative to other investments, business users tend to struggle to understand why it is a priority, and PDM tends to be bumped down on the list of investment priorities as a result.

On the contrary, when a strong and well-articulated business value story is created, I have seen PDM investments rise to the very top of the priority investment list. My advice: Spend the time articulating the business value story thoroughly before taking it forward. The strength in the business case will carry you over the long duration of the implementation and through adoption of the data into consuming systems down the road.

Building the Business Case

When writing the business case, I recommend working very closely with the consumers of the data (your stakeholders) to define the business objectives & outcomes that are expected from delivering strong Primary Data Management solutions. First, define a strong purpose statement that will support the program development.

For example, you may want to say something like:

> *"Our Primary Data Management Program will deliver fundamental and foundational data management capabilities to enable the company's transformation and empower employees, customers, and partners with highly reliable, trustworthy information when they need it."*

It's hard to argue with a purpose statement like this. Most stakeholders will agree, but also challenge you to be more specific. That's where your objectives come in. You should define 3-5 core objectives for the PDM Program, that will be your core focus in delivering for your stakeholders. Some examples include:

- Establish clear, aligned definitions and implement a unified customer data model, with high quality and enriched customer data fit for enterprise-wide use.

- Create a single-unified view of a customer, including a unique identifier, golden-source attribution for each customer at the most granular level, with multi-hierarchy management to support the needs of sales, marketing, customer support, and revenue operations, with consistency and trust.

- Establish a unified view of products, including a unique identifier, golden-source attribution and hierarchy relationship management to support product families, selling, and attribute-based pricing.

A Note on Scope of Program

You should be very clear about what is in the program (what will be delivered) versus what will be a part of post-program business as usual (BAU) work. For example, it is common to have adoption of the data published by a primary data management platform be a part of the initial program, but not for every system in the company, forever. Companies tend to deploy new technologies somewhat regularly, and if you keep your PDM Program up and running to support indefinitely, you will never finish the program. I recommend having the first few or key system adoption within the program, and once you have proven your approach to drive adoption (that is, consumption) of the data into target systems to be effective, you can complete the program and push everything else into BAU.

Capability Statements

As you build out the program, you should clarify for the stakeholders exactly what capabilities you will be deploying as a part of your program. Here are some example Core Capability Statements you might want to use:

- Golden Customer Record & Unique ID
- Single Source of Truth
- Assignment of Unique Customer Identifier
- Customer standardization and validations for accuracy
- Validated lineage transparency
- Customer status (current, former)
- Customer Maintenance, Workflow & Stewardship
- Customer look up search capability
- Add, update, delete customer
- 3rd party data enrichment
- Multi-Hierarchy Management
- Search for and classify customer relationship (i.e., customer, partner)
- Add, update, delete relationship
- Manage hierarchy
- Customer Classification, Segmentation, and Enrichment
- 3rd Party enrichment services (e.g., D&B, Lead Space)
- Address enrichment service
- Industry vertical assignment, grouping, & classification
- Geo, region, and location for sales and support services
- Tax ID, GULT, DUNS, NAICS assignment

Conceptual Architecture

Conceptual architecture generally defines what the ecosystem surrounding the Primary Data Management environment will look like. This allows you to provide the business and technology stakeholders with a perspective on how the ecosystem will function and interact when PDM is deployed.

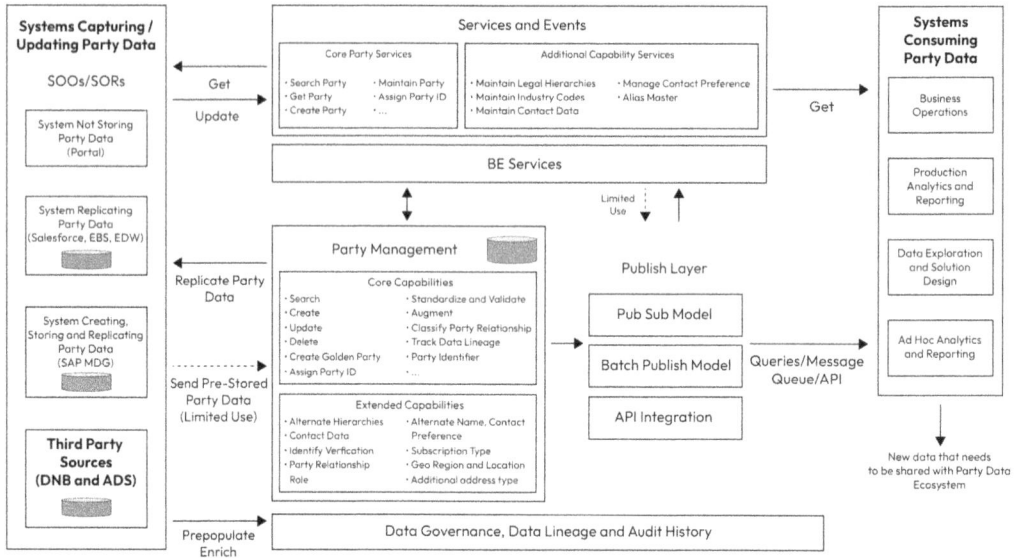

Figure 10.3 – Conceptual PDM Architecture

Directional Objectives & Specific Measures of Success

When defining the objectives of the program, for each objective you should define a specific measure and expected outcome to support each objective.

- Increased sales and marketing effectiveness: Targeted sales and marketing campaigns can be created and executed more effectively when contact master data is accurate and up-to-date.

- Improved customer service: Customer service representatives can provide better support to customers when they have access to accurate and complete contact information.

- Each customer is assigned a unique identifier in the PDM platform, which allows both the customer and the service representative to ensure the correct customer is selected for service.

- Reduced costs: Organizations can save money on marketing costs by eliminating duplicate contacts and targeting their marketing campaigns to the right audience.

- Improved lead conversion to sales. Measure the previous lead conversion before implementing PDM and again after final deployment.

- Number of qualified leads.

- Number of leads with a valid email address.

- Better business decisions: Organizations can make better business decisions by having access to insights into their customer base, such as customer demographics and purchase history.

- Each customer record will have valid contact information, verified by a 3rd party enrichment service, resulting in an increase in customer data quality (in this example, be sure to baseline the data quality before implementing your PDM platform, and then again at each release to show the measured increase).

- Automated customer segmentation to support sales planning process. Measure amount of manual intervention/time spent prior to PDM vs. after.

Business Benefits of PDM

Before we close out on this topic, I want to leave you with a very specific list of Stakeholders, Business Benefits, and KPIs to use as a starting point for your business case. You should always customize the list for your own company, but I hope you find value in this list as a jumping off point for defining the value of your PDM investment. Because these investments are usually multiple millions of dollars, involve rearchitecting business processes, implementing new systems, and driving new outcomes, they are hard to sell to the business. But, with clear business benefits, ROI statements, and measures of success (KPIs), I am confident you will be able to launch this capability at your organization.

Stakeholder Group	Business Benefit
Marketing	<ul><li>Increase in qualified leads.</li><li>Increased efficiency in account based segmentation and marketing.</li><li>Increased quality in contact to account linkage.</li><li>Increased ability to measure marketing lead ROI.</li></ul>

Stakeholder Group	Business Benefit
Sales	• Reduction in maintenance cost for sales/account planning. • Reduction in labor costs for sales/account planning. • Improved automation in sales/account planning. • Improved Sales Forecasting based on higher quality customer and account data. • Improved accuracy in Sales Commissioning due to improved reliability of forecast data. • Reduction in account proliferation, resulting in improved account visibility, and reduction in missed sales opportunities. • Improved quality of customer data. • Improved quality of contact data, resulting in improved customer engagement.
Finance	• Accurate Customer Count (for internal and external reporting) • Improved accuracy in revenue reporting due to improved account completion and order to customer unique ID mapping
Operations	• Improved operational efficiency through better account data hygiene and accuracy, consistent reporting • Improved cross-functional reporting quality, resulting in higher reliance on automated reports and streamlined decision making
Deal Management	• Reduced deal velocity from simplification of customer data across platforms, requiring less manual intervention across the cycle • Reduced cost to configure, price and quote deals
Legal/Compliance	• Improved compliance rigor due to single flag for do not sell to configurations • Less manual intervention and consultations from legal for deals • Reduced legal costs due to automation and reliability of customer information
Customer Success / Support	• Improved customer satisfaction scores due to improved customer data, ease of tracing customer information, and improved quality of customer interaction data through PDM to CRM • Improved quality of customer data to enable opportunity data to be more quickly visible to support representative in near-real-time

Table 10.6 - Business benefits of PDM

As you embark on your PDM journey, I hope that you have gained enough knowledge in this chapter to build a quality business case, explain the value of PDM, understand the types of PDMs, why consumption patterns matter, and how PDM is a great supplemental capability to any CRM.

Conclusion

Deploying PDM is much more than a way to improve the quality of your customer, product, vendor, or employee data, but a way to streamline and drive efficiency and effectiveness across your entire business. PDM is one of the most robust and potentially impactful capabilities that data governance can deliver for a company.

As we've covered in this chapter, there are four key skills that are required to launch a successful PDM capability in your organization:

1. The importance of PDM including why it is required for building successful data solutions.

2. How to design an PDM function.

3. The specific needs when it comes to implementation.

4. How to design an PDM solution.

Now that we've covered the importance of metadata management (both business and technical) as well as data quality and primary data management, our next topic, data operations, will cover how we operate these capabilities with ease and scale.

References

1. Gartner. MDM is Critical to CRM Optimization. Gartner, Inc. Refreshed 8 June 2015.

11
Data Operations

One of the less-focused-on areas of data governance, data operations, is often left out of the conversation. All companies have some sort of operational function focused on data, but they are often not visible to leaders. Data operations teams are often stuck behind visualization teams or governance functions, unknown to the company. What are they really? What do data operations teams provide to the company?

This chapter will dive into this topic. While I have shared previously that data governance tends to be unappreciated, I want to clarify that while true, I also believe it's data professionals who are largely to blame for this lack of value. In this chapter, we will dig into what *you* can do to help bring into focus the value data operations bring to your organization and how you can show measurable value to the executives you interact with.

Example

Imagine this: You are a sales executive, and it's crunch time. It's the last day of the quarter, and you have a big deal to close. You have a verbal commitment from the customer, and now you just need to get that final order over to them for processing so that the sale hits this quarter's books. Only there's one problem.

The transaction is stuck.

Somewhere in the flow of the transaction, between the quoting process and the order management process, the data isn't moving. Time is running out. Your customer is ready to sign, but you don't have the order for them to sign. This deal will mean meeting sales targets for the quarter and not closing the deal; well, it means you'll just barely miss.

Now what? What do you do?

Most likely, you wipe the sweat off your forehead and start dialing. Usual contacts include CIO, CDO, and maybe even all the way to the top. In time-sensitive moments such as these, it's not uncommon for the sales team to go straight to the top. However, there is a better way: calling your data operations team. They can help you in moments just like these.

I used this example because it is very real. I have seen this same situation play out in a number of organizations: some with great success and the ability to close deals such as these with ease. Others are not as fortunate. So, what's the difference between them? A strong data operations team.

We will cover the following main topics:

- Defining data operations
- Data operations capabilities
- The value of data operations
- Building an optimal data operations capability and setting up for success

Defining data operations

Data operations are often left unappreciated in a data organization. I think of data operations like electricity: it may not be appreciated until you don't have it. Data operations teams are often the glue that keeps things moving within a company, and depending on the way your company operates, the size and scale of the team may vary greatly. **Data Operations** (**DataOps**) is typically a set of practices, processes, and technologies that enable an integrated and focused perspective on data using automation and manual processes to improve the quality, speed, and collaboration of data across an organization. Data operations is a fairly evolving field, which includes both practitioner perspectives as well as an influx of vendors. Because companies are increasingly relying on data for decisions and general organizational operations, data operations is becoming a more essential discipline with additional focus.

Data operations often sit in the middle of various capabilities across an organization and are the glue that keeps everything working together:

Figure 11.1 – Data operations as the centerpiece of data governance

Data operations versus IT operations

There are some commonalities between data operations and traditional IT operations. Both are responsible for the overall health of the company's operations; however, traditional IT operations typically focus on activities such as the following:

- Monitoring IT systems

- Maintaining IT processes

- Implementation of IT systems

- Upgrading IT systems

- Ensuring ongoing data security and compliance are maintained

In many ways, data operations are not all that different, except instead of "IT," replace with "data":

- Monitoring data quality

- Maintaining data processing

- Implementation of data solutions

- Upgrading data processes and solutions

- Ensuring ongoing data classification and compliance

The goals and objectives are slightly different, but overall, both operations groups support the ongoing running of a company. The primary objective of IT operations is to ensure that IT systems are reliable, secure, and efficient, whereas the primary objective of data operations is to make data more accessible, usable, and valuable.

Data operations are occasionally a part of data engineering teams in that they are responsible for building and maintaining data pipelines. Data engineers are typically the profile and expertise hired to support data operations functions within an organization. The key distinction is data operations teams are more often brought in to fix and provide operational support versus building new, whereas data engineering teams are more often focused.

IT and data operations partnerships

Ever more, IT and data operations teams are working together. It is very important to align roles and responsibilities between these two teams so that there is no confusion about which team is responsible for what tasks. However, when both IT and data operations support each other, the results and seamless experience for the company become very fluid and effective.

By working together, these two functions can enable a breakdown in siloed work and improve the overall flow of data from source all the way to insight. In many cases, a business leader will request something to move through the organization "faster" but does not realize it takes both IT and data teams to make that happen. To move effectively, the IT and data teams must work together to deliver a delightful experience to the business leader. When the teams work together, you may design an interaction model such that the following outcomes are achieved:

- The data team meets with the business to understand the business needs and to define success

- The data and IT teams work together to define both business and functional requirements for both teams, as well as who will deliver on the requirements

- IT operations can provide the data operations team with the infrastructure and resources needed to build the appropriate data pipelines

- Data operations can provide IT operations data insights that can help identify where there may be issues stemming from IT operations

- The two teams can collaborate on governance and security to ensure that the business leader's solution is moved to production with governance and security built in by design

I have seen these lines blurred and, in some cases, combined. Unfortunately, when that happens, IT operations are usually distracted by their primary focus (that is, IT operations), and data needs tend to take a backseat to the operations of the IT systems. I strongly recommend maintaining a separation between these two functions to enable fluidity in the service of data to your organization.

Helpful Hint
When you have a strong data operations team, one great benefit is after-action reviews. Given data operations teams should be working from a ticketing system, you have great data about your data operations team's focus. This information about where your data operations team is spending their time is fantastic data to look at: problem systems, frequency of events, source of errors, and common types of issues. From this, you can identify opportunities to drive transformation and longer-term, more sustainable fixes.

Data operations capabilities

Data operations teams play a crucial role in enabling organizations to effectively manage and utilize their data assets. They provide a range of data capabilities that empower data-driven decision-making and enhance overall business operations. Data operations teams are often made up of individuals who have a wide-ranging understanding of a wide variety of systems, are deeply skilled in various computer languages, and can pivot quickly when issues arise.

Helpful Hint

Hire a leader for your data operations team who works well under pressure, can present well in front of executives, and can motivate team members to perform quickly and effectively. Your data operations leader is critical to the success of your entire data program.

Data operations teams are responsible for wide-ranging capabilities that may include "other duties as assigned" given their level of access and wide-ranging skillsets. Because of their need to have wide-ranging access to be able to fix issues as they arise, you need to have strong audit logging in place to be able to retrace steps and employ strong detective controls to see what was completed. Trust is not a control, so be mindful of their wide-ranging access.

Key data capabilities provided by data operations teams include the following:

1. **Data integration**: Data operations teams facilitate the seamless integration of data from diverse sources, including structured, semi-structured, and unstructured data. They employ data integration tools and techniques to harmonize data formats, eliminate inconsistencies, and create a unified data landscape.

2. **Data quality management**: Data operations teams ensure the accuracy, consistency, and completeness of data throughout its life cycle. They implement data quality monitoring and remediation processes to identify and rectify data errors, ensuring the reliability of data-driven insights, as defined by the data quality team. Data operations teams often serve as the technical enablement, configuring the data quality rules into the data processes as designed by the data quality team.

3. **Data warehousing and data lakes**: Data operations teams establish and manage data warehouses and data lakes, repositories that store and organize large volumes of data for analytical purposes. They design and implement data storage solutions that cater to specific business needs and support various data analysis workloads.

4. **Data pipelines**: Data operations teams build and maintain data pipelines, the pathways that automate the movement, transformation, and loading of data from source systems to target destinations. They optimize data pipelines for efficiency, ensuring timely and reliable data delivery for analytics and reporting.

5. **Data access and self-service**: Data operations teams enable self-service data access, empowering business users to explore and analyze data without requiring constant IT intervention. They implement user-friendly data access tools and portals, fostering a data-driven culture within the organization.

6. **Data governance and security**: Data operations teams enforce data governance policies and procedures defined by the data governance team to ensure the proper management, protection, and compliance of data assets. They implement data security measures to safeguard sensitive information and mitigate data breaches.

7. **Data experimentation and prototyping**: Data operations teams support data experimentation and prototyping by providing data sandboxes and agile development environments. They facilitate the exploration of new data-driven initiatives and enable rapid iteration of data-driven solutions.

8. **Data visualization and analytics support**: Data operations teams collaborate with data scientists and analysts to *enable* insightful visualizations and reports that effectively communicate data-driven insights to stakeholders. They may curate datasets for the data analytics teams to use for their analytical and visualization purposes. *For clarity: Data operations teams do not create visualization or analytics reports but focus on curating the data to enable the analytics team to perform their duties.*

9. **Continuous improvement and monitoring**: Data operations teams employ continuous improvement methodologies to identify bottlenecks, optimize processes, and enhance data capabilities. They implement data monitoring tools to track performance metrics and ensure the ongoing effectiveness of data operations.

10. **Change management and version control**: Data operations teams implement change management practices and **version control systems** (**VCS**) to manage changes to data pipelines, infrastructure, and data models. They ensure controlled and traceable changes, minimizing disruption and maintaining data integrity.

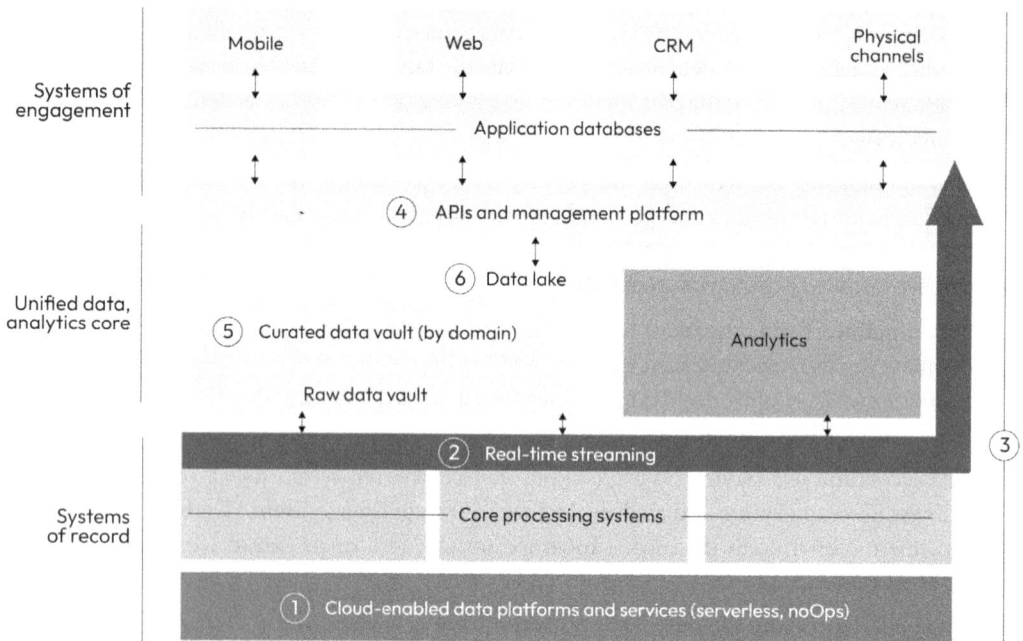

Figure 11.2 – Example data ecosystem

Looking at the data ecosystem as a whole, the collective capabilities across data operations are the glue across the ecosystem. While data architecture designs the ecosystem, and IT implements the systems, the data operations team is what keeps the data flowing, accurately, and with trust, across the ecosystem. They connect with all parts of the company (data governance, IT, and business groups) to ensure that the users of information have what they need when they need it. In summary, data operations teams provide a comprehensive suite of data capabilities that enable organizations to derive maximum value from their data assets. By effectively managing and utilizing data, organizations can gain a competitive edge, make informed decisions, and achieve their strategic goals.

The value of data operations

The value of data operations lies in its ability to streamline and optimize the way data is collected, processed, and utilized within an organization. In a word: simplification. As with data architecture (*Chapter 9*), the more simplified and streamlined operations can be, the less opportunity there is for breakdowns, errors, and business impact. Out of principle, when data operations are designed from a simplified perspective, the value is clearer to understand, and the time to resolve issues tends to be shorter. Less time is spent trying to troubleshoot the root cause (fewer places for issues to occur) and blast radius (impact of issues).

When evaluating the value of comprehensive and high-functioning data operations, there are a number of value-adds, but these are the key areas I recommend highlighting for your data operations function (whether building one or simply telling the value story). Here are some key aspects of its value:

1. **Improved data quality and accuracy**: Data operations practices ensure that data is consistently accurate and reliable. By implementing robust data validation and cleansing processes, organizations can reduce errors and improve the overall quality of their data. While your data quality team will set expectations, requirements, and so on, the data operations team will be employed to implement processes to clean and optimize the quality of the data directly.

2. **Enhanced collaboration and agility**: Data operations foster collaboration between data scientists, engineers, and business analysts. Because data operations professionals work across teams to create solutions and solve problems, the team is able to drive unity across teams to solve problems faster. This collaborative approach enables more agile responses to changing business needs and data requirements.

3. **Increased efficiency and productivity**: Automation of data processes reduces manual efforts and speeds up data-related workflows. This efficiency leads to increased productivity and allows teams to focus on more strategic tasks rather than routine data management. Your data operations team is well positioned to identify opportunities for automation. I have seen data operations teams act as automation seekers, finding all the options and creating a backlog to work through over time.

> **Helpful Hint**
>
> This is a *great* way to show the value of your data operations team—by accumulating the running count of hours saved by identifying and then automating data processes and capabilities across the organization. Most companies are shocked by how quickly this value adds up.

4. **Better decision-making**: With high-quality, timely, and relevant data, organizations can make more informed decisions. Effective data operations ensure that decision-makers have access to the right data at the right time. Because data operations are uniquely positioned to identify automation as well as simplification opportunities and deploy them rapidly, they can speed the time to insight and enable decision-making to happen faster, at the speed the business needs.

5. **Scalability and flexibility**: Data operations practices are designed to scale with the organization. As data volumes and complexities grow, data operations strategies help in managing these increases efficiently. With great monitoring, data operations professionals can identify where systems and pipelines are being stressed and can proactively suggest and deploy solutions.

6. **Risk mitigation**: Proper management of data through data operations reduces risks associated with data breaches, compliance issues, and operational inefficiencies. It ensures data security and compliance with regulations such as the **General Data Protection Regulation** (**GDPR**) and the **Health Insurance Portability and Accountability Act** (**HIPAA**) by ensuring consistent application of data protection controls throughout the data ecosystem.

7. **Enhanced customer experience**: By providing a better understanding of customer data and behavior, data operations can help organizations tailor their products and services to better meet customer needs, thus enhancing the customer experience. This can be achieved through data observability metrics implemented by data operations teams across data pipelines.

As your data operations team creates value from the activities outlined in this chapter, I recommend keeping a running total of the value contributed to the organization through your data operations team. It does not need to be complex, but you do need to decide what ways you will measure value upfront. My favorites are the following:

- Dollars saved/avoided
- Hours saved
- Risks mitigated (count or aggregate cost)
- Automations implemented

A simple four-column dashboard can do a great deal to showcase your data operations value. Additionally, you can also add trends by tagging the type of changes for each of these four categories to demonstrate where the biggest impact is coming from. A mock-up example may look something like this:

Data Operations Value Stream

| $39 M Dollars Saved | 190 Risk Avoided |
| 4,937 Hours Saved | 26 Automations Deployed |

Root Cause

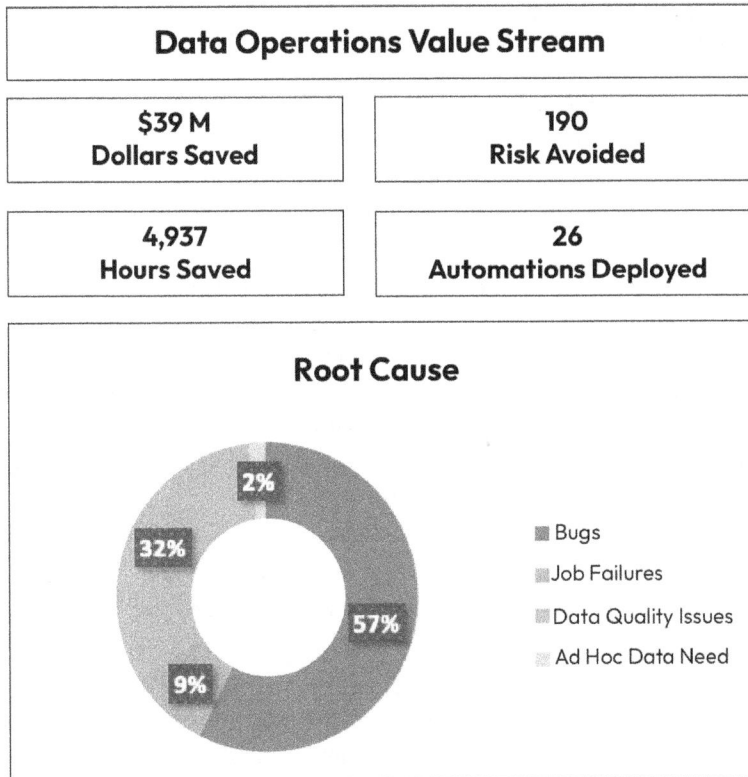

- Bugs
- Job Failures
- Data Quality Issues
- Ad Hoc Data Need

2%
32%
57%
9%

Figure 11.3 – Example data operations value stream dashboard

In summary, data operations bring significant value by ensuring high-quality, accessible, and secure data, fostering a culture of collaboration, and enabling more effective decision-making, *but you must capture the value clearly and transparently to help the return on investment (ROI) for the team become visible to the organization.*

The unsung hero of data governance

As I mentioned previously, data operations are often overlooked in organizations for several reasons. If you are working to educate your sponsor or perhaps your CFO to fund such a program, you may want to use these points to explain why this function is not always seen as a value-add, to help inform their decisions and dispel myths about an "operations" team:

1. **Lack of awareness**: Many organizations are not fully aware of the concept of data operations or its potential benefits. Without this understanding, they may not prioritize its implementation and/or funding.

2. **Legacy mindsets**: Some organizations are entrenched in traditional ways of handling data and may be resistant to adopting new methodologies. The shift to a more collaborative and agile approach can be challenging for those accustomed to siloed and hierarchical structures. I suggest explaining the data operations function like a data SWAT team. They are uniquely positioned to jump in and solve high-priority data issues at a moment's notice. They can then go back to fully remediating longer-term solutions, but no other team has the perspective and skill to solve data issues the "old way" and still meet the speed of business in today's fast-paced environment.

3. **Complexity and resource constraints**: Implementing data operations can be complex, requiring a blend of skills in data science, engineering, and business analysis. Organizations may lack the necessary resources or expertise to effectively implement data operations practices. This is where ensuring executive understanding is so important. Showing the value of such a function is important, which is where the dashboard shown previously comes into play. Make it transparent and accessible to everyone. Maintain backend data as well so that anyone who wants to see how numbers were created can do so with ease.

4. **Underestimation of data challenges**: Some organizations may underestimate the challenges associated with managing large volumes of data. They might not recognize the need for specialized operations to manage and utilize their data assets effectively.

5. **Focus on short-term goals**: Organizations often focus on short-term objectives and immediate results. By taking a strategic investment in data operations, you will require a long-term commitment that may not show immediate tangible benefits, leading to their undervaluation. Encourage a 6- or 12-month window to give the team time to show impact. The first few months may be a slow start, but the compounding of time and the trajectory will deliver.

Primary Data Management

In one company, we were beginning a large primary data management initiative. As a part of our business case, I had our data operations team go back and review all the issues and case data that they had maintained for the last 12 months to determine how many of their issues, how much of their time, and the investment made to address issues and/or cases that would be impacted by our primary data management initiative. It was shocking for everyone, including me. There were thousands of issues that had been logged related to customer hierarchy mismatches, incorrect or invalid contact information, invalid addresses for shipping purposes, and invalid industry codes, all of which would be enriched and standardized by our PDM implementation. The number of issues, the hours spent addressing these issues, and the cost to provide the data operations services to address the issues *alone* justified our cost to implement primary data management.

---

6. **Budget constraints**: Data operations require investment in tools and personnel. In organizations where budgets are tight, there might be a reluctance to allocate funds for what is seen as misunderstood as a non-critical function.

7. **Overemphasis on technology over processes**: There can be a tendency to focus on acquiring the latest data technologies rather than on improving data processes and collaboration. This tech-centric view can overlook the operational aspect of data management.

8. **Integration challenges**: Integrating data operations team members into existing systems and processes can be challenging. Organizations might be deterred by the perceived disruption and effort required to integrate new processes or make changes without fully grasping the return on that investment.

9. **Silos within the organization**: Data often exists in silos within an organization. Breaking these silos to implement a cohesive data operations strategy requires organizational change, which can be difficult.

10. **Competing priorities**: Organizations often have multiple competing priorities. Data operations might be deprioritized in favor of more urgent or seemingly impactful initiatives.

Addressing these challenges involves increasing awareness of the value of data operations, ensuring top management buy-in, investing in the right skills and tools, and fostering a culture that values data as a strategic asset. This next section will outline what you can do about these factors to gain the support you need to drive successful funding and positioning for data operations.

Making data operations more visible

As you work to bring the data operations team into the spotlight, making data operations more visible within an organization involves several strategic and practical steps. The path to support has been difficult for me, but the steps I outline next will help you get to the full support you need faster. I'd recommend following this order:

1. **Executive buy-in and advocacy**: Secure commitment and support from top management. When leaders understand and advocate for the value of data operations, they gain visibility and legitimacy throughout the organization. Spend time educating and showing the potential value. Use business examples with an impact that matters for their **business unit** (**BU**) or function.

2. **Education and awareness campaigns**: Conduct workshops, seminars, and training sessions to educate employees about the importance and benefits of data operations. Highlighting successful case studies and best practices can also help in raising awareness. Send out a monthly newsletter highlighting key wins for the month.

3. **Demonstrate value with pilot projects**: Implement data operations practices in small, controlled environments initially. Use these pilot projects to demonstrate tangible benefits, such as improved data quality, efficiency, or decision-making, which can then be communicated across the organization. Use these pilot projects to highlight the value of your education and awareness campaigns.

4. **Integrate data operations into business strategy**: This is a bit harder if your company and sponsor are resistant to investing in this area. However, it is important to position data operations as a critical component of the overall business strategy. This integration ensures that it is discussed in strategic meetings and considered in decision-making processes. Ask questions such as: What do we need to improve in our data ecosystem to make this process/report/metric/solution more efficient or effective?

5. **Create a data operations team and champion**: Establish a dedicated team and appoint a data operations champion (ideally, assign a business champion) who is responsible for promoting, sponsoring, and evangelizing data operations practices. This role can serve as a focal point for data operations initiatives and discussions. At times, focusing efforts on a single BU can be effective for gaining support. Your champion may emerge from this BU.

6. **Develop metrics and key performance indicators (KPIs)**: It may go without saying, but you should define clear metrics and KPIs to measure the impact of data operations. Regularly sharing these metrics with stakeholders can help in highlighting their importance and effectiveness. Use your education and awareness campaigns to highlight your metrics and KPIs with impact.

7. **Internal marketing and communication**: Regularly communicate the successes and progress of data operations initiatives through internal newsletters, meetings, and dashboards. Sharing stories and testimonials can also be effective. Testimonials are especially powerful when they come from senior executives.

8. **Encourage collaboration and cross-functional teams**: Foster a collaborative culture by forming cross-functional teams that include members from IT, data science, business analysis, and operations. This helps in breaking down silos and making data operations a part of the broader organizational conversation. You may want to form a core team of dedicated data operations but also have a network that supports or engages when crisis situations arise. Formally name those individuals so that there is clarity about what your team will need from them.

9. **Leverage technology and tools**: Utilize modern tools and technologies that can showcase the efficiency and impact of data operations. This not only improves operations but also serves as a tangible demonstration of their value.

10. **Feedback and continuous improvement**: Encourage feedback from all levels of the organization on data operations practices and continuously improve based on this feedback. This approach keeps data operations relevant and top-of-mind within the organization. The most expected feedback you will receive is about moving faster. That's a great thing—you can use that feedback to request additional support (funding and headcount) if your company is seeing the impact.

By adopting these strategies, data operations can gain more visibility and recognition as a key contributor to the organization's overall efficiency, data quality, and decision-making capabilities. By driving with an impact-led approach, your team will focus on making a difference versus closing cases. This mindset will ensure your team remains supported and is recognized for impactful work versus as a back-office function.

Building an optimal data operations capability and setting up for success

Building an optimal data operations function involves a blend of strategic planning, technology implementation, and fostering a culture of collaboration and continuous improvement. The core design of this team makes for a successful and organization-wide solution. Here are key steps to set up the optimal team for impact:

1. **Define clear objectives and scope**: Start by clearly defining what you want to achieve with your data operations function. This could include goals such as improving data quality, accelerating data pipeline development, or enhancing collaboration between teams. You may focus on one area that is in need first, and then grow to support other functions over time. If your company is going through a big transformation (for example, implementation of a new ERP), you may want to focus on supporting that initiative as a priority to ensure a successful program implementation.

2. **Assess current capabilities and needs**: Evaluate your current data management practices, tools, and infrastructure. Identify gaps, inefficiencies, and areas for improvement that the data operations function can address. Where do you have areas of need? Where can you demonstrate immediate impact?

3. **Develop a strategy and roadmap**: Create a strategic plan that outlines how you will develop your data operations capabilities. This should include short-term and long-term goals, milestones, and a roadmap for implementation. Perhaps you will address priority issues immediately, while you also build routines, rhythms, and processes to support your data operations team's strategic focus. Lay out the priorities and how you will build the function while you are delivering.

4. **Establish a cross-functional team**: Data operations require collaboration across different areas of expertise. Form a team that includes data engineers, data scientists, IT professionals, and business analysts. Ensure there is a clear understanding of roles and responsibilities. The most successful data operations teams I have led came from various parts of the company and formed a starter team together. The domain expertise from the business helped us gain momentum and deliver impactful solutions quickly. Outside hires came second, and that sequencing was critical to our early success.

5. **Invest in the right tools and technologies**: Choose tools and technologies that support data operations principles such as automation, version control, **continuous integration/continuous deployment (CI/CD)**, and monitoring. Look for solutions that integrate well with your existing systems. You don't need fancy tools to get started, but you may want to consider investing in more advanced tooling as you scale your team.

6. **Implement agile and lean methodologies**: Adopt agile and lean methodologies to streamline processes. This includes iterative development, sprints, stand-ups, and retrospectives to ensure continuous improvement. In most cases, you will need to move quickly. Prioritization will be key. Develop a methodology or triage process to support your agile processes.

7. **Automate data pipelines**: Automate as much of the data pipeline as possible, from data collection and processing to analysis and reporting. Automation reduces manual errors and frees up time for more strategic work. As your team becomes intimate with the data environment, you will organically identify opportunities for automation. Keep this logged so that when there are times between crises, your team can focus on these longer-term impacts. You may also consider splitting your team into crisis management and long-term automation to support the variation in need.

8. **Ensure data quality and governance**: Implement robust data quality checks and governance policies. This includes data validation, cleansing, and ensuring compliance with data privacy and protection regulations. Work very closely with your data governance leader.

9. **Foster a culture of collaboration and experimentation**: Encourage open communication and collaboration between different teams. Create an environment where experimentation and innovation are valued. Celebrate collaboration in meetings to encourage this culture.

10. **Regularly monitor, measure, and optimize**: Continuously monitor the performance of your data operations function. Use metrics and KPIs to measure success and identify areas for improvement. Make these metrics and KPIs outwardly available. Transparency is key.

11. **Train and develop skills**: Invest in training and development programs to ensure your team has the necessary skills and knowledge. This includes both technical skills and soft skills such as collaboration and problem-solving. I highly recommend rotating key talent into and out of this team. Spending time in data operations will expand their knowledge of how data is moving through the company and where the challenges are with first-hand experience. This perspective is valuable and will be a great asset for your high-potential leaders to gain.

12. **Align with business goals**: Ensure that your data operations initiatives are closely aligned with broader business goals and objectives. This helps in demonstrating the value of data operations to the organization, and focusing efforts on overall company priorities will enable transformations to be even more impactful. This provides higher ROI on larger investments, which is a great way for your data organization at large to show impact.

13. **Feedback and iteration**: Never forget that feedback is a gift. Create mechanisms for feedback from end users and stakeholders. Use this feedback for iterative improvements. Be willing and able to evolve as needs change.

Conclusion

Building an optimal data operations function is a continuous process that evolves with the changing needs of the organization and advancements in technology. It requires a commitment to best practices, ongoing learning, and adapting to new challenges and opportunities. In this chapter, you have learned the following:

1. The importance of data operations, including why it is required for building successful data solutions

2. How to design a data operations function

3. Specific needs when it comes to implementation

4. How to design a data operations solution

By understanding how to run the operations of a data organization, your team will be able to support a very broad capability with impact, including the running of primary data management, data warehouses, data lakes, and other authorized provisioning points managed by the data organization. This entire capability is the power by which all other data governance functions are running. Ensure you build and treat your data operations team accordingly. Without it, your team will not have the visible impact it needs to ensure executive support is achieved and grows.

Part 3:
Building Trust through Value-Based Delivery

In this part, we will take all we have learned from *Parts 1* and *2* and translate it into a successful program launch. In later chapters in this part, you will learn additional techniques to accelerate and optimize outcomes that your business stakeholders will value and understand. Finally, we will walk you through the virtuous cycles to help you win with velocity.

This part contains the following chapters:

- *Chapter 12, Launch Powerfully*
- *Chapter 13, Delivering Quick Wins with Impact*
- *Chapter 14, Data Automation for Impact and More Powerful Results*
- *Chapter 15, Adoption That Drives Business Results*
- *Chapter 16, Delivering Trusted Results with Outcomes That Matter*

12
Launch Powerfully

Any good data governance program can quickly lose impact if not launched properly. Even with a clear purpose, milestones, and great execution, the approach to launch will determine the success (or failure) of the program. The importance of the launch cannot be underscored enough. As we embark on *Part 3* of this book, we will walk through how to create simple and strong core messaging to engage and clearly articulate to the stakeholder community what and how the delivery will be accomplished. Then, I will lead you through the creation of a launch plan, a design of feedback loops to ensure continuous improvement, and finally, how to report on an ongoing basis for impact.

The next five chapters, which together make up *Part 3* of this book, take all the knowledge from the last 11 chapters and guide you through translating the information into a true data governance transformation. Be mindful that understanding the capabilities outlined to this point in this book is one thing, but turning the information into a successful data governance transformational program is another. Some of the best technical data governance leaders struggle with this translation into impact, because "being technical" is not enough. It is the basic requirement to be a data expert. However, without the ability to bring others along the journey with you, and translate it into impactful business outcomes, you will not be successful.

As you embark on your journey to launch a data governance transformation, it's so important that you get the early launch plan right. The focus of this chapter will walk you through this critical step. As a data leader, or a business leader, or if you are sponsoring a data leader, it's your job to ensure that the business deeply understands, is bought into, and will stand behind the data transformation for the duration of the program. Given that most data governance transformations take anywhere between 24 and 36 months, getting the entirety of the company to stand behind you for the long haul is of utmost importance. Some key capabilities, such as the primary data of management, data operations, and target architecture, will take far longer to deliver on the return on investment than others. Therefore, it is important to launch powerfully, which includes delivering quick wins (which we will dig into in *Chapter 13*).

The data leader, along with their executive sponsor, should craft a prolific future state vision that allows the company to visualize what the future will be like once a data governance transformation has been completed. As a data professional, you know that data work is never done. Much like getting into shape after a long period without exercise, there is a hill to climb. However, once you've climbed the hill, you can't stop exercising. No, you must keep exercising to maintain your level of fitness.

The same is true for data. You will need to deliver on a transformation (or implementation) to drive the capabilities outlined in *Chapters 6* to *11* into your company's DNA. Not just once, but in a sustainable way. This is the "getting into shape" part of the program. Beyond the transformation, you will maintain the company's level of "data fitness" through ongoing data practice, much like you would maintain a level of physical fitness. Your company should not be the same after you deliver your transformation.

We will cover the following main topics in this chapter:

- Assessing readiness for launch
- Simple and strong core messaging
- Executing a comprehensive communication strategy for data strategy deployment
- Designing feedback loops
- Setting and meeting expectations for program launch

Assessing readiness for launch

Before you prepare to launch, you need to pause and assess the current state. No, I don't mean from a data management maturity perspective, but the business readiness. If you head into your launch plan assuming that the business is more ready to change than you assessed it to be, you will face resistance and will be frustrated early. If you underappreciate the readiness, you might find yourself selling it on a transformation it is already bought into. This can be equally as bad. If the business isn't ready, you might be pushing for change they don't think they need. If it is beyond ready, you'll be talking about change when they are already wanting to see the change happening. You lose credibility and support in both scenarios. That's why assessing the readiness is so important.

The degree to what you need to assess has several factors to consider:

- Do you have an established data function?
- How trusted is your data by all levels of the company?
- Do you have core capabilities in production?
- What is your maturity score, and is it accurately reflecting your company's state of data maturity?
- Do you have an identified data leader? Are they positioned appropriately and supported to deliver a large-scale transformation?

Performing the assessment

To help you assess how ready your organization is for a data governance transformation, let's spend a moment reflecting upon the state of your organization. Plot the answers to the preceding questions here, so you can come back to reference them as we work through this chapter together on the following charts. The answers to these five questions do not necessarily mean your company is not ready—they are simply indicators as to the approach you need to take as you prepare to launch powerfully.

Established data function

The first factor—the existence and maturity of your data function—is a consideration but any answer is not a deal breaker. If you have an established data function, it is a consideration but having one isn't a barrier to get started. You can use the lack of a central function to drive investment in one, or to drive centralization if needed. If there is a central function already in place, you may be able to move faster to drive transformation. Therefore, when it comes to establishing your transformational program, having the team in place will help you to get down the path of transformation faster.

Figure 12.1 – Established data function

Highly trusted data

No one will argue with you, but having trusted data is no longer a *nice to have* but a requirement for any company. When you have high trust in data, it is a signal that the executive team not only relies on data for business decisions but also believes that the data they used to make those decisions is reliable. Not having trust in data shows up in a number of ways, including inconsistent information at the executive level, questions about the validity of the information, a clear lack of capabilities, data, and data quality, and ultimately, low trust in the data function.

When trust is low, painting a picture of a world where trust in data is not the exception but the norm can be very compelling. A great and simple use case is to ask your executive team which metrics (KPIs or OKRs) they use to measure the success of the company. Then ask how confident they are in the numbers. Is the executive team aligned that these metrics are correct and reliable? Do you trust them?

Most companies will tell you that they do not have alignment in the most critical metrics. Or, they will say they are confident in the number their team is responsible for but not others. This signals a low trust in data and can be a great use case to start with.

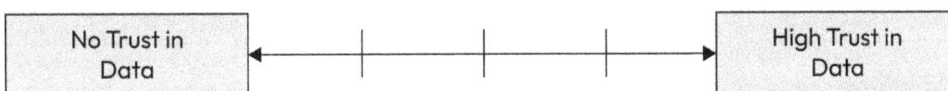

Figure 12.2 – Trust in data

Established capabilities

The next factor to consider as you are assessing the state of established capabilities is the fitness of your established capabilities in place prior to launching a data transformation. Prior to launch, assess the state of established data governance capabilities. Regardless of centralization, does your organization have councils, stewardship in place, Meta, date of management, capabilities, data, quality, primary data of management, or data operations? If yes, to what extent are these capabilities mature and available for use across the organization? Are they highly adopted? If yes, then you have a leg up on launching your program. Simply having these capabilities gets you off to a strong start in transforming the way in which they are utilized in support of strong data enablement.

However, not having established data management capabilities does not prevent you from launching a program. It's simply means that you need to build the capabilities as you transform the organization at large. As with the preceding factors, neither strong nor weak data governance capabilities will prevent you from launching powerfully; it is simply something to be aware of as you determine the degree of transformation that is required for your company.

Figure 12.3 – Core capabilities

Data management maturity

As we discussed in *Chapter 4*, you should use your data management maturity scores to bring awareness of the state of data governance at your company. A lower data management maturity score can help drive transparency and awareness to your executives regarding the true, unbiased state of data capabilities. This is a purer measure of the state of your organization versus simply assessing the existence of capabilities and the previous factor because data management maturity takes into consideration how embedded these capabilities are in day-to-day operations.

If you have a high data management maturity score, meaning a level of 4 or 5, it is unlikely that you need to do a significant data management transformation enterprise-wide. It may mean that you have focused pockets of improvement to deliver. Most companies remain somewhere between a 3 and a 3.5 on the data management maturity scale, although it varies based on industry. Financial services and healthcare, for example, tend to be more mature than other industries. The reason for this is the more intensive regulation around the control and protection of data.

Figure 12.4 – Data management maturity

Strong leadership

Finally, assess the state of your data leadership. Do you have a chief data and analytics officer? Do you have an executive sponsor? Do you have a path to secure ongoing funding? Do you have the support of your C-suite? If you do not have these things, gathering support to drive a data transformation will be very difficult. You may need to select a smaller program or project to focus on to drive credibility and visibility at the most senior levels of your organization as a first step. However, if you are fortunate enough to have senior leaders supporting you with funding in place or the opportunity to secure funding for a data transformation, then you are in a great position to launch a powerful data management transformation for your company. Most chief data and analytics officers would greatly desire to have this kind of support.

If you do not have executive support, there is one thing you can do to start to gain it. That is to socialize your vision (which we will cover here in a moment) and your corresponding plan. By going through the state of the union and helping to educate your executives one by one, you will help to open their eyes as to what the company is experiencing today because it is not mature.

My suspicion, having led this type of effort many times over, is that simply educating your executives and helping them see the truth about the state of the union will help you gain support. It may take time, but one by one, these conversations will help you build awareness that you need to launch powerfully.

Figure 12.5 – Data leadership

Common baseline

Most companies start their data journey with something like this:

- Some data teams scattered throughout the company (some may be more mature than others, but no consistency)

- Some trust in information, usually more in finance, due to financial regulations supporting regulatory and financial reporting

- Some capabilities, usually more manual; low consistency enterprise-wide

- Resulting data maturity isn't zero, but it's on the lower side due to the inconsistency and fragmentation of efforts

- There is a data leader appointed (usually one of the reasons a data transformation is possible, as they will champion it), but staffing and formalization are needed

Together, this becomes a snapshot view of your "As-Is" state of the union. The plot lines for the exercise may look like this:

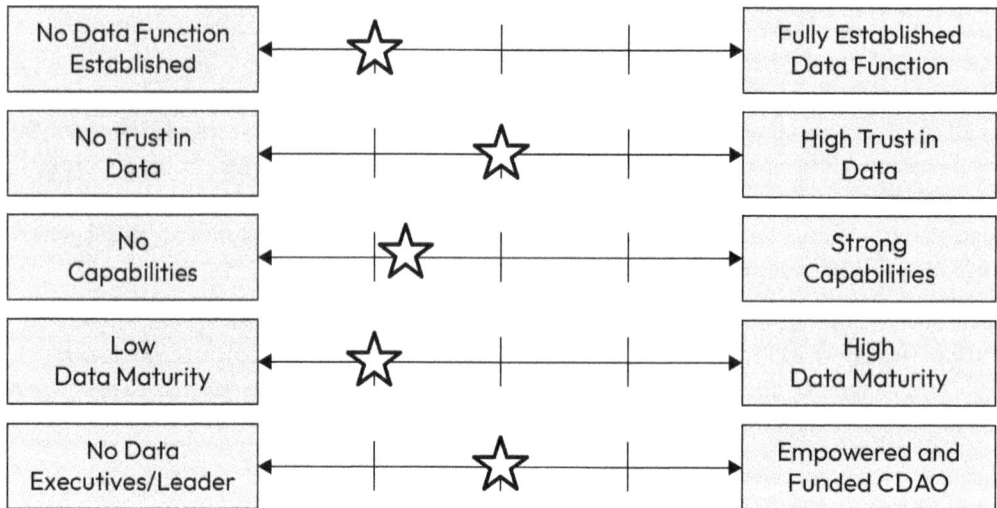

No Data Function Established	⟷ ☆			Fully Established Data Function
No Trust in Data	⟷ ☆			High Trust in Data
No Capabilities	⟷☆			Strong Capabilities
Low Data Maturity	⟷ ☆			High Data Maturity
No Data Executives/Leader	⟷ ☆			Empowered and Funded CDAO

Figure 12.6 – As-Is example

Now, you are ready to get started in crafting your messaging. These five assessment criteria will inform *how* you message the transformation, so that you can launch powerfully.

Simple and strong core messaging

As you embark on a formal data governance transformation, it is of utmost importance that you make your messaging simple and understandable to the masses. One great way to do this is to think about what life will be like once you've delivered. A great way to do this is to start by outlining your *as is* versus your *to be* state. I've seen this work well in a number of companies and as a clear way to depict the variance between before and after. This should be done in several ways, but first and foremost, it should be done from a business perspective.

For example, if it takes 18 days to complete a quote for a customer in the current state but, in the future state, we expect it to only take 8 hours, you should define this for the user. Show them and tell them *how* you're going to get there:

- Are you going to implement a new system?
- Are you going to automate processes?
- Are you going to remove redundant processes?

- Are you going to create new models?

- Maybe it's even a combination of all of the above

Ultimately, the more you can define the experience that *will be* compared to the experience *that is*, the better chances you will have to gain business support and be able to launch your transformation program powerfully.

Crafting a compelling vision

Before you start to socialize the broader plan to transform the company's use of data, you need to take the time to create a compelling view of the future. This is the time to craft an imagined future for your company. What will the company be like? How will it operate? What will the lived experience for employees, customers, and stakeholders be? What will they be able to do in that future state that they can't do today? What won't they have to do?

This is much more art than science in that it is your opportunity to really dream about the future state you and your team will create. It's the time to let the technical components sit aside and tap into the emotional parts of data. How will that future state feel?

Example

One of my very favorite data transformations began as a side project. There was a difficult reporting process that required consistency and primary data to allow for some of the most complicated regulatory reporting to occur. We started out by finding a couple of really good examples of what it took in the present state to complete this regulatory required reporting process. By fully understanding the efforts that it took to do large scale enterprise reporting, we were able to identify that there were hundreds of people manually touching the data in order to create a single report. A large amount of the manual intervention was in rationalizing data across systems that didn't align systematically. It required manual intervention.

We were able to craft a powerful vision that gave the company clarity around what a future state could be if we implemented common reference data and published the reference data for all systems to consume. Aligning the company to these common reference status sets enabled the inconsistencies to be remediated. It allowed for a dramatically simplified and much more automated process to support this data aggregation work across the organization at large. By showing this use case across the company to several executives, including the chief financial officer, the chief risk officer, and the chief data officer, we were able to get there rather easily.

The hardest part was making the story so crystal clear that anyone who heard it would understand and immediately support it moving forward. This is the way to launch powerfully. Bring clarity to your baseline so that everyone has a common understanding and will support you moving forward. In this example, the hardest decision became where the funding was going to come from—not whether we were going to get funding but where from. With three C-Suite executives supporting us, it was a big win.

Remember, the vision statement is intended to be a lofty long-term view. It is meant to be inspiring and high-level. A few examples follow:

1. Harmoniously orchestrate our disparate data sources, transforming siloed whispers into a powerful chorus of actionable insights, propelling us toward data-driven decisions at every level.

2. Empower every employee with self-service access to curated, trustworthy data, igniting a culture of data-driven problem-solving and innovation across the entire organization.

3. Leverage AI and predictive analytics to shift from reacting to trends to predicting them, anticipating market shifts, optimizing resource allocation, and navigating business landscapes with confidence.

4. Transform operational data into a potent elixir of efficiency, streamlining processes, reducing waste, and maximizing ROI through automated workflows and real-time insights.

5. Break down barriers between departments, democratize access to data, foster cross-functional collaboration, and harness collective intelligence for game-changing outcomes.

6. Craft a personalized journey for every customer, weaving data-driven insights into every touchpoint, exceeding expectations and building lasting loyalty.

7. Mine the wisdom hidden within historical data to anticipate and mitigate potential risks, building a resilient and agile organization prepared for any challenge.

8. Guide our environmental and social impact with purpose, using data to optimize resource consumption, minimize waste, and drive responsible growth for a sustainable future.

9. Transform data into a strategic weapon, uncovering market opportunities, outmaneuvering rivals, and establishing a dominant position in an ever-evolving marketplace.

10. Empower a data-driven culture, where every decision is informed by insights, every employee champions data literacy, and data fuels our relentless pursuit of excellence.

As Is versus To Be (aka current versus future state)

As you bring the vision to life, the As Is versus To Be state will bring that vision to a more grounded future state. Creating a specific and distilled view of what the difference is between the current state and the future state is a critical next step in clearly communicating the reason why change is needed. Crystalizing the future opportunity into a simple story that can describe the future, further building on the compelling vision you have defined, helps fuel the motivation that is required to bring your company along on the journey to transform. This will help build understanding and also serve as a backdrop for everything that you will do to drive to the imagined future.

By effectively defining this As Is versus To Be state view, you will be bringing to life the vision created. This will help further define exactly what is working as well. Maybe there are some components that are working well that you can acknowledge and highlight. This will make your imagined future credible and believable. One risk, especially if you are new to the organization, is that stakeholders assume (perhaps incorrectly) that you haven't taken enough time to understand the specific nuances of the company. By being specific in your As Is state, you will be able to further gain credibility by acknowledging what works well today that can be built on.

I recommend you start with two one-page views of the As-Is versus To-Be view:

1.   Describe succinctly what the current state is in a few bullets (e.g., it takes days to weeks for analysts to find the data they need to create insights) versus the future state (e.g., analysts will be able to find certified data sets in an enterprise data catalog, enabling insights to be produced in hours versus months)

2.   Visually depict what this will look like (e.g., a marketecture view) to help *show* rather than *tell* what the future will look like:

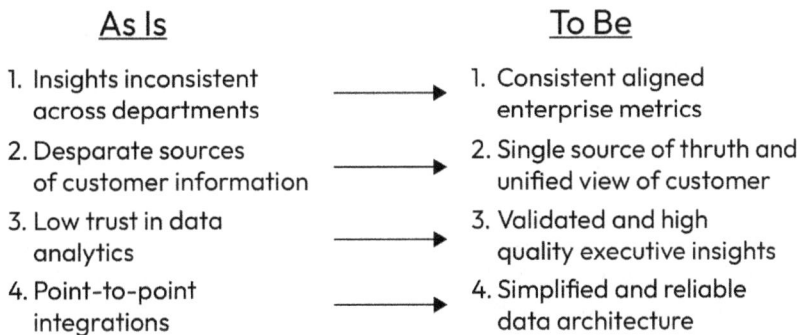

As Is

1. Insights inconsistent across departments

2. Desparate sources of customer information

3. Low trust in data analytics

4. Point-to-point integrations

To Be

1. Consistent aligned enterprise metrics

2. Single source of thruth and unified view of customer

3. Validated and high quality executive insights

4. Simplified and reliable data architecture

Figure 12.7 – As is versus To be concept

By leveraging both a succinct bullet approach for one page and a visual depiction for the second page, you cover your bases for visual versus verbal learners. If you are challenged to write it this crisply, start with a longer view and work toward a concise story. Ultimately, if you can't describe it this succinctly, you may struggle to get buy in. Most executives need a clear path to the outcome, and by keeping your future state crisp, your executive team will understand why this matters quickly. If you can't describe the outcome briefly, you may not be ready to drive the future.

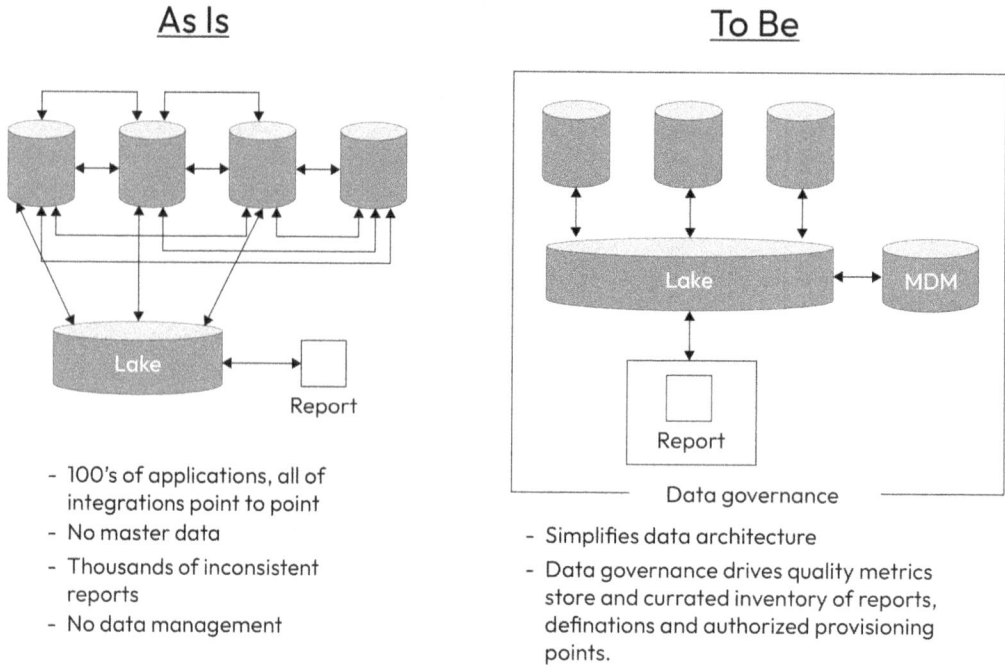

As Is

- 100's of applications, all of integrations point to point
- No master data
- Thousands of inconsistent reports
- No data management

To Be

Data governance

- Simplifies data architecture
- Data governance drives quality metrics store and currated inventory of reports, definations and authorized provisioning points.

Figure 12.8 – As is versus To be marketecture

To get to this target state and to outline the appropriate To Be state for your organization, you will need to leverage the work outlined in *Chapters 1* to *5*. You will also need to have a good understanding of the company's current state and a clear understanding of what needs to happen in order to define this view appropriately. This is one of the hardest steps in preparing to launch your transformation—to translate the needs of your company into the transformation that is needed. It will be unique to your particular situation and company. It will help to gather input from stakeholders, executives, and best practices from other companies, but ultimately, your strategy is for your company.

Getting crisp with your messaging

As you prepare to launch your strategy, you will need to take the work from *Chapters 1* to *5* distilled into a strategy and craft it into a crisp message that will resonate with your stakeholders. You should expect that different stakeholders will want different levels of detail. The first step in defining great messaging for launch is to determine which audiences you will need to message to, and what kinds of information they will need:

- **Individual Contributors/Front Line Managers**: Will need detailed information such as project plans and specific tasks assigned to individuals

- **Middle and Upper Management**: Will need a more aggregated and strategic view, as well as key milestones and aligned outcomes

- **C-Suite and Board of Directors**: Will need a highly summarized outcome-oriented plan showing what the company will achieve or experience as a result of this work

To meet the needs of these various audiences, you will need to write a few different types of strategic messaging material. However, one of the best recommendations I can offer, is to start with a *North Star* or strategic memo. This memo can not only serve as the backdrop for all that you will do but also shows any audience that you have a well-thought-out plan. I recommend you aim to keep this memo under 10 pages. It will force you to go into enough detail to explain what you will deliver, why, and how you will measure success without becoming overly verbose.

Writing a narrative memo

As mentioned, one of the best ways to crystalize your strategy is to simply write it. It sounds obvious, but many executives fail to move from pictures into a full description of the strategy. A memo is great for two reasons: it helps you fully crystalize your strategy and it defines the future state in a very specific way. It forces you to think through the details and refine the messaging clearly. In a picture or a slide, you have more liberty to skirt the details, whereas in a narrative, you are forced to be more thoughtful and specific.

Within the North Star strategy, you should cover three key areas: why there is a need to change, what will be changed, and how the company will get there. I recommend that you really take the opportunity to think through this as it will set the tone for the next few years of work; however, you should set an expectation that the document is living and will be updated regularly (at least annually) to ensure it continues to enable the company's strategy.

- **Why the company needs to change**:

  - What is missing from the current state?

  - What is the state of maturity?

  - What can the company not do today because of the current state?

  - What will the company be able to do in the future, once the strategy is delivered?

- **What will be changed**:

  - What capabilities will be deployed?

  - What will stay the same?

  - What will be enhanced or enriched?

  - What will be retired or decommissioned?

- **How you will get there**:

  - How will we get there?

  - How will the employees experience this change?

  - What are the key milestones? How will you deliver against them?

- **Who will be involved**:

  - Who from the C-Suite will need to support the strategy?

  - Who will be plugged in? When? How?

  - Who will not need to be a part of the strategy?

As you draft out the strategy memo for your company, iterate. Ask for feedback while you are drafting. I recommend identifying a few key supportive executives to contribute to the memo. This tip will enable you to enter into your strategy launch in partnership with your stakeholders instead of singularly attempting to change the company. You now have partners in the mission by bringing them into the drafting with you.

Design based on outcomes

A good business project starts with the end in mind. This means fast-forwarding in time and really thinking about what life will be like once you deliver on your program. You must start with your company's strategy, and the divisional strategies focused on delivering against the company's strategy. Your work must support and enable the strategy. Spend time outlining specifically what the company is aiming to deliver, and how your work supports that at a granular level. Is the company focusing on the operating margin? Show how your team's work is creating margin through cost savings activities. Be clear about *how*. Some key areas you may focus on are as follows:

- Driving product innovation or efficiency

- Increasing revenue

- Improving operational efficiency and/or reducing expenses

- Measurable improvement in customer satisfaction or experience

- Reducing risk to the business

By framing the work in your transformation into these categories and translating this into your North Star, you will help the business understand why what your team delivers is important to them and, therefore, their success.

One of the biggest risks for failure is to invest in programs or capabilities that do not clearly link to business outcomes. If the business does not clearly understand why the work you are leading for the company translates into impact for them, they won't support you. Furthermore, they could argue against you. Time, money, and resources are all finite. If you can't clearly articulate what you are doing in terms that impact their ability to be successful, you won't be successful.

It is easy to over rotate on operational efficiency and risk mitigation. These are important parts of your duty to the company. However, the more you can translate the work of the data office to revenue, the more successful you will be. At times, this will be a few steps removed, and that is okay. However, do not make the mistake of failing to connect to revenue, even if a step removed.

Helpful hint
As you work through the drafting to launch your data strategy, be sure to focus deeply on translating into business terms. Have a non-data professional read your strategy. Have them highlight any terms that are not explained or translated into business outcomes. By dropping the *data* terminology, you will ensure your data strategy is written for maximum impact.

Creating a repeatable process

As you prepare your launch plan, ensure you are prepared to educate wide and deep into the organization. You should plan to go on a roadshow-type communication tour, sharing the vision, the plan, and what the future will be. Tell them, tell them what you told them, then tell them again. You will need to leverage several types of communication mechanisms to ensure you have enterprise-wide understanding:

- **Memo**: Ensure your data strategy memo is published and available for review broadly. Transparency is a big benefit to launching powerfully.

- **Plan**: Build a plan to show what you will deliver and when. Be specific about what the stakeholders will be able to do at each release or publication, so they can digest what they can expect along the way (not just at the end).

- **Updates**: Plan out how you will update your stakeholder communities along the journey. You will need different updates for the board versus individuals directly working on the data strategy. Define what they will be upfront so that you can tell your stakeholders what they can expect from you.

- **Status reports**: Define what status reports will need to look like. Define how you will share them. Consider live verbal updates versus written async updates, based on your company's culture and preference. Do not shy away from making these open to a broad audience. Transparency builds trust (especially when it's *not* good news). If your stakeholders know they can trust you to share hard news, they will know they can trust the positive news too.

- **Budgets**: Although not relevant for all audiences, you should have a detailed budget that you use to measure financial aspects of your data strategy deployment.

- **KPIs and success measures**: Define how you will measure success. A best practice is to publish a scorecard that can show progress over time. Define what the measures are, and how they are calculated. Again, transparency is key, since you will be publishing your own metrics of success.

Remember, the entire data team and sponsors are all evangelists for the data strategy and corresponding implementation plan. Bring positive energy to every forum. When you are excited about the strategy and future of the company's use of data, others will be too.

Designing feedback loops

As you launch (not after), define how you will improve along your journey. You will only get better at delivering great outcomes if you establish routes for continuous improvement, and that includes a focus on feedback loops. As you launch, you should explain to all stakeholders (executives, managers, and individual contributors) how they can provide input, and encourage them to do so. If they see something that can be better, encourage them to say something.

You may want to establish a few options for this:

- **Verbal feedback through forums**: Stand up forums for individuals to learn about the delivery of your strategy. You may need a few different forums for various audiences. Leverage your Enterprise Data Governance Council or committee to provide updates to your executive stakeholders. You may also want to stand up a broader townhall-style forum to distribute verbal updates to larger audiences.

- **Formal feedback through surveys**: Periodically throughout your data strategy implementation, you may want to request formal feedback. A great way to do this for a wide audience is through the use of surveys. If you are going to request written feedback from a wide audience, you should define what you are going to do with the feedback. I recommend committing to share the feedback, good or bad, to your stakeholders.

- **Written feedback through workflows**: If your organization uses a workflow tool, you may opt to allow feedback to be continuously submitted for consideration by the data team. This allows freer flowing information during the implementation but requires your team to manage the workflow. Depending on the degree of change, you may consider this option for larger transformations that are moving quickly so you can adjust quickly.

As you work together with your stakeholders to share updates, listen for input, and adapt accordingly, you will ensure the stakeholders continue to gain value from the transformation that you are delivering through implementing your data strategy. By failing to create feedback loops and incorporate appropriate feedback as you deliver your strategy, you risk delivering outcomes that do not serve your company.

Setting and meeting expectations in the program launch

As you launch your program, you should define what success is going to look and feel like to your stakeholders. Define clearly what they can expect from you and when. As you deliver against your commitments to your stakeholders, make sure you tell them what has happened, in addition to showing them. There are several ways you can show progress throughout your program. This will help your stakeholders see and be reminded of progress. With each milestone, issue some kind of informational messaging:

- **Micro training**: Small individual training (either live or pre-recorded videos) showing what can be done now that the release has occurred.

- **Measured results**: Show the results in terms of KPIs or other metrics. Publish the information in an easy-to-access-and-consume mechanism such as a dashboard or internal website.

- **Before versus now**: Show what can be done now that couldn't be done before. Bonus: show what will be able to do in future releases to keep the excitement up among your stakeholders.

Here is one final suggestion. As you plan your launch meetings, don't wait to deliver. Get started now, and have a win already delivered since you started your strategy to show that you are not waiting to make an impact—the impact is already happening. Deliver the win ASAP, and announce it in your launch meetings. This will show the stakeholder community that you are anxious to deliver and you're not waiting to make a difference. This is a great way to launch powerfully, and build immediate trust in your data strategy delivery.

Conclusion

As you learned in this chapter, launching powerfully is the best way to create momentum in your company's data transformation. By moving quickly and comprehensively, and by anchoring in the maturity assessment (as covered in *Chapter 4*), you will have a firm foundation by which to generate significant impact to your organization. In this chapter, we covered the basics of a successful program launch, including the following:

1. How to speak clearly and in business terminology

2. How to design communication patterns leading up to and at launch

3. Building a launch plan

4. Creating feedback loops to gather inputs

5. Incorporating feedback for even more powerful messaging

In the next chapter, I will walk you through how to identify and construct quick wins to help build velocity to your data transformation's launch, so that you can gain the support and interest of your organization quickly and with impact. These two chapters build on each other to help you build tremendous credibility and support enterprise-wide. Be bold in how you launch your transformation, take appropriate credit for your team's impact, and deliver tremendous results iteratively to generate support along the way.

13
Delivering Quick Wins with Impact

As you launch your data transformation program, your team will quickly and consistently deliver results. Because of the nature of data governance, and skeptics of the practice of data translating into real, measurable results, you will need to shorten the time to first value as much as possible, and crisply and consistently show progress. In this chapter, I will walk you through how to create momentum with quick wins, how to communicate these wins effectively to and with the business, and how to ensure the business stakeholders understand how your results translate into their success.

In my experience, data leaders who bet exclusively on big, transformational platforms often lose stakeholder interest by the time their results are realized. You can't wait until your platforms or capabilities are launched to claim victory. In my experience, big-bang solutions are critical, but they can't be everything. No stakeholder group or company will wait 18-24 months to see results on their data investments. Results have to happen in bite-sized moments while you simultaneously deliver incremental results.

According to Deloitte's research (see the *Further reading* section at the end of this chapter), the average tenure of a chief data and analytics officer is approximately two and a half years, compared to other C-suite executives' average tenure of approximately five years. Because of this, it is critical that you show you can deliver sustainable, measurable success. Your success in the role depends on it. As you begin with this pressure in mind, do not let it paralyze you, but rather, use it for fuel. Be mindful that you must consistently show up, every day, and demonstrate impact.

First things first, you will need to determine what constitutes a "quick win." What will that mean? What's worthwhile for your stakeholders versus what is important to you? I recommend you start by answering these questions for you and your team. Hiring is an example of something you will need to do but it isn't a "win" in the eyes of your stakeholders. Fixing a long-standing data quality issue that is causing executive-level metric errors, however, is a win that you should celebrate and communicate. So, what does it take to identify a quick win? We'll start there.

This chapter covers the following topics:

- Finding quick wins
- Why policies, standards, and procedures can generate buzz
- Data ownership
- Applying a product mindset to data capabilities
- Building momentum through a continuous delivery model

Finding quick wins

As you were coming up to speed and meeting with your initial stakeholders, as we went through in *Chapter 2*, you listened to stakeholders' concerns, what was going well, and what wasn't going well, and you started to better understand what their needs were. Now is the time to work with them to develop the priority list of what they need now, and what they need in the long term. This is where you refine that priority list of needs with your team and with stakeholder groups so that you can make a big impact in your organization.

Identifying areas of need

As you continue to build these relationships, a key step in building trust is delivering what you said you would. As you met with stakeholders, you should have captured the list of their needs. In raw form, it might look something like this:

Sales	Marketing	Finance	Support
• Multiple versions of a customer • Unable to see the full history of transactions • Slow reporting at the end of the quarter • Inconsistent measurement of revenue by product	• Thousands of failed emails per campaign • Bad mailing addresses increase our costs • Unable to measure contribution to sales revenue	• Very manual aggregation for financial reporting purposes due to a lack of standardized data • Inability to improve quality – lack of ownership	• Can't see what a customer has purchased to determine what support they should have • Multiple versions of a customer

Table 13.1 - A sample of identified issues through stakeholder interviews

These are just a few examples of what you might have heard when speaking with your stakeholders. You could have dozens of issues identified that you heard during your listening tour. Write them all out by domain, even repeats across groups. Next, you should do the following:

- Share the individual lists back to the individuals you met with. A simple, "thank you for meeting me, this is what I heard, did I miss anything?" can be super helpful. It may spark new ideas and/or clarify anything you didn't capture correctly.

- Meet with your team, share the lists with them, and share what you heard. Ask the team for input. You may find they are aware of other issues that exist (of any size or scale) that you can add to the list.

Once you've landed on a stable list of current issues or missing capabilities that are impacting the business and/or back office functions from their success, the next step is to look at what exists across groups and what exists in individual groups. This means looking for common themes, but also where there are variances so that you can determine what needs to be done for multiple stakeholders, and what serves only a single group.

Rationalizing the list

As you review the list, you will see the themes. I have highlighted two consistent themes in the short example below for reference. Note, in one example, the wording is the same so it is easy to identify, but the second issue is not exactly worded the same. This is intentional. You must be well versed in the list. Simply having the list is not enough. You have to know the content well. The issue with consistent language would be picked up using matching logic in a spreadsheet (if you have a long list) but the other would not be. This is to provide an example of why it's important to be intimate with the list.

Sales	Marketing	Finance	Support
• Multiple versions of a customer	• Thousands of failed emails per campaign	• Very manual aggregation for financial reporting purposes due to lack of standardized data	• Can't see what a customer has purchased to determine what support they should have
• Unable to see full history of transactions	• Bad mailing addresses increase our cost		
• Slow reporting at quarter end	• Unable to measure contribution to sales revenue	• Inability to improve quality - lack of ownership	• Multiple versions of a customer
• Inconsistent measurement of revenue by product			

Figure 13.1 – Identified common issues across divisions

Helpful Hint

You may be shedding light on the commonality across groups for your stakeholders simply by creating this list. Consider sharing the full list with your stakeholders so they can see what issues other groups are struggling with. They may not realize other groups have the same issues they do (e.g., the preceding example regarding the history of transactions – this is the same issue as on the right, just phrased differently. It requires the same solution, but without data expertise, this connection might not be made). This can energize your stakeholder community to come together and work with you and one another.

You may want to re-format the list so that it is based on issues and then identify which groups are impacted by the issue, like this:

Issue	Sales	Marketing	Finance	Support
Multiple versions of a customer	X			X
Unable to see the full history of transactions (to determine historical purchases and to evaluate appropriate support levels)	X			X
Slow reporting at the end of the quarter	X			
Inconsistent measurement of revenue by product	X		X	
Thousands of failed emails per campaign		X		
Bad mailing addresses increase the cost per campaign		X		
Unable to measure marketing contribution to sales pipeline/revenue generated		X		
Very manual aggregation for financial reporting purposes due to a lack of standardized data			X	
Inability to improve the quality of data due to lack of ownership			X	

Table 13.2 - Identified common issues across divisions, reformatted

From this view, you should seek to identify which of these issues could be solved, at least in a meaningful way, in the short term. The idea isn't to necessarily solve all problems immediately, or completely, but to show meaningful progress for the stakeholders in a short time horizon. By solving quick wins, you drive trust with stakeholders that you can make meaningful change happen for them. This will demonstrate near-term urgency in service of a long-term, sustainable view.

Prioritizing the list

Now that you have the list, the next step in the process is to determine what you should focus on, and in what order. There are a few questions you and your team should ask to help prioritize the focus:

1. What is the impact of solving each issue?

2. How will you measure success? Time saved? Revenue generated? Cost avoidance? How will you quantify the impact?

3. What is the urgency?

4. What could be done now to solve an urgent issue versus what needs to be done more sustainably long term? Is it worth it to solve part of the issue now?

5. Do you have the people you need to solve the issue? Expertise?

Example – unable to see purchase history by customer

Scenario: In this example, the company sells a subscription product with add-on support services.

Needs for sales: Sales professionals need to be able to see what a customer has purchased so they can 1) sell them additional, complementary products and services and 2) know what to renew for future years. Without this information, the sales team is left asking the customer, "What have you purchased?" This can lead to a poor customer experience and a loss of revenue opportunity for renewal products. Customers are often not renewed, leading to attrition of the revenue.

Needs for customer success: Customer success agents are unable to see what customers have purchased, so they don't know whether a customer is entitled to a particular level of support when they call the call center. They have to trust the customer at their word and have no way to verify their eligibility for the services. This leads to the assumption of overserving the customer but at the expense of revenue.

Prioritization framework

Now that we've captured the list, let's define how to build a framework to prioritize the list. Consider the following:

- **The impact of solving issues on the business**: Both sales and service are risking a leakage of revenue, either in upsell or resell opportunities for sales, and for add-on services/support for customer success. Additionally, we may be over-servicing customers without adequately charging them for the services they need, increasing our cost to serve by over-serving customers.

- **How to measure success and impact**: Put yourself in the position of the business. Ask yourself the following questions: What will the business be able to do when this problem is addressed that they can't have or experience today? How will I measure that? In this example, revenue is a result of this problem, as well as over-providing services, which increases the cost per customer for services because we are providing services to customers (at least at increased levels) than they are entitled to. One measure is the percentage of revenue renewed, another is the cost to serve per customer, and the last, finally, is attrition.

- **Urgency**: Revenue leakage and costs to serve are usually pretty critical items for management. It is safe to assume sales, service, and executive management would be very interested in solving this issue with a high degree of urgency.

- **Immediate work versus long-term work**: In this step, you and your team should brainstorm ways to approach this issue both in the very short term, but also in a long-term and sustainable way. What is something you could do today, this week, this year?

- **Resourcing**: What investment might you need to complete this short- and long-term project? Do you have anything available at your disposal today, by reprioritizing or creating a stretch assignment for someone on your team? Do you need funding?

After assessing each issue like the preceding example, you should re-prioritize the list to the sequence in which you intend to solve the issues. You don't need to take them one at a time. In fact, you may want to select 5-10 problems and attack all quick wins with different parts of your team at once. If I were tackling this same list, I would put my data governance team on the ownership item from finance, the platforms/primary data team on the unified view of the customer issue, and my data operations team on this purchase history example we are exploring together.

Short-term versus long-term wins

Within a common issue or capability, you should have short-term solutions that qualify as a quick win, and long-term solutions for the same issue, which get to a stable solution for the long haul. So, how do you decide?

1. **Create optionality**: Come up with some options for your stakeholders to consider. Ideally, propose three options that address their problems.

2. **Involve stakeholders**: Get their perspective on the options you propose. Ask curious questions such as "What are we missing? What else could be impacted as a result of these options?"

3. **Use what you have**: Consider the resources you have. It can be seen as a red flag when you ask for funding and/or resources every time you need to do something new. What could you do without a single dollar or new headcount?

4. **Show progress (versus tell)**: Schedule regular check-ins with your stakeholders as you have progress to show. Showing the progress versus sending a status report is worth so much in credibility. Show them how you are helping them win.

5. **Iterate**: To demonstrate progress quickly, you need to show incremental progress. As you deliver features, show and solicit feedback quickly. Maintain a sense of urgency while you iterate.

6. **Demo**: Take your iterative solutions to your stakeholders and show them what you and your team have created. Get their early and frequent feedback so that you can demonstrate forward progress, and include any feedback as you deliver for them. Don't wait until the solution is built to show them what you've done in service of their needs.

7. **Go live**: Simply, turn your solution on. You will continue to iterate and deliver new features once you deliver the initial capability, so, go live with urgency.

8. **Communicate far and wide**: Share your solution with your stakeholders, but also with others. Add this new solution to a monthly communication, or a status report that you share with a broader community of stakeholders. This will be a great way to show others that you have delivered a solution with impact.

9. **Fail fast**: If the solution isn't working, or you need to change course, don't be afraid to do so. Just do it quickly. You can always pivot.

10. **Build the long-term solution**: After you have deployed or delivered the first iteration that quickly addresses your stakeholders' needs, get to work on building the long-term solution. That may mean delivering more sustainable solutions/releases than what you delivered as your quick win, or it could be a totally different sustainable solution. Either way, once you have delivered the quick win, the next step is to immediately get to stable long-term needs.

Example – unable to see a complete view of historical purchases by customer

- **Scenario**: In this example, the company sells a subscription product with add-on support services. In the current state, the sales and customer service teams were unable to verify what the customer had purchased, and therefore were running into two primary problems:

  - Customer service representatives were not sure which level of service package a customer was entitled to, which leads to over- or under-service.

  - Sales representatives were unsure what the customer had purchased previously and therefore were not sure what to renew. This led to revenue being left unbilled.

- **Short-term/quick win objective**: Build a simple lookup on top of the ERP data to identify the lost revenue that was not being renewed. This revenue leakage identification would be able to justify the additional spending for the long-term solution. (Note: this is a very common issue, and in large enterprises, it often results in 10s or 100s of millions of dollars of unbilled revenue being identified.)

- **Long-term objective**: Build a purchase history tool that shows all the history of customers for marketing, sales, customer services, and finance to be able to easily look up all of the history for any customer globally.

- **What to consider**: As you are starting to build the quick win versus the long-term portion of the solution, you'll need to look at what's available to you. Following the preceding 10 steps, you first need to come up with a variety of options for your stakeholders to consider. Ideally, you should be able to propose three or more options to address their problems. Second, you'll want to involve your stakeholders in the selection of these options. You should ask them questions about the options you prepared.

- **What we did**: In this example, we prepared options that included being able to take raw transactional data from our enterprise resource planning platform and curate a view based on that information, which was not of the highest quality but was enough to get the team started. This addressed *Step 3*, which is to use what you have. As we worked toward *Step 4*, we started to show the stakeholder groups what the raw data from the ERP system looked like. Even though the data was not very complete or comprehensive, it gave them a place to start from. We worked with our stakeholders to provide an iterative view of what we were able to remediate quickly based on other data sources that we had available in our ecosystem.

By iterating with our stakeholders, we also demonstrated our solutions by placing a very simple GUI interface on top of the data set, which allows the stakeholders to be able to search for the history that they need. Once we had enough confidence from our stakeholders that this would begin to address their problem, we made it live for them, and we communicated effectively that the data in this version was not fully reliable, but was enough to get started. We also shared this early iteration with other teams that we thought might be interested in this information. There were other teams in IT, finance, and marketing that were also interested in this initial view.

Long term, we needed to build a primary data management platform for customers, so we had full confidence we had a complete view of a customer and the hierarchies around a single entity. Ultimately, we automated the purchase history platform, linked the purchase history to the appropriate customer, and had the ability to see purchase history at the lowest legal entity, as well as the ability to roll up the purchase history to the ultimate parent (highest level). We iteratively delivered until the stakeholders involved had a fully automated end-to-end sustainable solution. We saved the company millions in operational efficiency and lost revenue.

Organizational readiness considerations

It may be surprising to note that a similar recommendation had been made a few years prior but was not approved by the business. Why might that be? Well, sometimes organizations don't understand what their opportunity is because of a variety of external factors. Or, it could simply be that the previous pitch was not made very effectively. Just because it didn't work before doesn't mean it won't work now. If your stakeholders don't accept your recommendations the first time, wait a period of time and then try again. Especially when there are leadership changes, you may want to consider that new leaders may have new ideas.

You should also consider the state of the company. If the company is going through a rough financial time, it's likely not the right time to request millions of dollars to push your data agenda. Get really focused on what you need to deliver, why the company needs it, and what the financial outcomes will be if you do. Simply stating your solution will deliver "revenue" isn't sufficient. Be clear on how and why. If the company is in a financial growth mode, it might be a better time to experiment and innovate.

Investment/funding models

Typically, there are a couple of ways to go about funding these quick wins. These different options may vary based on your organizational preferences. There are commonly three options to consider:

1. **CDAO office funding**: You use your own budget to fund this quick-win project. This is my recommendation for when you are trying to demonstrate your team's ability to deliver. This is often viewed as a "goodwill" attempt to show reputable results.

2. **Stakeholders' funding**: You ask your stakeholders to fund your quick-win project. I would recommend this only when you have a good standing you're your stakeholders and they are used to funding work for your team.

3. **Hybrid funding**: You ask your stakeholders to fund part of the solution and you offer to fund the other part of the solution. This can work when there is a bit more investment needed to get the project off the ground, appreciation from both sides that the quick win is critical, and alignment on the shared success of delivery.

In my experience, it's a stronger relationship builder when your team self-funds the quick win and goes to the stakeholder for funding only when you have demonstrated that your team can deliver. Only once you exit the "quick win" phase and move on to delivering the long-term sustainable solution should you request funding from stakeholders. Use your best judgment and follow the norms of your company's funding model.

Follow through

This should be a no-brainer, but you have to deliver excellent results in a quick win if you want to be taken seriously by your stakeholders. There's really no room for failure, especially if your stakeholder is funding your quick-win project. There are lots of ways to "win," but you have to deliver a result that meets or exceeds their expectation.

Once you deliver that very first iteration, you should immediately ask for input into the next iterations of your solution. Each and every delivery that you have in this quick-win phase builds small amounts of credibility and trust in your teams' ability to deliver what the business needs. Keep showing the stakeholders that they can depend on you for excellent results, and that you are their partner. Work with them to ideate on the next steps and keep delivering. This virtuous cycle of delivery will pay dividends when you move into the larger deliveries in your program.

Communicate effectively for support

After all the preceding work, identifying, producing, and iterating on results through continuous delivery, it is a shame that many data leaders fail to communicate appropriately. There tend to be two camps: over-communicating on less-than-impactful results or not communicating enough about impactful delivery. Think about it in this very simple view:

High impact / under communication	High impact / highly communicated
You've delivered great solutions, but you don't tell the story effectively to your stakeholders or users.	You've delivered great solutions and you have effectively communicated to your stakeholders.
Result: Stakeholders are unaware of your impactful quick win, and fail to support you appropriately for future investments and products.	**Result**: Stakeholders are aware of your impactful work and support you for future investments and products.
Low impact / under communication	**Low impact / highly communicated**
You've delivered low-quality or low-impact results, and you don't share the result broadly with your stakeholders or users.	You've delivered a low-quality or low-impact solution, but you've communicated broadly about it.
Result: You don't deliver and no one notices. You should go back to the drawing board and find another impactful data solution to deliver ASAP.	**Result**: You have tarnished your reputation. You've overcommunicated a low-impact solution, which lessens the chances of your stakeholders believing your results when you do produce something of high impact for them in the future. You may struggle to gain funding or support for your next product/solution.

Table 13.3 - Impact of quick wins and communication effectiveness

You want to be in the top-right box – high impact and effective communication. However, the next best place to be is the lower-left box. This is probably unexpected, however, the other two carry a higher degree of risk for the success of your team.

Measuring results

As you are communicating, do not forget what we learned in *Chapter 5, Aligning on Outcomes*. It is critical that you measure the impact of the results you deliver. For example, in the purchase history example we went through earlier, we identified unbilled revenue that customers had committed to renewing but hadn't been renewed by sales. In the example, from the financial transactions and order forms, we were able to identify the years of commitment, what had already been billed and paid, and what had not been billed and paid. The unbilled commitments were able to be measured and aggregated. The unbilled revenue totaled in the millions of dollars.

By reporting outwardly to all stakeholder groups, including finance, sales, and executive management, we were able to state very concretely that the team had identified the specific dollar amount of unbilled revenue. As sales took that data and followed up with customers, most were very happy to pay for the services, but no one had asked them to. They also were unaware. I have heard this exact same example play out in numerous other companies.

Data teams that can directly identify a revenue improvement from their work often find funding their programs much easier to do than when measuring results is less direct, or when there is not a direct revenue or operational savings tie. If you can, measure results specifically and share very clearly. Obtain your stakeholders' support for the number you identify and go together to executive management to share the outcomes. This will bolster your credibility and partnerships. Now that we've learned all about quick wins, in the next section, we'll explore how policies, standards, and procedures can help you achieve them.

Why policies, standards, and procedures can generate buzz

One of the easiest quick wins that you can deliver on the data governance side of your team is to establish effective and easy-to-understand policies, standards, and procedures. In my experience, some of your stakeholders will simply want to be able to self-deliver. I think this is a great signal. It means that you have highly qualified data professionals across your organization who want to be able to get started. However, if they are looking to your team to tell them what to do, how to do it, and how they want to do it in alignment with your team, then these are engaged stakeholders.

One of the best things you can do is provide them with the guidance that they are seeking. The easiest way to do this is to publish guidelines that they can use. While some of your data engineers and analytics professionals are delivering on other quick wins, focused on the more technical components of data governance, other team members can concurrently be focusing on delivering these documents, which can support the broader enterprise.

Especially if your team is small or new, producing simple, straightforward, and not overly complex policies, standards, and procedures is a great way to engage the entire company in data without a significantly sized team. Simply providing templates is a very easy way to engage your stewardship community on how to best document simple controls, define how to measure and report on the state of data quality, or perform simple data operations.

While the preceding example of purchase history gets deep in a single area, policies, standards, and procedures cut wide across your organization. By marrying a technical solution with a more generalized solution, such as a simple data policy, you will gain support from a few different stakeholder groups. This is another way to build effective momentum in your data program while enabling the company to know what they need to do and how they need to do it. After publishing policies, standards, and procedures, and delivering a data governance capability, one of the next best steps that you can take is to define clear data ownership. By assigning data owners, you can operationalize your data governance in a federated model that will deliver accountability across the enterprise.

Data ownership

In *Chapter 3*, we went through how to build a high-performing team. You may recall that building a high-performing team isn't just about your direct reporting staff, but also the entire data community across the company. One of the most important considerations in building a high-performing team is activating those who manage the data directly. These data stewards (both technical and business data stewards) are a key component to operationalizing all of the capabilities we discussed in *Part 2* of this book, but also in implementing policies, standards, and procedures.

One way to get a quick win is to activate your stewardship community. The data governance leader, which we covered in *Chapter 3*, should identify who data stewards are across the organization and use these stewards to implement the policies, standards, and procedures, but also to identify quick wins! The individuals closest to the data are the ones who see and experience the data issues day to day, and thus, are your biggest source of input when it comes to identifying quick-fix opportunities.

Be sure to keep track of who is providing you with these ideas as they come in. A few things you can try are as follows:

- **Create a hackathon**: Activate your community by capturing ideas that need solving. Then, push these ideas back to the community and create a contest-like forum to "hack" these ideas into solutions. Ask an executive to take the winners to lunch or host an **ask me anything (AMA)** as a prize. Note that this doesn't require funding.

- **Ask for submissions**: One way to gather ideas is to create a forum to submit ideas. You could use a Slack channel or simply collect them through a monitored email box.

- **Create a sign-up form**: Allow individuals to log their ideas on a form. Be sure to capture who submitted the ideas so you can acknowledge them.

By engaging the entire data community, your reach and idea set will become much richer and wider than if your team attempted to gather ideas or generate ideas exclusively on their own. There is a great deal of pride in ownership for ideas that are gathered, so, celebrate the individuals who brought them forward. When solutions are gathered, solved, and communicated, be sure to mention and publish who brought it forward. This is a great way to honor those who are supporting your team and data more broadly at the company. Now that we have learned what data ownership is, and how it helps define quick wins, we'll now learn how to apply the product mindset to finalize solutions.

Applying a product mindset to data capabilities

One of the best ways to continue to iterate on a solution is by adopting a product mindset to your data capabilities. This concept has been emerging in the data space for the last few years and I've driven this model in two teams I've led at the time of writing. The best way to think about adopting this mindset is to look at how products are deployed in the technology industry. It's a great time to think about this as you are building solutions under the data product mindset because it fundamentally aligns with product management.

Product management for data

As you start to build a solution, the idea is that you go live with an immediate **minimum viable product** (**MVP**) solution and continue to release new features periodically over time. Ideally, you should follow the following steps, at a minimum:

1. **Assign a product manager**: Each solution should have an assigned product manager who "owns" the solution. The product manager should be the expert on the solution, and accountable for the quality and performance of the solution. Much like you would see with a traditional technology product, this person is ultimately accountable, no matter what.

2. **Leverage a feature backlog and prioritize**: Collect all the features requested by stakeholders and those needed to improve the data product. Prioritize the features based on impact and needs.

3. **Build a roadmap**: Each product should have a roadmap with features being released iteratively over time. It should be clear and transparent to the stakeholders what they can expect, and when, with regard to the data product.

4. **Deliver iteratively:** As depicted on your roadmap, the data product should have clear, iterative deliveries over time. This roadmap should not "end" – you should adopt a continuous improvement model.

5. **Enable users**: As you deliver, be sure to enable the users with training so they can use the product to its full potential.

6. **Repeat**: Because you are deploying a product, you should continue to repeat this cycle indefinitely or until the product is retired.

Because your goal is to get a solution into production quickly, and to deliver that quick win, focus on delivering the MVP so that your stakeholders can get value as fast as possible. Leverage the preceding steps to get to your full solution, with future enhancements. Do not let perfect be the enemy of good; deliver with urgency.

Products versus non-product solutions

Once you see how effective this approach is, it may be tempting to apply the product management mindset to all data capabilities and solutions. However, not everything should be treated as such. It becomes very easy to become captivated by this model and want to apply the model to everything, but it does come with a cost: aligning a product manager and engineering team to each product is not scalable infinitely.

Helpful Hint
Get really clear with your team about what makes a data product a product, versus what is a service, versus what is just a dashboard or business intelligence metric. It's tempting to swing too far toward product management, so clarifying how you will treat solutions is an important early step.

Basic criteria

To aid your team in staying objective, you should create basic criteria to use for your company, which will define what constitutes a product, service, or asset. To get you started, I've captured the very basic criteria you can use as a starting point:

Product	Service	Asset
Will have continuous support. Will have continuous delivery. Requires new features or functionality.	Provides a capability to others for use in managing data or producing analytics and insights.	A single delivery that is produced and used.
The examples are as follows: • Early warning system • Purchase history system • Customer health score	The examples are as follows: • Data governance policy • Data catalog • Data quality tool	The examples are as follows: • Enterprise-metrics • Revenue dashboard • Customer attrition

Table 13.4 – Criteria for various data solutions

In the first organization that I deployed this model in, we went through every single thing we did, no matter whether it was a simple dashboard, a curated dataset, or a full-blown solution, and we determined which of the three buckets each solution fit into. Simply going through this exercise allowed us to retire a number of dashboards we realized not only weren't products, but weren't being used at all. It crystallized for us what we needed to be doing, versus what we could stop doing altogether. From there, we identified which solutions were true products, and we could start to iterative quick wins.

Product culture

As you focus on delivering quick wins with iterative delivery, a good best practice is to identify and appoint an individual to define product management best practices for your team. This individual will define the preceding criteria, establish forums for product roadmap reviews, manage the process for scrum, and partner with engineering teams to align both product and engineering to the same goals. By defining these expectations, you will begin to establish a culture of product management. Depending on the size of your company and data team, this could be a part-time role or a full team.

Training

You will need to define requirements for product management (both for quick wins and for ongoing product management). Especially if this concept is new to your company or your team, you will need to spend time training. There are some online programs focused on data product management, which could be a good place to start. If you find you have to DIY a training program that is customized for your company, you can. There's no single way to accomplish training. What's most important is that you assess the needs of your team and company, and train accordingly. Now that we've covered how to build quick wins and walked through some examples, we need to focus on momentum

Building momentum through a continuous delivery model

Quick wins are not just something that you create and deliver in the early phases of your tenure – they're quite the opposite. You should create quick wins to build momentum, and then keep delivering with velocity over time. The best way to create momentum is by devising a **continuous delivery model**.

Continuous delivery model

A continuous delivery model enables your team to further deliver against each solution, by adopting the product mindset discussed previously, as well as using the same model to identify and deliver new quick win opportunities. The same model applies to both an individual solution, as well as the process overall, which makes it easier to deploy across your team. For engineers, this may look a lot like an agile delivery model, which it is modeled after. For non-engineers, this is the opportunity to learn from our technical counterparts and adopt their processes more broadly to solutions holistically. The following image provides a visual representation of how the continuous delivery model operates. Note that there isn't an end to this model, rather, you should continue through the process as long as the data product is in production and used by your stakeholders.

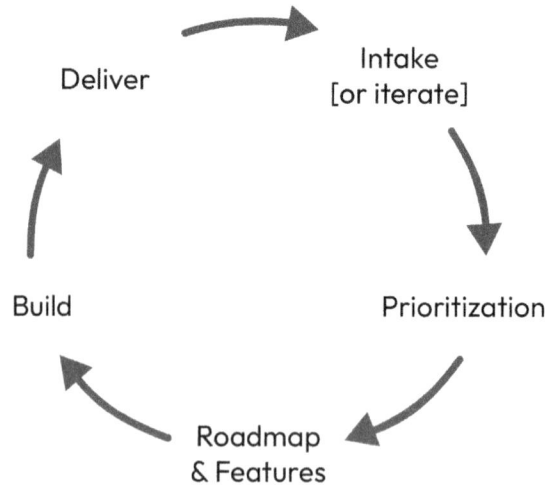

Figure 13.2 – Building a momentum flywheel – continuous delivery model

We will explore each stage of the model in the following subsections.

Intake

At a team level, you should create a process and mechanism to collect and document all the solutions that you will build, regardless of size. You may use a tool to do this, such as Jira or Asana, or you could use something as simple as a spreadsheet. Regardless of what tool you use, be sure to capture ideas both big and small.

At the solution level, you will need to capture new features or changes that are required for each individual solution you are building/maintaining. Because the model is continuous in nature, you should be evaluating enhancements, new features, and fixes on an ongoing basis.

Prioritization

At the team level, you should review the solutions that have been logged in your backlog for prioritization. Ideally, you would define a prioritization framework. It can be as simple or as complex as you need to fit your business needs, however, I find a lot of elegance in a simple solution such as the following:

- **Impact**: Low/medium/high
- **Cost/resourcing**: Low/medium/high

Seems simple, and simple can be great. To prioritize at the solution level, you are simply prioritizing these solutions to deliver rapid impact on the business. This prioritization framework can help you identify which solutions to go after based on your resourcing. For example, if someone has a week of capacity, and a week of effort is considered a "low" cost for your organization, you might search the list for a low-cost and high-impact solution to work on next.

At the solution level, you can use something similar to build prioritization at the feature level, such as the following:

- **Impact**: Low/medium/high
- **Cost/resourcing**: Hours/days/weeks

You could use the actual expected hours to complete the features (e.g., 2 hours or 36 hours). This will also help you prioritize the feature backlog for each solution you create.

Helpful Hint
Across both the team level and solution level, this prioritization approach will also help you identify where there is work to deliver that may not be considered "quick." Perhaps this process will identify where you have larger-scale needs, such as what was covered in *Part 2* of this book.

Building a roadmap and aligning features

At the team level, once you have the prioritization framework pulled together, you should build an integrated roadmap of the small quick-win projects your team will continue to deliver. This view will help your combined team have visibility into and understand what is being delivered. By providing micro-moments with stakeholders that your team is able to drive, you will delight your stakeholders, but you will also build confidence in your team's ability to deliver impactful work at velocity. This will inspire your team to find more quick wins and thus, will generate more momentum.

At the solution level, you should build a simplified view of the releases you will have for your quick wins. This should be shared not only with the individuals working on the solution but also with your stakeholders. By showing them what this will look like, they will understand better what features and/or functionality will be available to them and when. Be sure to not just mention what is available, but also what that will enable them to be able to do in business terms (e.g., a customer-level health score will enable the customer success team to proactively reach out to customers and delight them with an improved customer experience and a higher NPS score).

Building/engineering/analyzing

At the team level and the solution level, this step, simply put, is to execute your plan. Deliver the solution with excellence.

Delivering

At the team level, this is a great time to show the stakeholder community, perhaps through your enterprise data committee or council, on a quarterly basis, what has been delivered. Depending on the willingness of the stakeholders, it can be very powerful for the stakeholders to present in this forum what they are able to do now that they have received the solutions your team has delivered.

At the solution level, after you build the solution (for example, a dashboard, a curated data set, or a new pipeline), you should deliver this solution to your stakeholders. Don't forget to show them exactly what they can do with the solution and how to use it. Ask for immediate impressions and feedback.

Repeat/iterate

At the team level, continue to generate ideas, follow your intake process, and iterate through the continuous delivery model for impact. This is a great time to also add up the impact your team has created through the sum of your quick wins process. Consider the tracking time saved, revenue added, cost saved, and so on. Keep this information at the most granular level possible so you can provide the details. However, the aggregate number can add up very quickly to demonstrate the team's value.

At the solution level, after delivery, you should take the feedback and input from the delivery step, and repeat the entire flywheel, starting with intake. Ask what additional features or functionality they need, and continuously deliver through the cycle again. As long as the solution exists, this process should continue. Once the solution is no longer needed or used, then retire it, but until that time, continue to follow this continuous delivery model for impact.

Follow through

This may go without saying, but you must follow through on your commitments in these quick wins. They can't be wins if you don't deliver against them. By honoring your commitments to your stakeholders, you begin to build trust. If you find you are not going to be able to deliver, or you get into the solution build, and you determine it's far more complex than expected, go communicate with your stakeholders. Do not shy away from giving news regarding the success or failure of the quick win process. Not everything will work and that is OK.

Being transparent, working with your stakeholders, and truly partnering through these processes with visibility will continue to build trust. You may consider asking your stakeholders to co-develop with you for added business integration. This approach can be quite helpful if your team is new to the company, or you have a large number of new team members joining the team. Celebrate the wins, big and small, and also celebrate the failures. When a team member quickly realizes something isn't going to work and stops working on the solution (e.g., fails fast), that is also something to celebrate. It will create a culture of innovation where it is safe to try things and fail. Failure isn't failure – it's part of success. Be sure to encourage this on your team, so you keep motivation within your team.

Conclusion

As you establish a culture of building quick wins for impact, you are creating a machine of delivery within your team that will help build your reputation as a dependable and innovative team. Most organizations do not build this culture, and are constantly asking for the big projects, and unwilling to start small. There is no reason not to do both. By investing in quick wins and the process to deliver them early, you build momentum fast. By adopting the continuous delivery model and data product mindset, your teams can deliver incremental and powerful value in a predictable, scalable way.

Be mindful to capture how you will measure the quality and impact of your quick wins so that you are able to tell your value story quickly and effectively. There is a great deal of power in being able to quantify your impact on the company quickly and effectively. This will captivate your stakeholders, elevate your team's impact, and create additional demand for your team's services. Everyone wins with this model.

Starting strong is a key indicator of a strong data organization, as well as a strong leader in the data and analytics space. Building momentum early and continuously will carry you and your team to success. If you need ideas, consider bringing the team together to hack a list of ideas together. Whatever you do, don't go stagnant. Continue to deliver with a focus on high-quality outcomes of any size. You will build a delivery model that can't be beat. The next chapter will help drive even faster wins, through the incorporation of automation to further build your virtuous cycle of impact.

Further reading

CDO 2.0 – How the role of the CDO has evolved: `https://www2.deloitte.com/us/en/insights/industry/public-sector/chief-data-officer-government-playbook/2023/chief-data-officer-government-outlook.html`

14

Data Automation for Impact and More Powerful Results

Traditional data governance processes can feel like a program that is separate from the business. With the pace of today's modern business models, governance must be embedded into the process, and that requires a new way of thinking about data governance. In modern data governance teams, there is a shift away from too much committee work, with more emphasis placed on embedding data governance into processes by design. I refer to this newer model of governance as **data governance by design**.

This newer way of thinking requires data governance professionals to think and act differently when it comes to governance activities. Data governance by design requires professionals to think about how to embed data governance capabilities into a business process from the start, not alongside it after it has been built. The longer I have spent in the business of data, the more I see the demands of data increasing at a pace that does not have the patience to wait for governance to "happen." We must evolve now as a profession.

Extracting actionable insights from vast corporate data ecosystems at the speed of business needs also requires a powerful set of tools or data automation capabilities. This chapter dives deep into this transformative set of capabilities, equipping you with the knowledge and understanding to harness the potential of automated data processes. This is a key design component and set of capabilities that support and enable data governance by design.

Imagine a world where data flows seamlessly, users trust the information they receive, and insights emerge effortlessly. Automation is a lever that can be pulled to expedite data governance deliveries. By automating repetitive, manual tasks, we free our teams from the mundane task of data movement and manual manipulation, unlocking time and resources to focus on higher-level analysis and strategic decision-making.

This chapter covers the following topics:

- What is automation?
- What is Data automation?

- Types of data automation

- Benefits of data automation

- How to determine which type of automation to use

- Third-party enrichment

- Data solution examples powered by data automation

Before we get into the specifics, let's ground ourselves in key basic definitions.

What is automation?

Automation broadly refers to the use of technology to perform tasks with minimal human intervention. It encompasses a wide range of techniques and technologies applied in various ways. The key aspects of automation include the following:

- **Reduced human involvement**: The goal is to minimize the need for team members to manually perform tasks, leading to increased efficiency and productivity. A secondary benefit is team member satisfaction, which we will discuss later in this chapter.

- **Use of technology**: Automation relies on various technologies, from simple tools and scripts to complex artificial intelligence (AI) algorithms.

- **Pre-defined instructions or processes**: Automated tasks are typically guided by pre-programmed rules, instructions, or decision-making criteria. This could include primary data management algorithms, as defined in *Chapter 10*.

There are a number of types of automation beyond those covered in this chapter. For the purposes of this book, we will be focusing on data automation capabilities. The capabilities outlined here are specifically selected to enable your data governance capabilities and data governance program, so let's start to dive deeper by digging into the basics of data automation and how data automation applies to data governance.

What is data automation?

Before we go deep into this topic, we will ground ourselves in a few basics about what data automation is. **Data automation** is a broad term encompassing various methods for automatically handling data tasks. Data automation is a specific subset of automation techniques that apply technology to perform data governance with minimal human interaction. This can include a wide range of techniques, from data entry and data cleaning to more complex techniques such as analytics and reporting. We will go into the specific types of data automation in a few pages, but for now, let's focus on the value and benefits data automation brings to data governance.

Types of data automation

The data automation techniques included in this section should be applied comprehensively across all capabilities outlined in *Part 2* of this book. Data automation transforms the way you work with information and is a complimentary suite of solutions that unlocks additional value in your data capabilities. Consider the contents of this chapter to be additive to what you have learned to this point.

By applying data automation to data governance capabilities, you add exponential benefits and speed to the results and, in essence, you are creating embedded data governance by design into your data governance program, enterprise-wide. We'll delve into the diverse types of data automation in this section.

Data integration

Data integration is the ability to move data between systems without human intervention (or a significant reduction in human intervention), which breaks down data silos and enables a more seamless analysis experience for users. Data integration combines data from multiple sources into a unified view. There are typically a series of steps that are involved in integrating data well (known as ETL):

1. **Extracting data**: Gathering data from one or more sources (e.g., websites, databases, and spreadsheets).

2. **Transforming data**: This may include cleaning, formatting, or standardizing the data in some way to ensure it is consistent and/or comparable across the various sources that the data was extracted from. You may need to address issues such as formatting, inconsistencies, and null values, and you will need to build processes to resolve conflicting data.

3. **Loading data**: This involves putting the transformed data into a target source (e.g., a data lake, data warehouse, or other type of source, such as a report).

The purpose of data integration is to bring datasets that were previously isolated or trapped in other systems together, sometimes in different formats. These existing data silos make it difficult to analyze the data maintained in various locations (this is sometimes referred to as **data fragmentation**). By integrating data into common formats and locations together, this allows companies to do the following:

- Improve data quality

- See and leverage deeper insights from larger and more comprehensive datasets

- Improve decision making

- Increase operational efficiency

Examples of this include the following:

- Providing a centralized data source for business intelligence

- Enabling machine learning models by improving accuracy and performance by using a unified dataset

- Obtaining a unified view of a customer in a **customer relationship management** tool (**CRM**) by integrating multiple customer data sources

> **Data integration example**
>
> Instead of manually copying and pasting data from one system to another or spending hours crunching numbers in spreadsheets, data automation empowers you to set up **ETL processes** that do the heavy lifting for you. These ETL processes follow pre-defined instructions, ensuring that data flows seamlessly, tasks execute automatically, and insights emerge effortlessly.
>
> In some CRM environments, you may find up to 80–100 integrations that have been built to enrich the unified view of a customer. When acquisitions occur and customer data is stored in multiple CRMs, integrations can be used to bring customer data together prior to system integration as a temporary solution that enables the business to see all customer information ahead of the hard work of system integration and the decommissioning of legacy systems.

Overall, data integration is an essential process for organizations that rely on data to make informed decisions, improve operational efficiency, and gain a competitive edge. In today's economy, it is difficult to find a company that does not rely on data in this way, but in my experience, there are a plethora of opportunities to integrate data better for improved time to insight and improved operations.

Data transformation

Data transformation is the process of cleaning, formating, and manipulating data to prepare it for analysis by using a (more) standardized format for accuracy and usability. Data transformation converts data from one format or structure into another, which makes it more usable. Data transformation is a key step in data pipeline management and is often a part of data integration work. Data transformation (and integration) work is typically performed by data engineers in service of operations or analytics.

The purpose of data transformation is to convert data or enrich data to make it more useful for a specific purpose or set of purposes. There are many ways to transform data based on the specific need you are working to solve. Examples of this include the following:

- **Data Cleaning**: Removing errors, inconsistencies, and duplicates.
- **Standardization**: Driving consistency in data (e.g., dates 1/1/2011 to January 1, 2011).
- **Creating new fields**: Creating derived data by adding or converging data into new fields (e.g., totaling).
- **Aggregation**: Summarizing data by grouping it (e.g., average sales per month; total sales per month).
- **Filtering**: Extracting subsets of data based on a range of filters (e.g., current year sales).

> Data Transformation Example
>
> One of the most common types of data transformation is the use of **primary data management (PDM)** techniques. PDM, as we covered in *Chapter 10*, is a capability that I have implemented in three different companies. Typically, by bringing together multiple sources of customer data, I have seen dramatic improvements in data quality, which has a cascading impact on the way in which companies are able to rely on and use customer information to improve revenue, reduce costs, and improve insights. In all cases, the analytics improved as well; however, the main beneficiary was the business. Don't forget to focus on the impact made outside of your team. In the case of data transformation, the business often benefits the most from the speed and quality of improved data transformation.

Data analysis and insights

Data analysis and insights: They represent the ability to automate repetitive analysis tasks, such as generating reports and identifying patterns (e.g., trends), to drive decision-making. Automating these tasks extracts knowledge and insights from data and saves time and resources in terms of data analysts and data scientists. There are various components to data analysis and insights that can be automated, including the following:

Data acquisition and preparation: This process leverages tooling to automatically extract data from a variety of sources (systems, APIs, and spreadsheets), reducing the manual effort traditionally followed, and this enables error-prone processes to be completed consistently and at scale. This process may also include transformation to automate data cleaning (e.g., correcting the inconsistencies and formatting) to improve the data for further analysis.

Data exploration and analysis: Tools can identify the patterns and trends in data and any outliers that are normally identified through manual analytics work. This can also benefit data analysts by finding insights that are commonly overlooked or buried deep in the data. The scale of a large organization's datasets makes it difficult for a human to find trends without using long time frames and expensive tooling. Data automation can enable these processes, where scale is a historical challenge.

Insight generation and communication: Data automation tools can generate automated reporting and create visualizations (e.g., Tableau dashboards), which present insights in a format that is far easier for end users to explore and review.

The purpose of data analysis and insight data automation is to expedite and drive efficiencies that were once traditionally carried out by high value resources. This process enables data analysis to be completed on higher value work and frees up your data analysts and scientists to perform more high-value tasks.

Examples of this include the following:

- Automating reporting and insights so that analysts can focus on interpreting the results
- Reducing human errors in data handling so analysts have higher confidence in the reliability of the results, thus improving trust in the data

- Enabling the democratization of data insights so that a wider range of individuals can access and use insights at the speed of business

Data monitoring and alerting

Data monitoring and alerting is the process of using technology to continuously observe and analyze data sources, as well as automating the triggering of alerts when specific conditions are met. This capability enables organizations to identify problems when they occur before they become major problems. **Monitoring** includes collecting information from sources (e.g., databases, APIs, and network devices) and using tools to track very specific metrics (e.g., error rates, performance indicators, such as time to process, or specific data quality thresholds, such as percentage completed), as well as analyzing the data in real-time or on a regular candace (i.e., nightly). Another term for this type of process is **data observability**. Alerting occurs when a pre-defined threshold is met through monitoring; then, an alert is delivered through an email, SMS, or internal notification (e.g., Slack).

Examples of this include the following:

- Server failures
- Security threats
- Errors in processing
- A sudden drop in orders
- Suspicious activities (i.e., fraud)

Data cleansing

Data cleansing, the process of identifying and correcting errors and inconsistencies in data, is a crucial step in ensuring reliable and trustworthy information for analysis. Fortunately, this tedious task can be significantly automated, freeing up your valuable time and resources.

Types of data cleansing automation

There are several types of data cleansing automation that represent common techniques to improve the quality of data. There are a few common types that I will provide an overview of here, but please note that each of these types requires its own chapter to get into the technical implementation details. At a high level, the following are the various types of automation when it comes to data cleaning:

- **Rule-based automation**:
    - **Define rules**: Establish clear rules to identify and address common errors based on data formats, values, and relationships

- **Data profiling tools**: Analyze data to identify patterns and define any rules based on these patterns

- **Examples of this**: Standardizing date formats, removing outliers, and flagging missing values

- **Fuzzy matching**:

  - **Identify similar records**: Match records that have slight variations, such as typos or abbreviations

  - **Data deduplication**: Eliminate duplicate records based on fuzzy matching algorithms

  - **Examples of this**: Merging duplicate customer records and identifying inconsistent product names (e.g., PDM capabilities)

Some of the benefits of automating cleansing include the following:

- **Increased efficiency**: Saving time and resources by automating repetitive cleaning tasks

- **Improved accuracy**: Reducing human error and ensuring consistent data quality

- **Scalability**: Easily handling large datasets and complex cleaning requirements

- **Better insights**: Building more reliable and trustworthy models based on clean data

Considerations for the automation of data cleansing

Before selecting a type of automated data cleansing for your use case, you should consider the following as you evaluate your options:

- **Data complexity**: Complex data with diverse errors may require manual intervention or advanced algorithms

- **Rule development**: Defining effective rules requires understanding your data and common errors

- **Data security**: Ensure the chosen solutions comply with data security and privacy regulations

Begin with automating simple cleaning tasks and gradually expand as you gain confidence. By carefully selecting and implementing data cleansing automation, you can unlock the true potential of your data for informed decision-making.

Advanced data automation capabilities

There are several additional advanced capabilities that can be explored beyond the more common data automation capabilities above. Beyond these core types, the advanced capabilities include the following: data cleansing, machine learning and AI automation, and **robotic process automation** (**RPA**). These advanced capabilities are very helpful for capabilities that are standardized and repeatable. At a high level, there are two capabilities that are especially useful for data automation:

- **Machine learning and AI automation**: Leverages AI algorithms for deeper analysis, predictions, and data-driven recommendations. Some examples include the following:

  - **Training algorithms**: Train models on labeled data to identify and correct errors with greater accuracy and adaptability

  - **Supervised learning**: Training models on labeled data with correct and incorrect examples

  - **Unsupervised learning**: Use algorithms to identify anomalies and patterns to suggest potential errors

  - **Examples of this**: Identifying and correcting spelling errors and predicting missing values based on other data points

- **Robotic Process Automation** (**RPA**): Automating tasks that interact directly with user interfaces, such as data entry in web applications.

These advanced data automation capabilities are much more robust and involved and could warrant an entire book of their own. For now, be aware that these additional types exist; it is often beneficial to evaluate if they are fit for use in your organization once you have tackled the implementation of the data automation capabilities covered in this chapter. Next, we will dig into the benefits of data automation and how to measure the benefits.

Benefits of data automation

When it comes to automation, the benefits extend beyond efficiency. Efficiency is a great first principle, but data automation empowers us to do so much more. These benefits can and should be quantified as you build your business case, and as you realize the value, you should report on them to show the return on investment (ROI) for your data automation investments. The common benefits are wide-ranging, such as the following:

- **Ensure accuracy and consistency**: Data automation eliminates human error in data handling, leading to reliable and trustworthy information.

  - **Example**: Automating the enrichment of data for marketing leads to reduced errors and produces comparable, consistent results daily.

- **Gain deeper insights**: Analyzing vast datasets at scale, uncovering hidden patterns and trends that are invisible to the human eye.

  - **Example**: Automatically identifying the hidden patterns between product purchases and customer demographics, such as a situation whereby customers who buy raincoats are also likely to buy umbrellas when weather predicts rain within 48 hours in their location. Thus, the company would benefit from placing umbrellas at the front of the store to encourage a higher purchase rate.

- **Improve decision-making**: Driving data-driven choices by automating data analysis and reporting, providing real-time insights to inform actions.

  - **Example**: Data observability built into a data lake to alert when data volumes drop below expectations (e.g., by 5% or greater).

- **Reduce costs**: Streamlining workflows and optimizing resource allocation, leading to significant cost savings.

  - **Example**: Automating the data cleansing of customer records to expedite them leads to account matching in a CRM system.

- **Boost agility**: Respond faster to changing market conditions by automating data collection, analysis, and reporting.

  - **Example**: The automation of daily sales reports allows for the additional capacity of data analysts to be focused on anomalies.

- **Improve team member experience**: By automating data processes and basic reporting, team members are able to focus on more interesting and high-value activities.

  - **Example**: After automating daily sales reports, data analysts are able to focus on anomaly detection, and they are able to dig into anomalies and uncover additional sales opportunities for specific customer segments, increasing revenue opportunities.

Beyond identifying the benefits of data automation, it is critical to measure the impact of the benefits so that you can measure the return on the investment of implementing data automation techniques within your data governance program. As you work to build out this capability within your data program, ensure you leverage what was learned in *Chapter 5*. We will build on what was learned in the following section, with a specific tilt towards data automation.

Measuring the benefits

There are a few types of measurement to consider, including both quantitative and qualitative measures. Remember, quantitative measures are based on numbers and are more directly measured, whereas qualitative measures are based on experiences and are harder to measure directly. Both types of measures are important for your audience to understand, as they benefit your stakeholders in a variety of ways, including their experience of working for your organization.

Examples of quantitative measures

Some examples of quantitative measures include the following:

- **Improvement in customer conversion rate**: After implementing data-driven product recommendations based on next-best-action modeling, track the percentage of customers who make a purchase before and after the implementation of the automation.

- **Increase in revenue**: Measure sales before and after implementing a data automation capability. Be sure to take into account external factors such as market trends (adjust as needed). Examples of this include personalized marketing campaigns, optimized product placement, or dynamic pricing (e.g., airline ticket pricing).

- **Reduction in cost**: Measure the savings of person-hours achieved by automating tasks such as moving data and cleaning data by measuring the number of hours saved multiplied by a base all-in salary rate, including benefits and bonuses. Measure this of a time horizon, such as a week, a month, or a year, less the cost of automation.

Examples of qualitative measures

Some examples of qualitative measures include the following:

- **Customer satisfaction surveys**: By conducting customer satisfaction surveys, you can identify how effectively data automation capabilities are used to improve the customer experience. An increase in customer satisfaction after the implementation of data automation can indicate improved customer experience.

- **Employee surveys**: By conducting employee satisfaction surveys for those who benefited from data automation (analysts, business users, and so on) before and after, this can help identify and assess the impact of data automation on their employee experience. You should expect an increase in job satisfaction when mundane tasks are automated well.

- **Brand reputation analysis**: By monitoring online reviews and social media, you can determine how brand image is impacted among customer sentiment.

In Aggregate – Qualitative and quantitative measures

When joined together, both qualitative and quantitative measures should enable you to calculate the ROI in data automation activities:

Net Benefits / Total Costs

Here, net benefits (increased revenue, cost savings, and employee satisfaction improvement) are divided by total costs (investment, time, and so on). This assigns a financial metric to assess the overall benefit of the implementation of data automation capabilities.

> **Important note**
> Define the measures in advance of completing the work. This will result in a more objective calculation of the success of the project (in retrospect) than when the calculation of success is determined in hindsight.

By combining quantitative and qualitative data, businesses can gain a comprehensive understanding of the value generated through data automation in this specific example. This multifaceted approach allows for a more holistic evaluation of the impact on both business metrics and customer experience.

In the next section, I will walk you through how to evaluate the data automation types previously explained and define a process that you can use to select the appropriate data automation capability for your needs.

As we explore this determination process together, you will be equipped with the knowledge to do the following:

- **Identify your automation needs**: Assess your current data challenges and determine the most suitable automation solutions

- **Select the right tools**: Navigate the diverse landscape of data automation tools and choose the ones that best fit your requirements

- **Implement effectively**: Understand the key considerations for successful implementation, ensuring smooth adoption and maximized impact

As we walk through this next section, it may be helpful to have a use case in mind so that you can evaluate this process against it.

How to determine which type of automation to use

There is a fairly straightforward process to identify your needs, select the right tools and techniques, and implement them effectively. We will walk through exactly how to determine which type to use and how to execute the process for your company.

Step 1 – Identify your goals

Start by exploring the problem. A few key questions to ask include the following:

- What are you trying to achieve?

- What is working well and needs to be retained?

- What are the current challenges?

- What outcomes would indicate a successful solution?

These exploratory questions can help you determine if you need to increase efficiency, improve data quality, or if you are looking for a deeper result, such as finding deeper insights or meeting regulatory expectations. Perhaps you uncover that you are spending far too much of your team members time on low-value work, such as manual data cleaning, or you are struggling to identify problems proactively. This step will help you identify these goals.

Step 2 – Identify the existing process and pain points

Next, begin to explore the current state. Ask the following questions of your team and your stakeholders:

- What is the current process?

- Have we reviewed the data flow, and are there obvious inefficiencies?

- What are the current systems and datasets? (e.g., structured, unstructured, databases, or APIs)

- Where in the process are there manual steps?

Once you have the answers to the current state, you can begin to formulate specific steps to address the problem.

Step 3 – Agree on the problem statement(s)

As you frame the situation in Steps 1 and 2 above, you are ultimately working towards an agreed problem statement (or statements) that define the current state. It's important to ensure that you have agreement on what the problem is prior to defining any paths forward for the options in Step 4. Without firmly aligning all parties on the problem, you are much more likely to run into issues when it comes to later steps in the process, especially when affirming the solution when working as it was designed.

Step 4 – Align on the approach and ROI calculation

After (or concurrently) aligning on the problem statement, you should put together at least one (ideally, two or three) option(s) for how you can approach the solution. This alignment may include a combination of data automation techniques and may also vary in complexity and the extent of the solution. In the following example, the problem statement comes into play because if the general consensus is that reporting isn't the issue, it's unlikely to be supported and receive money to automate it:

Approach A	Approach B	Approach C
Automate data pipelines and implement data monitoring and alerting capabilities.	Automate data pipelines and implement data monitoring and alerting capabilities.	Automate data pipelines and implement data monitoring and alerting capabilities.
No change to analytics.	Automate basic analytics work.	Automate basic analytics work.
No change to reporting.	No change to reporting.	Automate daily reporting processes.

Table 14.1 – Example of an approach proposal

Example menu of data automation capabilities

The following list represents a "menu" of data automation capabilities to choose from:

- **Data integration**: Use this if you need to move data between different systems regularly, regardless of the format or source

- **Data transformation**: Choose this if your data requires cleaning, formatting, or manipulation before being further used

- **Data loading**: Implement this if you need to automate the final step of depositing transformed data into your target system

- **Data analysis and insights**: Consider this if you want to automate repetitive analysis tasks and generate insights without manual intervention

- **Data monitoring and alerting**: Choose this if you need proactive notifications based on specific data conditions to identify and address issues quickly

- **Machine learning and AI automation**: Explore this if you want to go beyond simple rules and leverage AI for deeper analysis, predictions, and data-driven recommendations

Return on investment

If you can explain the ROI of the proposals, this adds another layer to the decision-making process. Providing a proposed ROI for each solution at this stage directly exposes the value of the possible solutions, and this tends to result in a very different outcome than if ROI is strictly calculated upon the completion of the project. In this example, you may want to add an ROI calculation to each row:

Approach A	Approach B	Approach C
Current resourcing hours * personnel cost of manual support Less new cost: Resourcing hours * personnel cost of maintaining the automated pipelines going forward (post-implementation) = Cost savings of automation Consideration: Resourcing hours * personnel cost to automate (one-time costs)	Current resourcing hours * personnel cost of manual support Less new cost: Resourcing hours * personnel cost of maintaining the automated pipelines going forward (post-implementation) = Cost savings of automation Consideration: Resourcing hours * personnel cost to automate (one-time costs)	Current resourcing hours * personnel cost of manual support Less new cost: Resourcing hours * personnel cost of maintaining the automated pipelines going forward (post-implementation) = Cost savings of automation Consideration: Resourcing hours * personnel cost to automate (one-time costs)
No change to analytics.	Current resourcing hours * personnel cost of manual support Less new cost: Resourcing hours * personnel cost of maintaining the automated pipelines going forward (post-implementation) = Cost savings of automation Consideration: Resourcing hours * personnel cost to automate (one-time costs)	Current resourcing hours * personnel cost of manual support Less new cost: Resourcing hours * personnel cost of maintaining the automated pipelines going forward (post-implementation) = Cost savings of automation Consideration: Resourcing hours * personnel cost to automate (one-time costs)

Approach A	Approach B	Approach C
No change to reporting.	No change to reporting.	Current resourcing hours * personnel cost of manual support Less new cost: Resourcing hours * personnel cost of maintaining the automated pipelines going forward (post-implementation) = Cost savings of automation Consideration: Resourcing hours * personnel cost to automate (one-time costs)
Add together each row for Total Cost of Savings for Approach A	Add together each row for Total Cost of Savings for Approach B	Add together each row for Total Cost of Savings for Approach C
Add the sum of the cost of the automation project (row 1)	Add the sum of the cost of the automation project (row 1 + 2)	Add the sum of the cost of the automation project (row 1 + 2 + 3)

Table 14.2 – Process for calculating the value of an automation project

This process becomes the expected ROI for the project. You should go into the project with this as a "working assumption." Upon the completion of Step 6, you will measure the actual results to determine the ROI for the project. Do not let this prevent you from sharing the assumptions with the stakeholders as you enter into the project. Even if you end up materially different than your expectations, this process will build transparency and trust. Your stakeholders may provide valuable input into your ROI modeling by sharing the model with them upfront.

Additional factors to consider

There are a number of factors you could consider, but the following are typically the most important to evaluate for your particular project or solution:

- **Available budget**: What financial resources can you afford to spend on this project?

- **Resourcing**: Do you have the time and personnel to complete this project?

- **Technical expertise**: Do the resources that you have (onboard) also have the technical expertise to complete the work, or do you need to supplement this with outside resources?

- **Security or compliance**: Are there specific requirements you need to consider to remain compliant with laws, regulations, or customer contractual obligations?

- **Scalability**: If your company is growing or your data volumes are expected to grow, can the solution handle future projected volumes? Or will you need a new solution down the line?

In this ROI example, keep in mind that it is typical to combine multiple types of data automation together to optimize the results. If you are considering an example such as the one outlined in the previous part for Step 4, the maximum result will be realized by adopting Approach C.

Step 5 – Execute

While this step in the process often takes the longest amount of time, it is pretty straightforward. In this step, you execute the option you selected. If you find that you need to adjust your plan as you progress through the project, make adjustments. My advice is to be transparent when you do, with this forming a part of your ongoing messaging and reporting about the project to your stakeholders.

Step 6 – Measure and report

Upon completion, calculate your results based on the model you produced in Step 4. Any deviations (from the expectations) that require you to reassess or redesign your model are OK; just be clear about why this is and what the impact on your measurement is. The last thing you want is to complete this work only to erode trust by failing to measure and report transparently. Now that you have completed this six-step process, I will explain some additional options for automation that you can buy and incorporate into your environment versus building them.

Third-party enrichment

One very common type of data enrichment is the use of third-party data enrichment services. Third-party refers to the use of external data. This type of data is typically purchased from an outside data vendor and added to the data your company creates (referred to as first-party) to create a more enriched and higher-quality dataset.

When you are considering using a third-party data source, consider the following factors. Not all data enrichment is high quality, and using a third-party source that does not meet the expectations of your business can reduce the quality of your data versus improve the quality of your data:

- **Data quality and accuracy**: Ensure the data is reliable and consistently updated
- **Data coverage and relevance**: Verify the data aligns with your specific needs and target audience
- **Data privacy and compliance**: Check for compliance with relevant data privacy regulations
- **Pricing and cost models**: Understand the pricing structure and choose a solution that fits your budget
- **Security and integration**: Ensure secure data access and compatibility with your existing systems

Remember, it's often beneficial to evaluate different sources and compare their offerings before committing to one. By carefully evaluating your needs and the available options, you can choose the best third-party data sources to enrich your data for your business needs.

> **Important note**
>
> This is not an endorsement of any of the third parties listed (or not) in the following section; this is simply an example list of the types of third-party enrichment services available that you may have heard of. As with any technology selection process, you should assess the needs of your business and your cost/budget, making a selection based on your company's process.

The best sources will depend heavily on the needs of your company and the type of data you are working to enhance. I have provided examples of several types of data to help you understand what types of third-party data enrichment are available, and I provide some examples of each:

1. **Contact and company data:**

   A. **LeadGenius/ZoomInfo**: Provides comprehensive B2B contact and company information with high accuracy and real-time updates

   B. **Clearbit**: Offers enrichment for email addresses, domains, and companies, including firmographics, technographics, and social media insights

   C. **Dun & Bradstreet**: Features extensive business data with global reach, including financial information, credit reports, and business relationships

2. **Demographic and lifestyle data:**

   A. **Experian**: Delivers consumer credit, marketing, and risk analysis data to understand individual demographics and purchasing behaviors

   B. **Equifax**: Offers consumer credit reports, risk assessment tools, and marketing data for individual-level enrichment

   C. **Mosaic (Nielsen)**: Uses segmentation techniques to categorize individuals based on demographics, lifestyles, and purchase behaviors

   D. **Claritas (Claritas)**: Provides consumer segmentation data based on demographics, spending habits, and media consumption patterns

3. **Location and geospatial data:**

   A. **Mapbox**: Delivers mapping, geolocation, and geospatial data services to enrich data with geographical context

   B. **Google Cloud Location Intelligence**: Utilizes Google Maps data to offer insights on demographics, travel patterns, and spatial relationships

C. **HERE Technologies**: Provides location-based data APIs and services for mapping, routing, and geospatial analysis

D. **Foursquare**: Features insights on points of interest (POIs), foot traffic patterns, and competitor analysis based on location data

4. **Social media and web data**:

A. **Brandwatch**: Tracks and analyzes social media conversations and online discussions relevant to your brand or industry

B. **Sprout Social**: Offers social media listening and analytics tools to understand audience sentiment and brand mentions

C. **Similarweb**: Provides competitive intelligence on website traffic, audience demographics, and online marketing strategies

D. **Buzzsumo**: Helps identify trending content and influential figures in your domain to inform content marketing efforts.

5. **Custom and specialized data**:

A. Numerous specialized data providers exist in various industries, such as healthcare, finance, and technology

B. Conduct research specific to your industry and data needs to discover niche providers focused on enriching your particular dataset

Remember, there are hundreds of options when it comes to third-party enrichment services. You need to evaluate and select these based on the needs of your organization. This list is intended to offer examples and to get you started and is not an endorsement of any particular third-party data solution.

Data solution examples powered by data automation

Now that we have gone through the types of data automation, the benefits of data automation, how to calculate the return on your data automation investment, and what to do to implement it, the hardest remaining part is identifying where to get started. I recommend you select an area of the business that is exceptionally manual and begin. Yes, just begin. By focusing your efforts on one area, you can show dramatic results. If you spread your data automation efforts across divisions, it may become hard to feel the dramatic improvement that can be realized through data automation capabilities. By focusing your efforts, stakeholders in other divisions will take notice, and you can, over time, move into new parts of the organization.

Here are 10 strategic areas to consider starting with when it comes to designing your data automation capability in your organization:

Customer domain

First, in the customer domain (every company has customers, so this likely applies to your organization), there are several options for accelerating your data solutions with automation. Consider the following five common opportunities:

1. **Enhance marketing campaigns**: Automate personalized email marketing, A/B testing, and lead scoring, driving higher engagement and ROI

2. **Streamline customer onboarding**: Automate data collection, account creation, and initial communication, making the process faster and smoother for new customers

3. **Personalize customer service**: Utilize chatbots and AI-powered assistants to answer common questions, resolve issues, and enhance the customer experience

4. **Automate reporting and analytics**: Generate routine reports and dashboards automatically, empowering data-driven decisions across departments

5. **Accelerate product development**: Automate market research analysis, customer feedback integration, and competitor monitoring, informing efficient product development cycles

Operations domain

Like customers, every organization has operations to manage their business. Consider optimizing operations with the following data automation use cases:

1. **Optimize order processing**: Automate order intake, inventory checks, and shipment management, minimizing errors and improving delivery speed

2. **Optimize supply chain management**: Automate inventory tracking, supplier communication, and logistics planning, which leads to cost-efficiency and improved responsiveness

3. **Improve financial management**: Automate invoice processing, expense tracking, and budget monitoring, ensuring accuracy and timely insights

4. **Boost HR efficiency**: Automate payroll processing, benefit administration, and employee onboarding, freeing up HR resources for higher-level tasks

5. **Enhance risk management**: Implement automated data security scans, threat detection, and compliance reporting, ensuring a proactive approach to security

While these are only a few examples, they are great places to get started in building out your data automation capabilities. As with other capabilities, be sure to build in feedback loops and effective communication patterns for your stakeholders to understand what you are delivering and how to build virtuous cycles of improvement as a standard in your program overall.

Conclusion

Data automation is a specific technique that is additive to the capabilities that are already deployed in your organization. There are several types of data automation that are available to you, and we have covered these. Typically, this capability is a great place for your data engineers and data analytics professionals to drive additional value to your organization. If traditional data governance capabilities are effective at getting from place A to B on a bike, adding data automation capabilities to existing data governance capabilities is like using a car to get from A to B. It will move you faster and with velocity. However, be careful. Moving faster isn't always the best answer. You must be sure you are automating a strong process; otherwise, you are simply moving problems through your organization faster. As we covered previously, there are several options at your disposal, including using third-party enrichment, implementing additional tooling, such as RPA, and improving data cleansing with services. Consider where automation is beneficial to the business.

As you embark on your data automation journey, remember to do the following:

- Identify the types of automation that would best support data transformation

- Identify where to apply automation in terms of data products and solutions

- Learn how to obtain support for automation solutions, what types of skills are needed, and how to communicate the results to leadership/sponsors

Above all else, partner closely with your stakeholders. Focus on aligning expectations and what "good" looks like so that you are tightly aligned on the results that drive tremendous impact and trust in data. Not every single step of every process is a great candidate for automation. As we covered previously, it's important to evaluate the options and deliberately apply automation where it will drive the most significant ROI.

In the next chapter, I will pivot to the topic of driving the adoption of your solutions. In this chapter, we will carry forward the learnings we have obtained thus far, and we will discuss how to make the solutions "sticky" or more highly adopted within your company. This helps further your ROI by increasing the use of your solutions.

15

Adoption That Drives Business Success

Now that we have covered what data governance is, how to gather support, design a program, baseline the organization, and launch and deliver against the plan, we need to be able to ensure solutions are used by the business. Driving the adoption of data solutions is not a one-time activity, nor does it end after the delivery of the program. While there should be initial adoption done during implementation, adoption is an ongoing activity that you and your team must master in order to ensure maximum impact is realized from data investments.

In short, your long-term success is tightly coupled with your ability to deliver value into perpetuity. Your data solutions will live or die based on the post-go-live, but most teams stop short of success by considering "go-live" the end milestone. This chapter will delve into the crucial, and often overlooked, aspect of data governance: adoption. We will explore why driving widespread use of data solutions is absolutely critical for maximizing impact and achieving your desired **return on investment** (**ROI**).

Data is the lifeblood of your organization. Businesses of all sizes and shapes are collecting and storing momentous amounts of data, recognizing its potential, but unfortunately, simply collecting and storing data is not enough. The true power of this data comes when it is unlocked through effective solutions. As we covered these in the first 14 chapters of this book, you know the key building blocks of data governance. You know why these capabilities matter, and you know how to discuss their value with stakeholders. Now, we need to focus on further adoption to drive business success long-term.

If adoption were easy, we would not need to dedicate an entire chapter to reinforcing the importance and discussing examples to drive adoption in your organization well. I will walk through challenges and opportunities associated with driving the adoption of data capabilities, as well as key factors that influence users' willingness to use and adopt data solutions. We'll also dig into strategies that can help you foster a culture of data adoption in your organization.

Before we begin, I am assuming you have a firm grasp of the concepts outlined in the previous 14 chapters. This chapter is solely focused on the adoption of the capabilities previously explained, and the assumption is that these capabilities are either "in development" or "live" in your environment, for the purposes of exploring adoption. In the context of this chapter, I will be working from this assumption unless otherwise noted.

Before we wrap up this chapter, you will have a firm framing of the importance of ongoing adoption to empower you and your teams to drive endless adoption of core, critical data solutions in your organization that have staying power, long after you move on to the next project or program (or even role!). Together, we will define what success looks like for your organization and how to ensure you nail the basics of adoption.

We will cover the following main topics:

- Why adoption matters – getting started

- Low adoption is costly

- Why does adoption fail?

- How to succeed at driving exceptional adoption

- Recovering from failed launches

- Post-deployment

Why adoption matters – getting started

Driving the adoption of data governance solutions within a company requires a multi-faceted approach that addresses both the technical and human aspects of change, including employee responses to change, attitudes, and the overall organizational culture. There are some key, basics to start with as you frame out your adoption approach.

Start with the why

To bring people along on the journey to drive change, it's best to start by explaining why change is required. What is or is not working well today that can benefit from the change? You should start by addressing three key areas when building your messaging:

- **Align data solutions with business goals**: Clearly communicate how the solution will solve specific pain points, improve efficiency, or generate new opportunities. Use real-world examples and quantifiable metrics to demonstrate the value proposition.

- **Listen to feedback**: Hear your stakeholders' feedback about concerns they have. Be thoughtful about how you address the feedback, and adjust messaging to support their concerns transparently.

- **Focus on user needs**: Understand the challenges and priorities of different user groups and tailor the solution and training accordingly. Address concerns about job security and emphasize the benefits of data skills for career development. For example, a policy will enable compliance and will likely be well received out of principle, but an engineer may need more convincing and will need to better understand how policy requirements will help them to do their job more effectively.

Adjust the solution (if needed) and make it easy to use

As you meet with stakeholders, to help drive adoption, if they are providing feedback regarding the solution, specifically, with ways that will make it more useful for them, listen. Feedback is a gift and can be used to adjust and improve your solution to drive adoption rates up. These are a few things to specifically listen for:

- **Invest in user-friendly tools and interfaces**: Ensure the technology is intuitive and accessible, even for those with limited technical expertise

- **Provide robust training and support**: Offer comprehensive training programs, user guides, and readily available support channels to help users overcome obstacles and learn to leverage the solution effectively

- **Promote self-service options**: Design data dashboards and reports that empower users to access and analyze information without relying solely on data analysts

Don't forget about culture

As you are adjusting the solution as needed and making it easier to use, do not forget to think about the culture. Is your company spreadsheet first? Are people operating inside solutions, or are dashboards commonly used? Really thinking about where people work, how they work, and the openness of the culture at your company to change is critical in driving adoption. If you are trying to change the culture of people using spreadsheets to be more dashboard-driven, for example, you may need to start with a single group or leader to drive the change you seek. A few great ways to influence broader cultural shifts include the following:

- **Lead by example**: Encourage senior management to use and champion data-driven decision-making, setting the tone for the organization

- **Communicate success stories**: Share real-world examples of how data-driven insights have led to positive outcomes within the company

- **Recognize and reward data-driven behaviors**: Acknowledge and celebrate employees who actively use data solutions and leverage insights to improve their work

- **Organize data-driven events and workshops**: Promote data literacy and encourage collaboration across departments through workshops, hackathons, and data visualization contests

Address barriers to adoption

As you work through the preceding feedback and hear from your stakeholders, use their feedback to continuously improve your solution and drive further adoption. Make sure you consider the following barriers:

- **Identify and address concerns**: Actively listen to user feedback and address concerns about data privacy, security, job displacement, and potential ethical implications.

- **Ensure data quality and governance**: Implement data governance practices to ensure data accuracy, reliability, and ethical use.

- **Prioritize data security**: Implement robust security measures to protect sensitive data and build trust among users.

- **Measure and iterate**: Track adoption rates, user feedback, and the impact of data solutions. Use this data to continuously improve the user experience and adjust your approach for maximum impact.

Remember – change takes time. Be patient and persistent in your efforts. Building a data-driven culture requires sustained commitment and continuous improvement. Collaboration is key, and you will need to involve stakeholders from across the organization in the planning, implementation, and adoption of data solutions. It's important to take time to celebrate progress. Recognize and celebrate milestones to maintain momentum and keep users engaged. If you identify an early adopter of your solution, be bold in showcasing their success to the company. By implementing these strategies, you can create an environment where data solutions are embraced by employees across the company, unlocking the true potential of data-driven decision-making for your organization.

Low adoption is costly

Imagine this: your company spent millions of dollars deploying a wonderfully crafted, embedded data governance-by-design program, only to move on to the next project, and the benefits realized at go-live evaporate.

This happens. Every. Single. Day.

Everyone has good intentions. We build a great business case. We deliver the program. We drive adoption with initial teams, groups, or systems. But over time, that adoption atrophies. Let's dig into a specific example that is easy to understand.

> **Amazing visualization**
>
> Imagine a scenario where your company, eager to realize the full power of your data, invests in best-in-class data visualization technology. After months of vendor selection, procurement, development, and deployment, the solution sits unused, with minimal visualizations being built, in favor of using our old favorite: spreadsheets.

In this scenario, the data team that advocated for and gained approval to implement the solution loses credibility with the executive team because the visualization tool was only adopted by the data team, versus enterprise-wide as proposed. The ROI is not fully realized because the ROI was calculated at an enterprise, not divisional, scale. Your credibility is shot, and you are labeled as a "buys shiny objects" executive, and future investments are heavily scrutinized. Unfortunately, this paints an all-too-familiar picture for many organizations grappling with the critical challenge of data solution adoption.

Now what?

In short, you have work to do. You can't go back in time and make a different plan, but you *can* make a change for how you drive adoption in future initiatives (and also repair failed adoption of past deployments, which we will cover in just a few pages in the *Why does adoption fail?* section).

Quantitative costs of low adoption

Low adoption costs come in many forms, both quantitative and qualitative. It's important to understand both types so that you can appropriately ensure that you and your team do not undersell the importance of driving comprehensive and sustainable adoption of your data solutions. Let's start with quantitative costs of low adoption, focusing on tangible costs:

- **Financial**: The initial investment in acquiring, implementing, and maintaining the data solution goes to waste. This includes software licenses, hardware costs, and team members dedicated to the development and maintenance of your solution.

- **Duplication of effort**: Teams continue to rely on outdated methods or manual data analysis, wasting time and resources. Now, your teams are paying for the "old" method *and* the "new" method, thus incurring a higher cost of ownership.

- **Inefficient operations**: Without widespread adoption, valuable data remains siloed and inaccessible, hindering collaboration and hindering the organization from leveraging the solution's potential for streamlining processes.

> **Quantifying inefficiencies in time and opportunity**
>
> These inefficiencies can be quantified by extrapolating the cost of the time required to access and drive solutions and the lost opportunity. This is a bit harder to quantify than others and will require some assumptions, but can be quantified.

Qualitative costs of low adoption

Low adoption costs do not stop at easy-to-quantify measures but are also inclusive of the qualitative impact of low adoption. These types of issues tend to be more about the employee or customer experience, the general culture of the organization, and the sentiment of all stakeholders. These costs are harder to move and thus have real staying power within an organization. It would be a mistake not to make sure these costs are clearly articulated and built into your business plan.

It is *valid* to articulate the risk to future programs as a risk to the success of the program you are working on. Especially when driving data capabilities in an organization that has not seen success in data previously, each failed adoption will drive a significant blow to the future success of other capabilities. This is often missed or significantly underrepresented.

Some key qualitative costs of low adoption include the following:

- **Frustration and resistance**: Low adoption can breed negative experiences and resistance among users who feel the solution is imposed, irrelevant, or cumbersome.

- **Hinders future adoption efforts**: Negative experiences can discourage other users from embracing new data solutions, creating a domino effect of resistance.

- **Erodes trust in data**: Users who perceive the solution as unreliable or unhelpful may lose trust in the value of data-driven decision-making altogether. This is the largest and most difficult risk to your success. Once trust is lost, it is very difficult to repair.

- **Drains morale and productivity**: Frustration with a poorly implemented solution can negatively impact employee morale and productivity.

- **Delayed decision-making**: Lack of access to real-time insights can lead to slow and potentially inaccurate decisions.

- **Missed opportunities**: Organizations may miss out on opportunities to optimize processes, identify trends, and unlock hidden potential within their data.

Costs associated with the failed adoption of data governance solutions are significant. This information is great to put alongside the "why" section of your business case early on in your journey. You should include a rationale for why you should deploy the data governance capability, but that should be inclusive of why you also need to drive adoption post-development of the capability.

> **Comparing data governance policy approaches and outcomes**
>
> I have worked in two separate companies that had really low-quality data governance policies. In both organizations, we rewrote the policy as one of the early-stage focus areas because, in both cases, we were getting questions about what stewards should be doing to manage their data well. In one company, we were very short on resourcing, and thus, all we could do was re-publish the updated policy and answer the occasional question. In the other organization, we published the updated policy and drove an implementation plan that included walking the stewards through the adoption of the policy and had a much more "in the trenches with you" approach versus standing on the sidelines.
>
> As you can probably predict, the company where we rolled out the policy *AND* that supported the adoption of the policy had a much higher data management maturity score (by about a whole point or so), and a more effective data management culture. Additionally, our data had fewer issues and higher trust in additional solutions we deployed over time.

Why does adoption fail?

There are a number of reasons that lead to the failure of data governance solutions. I have had success bucketing them into a few key themes, to help you identify where solutions go wrong and how you can prevent these failures from happening in your own adoption journey. They are broken into three core categories:

- The solution

- The company

- The leader (you)

All three reasons are common, and all three reasons are very possible for any data governance solution failure.

The solution is the problem

The first and most commonly blamed barrier to success is the solution itself. This means that the solution built or created for your stakeholders is just not the right solution. Either it was the wrong solution altogether or the process and/or technology isn't working as intended. In short, the solution isn't going to work for your company's needs. Usually, the solution issues are one or more of the following:

- **Usability and ease of use**: An intuitive interface, clear functionality, and a minimal learning curve are essential for encouraging user engagement. A complex or poorly designed solution can create frustration and hinder adoption.

- **Relevance and value proposition**: The solution must address users' specific needs and demonstrate clear value in improving their work or providing valuable insights. If users do not see the relevance of the solution to their daily tasks, they are less likely to adopt it.

- **Data quality and reliability**: Users need to trust the accuracy and reliability of the data within the solution to make informed decisions based on its outputs. Inconsistent or unreliable data can undermine user confidence and hinder adoption.

- **Integration with existing workflows**: The solution should seamlessly integrate with existing workflows and tools to minimize disruption and maximize user acceptance. A cumbersome or disruptive solution can create additional work and discourage adoption.

These issues come up when either the team driving the work doesn't fully understand the need or is unwilling to accept feedback as the solution is developed and/or deployed. You can counteract this risk by seeking to understand needs and feedback from and for your stakeholders and maintaining a willingness to adjust course when it looks like you aren't going to meet their needs.

Your company is the problem

Unfortunately, your company can also be a barrier to success. When the company isn't ready for data governance or is unwilling to consider new paths to new successes, the company can be the root cause of your failed adoption. It usually comes down to a few core reasons:

- **Lack of leadership buy-in**: Strong support and commitment from leadership are essential to create a culture that values data and encourages its utilization. Without leadership buy-in, data initiatives can lack the necessary direction and resources to succeed, fostering a skeptical attitude toward adoption.

- **Ineffective change management**: Effective communication, training, and support throughout the transition period are crucial to address user concerns and facilitate a smooth adoption process. A lack of clear communication and support can lead to confusion, resistance, and ultimately, low adoption.

- **Poor organizational culture**: A data-driven culture fosters openness to new information, encourages using data for informed decision-making, and values data literacy across the organization. A culture resistant to change or skeptical of data can significantly hinder adoption efforts.

This is the hardest of the barriers to overcome because while you can influence change, you are just one person. A company has to be open to change, willing to move away from old patterns, and effective at adopting new solutions (not just for data, but across many disciplines). This is why company-level change is such a hard barrier to overcome.

You are the problem

Hard to admit, but can be true. I have lived this experience, and yes, it is hard to admit and harder yet to acknowledge publicly and address. However, sometimes the problem is the leader sponsoring or deploying the solution. There can be many reasons why you are the barrier, but here are a few words of encouragement:

- You can move aside and allow your team to flourish

- You can ask for feedback, adapt, and improve

- You can adjust your approach and try new pathways

If you find yourself in a situation where you can't seem to break through to a stakeholder or a group, you might try reviewing the preceding bullets, meeting with your stakeholder 1:1, asking for the coaching of a mentor or sponsor, and reconsidering your approach. This is not as difficult to overcome as the company barrier, but it requires a humble heart posture and a willingness to change approaches when you are running into headwinds.

How to succeed at driving exceptional adoption

The number one piece of advice I can give you to help you drive exceptional adoption in your organization and maximize your value in data governance solutions is very simple:

Focus ruthlessly on adoption.

That's it! That's the advice. Those who focus intently on driving value from adoption, measure adoption metrics, and focus on squeezing the most from the investments they have already made will get the best ROI on their solutions.

> **Primary data management metrics**
>
> In my first PDM deployment, we set very specific measurements to, you guessed it, measure the value of our solution. Seems straightforward, but we really pushed ourselves to think beyond simply go-live and focused our measurement on adoption as well. We did publish specific metrics about standing up the capability (for example, # of attributes published), but we pushed ourselves to also track, for each attribute, # of systems adopted. This forced us to look beyond simply making the data available but also downstream to which platforms were consuming our newly published primary data.
>
> If I were to run that program again, I would push us to go a step further and also track the # of key reports published using the primary data. Would it be tough to verify this? Yes. Would it show the full downstream impact of maximizing value in our investment? Also, yes.

As you work to drive exceptional adoption in your organization, there are a few focus areas to help you be successful:

- **Demonstrate value early**: Showcase real-impact use cases and quantifiable benefits achieved through the data governance solution, emphasizing how it can address users' pain points and improve their work. This can involve creating pilot deliverables in specific departments, sharing success stories, and quantifying the impact of the solution on key metrics.

- **Transparency and clear communication**: Keep users informed about the solution's purpose, benefits, and implementation timeline throughout the process. Address concerns and answer questions transparently. This fosters trust and reduces anxiety about changes.

  - **Bonus: create targeted communication**: Tailor communication channels and messaging to different user personas based on their needs, technical expertise, and preferred communication methods. This ensures they receive relevant information in a way that resonates with them.

- **Build feedback loops**: Encourage user feedback through surveys, focus groups, and open communication channels. Consider their suggestions for improvement and address their concerns. This demonstrates the organization's responsiveness to user needs and fosters a sense of ownership.

- **Invest in user experience**: Prioritize user-friendly design, intuitive interfaces, and robust training programs to minimize the learning curve and ensure users can leverage the solution's functionalities effectively. This includes features such as intuitive navigation, clear visualizations, and readily accessible documentation.

- **Training and ongoing support**: Provide comprehensive training programs that cater to different learning styles and are readily accessible. Offer ongoing support through dedicated help desks, online resources, and knowledge-sharing platforms. This empowers users and addresses their questions as they navigate the data governance solution.

  - **Hint**: Do not stop at the go-live. Offer ongoing user training beyond go-live so that users who onboard later have the same delightful onboarding experience as anyone who was there at launch. Consider offering a monthly or quarterly session to bring new users up to speed and answer questions. Content is reusable, but the value of meeting the user where they are is worth the repetition.

- **Foster a data-driven culture**: Encourage leadership to lead by example by showcasing data-driven decision-making in meetings and presentations. Promote open communication around data utilization and celebrate successes achieved through data-driven insights. This creates a visible commitment to data and helps users understand its value.

In summary, the key to success is to think all the way to the ultimate individual who is impacted by the work you are doing. We often think about the person we provide the solution directly to, but when it comes to data solutions, so many of the capabilities we drive have a ripple effect. They impact the person we are working with directly – yes, but the capabilities impact so many more.

Consider the previous data governance policy example I shared for a moment. While the policy is directed (primarily) at stewards and users of data, they aren't the full story. Ultimately, you must think about who else is impacted by the policy: the customers, the employees, the users of systems, the readers of reports, the executives making decisions, the Board of Directors, and stakeholders across the enterprise as a whole (to name a few). I try to put myself in the customers' shoes. What will my experience be, as a customer, when this new data governance capability is fully realized and I can feel it?

The answer to that question is what good adoption should be based on. Not the deployment itself, but the felt and lived experience of the ultimate individual person who is impacted by the success of your team. That person, whom you may never speak to and may never know. Impacting their experience is what it is all about. The more you can put yourself in the embodiment of their journey, the more successful you will be at driving great adoption in your organization.

Recovering from failed launches

We all have these moments. You've built an amazing solution. You are so proud. The team is excited, it works great, and you can't wait for the users to get their hands on it and use it.

And then, it's quiet. No one is excited. The user metrics are – well, they're low. You are left scratching your head. You might be pondering the following:

- What went wrong?
- Why is there no buzz?
- Doesn't anyone care?
- Where did all the excitement go?

Unfortunately, what you are experiencing is a failed launch. It happens to everyone. You think it's going well, and then…nothing. You have no more support, and all your expected users have either moved on to the next thing or are reverting back to their old solution.

The question is, what can you do about it?

Uncover the root problem

First, you need to identify why your program failed. The preceding questions can help you start to identify what went wrong. It usually comes back to one or more of the following probable causes:

- **Misdiagnosed problem**: Without fully exploring the problem, you could have not fully addressed the problem statement, and thus did not address the issue the stakeholders truly need to be addressed

- **Misinformed decisions**: Continued reliance on intuition or outdated data can lead to inaccurate assessments, hindering strategic planning

- **Poor resource allocation**: Resources may be allocated to the wrong areas based on faulty assumptions or inaccurate data

- **Only partial solution**: You may have deployed a great solution, but if it doesn't address all of the problems the stakeholder is facing, you might not get their buy-in to adopt the part of the problem you did address

When you experience this moment of reckoning, having to reevaluate why your solution did not get the adoption you expected, you haven't failed. This is a bump in the process, but all hope is not lost. What you can do is start by asking for partnership with your stakeholders. Start by asking for their support and collaboration to drive forward.

Collaboration (almost always) wins

Effective communication and collaboration are crucial elements throughout the data solution adoption journey, but especially critical when you have a failed launch. Ask your stakeholders to evaluate the following capabilities, and sharpen your approach going forward to improve and establish them:

- **Establish clear communication channels**: Create dedicated communication channels, such as email newsletters, internal wikis, or designated forums, to keep users informed about the solution, its progress, and any updates. Ask if previous channels worked or if there needs to be adjustments to incorporate feedback loops (see the *How to succeed at driving exceptional adoption* section).

- **Empower data champions**: Identify and empower "data champions" within different departments who are enthusiastic about the solution and can advocate for its benefits among their peers. These individuals can provide hands-on guidance and address common concerns within their teams. Consider spotlighting a stakeholder on a regular basis to share their personal story of how adopting the solution has changed their employee experience.

- **Foster collaboration and knowledge sharing**: Encourage collaboration and knowledge sharing across departments through events, workshops, or online communities dedicated to data and the implemented solution. This allows users to learn from each other's experiences and best practices.

Post-deployment

Whether your deployment went well and adoption is progressing nicely, or you had to reapproach adoption as outlined in the section directly before this, you will need to focus on the adoption that occurs post-deployment. Early adopters aside, what happens after go-live is just the beginning of your success as a data professional.

First, assign someone on your team to build out a post-go-live adoption framework. This will include key capabilities such as the following:

1. What is required for post-go-live adoption from us? From stakeholders? From users?
2. What is a reasonable onboarding timeline?
3. How will adoptions be funded?
4. How will we measure success?
5. How will we measure ongoing ROI?

This framework should be flexible enough to be leveraged for any data governance solution that your team deploys but focused enough that your stakeholders know what to expect from you on an ongoing basis.

Adoption roadmap

One of the key areas of your post-go-live adoption framework should include the building of an adoption roadmap. Given that the adoption process is ongoing, you should be refreshing the roadmap on an ongoing basis. I recommend you build a value stream for each onboarding event (for example, system, report, user, as applicable for your solution), with the "go-live" for their adoption, plus any hypercare or ongoing support you will provide post-go-live.

Monitoring activities

After the adoption for each group, you should ensure you are tracking appropriate metrics to monitor the impact of your solution. This may be captured in a number of ways, but I would recommend considering at least the following monitoring metrics:

1. Hours saved
2. Dollars saved
3. Data quality improvement
4. Employee/team member experience improvement

You should capture this information for each go-live but also keep a running total of the aggregate for your solution. As with any value measurement, be sure to validate the methodology and/or calculation with the beneficiary of the solution, and separately validate the output of that methodology and/or calculation.

Lastly, don't forget to report the value achieved by group and in aggregate as one of your program-level value metrics. This is a key portion of how you measure the success of your team's impact on the company. It's very difficult to go back and try to measure this later, so be sure to capture it now.

Baking adoption into SDLC practices

Once you have a stable solution that is widely adopted, the final best practice is to embed the solution into a standard **System Development Life Cycle** (**SDLC**) process to ensure it is a part of any future development. Depending on the type of solution, you may also want to include it in your standard project management office process (for example, data policy). Next are some key strategies you can implement.

Start early and integrate throughout

As you work toward broadscale adoption of data governance, a great place to drive wide-scale implementation is through embedding data governance requirements into the SDLC process. This will enable your company to go live with new solutions with data governance by design:

- **Involve data stakeholders in requirement gathering and planning**: Include data analysts, scientists, and business users in discussions to understand their needs and ensure the solution aligns with the data strategy

- **Conduct data feasibility assessments**: Evaluate the quality, accessibility, and relevance of existing data before development begins

- **Design for usability and interoperability**: Prioritize user-friendly interfaces and integrate them with existing systems for seamless data flow and adoption

Imagine going live with data dictionaries, data stewards, and great end-to-end data lineage available from day 1. Starting early in the SDLC process enables you and your team to drive data governance through each release into production.

Implement data governance and quality

As you implement data governance into the SDLC process, be sure to focus on the following key components for the most significant impact:

- **Define data standards and guidelines**: Establish clear rules for data formats, naming conventions, and access controls to ensure consistency and reliability

- **Integrate data validation and testing into SDLC stages**: Automate data cleaning and verification processes at every step to maintain data quality

- **Promote data literacy and training**: Equip developers and users with the skills to understand, manage, and interpret data effectively

Focus on collaboration and communication

Data governance is a team sport. Be sure to establish the collaborative forums necessary to ensure everyone exits the SDLC process with a win. Focus on ensuring you complete the following:

- **Establish clear communication channels**: Regularly share progress updates, address concerns, and gather feedback from data stakeholders throughout the development cycle

- **Form cross-functional teams**: Break down silos and encourage collaboration between developers, data teams, and business users to foster joint ownership and understanding

- **Document data requirements and usage**: Create clear documentation for data sources, transformations, and usage within the solution, ensuring future maintainability and adoption

Continuously monitor and iterate

As you continuously work through the SDLC process, there are a few key ways you can monitor for continuous improvement and iterate your solutions for even better adoption:

- **Track key adoption metrics**: Measure usage rates, user satisfaction, and the impact of data solutions on business objectives

- **Gather user feedback through surveys and interviews**: Identify pain points, suggest improvements, and ensure solutions meet evolving needs

- **Agilely iterate and adapt**: Based on feedback and metrics, continuously refine the data solution and user experience to drive broader adoption and value realization

Leverage automation and tools

Finally, as you consider how to drive further adoption, consider ways to automate solutions, improve the way work is completed, and automate data pipelines where appropriate. If you can make it easier for your stakeholders to consume your solutions by automating when data assets are embedded in their flow of work, they will be more likely to consume them. Consider the following:

- **Automate data pipelines and integrations**: Eliminate manual data tasks and reduce the burden on teams, fostering smoother adoption

- **Utilize data visualization tools**: Create user-friendly dashboards and reports to make data accessible and actionable for diverse audiences

- **Explore self-service data access options**: Empower users to explore and analyze data independently, increasing engagement and data-driven decision-making

You should tailor your approach to your specific context. Consider factors such as organizational size, culture, technical expertise, and data maturity when implementing these strategies. You should seek ongoing buy-in from leadership as well.

You can and should emphasize the strategic value of data solutions and secure top-level support for sustained adoption efforts. Lastly, invest in change management. Provide training, resources, and clear communication to support individuals through the transition to a more data-driven culture. By baking adoption into your SDLC from the start and using these strategies throughout the process, you can increase the chances of successful data solution implementation and maximize their impact on your organization.

Conclusion

Adoption is a continuous journey. Until the solution is retired or decommissioned, you will be driving ongoing adoption of your solution. Data solutions are powerful tools, but their true power lies in their widespread adoption and utilization. By understanding the cost of low adoption, the factors influencing user behavior, and the various strategies for fostering engagement, organizations can create a culture of data-driven decision-making and unlock the full potential of their data investments.

Data adoption is not a one-time event; it's a continuous journey requiring ongoing effort, engagement, and commitment to building a data-driven culture within your organization. By embracing the strategies outlined and fostering an environment that values data and user experience, organizations can navigate the path toward successful data adoption and turn data into a powerful engine for success.

16

Delivering Trusted Results with Outcomes That Matter

As the implementation of data governance occurs, the chief data and analytics officer and their leadership team must keep all messaging on delivering trusted results that are framed in business outcomes. This mindset requires CDAOs and their teams to think beyond "data metrics" into outcomes that matter to the business. In this chapter, you will learn how to ensure consistency in what was promised to stakeholders versus what was actually delivered, how to explain variances in expected delivery versus real results, and why that is trust building. Last, you will learn how to message back to stakeholders powerfully during delivery for impact.

As we dig in, I want to reframe much of what we have covered in this book to bring us to a final view, and that is to pull together a standard end-to-end data governance approach. As we have covered over the last 15 chapters, you will have to customize this model to meet your individual needs. I also want to highlight that this model is not unique. Over the last 10-plus years, I have seen variations of this model produced by endless consultants in every firm I've interacted with. Thus, this is my twist on a model that I have seen over and over again.

Part of building trust is setting expectations, delivering what you say you will, adjusting where needed, and staying focused on making an impact that can be measured. All along this journey, message clearly what you must do to set up capabilities that may or may not be "felt" or measurable to the business, and also what is directly impacting the business that they can feel and we can measure. Don't be afraid to state when something is foundational that will serve another capability. This delineation and clarity is critical.

This chapter covers the following topics:

- How to message stakeholders
- How to communicate unexpected results and variances from commitments
- How to deliver results to build trust
- Capability review

How to message stakeholders

When messaging stakeholders about new data solutions for impact, it's crucial to tailor your approach to their interests and concerns. Remember that any variance from what their perception is (not necessarily what you told them, but what they expect) is a cause for questions. The burden lies with you to support their understanding with credible facts regarding your teams' impact. It's important to deliver trusted results with the stakeholders in mind. Let's recap a few key components of how to frame messaging.

> **Example of low-impact messaging**
>
> When launching a new team, take the time to customize messaging, especially if meeting one-on-one with stakeholders.
>
> One of the worst examples of messaging with stakeholders I have been a part of was meeting individually with top leaders but with overly generic materials. When you take time to meet individually but use generic materials, it does not take advantage of the incredible opportunity you have as a leader to showcase exactly, and with specificity, what you and your team do for the stakeholder group. By using generic materials, you miss out on a much more enriched conversation about the stakeholders' specific benefits received from your team.
>
> If you are presenting in a large forum with stakeholders, it can still be disheartening to be generic. Use specific use cases to demonstrate how your team is adding value to stakeholders, and, better yet, have the stakeholders present those examples for even more high-impact communication.

Focus on value and impact

Put communications in terms of value and impact. Be sure to use the *value measurement methodology* we defined in *Chapter 5*. Use business impact to frame the calculated impact for even more powerful, trusted results:

- **Start with the "why"**: Clearly articulate the problem the solution addresses and how it directly impacts their specific goals or concerns. Use quantifiable metrics and real-world examples to demonstrate the potential benefits.

- **Align with their priorities**: Frame the solution in the context of existing initiatives and pain points. Show how it aligns with their strategic objectives and addresses key challenges they face.

- **Emphasize impact over features**: As we covered in detail in *Chapter 5*, focus on the tangible outcomes the solution will deliver, not just its technical features. Show how it will lead to improved decision-making, stronger processes, or better financial performance. The business doesn't care what feature you release. They care about what they can do now that they couldn't do before, now that it's available.

Speak their language

You must use language that is common to the business, not common to data professionals. Huge frustration for most data professionals who struggle to get business buy-in is the lack of "data understanding" or "data literacy" the business has:

- **Avoid technical jargon**: Use clear, concise language that resonates with your audience. Explain complex concepts in layman's terms and focus on the practical implications. This is one of the biggest mistakes I see data professionals make. They get frustrated when the business "doesn't get it" or "isn't data literate." It is your job to make the data capabilities translate into language that speaks to the business. Not the other way around.

- **Tailor your message to each stakeholder group**: Understand their priorities and communication preferences. It may seem like a lot of extra work to tailor it in this way, but so is delivering a great solution that no one understands and, therefore, doesn't use.

- **Use visuals, analogies, or case studies relevant to their interests**: Highlight ease of use and accessibility. Demonstrate how the solution will be intuitive and accessible to their teams, regardless of their technical expertise.

Address concerns and build trust

As you meet and build relationships with your stakeholders, it is important to remember you are there to serve the company's needs. This means it is your job to listen deeply to what challenges exist and work with your stakeholders to provide solutions that optimally deliver results with impact. By starting from a posture of service, you will build trust with your stakeholders each time you deliver a solution that supports their needs. As you work to address their concerns and build trust, remember to do the following:

- **Listen to understand**: Do not listen to respond; listen to hear your stakeholders, and then address their concerns. This isn't a debate. You provide a service to them. Listen to their concerns and address the feedback in whole to build trust.

- **Acknowledge potential challenges**: Anticipate their concerns about data privacy, security, job displacement, or ethical implications. Address them proactively and transparently.

- **Explain data governance and security measures**: Demonstrate your commitment to responsible data use and robust security practices. Emphasize compliance with relevant regulations. Be clear about what data governance does to enable other capabilities and why these fundamentals power more advanced data capabilities to deliver business outcomes.

- **Provide opportunities for feedback and participation**: Involve stakeholders in the planning and implementation process. Address their concerns and incorporate their feedback to build trust and ownership.

Use clear and compelling communication

The best way to grab stakeholder attention is to be very specific and refined in what you say and show. Nothing loses the attention of stakeholders faster than too many non-specific words. Put yourself in their shoes, and write messaging like you would want to hear it. A few key ways to grab their attention include the following:

- **Keep it concise and engaging**: Capture their attention with a strong opening and present key points in a clear, structured way. Avoid information overload.

- **Use storytelling and data visualization**: Incorporate anecdotes, case studies, and data visualizations to make the message more impactful and memorable. Show the result; don't just tell.

- **Offer next steps and resources**: Be clear about how stakeholders can learn more, get involved, or provide feedback.

Remember – you are responsible for being the champion of the solution. Be passionate and enthusiastic about the data solution and its potential impact. This will inspire confidence and encourage adoption. It's a good idea to start small and build momentum. Focus on a pilot project or quick win to demonstrate the solution's value and gain initial buy-in. Measure and communicate success in bite-sized chunks. Track the impact of the data solution and share positive results with stakeholders to reinforce its value and encourage ongoing support. By following these principles and tailoring your message to your specific audience, you can effectively communicate the value of new data solutions and drive stakeholder adoption for lasting impact.

Now that we've covered the basics around communicating effectively, we will pivot to a more difficult communication pattern: how to communicate when things do *not* go as planned.

How to communicate unexpected results and variances from commitments

Communicating unexpected results and variances from commitments in data solutions requires transparency, proactiveness, and a focus on solutions. Here's how to navigate this situation effectively:

- **Be proactive and timely**: Don't wait until deadlines or meetings to disclose the issue. Inform stakeholders as soon as you identify deviations from commitments or unexpected results.

- **Schedule a timely communication session**: Depending on the severity of the variance, organize a dedicated meeting or briefing to address the issue directly.

Offer clarity and context

Don't be afraid to refine and clarify what happened. Be specific, and don't beat around the bush. Get right into what happened, why it happened, what the impact is, and what you'll do about it. Start by doing the following:

- **Clearly explain the nature of the unexpected results or variances**: Provide concise summaries and avoid technical jargon.

- **Quantify the impact**: Express the deviations in measurable terms, such as percentages or numbers, to convey the actual significance. Leverage the model from *Chapter 5* to articulate just how impactful the variance is, and establish a new measure for the future.

- **Contextualize the situation**: Explain the root cause of the variances, whether it's due to data issues, technical limitations, or external factors.

Focus on solutions and next steps

It's not enough to offer clarity and context. You must also steer the conversation forward. How will you solve this unexpected outcome? What will you do to help achieve the goals at hand? It's important to explain and understand the impact but focus on moving forward. Quickly, but directly, focus forward. Ensure you include crisp communication by doing the following:

- **Don't just dwell on the problem**: Offer concrete solutions or mitigation strategies to address the deviations.

- **Outline a realistic action plan**: Describe the steps you'll take to rectify the situation and get back on track. Include timelines and responsible individuals.

- **Be transparent about potential future adjustments**: If necessary, communicate potential adjustments to commitments or expectations based on the new information.

Maintain transparency and open communication

Being transparent when expected is one thing, but maintaining open dialogue and communication patterns is optimal. There are a few things you can do to keep open, trustworthy communication going between key meetings and forums:

- Actively listen to stakeholder concerns and answer their questions openly and honestly. Acknowledge their frustrations and address any anxieties.

- Maintain open communication channels. Encourage stakeholders to reach out with further questions or concerns throughout the process.

- Provide regular updates. Share progress on the implemented solutions and keep stakeholders informed about developments.

Tailor your communication to the audience. Adapt your messaging style and level of detail based on the stakeholders' specific needs and roles. You will build rapport by focusing on positive framing. While acknowledging the deviations, emphasize your commitment to resolving the issue and achieving positive outcomes. This will keep both your team and your stakeholders moving forward, together. Learn from the experience, as a team. Reflect on the root cause of unexpected results and implement measures to prevent similar occurrences in the future.

> **Failure builds trust**
>
> One of the best ways I've found to build trust is to be open and vulnerable when things do not go well. In transformational programs, when things start to slip or don't go as planned, it is typical for leaders to work to make things green or paint a picture that is optimized for steering committees or other forums where reporting is communicated.
>
> In my experience, the opposite is often much more effective in building trust. If you are open and transparent with leadership when you are in a yellow or red status and are not fearful of putting your body of work in these statuses, they tend to believe your reporting and delivery as effective, more so than a team that is continuously in green.
>
> In fact, one company I worked for had an executive who stated, "If we aren't in yellow or red periodically, we might not be pushing our teams hard enough."

By following these steps, you can effectively communicate unexpected results and variances in data solutions while maintaining stakeholder trust and fostering a collaborative approach to finding solutions. Remember – clear, proactive, and solution-oriented communication is key to building trust and navigating data challenges constructively.

How to deliver results to build trust

Building trust in data solutions goes beyond just the data itself. It's about establishing a foundation of reliability, transparency, and accountability across the entire process. The most trusted solutions I have delivered in my career started with strong transparency, my willingness to take full and unwavering accountability, and delivering against commitments, thus establishing myself and my team as reliable partners.

Prioritize collaboration and communication

When you are working with stakeholders, bring them into the build process. It can be unusual but effective to bring stakeholders into iterative design processes versus waiting until you have a fully baked solution to show them the outcome. Being open about interim steps can help them see a few things: 1) the complexity of the solution and 2) when something isn't going to serve them early so that quick pivots can be made. A few considerations to enable collaboration and communication include the following:

- **Involve stakeholders throughout the process**: Engage data users, business owners, and IT teams in planning, development, and implementation. Understand their needs and concerns.

- **Communicate proactively and regularly**: Share updates, address concerns, and gather feedback throughout the solution life cycle. Be transparent about challenges and successes.

- **Establish clear governance and expectations**: Define roles and responsibilities, data usage policies, and escalation procedures for addressing data-related issues.

Demonstrate expertise and competence

Another key component to building trust is ensuring your team is appropriately trained for the work they are completing. One of the most damaging risks to your team is to build a reputation of "incompetence." If the company does not believe you have the credibility to deliver, you will have a hard time building trust. To build a team that is trusted, start by demonstrating competence and expertise by doing the following:

- **Build a team of skilled data professionals**: Invest in developing the expertise of your data team to ensure they can handle complex data challenges and implement solutions effectively

- **Stay up to date with industry best practices**: Continuously learn and adapt your approach based on evolving data standards, regulations, and technologies

- **Share successes and learnings**: Showcase positive outcomes achieved through data solutions to build trust and encourage further adoption

Foster a culture of openness and accountability

Creating a culture of psychological safety starts with you. You have to create a culture where openness and accountability are the normal way in which business is conducted. This means holding your team accountable for results but doing so in a way that allows people to make mistakes without fear of retribution. If you set expectations for results, you need to hold your team accountable for the results. A great way to model this is by stating something like, "I see we didn't hit our goal here. What can we do to help?" This acknowledges the expected results were not met, but also indicates that you are in the problem with your team. This is critical because nothing demotivates a team more than when poor results are not addressed.

Have the courage to state clearly when results are not as expected, and be brave enough to hold team members accountable to deliver. Be human about it. You can do this with empathy and care while still holding your team accountable to deliver the results expected. A few ways to ensure a culture of openness and accountability is created are the following:

- **Encourage a culture of data-driven decision-making**: Promote the use of data to inform strategy and actions, empowering stakeholders with insights.

- **Embrace mistakes and learning opportunities**: Encourage open communication about errors and near misses, learning from them to improve future solutions.

- **Be accountable for results**: Track the impact of your data solutions and measure progress toward agreed-upon goals. Share results and address any gaps.

Building trust takes time and effort. It's an ongoing process that requires a consistent commitment to these principles. You will need to tailor your approach based on your specific context and audience. What works for one organization may not be suitable for another. Continuously evaluate and refine your approach. Seek feedback from stakeholders and adapt your strategies based on their needs and perceptions.

By focusing on these principles, you can develop trust in your data solutions and create an environment where data is used effectively to drive positive outcomes for all stakeholders. The core tenet of building trusted results all comes down to the principles described previously. You bring a critical skill to the table: excellence in data governance. You are in your role because the company has entrusted you to deliver great results with impact. Don't forget that. You are in that role for a reason. Lean into the lessons in this book. Deliver with transparency, be willing to fail, but most of all, build trust in everything you do.

Before we transition to the final chapter of this book, which is a case study of a fictitious company and how I would suggest a data leader handle that scenario, I want to recap how all the capabilities we went through in this book come together. It's a difficult task to weave all of the powerful data governance solutions together into a view that transcends industries, but I want to leave you with a strong summary as you digest the contents and context of this book, before heading into the case study in *Chapter 17*.

Capability review

Let's review each of these capabilities one by one, to show how to deliver trusted results with outcomes that matter for the business. This section is meant to be a reference guide.

Data governance

Data governance is a practice that ensures an organization has trustworthy information. Data governance typically includes policies, standards, processes, tools, and people to enable effectively. Data governance helps organizations make better decisions, reduces risks, and improves operational efficiency.

Stage	Capability/Deliverable	Impact
Define	Define DG organizational AND operational model	Stakeholders understand how your team will be organized and how they should expect to engage with you
Document	Document DG policy and standards	Stakeholders know what is expected from data governance and how the policy should be implemented
Analyze	Perform data management maturity assessment	Stakeholders understand the state of the union and how the company's maturity level compares to their industry
Optimize	Develop a DG deployment roadmap	Stakeholders understand what is going to be deployed and when
Sustain and Test	Measure the effectiveness of the data governance program	Stakeholders understand the value provided by the data governance program and the results they can measure

Table 16.1 - Data governance stages

Metadata (business and technical)

Metadata is often described as "data about data," which provides information about the data but isn't the content itself. There are two types of metadata in this book: business metadata and technical metadata. Business metadata is descriptive metadata that explains what the data is in plain terms. Technical metadata is more structural in nature and describes the physical aspects of the data. Metadata helps find information, understand it, and manage data more effectively.

Stage	Capability Deliverable	Impact
Define	Define key data elements/sources and metadata standards.	Stakeholders understand what data is in scope, where it comes from, and how it should be managed.
Document	Document business and technical metadata.	Stakeholders have clarity and can find business and technical metadata for data that matters to them.
Analyze	Use metadata to gain insights about data sourcing, use, and data quality.	Stakeholders understand where optimization opportunities exist.
Optimize	Optimize controls, process, sourcing, and data flow.	Stakeholders can begin to drive simplicity in their environment and use trusted data sources.
Sustain and Test	Measure the effectiveness of metadata.	Stakeholders understand the reliability of the metadata.

Table 16.2 - Metadata stages

Data quality

Data quality defines how a dataset or data asset meets the needs of its intended purpose. Data quality includes dimensions such as accuracy, timeliness, and validity. Data quality is critical because it ensures the data used is reliable and meets expectations.

Stage	Capability/Deliverable	Impact
Define	Define data quality rules, metrics, and thresholds.	Stakeholders understand what good quality data is and how data will be measured.
Document	Develop business data quality rules that support the outcomes the business needs.	Stakeholders document and clarify what data quality levels are appropriate for their business outcomes.
Analyze	Implementation of data quality rules, measure quality, and report on outcomes.	Stakeholders gain clarity of where data is below quality expectations and should be used with caution and where data is trustworthy.
Optimize	Optimize data quality measurement, gaps, and depth of coverage where issues were identified to find sourcing and provide remediation.	Stakeholders become empowered to find the root causes of data quality issues and remediate them accordingly.
Sustain and test	Measure DQ in monitoring in business as usual process.	Stakeholders are able to routinely receive alerts regarding data quality issues that fall below thresholds and are empowered to address issues as they arise.

Table 16.3 - Data quality stages

Data architecture

Data architecture is the blueprint of how a company manages its data. Good data architecture defines how data is collected, stored, accessed, and processed and how it moves and is consumed. Data architecture is useful to ensure data moves in accordance with business needs and is accessible in the flow of business activities effectively.

Stage	Capability/Deliverable	Impact
Define	Define architectural principles for the requirements of the business.	Stakeholders understand the North Star for architecture and how the environment should be designed.
Document	Development of the to-be/future state architecture is defined and documented.	Stakeholders see and can contribute to how the architecture is intended to be designed.
Analyze	Development of the gap assessment between the to-be/future state and current state.	Stakeholders see and can determine the level of effort and complexity between what is and what can be.
Optimize	A strategic plan to drive as-is/current state to to-be/future state.	Stakeholders understand where the future state will be different from the current state and can prioritize investments accordingly.
Sustain and test	New investments can be evaluated against the to-be state to ensure investments are made with the end in mind.	Stakeholders are able to pressure test investments with a framing toward the future.

Table 16.4 - Data architecture stages

Data operations

Data operations (often referred to as DataOps) is a consistent set of processes and technologies that are designed to improve the flow and management of data within a company. Usually, DataOps functions are focused on automating processes, driving effective collaboration, improving data quality and **time to insight** (TTI), and reducing costs to serve. More mature DataOps functions focus on increasing innovation and exploration of data and may create new data assets for scale across the company.

Stage	Capability/Deliverable	Impact
Define	Define integration patterns, tooling, and value stream.	Stakeholders are able to see the optionality for optimizing data movement enterprise-wide.
Document	In partnership with data architecture, identification of opportunities to streamline data movement can be identified and prioritized.	Stakeholders are able to see where data can move faster to support their business outcomes.
Analyze	Plans to drive optimization for data movement are built in support of the future state.	Stakeholders can determine which investments will expedite their outcomes through intentional investments in data operations.
Optimize	Investments in data operations can self-fund future investments because of the easy value stream of hours and costs saved.	Stakeholders can build a flywheel of improvement by self-funding data operations optimization.
Sustain and test	New investments can be evaluated against the to-be state to ensure investments are made with the end in mind.	Stakeholders are able to pressure test investments with a framing toward the future.

Table 16.5 - Data operations stages

As you create new assets or improve old ones, all of the capabilities summarized here should be wrapped around the solutions you and your team produce. By staying focused on iterative improvement, you will continue to build better and better solutions that are effectively used by your organization.

Conclusion

This chapter concludes the core content of the book. After over 300 pages of content, it's now up to you and your teams to activate the lessons in this book into outcomes for your company. There are so many evolving capabilities and new applications of old, which means this book will one day become out of date. I find that exciting! After working as a practitioner and passionate advocate for data governance for over a decade, I know there is so much more that can be done to optimize data governance capabilities. With improvements and innovation occurring every day, I have so much hope for the future of this discipline.

Companies need great data to deliver great results. They need practitioners like you and me to help them get there. If you take nothing away from the contents of this book than to be a humble partner for your business stakeholders, not working in parallel, but in the trenches of delivering great results with them, together, then that's good enough for me. Data governance serves the company. As a data governance leader, that means you serve your stakeholders. Never lose sight of that. By striving to support the company, support great outcomes, and do so in a simple, straightforward manner, you will deliver trust in data. In the very last chapter, we will take all of the lessons from the book and apply them to a case study for a regulated entity: a bank.

Part 4:
Case Study

In this part, we will walk you through a case study of a fictitious company and show you how the previous 16 chapters show up in a hands-on approach. Throughout this use case, best solutions will be highlighted, as well as alternative options that could have been chosen but were not, with explanations as to why.

This part contains the following chapter:

- *Chapter 17, Case Study - Highly Regulated Intitution*

Case Study – Financial Institution

In this final chapter, I will walk you through the steps to apply many of the capabilities and approaches discussed in the first 16 chapters. This real-world example will show you exactly what I would do (or lead my team to do) if I were presented with a similar scenario. While there are commonalities between real-world financial institutions and the case study in this chapter, this situation is fictitious.

Together, we will see how to apply the topics we have covered to highly regulated institutions. For this example, we will walk through a bank, but similar principles may apply to other highly regulated entities such as insurance or healthcare. I will focus on how to identify specific requirements for each forthcoming scenario, and how to modify the guidance in the previous chapter to meet the unique needs of the case.

There are three problem sets we will explore together:

- How to identify quick wins during periods of regulatory pressure

- How to message long-term solutions with high-value investments to executive team members

- How to design iterative delivery with impact

Scenario - highly regulated entity – banking institution

Over the last several years, data in financial institutions has moved from being a risk that needs to be controlled to recognizing that data assets represent strategic sources of insight to be leveraged across the enterprise. The role of Chief Data and Analytics Officer (CDAO), therefore, has moved from being more focused on the defensive angle to data and analytics (preventing bad things from happening) to offensive (using data and insights to drive additive revenue and customer experiences to the company). This change has moved the CDAO into the role of being a trusted business executive and out of the back office.

For the purposes of this case, we will look at *The Bank of the Midwest*. *The Bank of the Midwest* is a fictitious company serving approximately 25 states in the middle of America. It provides core financial products to its customers including checking, deposit accounts, retirement services, personal banking, mortgage and other loan products, and credit card services. *The Bank of the Midwest* also specializes in small business banking and prioritizes supporting small and medium-sized enterprises with customized solutions. Recently, *The Bank of the Midwest* has been under pressure from its primary regulator for some cash-handling malpractice and liquidity concerns in the current economic environment. As a result, the regulators have been focusing their examinations on their liquidity reporting process, as well as their data and reporting processes across the bank.

The Bank of the Midwest faced three primary challenges that needed immediate attention:

- The regulators and the executive team are experiencing a tremendous amount of pressure to determine what can be done to fix the problems at The Bank of the Midwest. They expect swift action with results. You will need to determine what can be done quickly to show good-faith progress, and fast.

- The bank is unclear on what the long-term plan should be to address the data and reporting challenges at all levels. Many senior managers are unfamiliar with data platforms, and you will need to figure out how to message these stakeholder groups in a way they will understand to support your needs and the needs of the company.

- Finally, you will need to deliver iterative results, and as such, you will need a plan that shows quick wins and iterative delivery for the long term.

It's important to note that you were hired to lead this effort and are the first chief data and analytics officer the bank has had in the role. There is a sense of urgency for you to join and make an impact quickly, but your stakeholders are also not sure what a CDAO does, and you will need to spend some time educating them as to what your job may be and how you are going to be able to help them with this pressurized situation.

As the leader of this effort, the following pages explain what you would do in this scenario.

Identifying quick wins

The Bank of the Midwest hired you as their chief data and analytics officer. You joined the company in the middle of Q1. After a bumpy Q4 and year-end closing process, the regulators discovered that the liquidity reporting used to manage the short-term cash position of the organization was full of inaccuracies. The primary regulator requested a full review of the report production, including all underlying systems and data flows, and a review of the company. This report is critical for banks because it compares their short-term assets (cash, convertible securities, and so on) and their short-term liabilities (deposits, short-term loans, and so on). By comparing the values, the bank is able to determine its ability to cover its obligations and avoid a liquidity event where the organization becomes insolvent.

You sat down on your first day with your manager: the chief operating officer. They explained that while your role as the CDAO is broader than addressing the concerns of this one report, it is a critical issue that you've been asked to lead the remediation of.

> **Alternative option**
>
> You could choose to push back on this request and suggest that you should focus on all key reports, with a focus on long-term solutions only. This option may provide a more strategic, long-ranging option; however, it will not address the immediate, urgent issue at hand: governance of the data and reporting process for the liquidity report.

Your ownership of this remediation effort was not well received by the chief risk officer because they are responsible for the company's risk management process and are the owner of the liquidity risk oversight process, including report production. You taking the lead on this remediation project, and this is stepping into the CRO's remit a bit. However, the regulator determined that the chief risk officer had failed to properly execute her duties as CRO in this situation and has been asked not to be a part of the remediation team by the CEO as a result.

> **Alternative option**
>
> You could suggest that the CRO retain this work and support them as a peer. This option could work if the CEO had not specifically requested you to take the lead. There are likely additional factors that you are not privy to that are leading to the CRO being excluded from this remediation work. You should work with the CRO to build rapport for your own onboarding and to understand how this situation unfolded. However, by deflecting or suggesting the CRO take the lead on this, you may undermine your own credibility, which is still being built as a new hire.

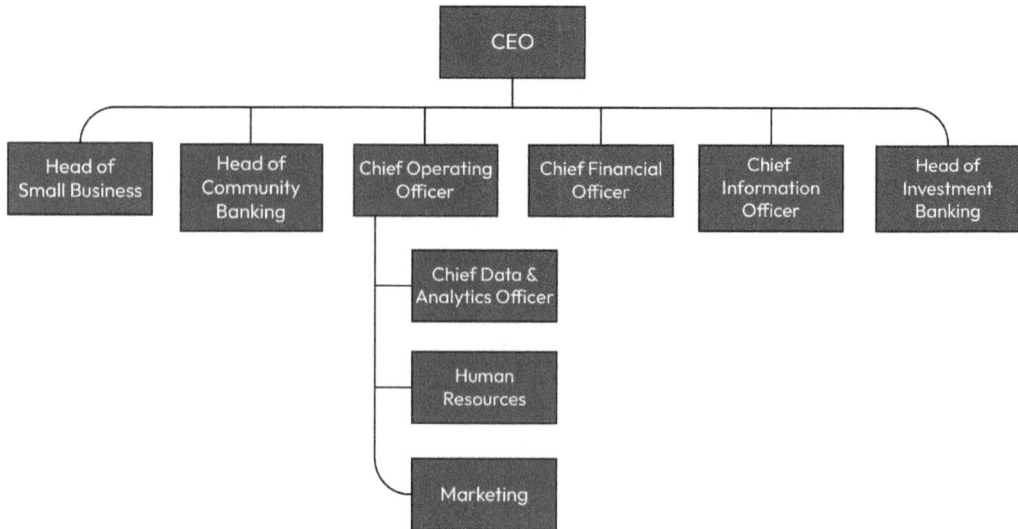

Figure 17.1 – Partial organizational structure, The Bank of the Midwest

Initial discovery

You began by setting up conversations 1:1 with each of the CEO's direct staff members, collectively referred to as the **Executive Leadership Team** (**ELT**). The ELT held a closed-door meeting without the CRO present to discuss the approach to handling this issue. You were asked to present at this meeting during the end of your second week on the job. Therefore, you had less than 2 weeks to understand as much about the problem as possible and frame out a rough plan for how to address it.

ELT

You requested to meet with each of the ELT members, as well as select members of their respective staff to collect knowledge about the failures at The Bank of the Midwest. Everyone was willing to meet, including marketing—who shared this had been a real blow to customer sentiment. You also met with the lead regulator to gain insight into their view of the failures at the bank.

> **Alternative option**
>
> You could prepare an approach without meeting with the executive team to remove bias from existing team members who may have had a role in the company ending up in this situation. However, if you proceed without involving the executive team, you may risk burning bridges with key supporters you need to be successful as a new leader of the company. Secondly, you may miss key context that is required to build a successful remediation plan.

They all said that the report was currently consolidated by the risk team but was a cross-functional effort. Data was collected from the Small Business, Community Banking, and Investment divisions. Data from each **Business Unit** (**BU**) was submitted to Sally in Corporate Risk for consolidation and for final review and presentation to the Enterprise Risk Committee by the CRO. The CRO was recently layered under the COO as a result of this situation. After review by the Enterprise Risk Committee, the report is then published to the regulators, as required.

Chief risk officer

Additionally, you asked the CRO to meet with you. After some deflecting, the CRO agreed to meet with you. You told her you were not there to pass any judgment, just to understand what she knew about the situation that would be important to work to solve. She explained that it was known to her that the liquidity reporting was very manual and that the team responsible for the report was very junior and lacked training on the importance of data quality. Because of this history, she had appointed Sally to consolidate the data provided by the various teams to enable "someone to do the job," yet she acknowledged this wasn't the right course of action, and someone in the BU should really be producing the report.

> Alternative option
>
> You could choose *not* to meet with the chief risk officer. Since she is being positioned as the person responsible for the issue at hand, you could avoid involving her in the remediation process. However, since she is still employed and still the chief risk officer, she still has a role to play, although a smaller one than before this issue emerged. You could choose to include or exclude her, but both options come with risks for you. I believe the complexity of the reporting process requires as much context as possible, and including her is an act of good faith.

She also mentioned that liquidity data was coming from various BUs, and ownership/accountability was unclear. When issues were raised, there never seemed to be a single person who would take on the task of solving them. Issues remained open for months or years in some cases. Therefore, there were known data issues with the report that continued to persist for long periods of time.

Report preparer

You sat down with Sally, who was currently in a position of being the report preparer. She was clearly frustrated and a bit frazzled when you met with her. She was aware it was not "her job" to prepare this report, but it had fallen on her shoulders because no one else had been doing the job. Due to turnover in the business over the years, Sally had a lot of knowledge about how the report came to be. As the "natural historian," she ended up in this role. Sally explained the following:

- She knew there were many issues with the report and, despite her best efforts, had not been able to get anyone to help her remediate problems in data feeding over to her (much of which was captured in spreadsheets)

- She often received files with errors requiring fixes that went unaddressed

- Sally had most of this knowledge in her head and was grateful someone was finally listening to her

You suggested that while it was very appreciated that she had stepped in to support the company in preparing this key report, you were committed to finding the right person to run this process going forward, and she could resume her appropriate role of providing oversight. You asked Sally to document issues that were known to her to help get this process rolling, and she obliged.

Key themes

The ELT surfaced a few key observations that you put into your immediate action plan, which were further supported by the CRO:

Theme	Observation
Failed to appropriately segregate duties	Sally should not be preparing the report and reviewing the report, as this creates a segregation-of-duties problem between frontline and second-line management. This eliminates the oversight of risk management.
Training gap	The liquidity process at the bank lacked appropriate understanding, which traced back to a lack of training on the importance of how to handle data and reporting properly, including what the data is going to be used for.
Communication gap	If someone identified an issue with the data or the reporting, there was a lack of clarity about who that information should go to or what would be done. Many issues went unreported, and known reporting errors persisted.
Ownership and accountability	It was unclear who owned the production of the report (versus who was doing the work as a default). It was also unclear who was ultimately accountable for the report.
Data quality	Many known data quality issues came up in discussions with the ELT. It was unknown how material or immaterial the issues were.

Table 17.1 – Key observations from the report

Quick wins

Based on the key themes, you immediately implemented the following changes, which you included in your 2-week report going out to the ELT:

- **Accountability**: Identified a report preparer, Asha, in Corporate Finance to consolidate the data from all divisions into a single report. Because of the skillsets in the Finance department, this immediately increased the understanding and importance of effective controls over key data elements.

- **Segregation of duties**: Separated the roles of report preparation and report oversight to allow for an appropriate second line of defense over the liquidity risk reporting capability. This effectively allowed Sally to review and provide oversight of the report, which was her appropriate job.

- **Training**: Appointed the report preparer to own accountability of training everyone involved in preparing the report, including data stewards, data governance, risk management, report owner, and the CRO, to be educated on what the report was, how it was used, and the importance of following appropriate controls in preparing the report. This training focused on each person's role and why it was critical, as well as what to do when problems were identified.

- **Documentation**: Report preparer, Asha, documented, in partnership with the technical data stewards, how data flows from source to report, which increased visibility into the complexities of the data used in the report and the process to prepare the report.

- **Ownership**: Appointed the chief risk officer, Sally, as the report owner, clarifying accountability.

- **Data quality**: Gathered a list of known data and reporting issues. Created a process for Asha to continuously obtain and prioritize known issues.

You took a three-page summary presentation deck to the ELT outlining the scenario you found and the immediate steps taken to address the findings:

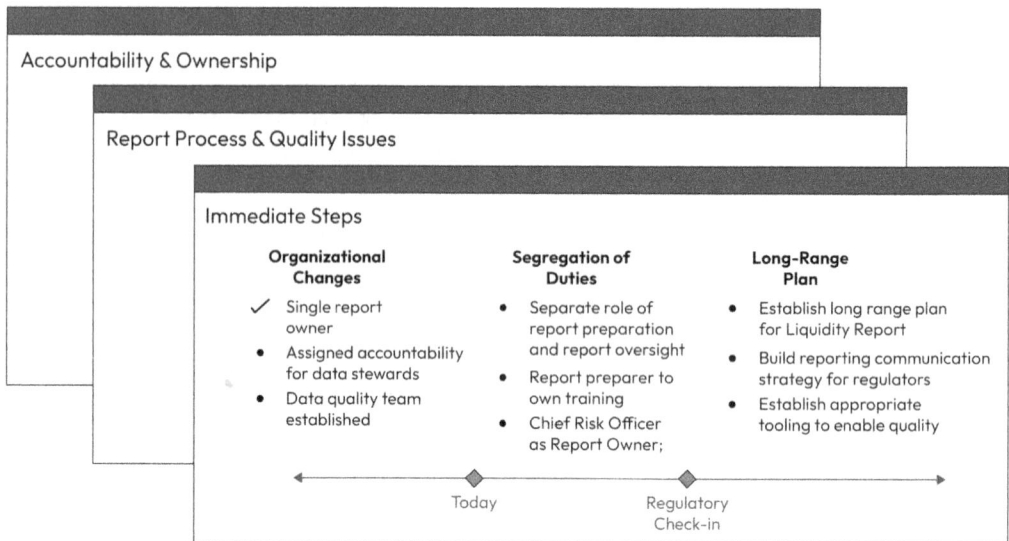

Figure 17.2 – Summary materials for ELT

Messaging long-term solutions to the executive team

After meeting with the ELT at the end of week 2 at the company, you were given full support to move forward with the next phase of the program: long-term sustainability. You put together a plan of attack for the long-range solution and reverted back to the ELT 2 weeks after the initial readout with the following plan:

- **Establish data and reporting governance**: This specific case became critical as the regulators identified concerns with this specific report. However, there is a lack of governance over all key reports reviewed by the ELT, which should be assessed, evaluated, and governed appropriately.

- **Create policies**: There is a need for formal policy requirements for how key reports are identified, the various roles needed to drive effective governance, the requirements for each role, and the location where key information is to be stored.

- **Establish appropriate tooling**: The company lacks appropriate data tooling to enable effective data governance. A data catalog, as well as a data quality tool, are needed as a bare minimum.

- **Build a data quality framework**: The company needs to appoint a data quality leader who will define a data quality framework for the enterprise. This individual will set and define requirements for data quality, aid in the selection and operation of tooling, and support the measurement and reporting of transparent data quality across the enterprise, up through the ELT.

- **Automate reporting processes**: The process of constructing the liquidity report highlights the manual nature of how critical reports are produced across The Bank of the Midwest. Where possible, automation of the reporting process will add speed to the process and reduce the risk of manual errors. This process will need to be designed and implemented on a continuous basis.

- **Centralized data platform**: The degree of manual intervention and use of spreadsheets to move data throughout the enterprise creates an environment with a high degree of manual time spent, as well as increased risk of error. There are hundreds of spreadsheets shared simply to produce the liquidity report, and when extrapolated across all key reports, this number increases sharply. Long term, there needs to be a centralized data platform implemented to provide a single source for data used to produce key reports and run the business.

You presented three options for how to move the long-term plan forward, including a variance in speed, staffing, and cost. The ELT ultimately approved a budget of approximately $8m to support the fastest and most sustainable plan you put forward. This plan included the strategic hiring of key personnel outlined in your plan, as well as the immediate hiring of contractors to get things moving quickly. The CFO and COO agreed to co-sponsor this work at the ELT level and will co-chair the Enterprise Data Committee to oversee this work going forward. Next, you presented these plans to the regulators.

Messaging to the regulators

After meeting with the ELT and securing funding, you met with The Bank of the Midwest's primary regulator. In the first meeting, you explained your role and the immediate ask to address issues with the liquidity report and to drive overall data management for the company. You used the same materials from the ELT meetings (2 weeks into your role and the following meeting). The regulator specifically mentioned that he appreciated the transparency and consistency in sharing what was presented by management with him and his team.

Overall, the regulator liked the approach and the plan you had constructed in partnership with the CFO and COO. The only feedback he had was based on his confidence in The Bank of the Midwest and the duration of time between the identification of the problem and when you were brought in. Because of this, he requested that you add consultants to your plan to move the plan to execution a bit quicker and to validate your approach with a third party.

Your manager, the chief operating officer, was present at the meeting and supported the regulator's request to bring in additional consultants to provide an outside opinion of your plan. This additional funding was also approved.

How to design for iterative delivery with impact

Next, you had to deliver on your plan. You set up a regular, monthly cadence with the Enterprise Data Committee to provide ongoing oversight of the program's success, to ensure transparency and ongoing sponsorship of the work. You divided the work into three buckets:

1. Immediate oversight of the liquidity report transformation
2. Long-range transformation for all in-scope data and reporting
3. Long-range implementation of data management and analytics strategy

As you progressed through the design of this plan, each of the three buckets received time at the Enterprise Data Committee for an update. You presented a mix of short-term updates and long-range updates. For example, one area you focused on consistently was data quality.

In the first meeting, you presented the state of data quality: no framework, no leader, and no tools for measuring data quality existed. You leveraged the consultants to gather the state of data quality for the liquidity report to further quantify the issue:

*   70% of issues identified are related to gaps in basic data quality
*   75 people are manually deployed to reconcile data for each report
*   15 contract resources are used to manually clean data
*   8% of records are duplicated across spreadsheets

Short term, you presented how contractor resources funded by the program were able to reduce the number of these issues immediately. Longer term, you showed iterative improvement through automation and implementation of a central database and were able to measure the impact based on this initial baseline of data quality.

You followed a very similar approach for each area of your long-range plan, demonstrating not just the "win" at the end of the milestones, but specifically leveraging the information in *Chapter 5* to quantify the impact of the results at each milestone, focusing not just on what was delivered but why that was impactful to the business. You might have considered the following:

*   Percent improvement in data quality (for example, 40%)
*   Increase in speed of production of the report
*   Reduction in manual processes

Your team developed a "trustworthy" indicator for reports as a part of the program. This indicator articulated the confidence level in the report. If the report was fully documented, had lineage, and the quality was measured and within the threshold defined by the report owner as acceptable, the report was marked as "Certified." This provided a level of confidence to the ELT that the report had been blessed by the chief data and analytics office and could be relied upon.

Further, the regulators were presented with the same materials as the Enterprise Data Committee, 2 weeks following each meeting. The regulators then had the opportunity to comment and provide feedback or ask questions. They became confident over time in the approach and eventually reduced the frequency of meetings.

Results

You were able to make these changes quickly due to the visibility of the problem at the ELT level and the regulatory push to make changes swiftly. You received great feedback for immediately taking action and implementing quick influence in the organization. Not only did this have an immediate impact on the company, but also established yourself as a key business leader. Here's an overview of what you achieved:

- **At 3 months**: You were able to demonstrate the end-to-end flow for how the report was created, had clear ownership and accountability for all key roles, and had a draft policy published for comment and review. You had begun vendor assessments for required tooling and were narrowing down the selection. You built a data quality framework, leveraged consulting resources, and began to implement manual quality checks with contractors.

- **At 6 months**: You were able to show fully approved policies, a framework for scoping in key reports, clear ownership and accountability across all key reports, tooling implementation plans in place, remediation of immediate issues, and that the regulators had reduced their level of concern over The Bank of the Midwest.

- **At 12 months**: Your team was fully functional. Implementation of the first releases of key platforms and tools was in production, and on-ramping was in progress. You had reduced the number of data quality issues by over 50% and automated 20% of all manual processes. The liquidity report had become the gold standard for your organization, and your team was able to move to other reports for further enhancements.

Never waste a crisis. When you have the attention of a leadership team, as in this case study, you have the opportunity to show (not just tell) what can be done better, in a more trustworthy way, to manage data well. This is a great example of how to drive immediate value but also demonstrates what could be better with long-term investment.

Conclusion

As you reviewed the approach in this use case, in concert with the previous 16 chapters, I hope it is abundantly clear that there is no single approach for data governance. Every company and every situation is unique. What works at one company won't work for a similar company in the same industry. This is why I offered alternative options in this chapter and examples throughout the book to showcase what has and has not worked previously for me. Ultimately, any data professional will have successes and failures in their career. One of the hardest lessons to learn (for me) is that what was recommended this year may have been recommended in the past but now is effective because the company is facing new challenges or priorities. Thus, sometimes, just changing circumstances will allow for the same suggestion to work in your environment now, whereas it was rejected previously.

The context matters. Your willingness to spend time to build trust in the capabilities outlined in this chapter will make all the difference in the success of your overall data governance program. The best advice I can offer, beyond what is technical based on the capabilities in *Part 2* or specific examples provided throughout the book, is to listen.

Your stakeholders are speaking with you about data because they believe, at some level, that you can help them. The best and most effective way to build solutions that matter, that truly make a difference, is to listen to your stakeholders and co-develop solutions that work for them. Conversely, the worst thing you could do is to come into an organization and apply a uniform set of suggestions that are not in any way unique. Start by listening. Then build, together.

The best way to make a difference is to do what was outlined in this case study. Listen, start to deliver small yet quick wins, message effectively to gain support, and deliver iteratively for impact. Finally, be sure to measure and report on your progress, transparently and often. By laying a foundation for open communication and continuous delivery, you will build trust in data.

I'm cheering you on!

Index

U

V

‹packt›

Other Books You May Enjoy

If you enjoyed this book, you may be interested in these other books by Packt:

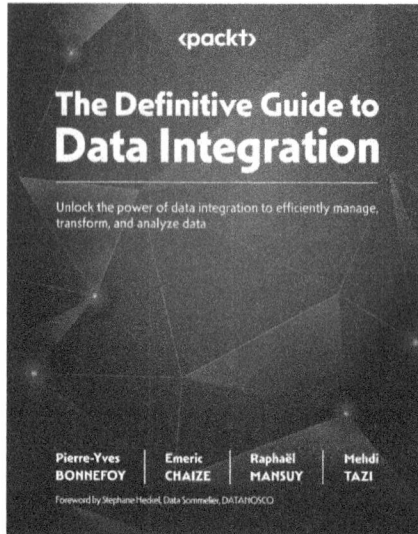

The Definitive Guide to Data Integration

Pierre-Yves BONNEFOY, Emeric CHAIZE, Raphaël MANSUY, Mehdi TAZI

ISBN: 978-1-83763-191-9

- Discover the evolving architecture and technologies shaping data integration
- Process large data volumes efficiently with data warehousing
- Tackle the complexities of integrating large datasets from diverse sources
- Harness the power of data warehousing for efficient data storage and processing
- Design and optimize effective data integration solutions
- Explore data governance principles and compliance requirements

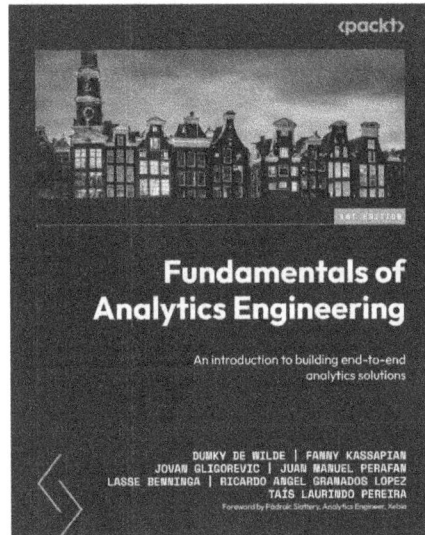

Fundamentals of Analytics Engineering

Dumky De Wilde, Fanny Kassapian, Jovan Gligorevic, Juan Manuel Perafan, Lasse Benninga, Ricardo Angel Granados Lopez, Taís Laurindo Pereira

ISBN: 978-1-83763-645-7

- Design and implement data pipelines from ingestion to serving data
- Explore best practices for data modeling and schema design
- Gain insights into the use of cloud-based analytics platforms and tools for scalable data processing
- Understand the principles of data governance and collaborative coding
- Comprehend data quality management in analytics engineering
- Gain practical skills in using analytics engineering tools to conquer real-world data challenges

Packt is searching for authors like you

If you're interested in becoming an author for Packt, please visit `authors.packtpub.com` and apply today. We have worked with thousands of developers and tech professionals, just like you, to help them share their insight with the global tech community. You can make a general application, apply for a specific hot topic that we are recruiting an author for, or submit your own idea.

Share Your Thoughts

Now you've finished *Data Governance Handbook*, we'd love to hear your thoughts! Scan the QR code below to go straight to the Amazon review page for this book and share your feedback or leave a review on the site that you purchased it from.

`https://packt.link/r/1-803-24072-5`

Your review is important to us and the tech community and will help us make sure we're delivering excellent quality content.

Download a free PDF copy of this book

Thanks for purchasing this book!

Do you like to read on the go but are unable to carry your print books everywhere?

Is your eBook purchase not compatible with the device of your choice?

Don't worry, now with every Packt book you get a DRM-free PDF version of that book at no cost.

Read anywhere, any place, on any device. Search, copy, and paste code from your favorite technical books directly into your application.

The perks don't stop there, you can get exclusive access to discounts, newsletters, and great free content in your inbox daily

Follow these simple steps to get the benefits:

1. Scan the QR code or visit the link below

https://packt.link/free-ebook/978-1-80324-072-5

2. Submit your proof of purchase
3. That's it! We'll send your free PDF and other benefits to your email directly

Printed in the USA
CPSIA information can be obtained
at www.ICGtesting.com
CBHW081628101024
15669CB00041B/I454

9 781803 240725